# THE AIRMEN

*Other Books by Edwin P. Hoyt*

KAMIKAZES

GUADALCANAL

THE MILITARISTS

JAPAN'S WAR

U-BOATS: A PICTORIAL HISTORY

AMERICA'S WARS AND MILITARY EXCURSIONS

DEATH OF THE U-BOATS

HITLER'S WAR

THE GI'S WAR

THE RISE OF THE CHINESE REPUBLIC

CARRIER WARS

YAMAMOTO

THE DAY THE CHINESE ATTACKED

# THE
# AIRMEN

*The Story of American Fliers in World War II*

# by Edwin P. Hoyt

McGRAW-HILL PUBLISHING COMPANY
New York   St. Louis   San Francisco
Hamburg   Mexico   Toronto

1 2 3 4 5 6 7 8 9 DOC DOC 9 5 4 3 2 1 0
ISBN 0-07-030633-8

**Library of Congress Cataloging-in-Publication Data**
Hoyt, Edwin Palmer.
   The airmen.

   Includes bibliographical references and index.
   1. World War, 1939–1945—Aerial operations, American.
   2. World War, 1939–1945—Personal narratives, American.   I. Title.
D790.H72   1990          940.54′4973          90-6563
ISBN 0-07-030633-8

Book design by Eve Kirch

This book is for Jake Jones, who, like millions
of other Americans of his generation, served
his country faithfully in World War II.

# Contents

*103*

# Acknowledgments

I am indebted to a large number of people who gave vital assistance in the preparation of this book, ranging from officers of the U.S. Air Force, to enlisted men, librarians, booksellers, and many others in the United States and Great Britain. For the idea and a thousand other things, I am indebted to my wife, Olga G. Hoyt, who sent out hundreds of inquiries to squadron associations and other groups of airmen from World War II.

The Air Force History Division at Maxwell Field, Alabama, provided basic information about veterans groups, as did the Air Force Headquarters in Washington, D.C. As usual, Kathy Lloyd of the U.S. Naval History Center gave valuable aid. Many others helped with guidance and information: L. Wayne Hudgins of the U.S. Naval Weapons Center, Art Cavanagh, the staff of the Mathews Memorial Library, and Granville Hall, all of Virginia.

Corporal Jake Jones wrote his World War II military autobiography, a very important one to this book, for me. For every man and every unit that saw action on the far-flung fronts of the war, there were hundreds of units and many thousands of Air Force men like Jones, in the air and on the ground, who served in administrative jobs and training commands in the United States, reaping none of the glory and still some of the danger.

General Thomas Jeffrey granted me a long interview in which we discussed his distinguished war career in the Western Hemisphere. Edison B. Vail spent considerable time talking to me, as did Joe Layer, Gordo Cruickshanks, and Kenneth Kinsinger.

Among the voluminous replies I received to my requests for individual experiences, I am indebted to the following:
Jeffrey Acosta of MacArthur Memorial Museum, F. E. An-

derson, James A. Bancroft, Art Berkey, Charles Bortzfield, George Brooks, Donald L. Caldwell, Joseph Carciotto, Bernard J. Chisholm, Forrest S. Clark, Robert L. Cloer, John P. Conlon, Chester W. Driest, Wilson V. Edwards, Donald F. Flaherty, Armand J. Galfo, Harry Gann, Jack Garnett, Henry J. Gelula, Fred I. Gilman, Samuel C. Grashio, Cliff Hall, Robert W. Halliday, Frank Halm, Jenny Hamilton, Ian L. Hawkins, Oscar Herem, Edmund Hicks, Fred H. Hitchcock, Jr., Charles P. Huntington, George P. Jahnke, Eino E. Jenstrom, George Kay, Edgar F. Kipp, James R. Knaub, Rudolph C. Koller, Jr., Curtis H. Krogh, Oliver S. Larouche, John Mahan, John G. Martin, Frederick Mears, the Naval Air Systems Command Headquarters, George Olson, Ralph K. Patton, George W. Pederson, Paul W. Pifer, Virgil W. Preston, Jack Purdy, Jim Ratelle, Frank Roth, Dennis R. Scarlan, Jr., Robert C. Sellers, Arthur Silva, Major Lester A. Sliter of Maxwell Air Force Base, Benjamin Smith, Jr., Hans-Heiri Stapfer, Ray B. Stone, Reade Tilley, James C. Van Nada, Mark L. Ward, Sr., William H. Watkins, Floyd G. Whitney, Jr., and Joseph J. Yuhasz.

Special thanks must go to those airmen who wrote their accounts, which were unpublished manuscripts, or privately printed, or otherwise published, as listed in the bibliography. In addition, special permission to use material from their writings was kindly granted by Samuel C. Grashio and Benjamin Smith, Jr. Thanks also for permissions from Robert W. Waltz, President of the 390th Memorial Museum Foundation; Richard F. Downey of the 449th Bomb Group Association; Harry H. Crosby of the 100th Bomb Group Association; Harry C. Bayne, Chairman of the Board of The China-Burma-India Hump Pilots Association, Inc. Thanks are also due to Doubleday, a division of Bantam Doubleday Dell Publishing Group, Inc., for permission to use excerpts from Frederick Mears's *Carrier Combat*, copyright, 1944; to Ziff Davis Publishing Company, for use of passages from *The Eagle Squadrons* by Vern Haugland, copyright, 1979; and of course, to Eino E. Jenstrom, whose experiences in the *Eddie Allen* were written for *Air Force* magazine, which also graciously granted permission to use Jenstrom's account, along with other material he contributed.

# Preface

*The Airmen* is a companion piece to *The GI's War*, which McGraw-Hill published several years ago. But whereas it was relatively easy to deal with military events in the North African, Italian, and European theaters of operation chronologically, dealing with the airmen was a more complex problem. Air forces and units varied greatly in size and complements. The Eighth Air Force was huge, the Seventh Air Force minuscule.

Still, I have tried to follow some sort of chronological sequence, which is why the book begins with Spain, the Battle of Britain, and China. Most of the book relies on tales told by the fliers themselves. As with *The GI's War*, very little comes from official records, for what I wanted to do was reproduce the feelings and fears and glories of the day.

Most important, I wanted to give a feeling for the war as it was fought in the air. Veteran airmen, and particularly the bombers, are very sensitive to the statements of naval officers and others that the air war was not particularly effective. It is very easy to make such a claim after the fact. The B-29 high-explosive bombing of Japan's air power sinews is a case in point. Despite repeated bombings, the Mitsubishi engine works in Nagoya, which made most of the engines for Japan, was still going strong at war's end. In Germany aircraft production actually increased during the height of Allied bombing. But the reason for this continued stability and even increase in production was that the Japanese and German governments spent enormous sums to protect their essential industry, an effort costly to them in resources and manpower.

It is true that the boast that air power could win wars single-handedly was proved wrong, but that in no sense adulterates the fine record of the airmen in helping to win the wars in both the Western and Pacific worlds.

For the combat crews the war was exciting and frightening. For the ground crews there was great responsibility and a good deal of boredom. But all of these airmen of World War II did their jobs, no matter how boring or lowly, and they established a proud tradition in the United States Army, Navy, and Marine Corps that has been carried on now, too, in the United States Air Force. As it was with *The GI's War*, I could not hope to give a complete story of even a single unit, but I hope that I have succeeded in giving a glimpse of the sorts of war, very different in different areas, that the airmen fought in World War II.

Edwin P. Hoyt
Hallieford, Virginia, 1990

# ONE

# Corporal Jake Jones— 13144734 USAAF 1942

You might say Jake Jones came from a line of American citizen-soldiers. His grandfather had fought in the American Civil War for the Confederacy, with the First Virginia Regiment, Pickett's Division, Longstreet's Corps, Lee's Army. His father fought for the United States in World War I as a soldier with the First Air Service Mechanics. He remained in France until 1919, working on the famous Liberty aircraft engine.

Young Jake was very regretful that his grandfather had died before he was born, for he would have liked to question him about the great Civil War. But he did have his father's shared memories, and during Jake's boyhood his father spent many an evening regaling him with tales of the great war to end all wars.

Thus at a very early age Jake Jones was bitten by the air bug. When he was nine years old he discovered the pulp magazines. For a dime he could buy a copy of *Flying Aces, Wings, Daredevil Aces*, or half a dozen other magazines that catered to the young and the young at heart. They featured stories about real air heroes like Baron Manfred von Richthofen and his Flying Circus, and Eddie Rickenbacker, as well as a host of mythical air heroes, mostly on the Allied side of the war. And then there were books about the air war, about Zeppelins and the Lafayette Escadrille and other heroic squadrons.

Jake read all the books in the local library, and at night he put himself to sleep with fantasies about the air service and his future. He was determined to be a fighter pilot when he grew up.

The Jones family lived in Washington, D.C. Sometimes Jake's

father would take him over to Bolling Field, where he could actually touch an airplane, or to Hoover Field, where the Pentagon now stands, to watch the airplanes taking off and landing.

Summers and on school holidays Jake Jones passed many happy hours in the Smithsonian Institution's air museum, a little metal temporary building in back of the Smithsonian itself. There he could ogle the French Spad, the famous Allied single-seat fighter plane of World War I; the first Army "round the world" plane; the hull of the famous flying boat NC-4; Lindbergh's *Spirit of St. Louis*; and other famous relics of American aviation's early days.

Sometimes Jake palled around with another kid who also read the flying magazines. They would spend hours discussing the relative merits of Spads, Nieuports, DeHavilands, Camels, Albatrosses, Fokkers, Pfalzes, Bleriots, Rumplers, and Gothas; and the relative virtues of one, two, or three wings.

With his pals Jake saw *Wings, Dawn Patrol*, all the combat movies.

While Jake was still in grade school, Mussolini marched into Abyssinia, and in 1936 the Spanish Civil War broke out. This added a whole new dimension to warfare and aerial combat, very exciting for young air enthusiasts.

Interest was soon focused on the new aircraft carriers and their carrier planes, and on the realities of the Spanish Civil War.

# TWO

# Leading the Way: The Mercenaries and the Starry-Eyed Ones

Where and when did World War II begin? For some it began at Versailles, in the harsh treaty imposed on Germany by the victorious western Allies. This peripherally also affected Japan and China, stoking but not satiating Japan's imperial designs. (Japan received the German colony of Kiao-chao but soon had to return it to China.) Germany was pressed down, its industrial output mortgaged to the Allies for years to come. Japan was forced to relinquish China's Shandong province, and the prime port of Qingdao, which it had occupied. Fifteen years later, in the anguish and confusion of an infant Chinese Republic, the Japanese wrenched off a large piece, the six provinces of Manchuria, and created the new puppet state Manchukuo. Some say *that* was the beginning of World War II.

Others point to the rise of Fascist totalitarianism, Benito Mussolini's creation of empire in Africa in the mid-1930s. Still others look to the Spanish Revolution of 1936, which became a proving ground for German, Italian, and Soviet weapons and tactics. It was here that Americans entered the fray, on the side of the Republicans, the Soviet-backed government of Spain, which was challenged by the professional army forces under General Francisco Franco. And it was here that American airmen first took a hand in the international war.

One of the American airmen was Frank Tinker, a mercenary pilot who flew for the Republicans under the name of Francisco Gomez Trejo. But in this particular war, even the mercenaries seemed to develop passionate political emotions. Two of the mercenaries, Derek Dickinson and Eugene Frinck, addressed a letter to U.S. Secretary of State Cordell Hull, protesting the refusal of the American government to sell military supplies to the Republicans. "We are not fighting for war," they said, "but to prevent another catastrophe equal to the 1914 European Conflict."

Washington was not responsive; the American position of complete neutrality was unchanged. But a number of Americans joined the Republican ranks to fight in the air against Adolf Hitler's Kondor Legion and the Italian air force pilots who were sent to help General Franco. That was how Frank Tinker got to Spain in 1937. He had an itch to get into the air war, and for a time he did not seem to care which side he fought on. When he learned that the Nationalists were bombing Madrid with German Junker bombers, however, his hostility toward Hitler made him decide to fly for the Republicans.

Tinker's credentials were impressive. He had attended the U.S. Naval Academy, started flight training at the army school at Randolph Field, Texas, and graduated from the navy flight school at Pensacola, Florida. Through the Spanish ambassador to Mexico, Tinker signed a contract to go to Spain and fight as an aerial mercenary, to be paid the enormous sum of $1500 a month plus $1000 for every Nationalist plane he destroyed.

In Spain, Tinker joined three other American fliers: Harold "Whitey" Dahl, James Allison, and Charles Koch. All four were sent to Manises Airfield to join with a number of British volunteers in an Anglo-American squadron. They flew French Breguet single-engine bombers for a time, but were then transferred to a fighter unit that was getting fast biplanes called Chatos from the Soviet Union (where they were called Polikarpov I-15s).

Koch dropped out of the unit with stomach trouble, but the other three went to Guadalajara. There they met an intensely political young American Communist named Ben Leider, who had some flight experience and who had, for idealistic reasons, come to Mexico to prepare to fight for Spain. Here Leider and the remaining three became known as the American Patrol.

The first American aerial victory was scored by Leider early in February, when he chased a German in a Heinkel 51 down to treetop level. The German misjudged, a wing caught a treetop, and the plane went cartwheeling to the ground. Leider had a "kill" without firing a shot from his four 7.62 mm machine guns.

But the fortunes of war were not with Leider for long. A few days later, the squadron encountered a large number of Heinkel 51s, and the squadron leader ordered his men into a circular defensive pattern. Earlier he had warned them that the enemy planes could dive faster than the Chatos, and the pilots were thus to avoid dogfights.

The squadron went into formation, but Leider could not stand restraining himself. He broke loose, dived after a Heinkel, and was pounced on by several of them. They came after him from several angles, firing, and Leider's Chato went out of control and plunged to earth.

Pilots Allison, Tinker, and Dahl were also hard hit in this encounter. Allison's plane was damaged by a Heinkel, but he managed to limp toward home base. Unable to make it, he crash-landed nearby. Dahl's Chato was so badly damaged that he had to parachute to safety. Tinker got into a dogfight with a Heinkel but managed to hold out until help came in the shape of six fast single-winged Soviet Moscas. The fastest fighters in the area, the Moscas proved to be more than a match for the German planes. Half a dozen Heinkels were shot down.

Back at the airfield, Tinker learned that Allison had been sent to the hospital with a wounded leg. Dahl had landed in an olive grove and been sent back to duty aboard a donkey. But Leider was not heard from—obviously he was dead.

The American Patrol was involved in several more missions in this winter of 1937, bombing and dogfighting. But in the early spring of 1937 the war changed. Dictator Mussolini sent a brigade of Italians to fight in Spain alongside the Franco forces. Mechanized troops with tanks began advancing on Madrid from Saragossa, and Tinker's squadron was ordered to stop them. Raid after raid was launched; the Chatos, along with Soviet bomber teams and the Mosca fighters, dropped down to bomb and strafe the mechanized columns. The attacks were most effective because the sides of the macadam road were ditched, and the ditches were mud traps for vehicles in this rainy season. The Republican air attacks were so successful that the Italian column was completely disrupted and the Loyalist army forces were able to stop the Italian drive on Madrid for a time.

The squadron, under Spain's Captain Garcia LaCalle, continued the attacks. Sometimes they fought Germans. Sometimes they fought Italian pilots in Fiat fighters, which were faster than the Chatos. Pilot Tinker used his considerable aerobatic skill one day to evade four Fiats that had ganged up on him when he got away from the squadron. One fighter would come after him and get on his tail. As the fighter came to the firing point, Tinker would bank sharply to the left and up, the fighter would scream by him, and he would be on *its* tail. He would then fire a few rounds, but by that time another Fiat would be after him. He had to repeat this maneuver four times, and finally found cloud cover that saved him from these not very skillful enemy pilots.

For a while, Dahl was ill with the stomach trouble that had already sent Koch home. Allison went back to America because of his wound. This left Tinker, who joined with another American named Al Baumler to fly fighters. They were so skillful that they were promoted to flying the coveted Mosca fighter from the Soviet field at Alcala de Henares.

Late spring and early summer were spent flying escort for squadrons of Russian bombers, but the sameness of it was boring to these young American adventurers. At the end of July Tinker decided to resign his commission and go home to America.

Whitey Dahl was shot down by three German Messerschmitt fighters one day. He managed to parachute out of his burning Chato, but he landed in a unit of Nationalist troops and was captured, sent to Salamanca, and imprisoned. There Dahl was tried and, on October 5, 1937, sentenced to be shot. His wife, Edith, a showgirl who had followed him to Europe, wrote a pleading letter to General Franco, asking that Dahl's life be spared. Surprisingly, it was. The letter had apparently reached Franco's staff, and the accompanying picture of Mrs. Dahl in a white bathing suit had persuaded some officer to let her husband go. He was held in prison until February 1940, a year after the Civil War ended in Franco's victory. Later he returned to America, went to Canada, and joined the Royal Canadian Air Force to become an instructor. (Edith left him and went back on the show circuit as a lady violinist, billed as "The Blonde Who Spiked the Guns of General Franco's Firing Squad.")

Al Baumler was wounded in the back by explosive bullets from a German Heinkel, and after that his health was slow to improve, so in the later summer of 1937 he returned to America. Baumler promptly applied for readmission to the U.S. Army Air Corps. He had been dismissed as an air cadet for failing to show proficiency in flying, but that was all forgotten now. He was an ace who had shot down five enemy planes during the Spanish Civil War, and late in the 1930s the Army Air Corps had begun to realize the necessity of strengthening its manpower and training programs. Baumler was accepted and began flying for the Air Corps again.

When Frank Tinker returned to the United States in the late summer of 1937, his passport was seized by the immigration authorities. The Spanish Civil War had become an American political problem, with the left wing demanding intervention on the part of "democratic" forces of the Republic, but the U.S. government was more afraid of the Communist influence on the Republicans than of Nazi and Fascist influence on Franco's Nationalists. Many young Americans had, like Ring Lardner's son, gone to Spain to fight in the "International Brigade." To discourage these enlistments the Department of State took a hard line with some of the returnees, and Frank Tinker was one of the victims of this policy.

He could find nothing to do that interested him. The armed services did not want the problem of dealing with this veteran of the Spanish war. He returned to his native Arkansas, but found himself bored there, too. He published an autobiographical account of his experiences. For excitement, he paddled a canoe down the Mississippi River.

Tinker announced boldly that he would defy the Department of State and fly a plane nonstop across the Atlantic to Spain. It could be done in the modern day of 1938, but first he had to have an airplane. He had already had too much publicity, and the Department of State enlisted the forces of government against him. The Civil Aeronautics Authority announced that if he tried to fly to Europe, he would be stopped at any airport.

Tinker then tried to rejoin the armed forces, but was turned down everywhere. Again, there had been too much publicity. He yearned to return to Spain, and spent hours studying flight logs and trying to find support for his project. None was forthcoming, and he began to despair. His world ended when the Spanish Republicans surrendered in 1939. There was talk in aviation circles about a new corps of mercenaries being organized by Chiang Kaishek in China to fight against the Japanese, but Frank Tinker had left his heart in Spain. On June 13, 1939, in a Little Rock hotel room filled with Spanish memorabilia, he committed suicide with a pistol. He was 29 years old.

# THREE

# *Flying Tigers*

On the other side of the world, in China, in 1936 General Chiang Kaishek saw the coming of war with Japan, and moved to build up the infant Chinese air force, which had only about 100 aircraft. Chiang turned the job over to his wife, Soong Meiling. She in turn enlisted Claire Chennault, a retired U.S. Army Air Force officer, for $1000 a month. Chennault had scarcely reached China in 1937 when the Sino-Japanese War erupted in fury at Marco Polo Bridge, near Beijing.

Soon Chennault had acquired two dozen Vultee V-11 bombers and hired American mercenary pilots to operate them. But the American mercenaries who arrived were a tawdry lot who, as Chennault said, "subsisted almost entirely on high-octane beverages." The propensity for strong drink almost destroyed the volunteer group in the beginning. Chennault planned a maiden attack with the two dozen bombers on the town of Jinan in Shandong province, but the fliers talked openly about the mission in the bars, and Japanese agents were listening. On the night before the mission Japanese bombers appeared over the airfield and blew the two dozen bombers into little pieces. Chennault persevered, however, and soon developed an early warning network. Chinese all over the country reported by radio, telephone, and telegraph on the movement of Japanese aircraft, thus enabling Chennault to use his slender resources fully to meet attack.

In 1940 Chennault returned to the United States, where he was advised by T. V. Soong, Chiang Kaishek's brother-in-law and ambassador to the United States. Chennault's mission was to secure planes and pilots for China. Through political connections close to President Franklin D. Roosevelt, Chennault and Soong managed to buy 100 Curtiss P-40 fighter planes. This was no mean feat at a time when the United States was committed to supplying Britain with aircraft and was beginning to build up its own air force.

Securing competent pilots was also a difficult matter. Chennault turned to the U.S. Army Air Corps and the U.S. Navy Air arm, but General H. H. Arnold of the Air Corps and Admiral John Towers of the Navy refused to help him recruit within the services. Then President Roosevelt took a hand and, in April 1941, issued an executive order permitting American servicemen to resign their commissions, go to China to fight for a year, and then come back and resume their rank and service with the military air services.

For the next few weeks recruiters worked the army, navy, and Marine Corps air bases and assembled several groups of pilots. The first group reached Rangoon by ship in September 1941 and then went to the British Royal Air Force base at Toungoo, 160 miles north, for training. Not one of them had any combat experience. After training they would go to the town of Lashio, where they would cover the Burma road that led up to China's Yunnan province. There one pilot, Eric Shilling, designed the shark face insignia that would be painted on the P-40 planes and would become world famous as the sign of the "Flying Tigers." In China, the tiger symbolizes ferocity.

The American Volunteer Group (AVG) was divided into three squadrons: Hell's Angels, the Panda Bears, and Adam and Eve. They were in training when the Japanese attacked Pearl Harbor and the United States was drawn into the war. The Hell's Angels squadron was then left at Toungoo to support the British defense of Rangoon, and the other two squadrons left for Kunming, the capital of Yunnan province.

Flying Curtiss CW-21 fighter planes across the Himalayas, three pilots ran into difficulties. Eric Shilling had engine trouble and had to crash-land in the mountains of China. He was found by Chinese villagers, who first took him for a Japanese, but then decided he was not and took him down to a village below the mountains. There Shilling learned that his two companions had also crashed. Lacey Mangleburg had been killed, and Kenneth Merritt had survived the crash.

When Shilling got to Kunming and told of his troubles, Chennault developed a back patch which showed a Chinese Nationalist flag and Chinese writing explaining the pilot's identity and offering a reward for helping him. This became another badge of the American Volunteer Group, and was later copied by the Fourteenth Air Force in China and the Tenth Air Force in India and Burma.

On December 20, 1941, the Flying Tigers went into action. Chennault's early warning air raid system announced that Japanese planes were coming in from the Hanoi area. For a year, the Japanese had been bombing Kunming without meeting resistance. This day, they came in confidently to do the same with ten Mitsubishi twin-engine bombers. But this time they were met by two squadrons of P-40s with grimacing open sharks' mouths, and soon nine of the Japanese bombers were shot down. One bomber escaped and returned to Hanoi. Pilot Edward F. Rector gave chase, until his plane ran out of gas and he had to crash-land. His was the only casualty to the AVG that day.

On December 23, the Japanese made a massive air assault on Rangoon, and the AVG Hell's Angels squadron was sent up from Mingaladon airfield to intercept.

First, in came eighteen Nakajima twin-engine medium bombers. They surprised the British defenders and attacked before any fighters could be sent aloft. They left the Rangoon docks ablaze.

The second wave, coming in from an air base in Bangkok, consisted of thirty more bombers escorted by twenty Nakajima fighters. But by this time the British were alert, and the Japanese were met by twenty RAF Buffalo fighters and the Flying Tigers' sixteen P-40s.

Chennault had trained his Flying Tigers to attack in teams of two. The P-40 was already "obsolete" in 1940 (although 14,000 would be manufactured and used by nine nations during the early days of the war), which is why the Chinese got 100 of them. But the airplane had certain positive characteristics. It was very heavy, which meant it could achieve great speed in a dive, perhaps 500 miles an hour. Chennault taught his pilots to use that speed as their principal weapon, to dive on an enemy and then to break away and make another climb and another pass. The Flying Tiger teams dove down on the enemy, firing as they came. Kenneth Jernstedt knocked down a bomber with the first burst from his guns. Charles Older shot down two bombers, but the explosion of one of them damaged another P-40, which crashed into the Rangoon River. Henry Gilbert's P-40 was shot down by a Japanese bomber tail gunner, and he became the first Flying Tiger to die in combat. Pilot Paul Greene was cornered by two Japanese fighters, and his P-40 broke up in midair. He parachuted to safety, but all the way down to the ground the Japanese fighters circled his parachute and fired on him. Soon the chute was a mass of bullet holes, but it held together long enough to get him down. Luckily, Greene was not hit by any of the bullets.

The second Japanese wave turned back without bombing. They had lost six bombers and ten fighters, while the British lost five Buffaloes and the AVG four P-40s.

On Christmas Day the Japanese returned with an even more massive air raid: sixty bombers accompanied by twenty fighter escorts. This time the British were not surprised. Three AVG pilots had been up on patrol, watching for the enemy, and they reported them before the Japanese reached Rangoon. Soon a dozen P-40s were in the air, along with sixteen Brewster Buffaloes. From the first wave the Flying Tigers shot down eight Japanese bombers. Altogether that day, the Japanese lost forty-five planes, the British lost nine fighters, and the Flying Tigers lost two. Robert Hedman shot down five planes to become the first American ace of the war in Asia.

But the Japanese advance to conquer Burma continued, and on the ground the Japanese were moving fast. So the Japanese air force came again and again. For seventy-five days the air battle over Rangoon continued. To try to stem the tide, General Chennault moved the Panda Bears squadron, and later the Adam and Eve squadron, to Rangoon.

On the morning of January 26, 1942, the Japanese sent fifty fighter planes over Rangoon on a sweep. Their leader had been studying the AVG tactics and the P-40 aircraft, and came up with a new wrinkle. As usual the P-40s climbed above the enemy planes, and came screaming down on them in pairs. But this time the Japanese opened their formations and let the P-40s scream by without hitting anything. Then the Japanese fighters executed split S maneuvers, flipping on their backs and making a half loop, and dived on the Americans who had gone by them. Immediately they shot down one P-40.

So the Flying Tigers learned that day not to try to outmaneuver the Japanese, whose unarmored fighter planes were much lighter and more maneuverable than the P-40s. Instead, the new technique was to lure a plane away from its formation, and then to trap the pilot and shoot him down. They shot down scores of Japanese planes, but they could not win the battle of Burma. The Japanese army reached the outskirts of Rangoon at the end of February, while the Flying Tigers picked up and moved to Magwe in northern Burma and then back to Kunming.

In the spring of 1942, the war changed. In March, the United States Army Air Corps was rechristened the United States Army Air Force and plans were made to establish air forces in various theaters of combat. Lieutenant General Joseph W. Stilwell made a trip to Kunming to confer with General Chennault, and Chennault was returned to active duty in the Army Air Force as a brigadier general. The Flying Tigers were asked to give up their mercenary status and join the Fourteenth Air Force, which would operate under Chennault in China.

But most of the Flying Tigers were tired, and the officer sent from America to recruit them was heavy-handed and unpopular. Only about half a dozen Tigers changed over to become Army Air Force fighter pilots in China. The rest opted to go home. On July 4, 1942, the American Volunteer Group was disbanded, and the Flying Tigers became just another memory.

# FOUR

# The Eagle Squadrons

When war with Germany broke out in September 1939, Britain immediately began reorganizing and strengthening the air arm of its defense forces, the Royal Air Force. In the colonies, too—in Canada, South Africa, Australia, and New Zealand—men rushed to the colors. Soon many young Americans were trying to join up, some of them because they wanted to learn to fly, but most of them because they wanted to fight Nazi totalitarianism.

The genesis of the American Eagle Squadrons in the Royal Air Force came from an Anglo-American family named Sweeny which had a history of involvement with uprisings and wars all over the world. They recruited young Americans to join the Royal Air Force (in England) and the Royal Canadian Air Force. The Canadians established a recruiting commission headed by Air Vice Marshal Billy Bishop, one of the leading aces of World War I. Recruiting was soon going full blast.

The three initial Eagles had begun by trying to join the French Air Force, remembering the tradition of the Lafayette Escadrille of World War I. They were Shorty Keough, a pilot and professional parachute jumper from New York, Gene Tobin, a Los Angeles boy who had learned flying there, and Andrew Mamedoff, a charter pilot from Connecticut. The three met in the spring of 1940 in Montreal where they had been drawn by the Sweenys, who were then recruiting for the French. As they took ship for France the Germans were breaking through the Netherlands and Belgium, bypassing the French Maginot line, and moving so fast the French could not keep up with them. So the French air recruiting program failed, and the three young men were left stranded and in danger of being captured by the Germans. They managed to escape by ship and get to England, where they tried to enlist in the RAF.

At first the RAF turned them down. But Winston Churchill and some others recognized the propaganda value in America of having Americans fighting for Britain in this period when pro-German and antiwar elements exercised a great deal of influence in Washington. Besides, the war had changed for Britain. With the fall of France that summer, the British knew that they would soon come under attack from the full force of the Germans. On July 5, 1940, the three pilots were accepted, given four weeks of training which ended up with flying a Spitfire fighter plane, and sent with volunteers from other nations to 609 Squadron in Dorset, across the English Channel from Cherbourg.

They finished training just in time to get into the Battle of Britain.

On July 10, 1940, Marshal Hermann Goering's Luftwaffe opened an attack on Britain that Goering promised would destroy British air defenses and make the proposed cross-channel invasion of Britain a simple matter. The initial attacks were on British shipping, but on August 13—Adler Tag, ("Eagle Day") the Germans called it—the move to destroy the RAF was started. Fifty Stuka dive bombers attacked airfields in and around Dorset, and 609 Squadron went into action against them. That was the beginning of sustained German effort. On August 15, the three young Americans were in the fight, and Tobin shot down a Messerschmitt fighter.

For the next month the Luftwaffe fought the Battle of Britain, trying to destroy the RAF. Tobin, Mamedoff, and Keough were in the thick of it. On September 15 Goering unleashed the whole of Germany's air power, but failed to knock out the RAF. That day Gene Tobin shot down a Dornier bomber and probably an ME-109. Four days later the three Americans were sent to Church Fenton to be a part of 71 Squadron, which the Sweenys had organized. In command was an American Marine Corps pilot named William Taylor, who had been in England on vacation when war came and who then began flying for the Royal Navy. Americans were being assembled from many places to join 71 Squadron.

At a press conference Taylor was made squadron commander and Robert Sweeny was made adjutant of the new squadron. They went to call on the air officer commanding the area, Air Vice Marshal Trafford Leigh-Mallory, who was very cool, as Taylor recalled:

"He said he was very strongly opposed to having a squadron of Americans. From his experience with them in the First World War he had found that individually they were charming, but as a group they were completely undisciplined. I kept my mouth shut except to say that the squadron's formation was already a *fait accompli*."

But Leigh-Mallory was not to be dissuaded, and for months Taylor found himself a figurehead, with a British officer actually in command of the American squadron. It was not until January 1941, after Air Vice Marshall Leigh-Mallory had been transferred to other duties, that the original Eagle Squadron was really established.

Marshal Leigh-Mallory's opinion of the Eagles was confirmed by American Air Corps General H. H. Arnold, who regarded them as a bunch of prima donnas. And in fact at first they did not do very well or get much respect from their RAF counterparts. The Eagles first went into battle on April 13, 1941, near Calais. Pilot Officer John Flynn was being pursued by a Messerschmidt 109, when Pilot Officer James Alexander went after the German. The ME-109 went off trailing smoke, but Alexander's bullets also hit Flynn's plane, which was so badly shot up it had to land near Manston. This gave the RAF boys the laugh that the Americans drew first blood by shooting each other down.

In their first weeks of combat at Martlesham Heath, the Eagles of 71 Squadron suffered from very low morale, created by the unkind remarks about their abilities. Everyone in the RAF knew that Prime Minister Churchill had formed the squadron for propaganda purposes, over the objection of practically everyone in the RAF.

The Eagles were a sloppy lot and, since most of them had lied about their hours in the air, not very skillful as a group. They had many operational accidents—too many. Although Squadron Commander Taylor worked hard at knocking them into shape, before he could accomplish this he was promoted out of the squadron. The command was given to another British officer, Squadron Leader Henry de Clifford Anthony Wood. Soon the Eagles were transferred to another station, north of London.

On May 14, 1941, a second American squadron, 121 squadron, was organized under one of the heroes of the Battle of Britain, Squadron Leader Robin Peter Reginald Powell, who had shot down seven German planes. Then on August 1, a third Eagle squadron was established—133 Squadron at Colishall, in Essex, under Flight Lieutenant George A. Brown.

Like the other two American squadrons, 133 started out badly, with more than its share of operational accidents. But by the summer of 1941, the Americans were getting into shape and began to produce positive results. On July 2, Gus Daymond and Bill Dunn, flying Hurricane fighters, each shot down a German plane near Lille, France, and a few days later each shot down another. A tense duel for leadership in victories began. Dunn became the first to shoot down five planes and become an ace. He flew his last mission with the Eagles on August 27, when his 71 Squadron was part of an escort of 100 Spitfires for nine Blenheim bombers that were attacking the steel mill at Lille. Here is Dunn's account:

"I dived on one of two ME-109Fs, fired from a distance of 150 yards, and fired again to within 50 yards. Pieces of the aircraft flew off, and engine oil spattered my windscreen. The plane looked like a blowtorch with a bluish white flame as it went down.

"Tracers from another 109F behind me flashed past my cockpit. I pulled back the throttle, jammed down the flaps, and skidded my plane sharply out of his gunsight. The German overshot me by about ten feet, and as he crossed overhead I could see the black cross insignia, unit markings, and a red rooster painted on the side of the cockpit.

"The 109 was now within my range. With a burst of only three seconds I had him out of commission. A wisp of smoke from the engine turned almost immediately into a sheet of flame. The plane rolled over on its back. As it started down, the tail section broke off. I had claimed my second victim of the day.

"I fired at another ME-109 and saw smoke coming from it. Just as I started to press the gun button my plane lurched sharply. I heard explosions. A ball of fire streamed through the cockpit, smashing into the instrument panel. There were two heavy blows against my right leg, and as my head snapped forward I began to lose consciousness.

"My mind cleared again and I realized that the earth was spinning up toward me. I tugged back on the control column and pulled back into a gradual dive toward the English Channel, fifty miles away.

"I checked the plane for damage. The tip of the right wing was gone. The rudder had been badly damaged. The instruments on the right side of my panel were shattered.

"There was blood on the cockpit floor. When I looked at my right leg I saw that the toe of my boot had been shot off. My trouser leg was drenched with blood. I could feel warm, sticky fluid seeping from under my helmet to my neck and cheek. I gulped oxygen to fight off nausea.

"Releasing my shoulder harness, I started to climb out of the cockpit. For some reason I paused. The engine was still running all right and the plane seemed flyable. I slid back into my seat. I would try to make it home. . . .

"Crossing the Channel the engine began to lose power. I switched on the radio telephone and called May Day. Within a few moments I had an escort of two Spitfires.

"They led me across the coastal cliffs to the grass airfield at Hawkinge, near Folkestone. The escorting pilot signaled to me that my landing gear had extended.

"I dropped smoothly onto the newly mowed turf and taxied to a waiting ambulance. An airman climbed up on the wing and shouted at me that I was in the wrong area and must taxi over to the dispersal hut if I wanted fuel and ammunition. Then he saw my bloody face and helmet and called the medical officer.

"I awoke thirty hours later in a bed in the Royal Victoria hospital in Folkestone and learned that the front part of my foot had been shot away, that there were two machine gun bullets in my right leg, and that another had creased the back of my head. I spent three months recuperating there and at the RAF hospital at Torquay."

By late summer of 1941 the Eagle squadrons had proved themselves and were no longer the subject of wry remarks by the rest of the RAF. They had much to boast about: 71 Squadron was known for its spit and polish, and for its effectiveness as a close escort squadron.

But not all missions ended in victory and heroism. Sometimes it was another story, as with Eagle Pilot Officer William Geiger. With thirty missions behind him, he was among pilots assigned on September 17, 1941, to escort a daylight raid of Blenheim bombers. Over Dunkirk they ran into German fighters, and Geiger was shot down. He parachuted into the English Channel, got into his dinghy, and rowed but got nowhere. That night he was picked up by the crew of a German E-boat, who turned him over to the army. Geiger went to prison camp, where he spent the next three and a half years.

The Eagles came in all shapes and sizes, and some of them were very, very young. The youngest was Gilmore Cecil Daniel, an Osage Indian. He had joined the RCAF in December 1939, using a forged birth certificate showing that he had been born in 1921. He was actually fourteen years old. Before he was finished he had served in all three Eagle squadrons and six other RAF squadrons.

On October 13, 1941, Pilot Officer Daniel was escorting Blenheims on a mission to Bethune, France:

"I had broken formation to attack three 109Fs. I shot the lead one up and he exploded, knocking the other two down also. I was so surprised and excited that I turned for England, forgetting to watch out for other enemy planes. I was soon being fired on by other 109Fs.

"I don't know to this day why I was not killed, because the cockpit was a shambles. I looked over my left shoulder and saw a plane off my port wing shooting at me in a 90-degree deflection.

There was an explosion in my starboard wing. I could see a big hole where my cannon ammo had been, so I started to dive at 28,000 feet.

"Smoke was pouring from two holes in the gas tank in front of my legs. I knew it would be just seconds before fire broke out. I jettisoned my canopy and when I pulled my Sutton harness pin I flew out, hitting the tail. I opened my chute immediately, not realizing how high above the earth I was.

"The 109Fs kept buzzing me and even shot at me until I waved at them. Upon hitting the water I released my chute. Then I knew I had been hit by shell fragments. My leg hurt like hell.

"The 109Fs went away and then darkness came. I had a grandstand seat for the bombing of Calais that night. I was about five miles from Dover, so I wasn't worried about being picked up; but the next day when Lysanders flew over me and I waved they did not see me. Then I started to worry. I waited all day and saw many fighters and a Walrus flying boat, but no one saw me.

"Night set in again and it was like the night before. The next day it started to rain. It was very cold and my face and hands were out of the water. My leg hurt and my wounds were very sore. Still I wasn't picked up.

"Nighttime set in again. Hours later I could hear the roar of the surf and distinguish land. Some time later I was thrown up on the beach. I crawled as best I could as soon as I felt ground. That was the last I knew until a very bright light was shined on me and I heard foreign voices.

"Later in the evening I awoke in a bed with a German sitting beside me in a chair. He asked in English how I was and whether I wanted something to eat.

"I had been in the water in my dinghy for seventy-eight hours. The water had helped to sterilize my wounds and kept me from freezing, but I did have frostbite and a cracked or broken leg.

"I was taken to St. Omer hospital and given very good care, and then was removed to a hospital at Lille. Later I was taken to Germany and put in Stalag Luft III, where I remained for over three years."

*        *        *

There are many tales of airmen dropping into occupied territory and then getting out with the aid of the Maquis. But not all Frenchmen were Maquis, and some, like Pilot Officer Jack Fessler of 71 Squadron, did not escape:

"My last day as an Eagle: October 28, 1941. It was a dawn rhubarb over France. . . .

"I started a gentle dive at a large freight train engine in the marshaling yards at Boulogne, firing with cannon and machine guns.

"I continued the attack until I had to pull up to clear the engine. At that moment either the freight engine blew up or I flew into it—I'll never know. I felt no impact, but my oil cooler and radiator cooling had both been damaged, and my engine was missing badly. I pulled up to about 2000 feet, looked for a place to land, and set down in a plowed field just outside Boulogne. I used a post fire to ignite my plane and then took off on foot. It was 6:15 a.m.

"Within fifteen minutes search parties with dogs were after me. I kept to the streams, using hedgerows for cover, and we played hide-and-seek until the searchers gave up in midafternoon. At one point I hid in a clump of bushes not seventy-five feet from men and dogs assembled at a crossroads intersection. Luckily I was downwind from them.

"I watched a farmhouse for the rest of the afternoon and evening. At about 9 p.m. an automobile drove up and the occupants went into the house. At eleven o'clock I went to the back door and knocked. A farm woman in a long nightgown let me in, and the farmer appeared in long johns. They invited me to sit in the kitchen and the woman stirred up the fire and started warming some soup.

"The farmer's daughter came into the kitchen and then two French gendarmes pulling their pants on over long johns. One had a pistol in his belt. The police officers were the persons who had come in the car. They were billeted in the farm home.

"We all discussed my situation. I had with me an English-French pocket dictionary and had also studied French in school. We could understand each other.

"They fed me soup and offered me wine.

" 'The Germans know you are in this area,' one gendarme said. 'Tomorrow they will be back with larger search parties. If your scent leads them to this house and they do not find you, they will know we helped you. They will cut all our throats as a warning to other French people not to aid the enemy. We know they will do this because they have done it before.'

"I knew they were telling the truth. I wondered whether the gendarme with the pistol would fire at me if I were to run out the door into the night. At the same time I wanted none of these people killed because of me. Therefore I allowed the gendarmes to take me with them and turn me over to the German authorities. Thus began my three and a half years as a prisoner of war."

On the day that Pearl Harbor was attacked, two of the Eagle squadrons were in England and the third was on a sort of R and R in Northern Ireland. Immediately the two squadrons in England sent emissaries to London to see the American ambassador. While they were at the embassy, Ambassador John G. Winant spoke to President Franklin D. Roosevelt and it was agreed that the Eagles would be transferred to the Army Air Corps as soon as possible. (In fact the transfer was not accomplished until September 1942.)

When the change came, the three Eagle squadrons of the RAF marched to the parade grounds at Debden one rainy day, led by their squadron leaders. When they marched out, they were the Fourth Fighter Group of the United States Army Air Force. Air Chief Marshal Sholto Douglas presented them to their new commander, Major General Carl Spaatz. And the RAF made note of their accomplishments. In eighteen months the Eagles had certainly destroyed at least 73 enemy planes and had probably destroyed many more, perhaps twice as many.

# FIVE

# Airman Jake Jones

In the winter of 1940 Jake Jones, contemplating life after high school, took a civil service examination for a machinist apprenticeship at the Washington Navy Yard. He passed. When he graduated from McKinley Technological High School he started work in the assembly and fuse shop at the yard. It was July 1941, and the pressure of the American defense buildup was on.

"For the first few months most of us kids were put at benches and given a file to file the rough edges off various parts that were being assembled there. Then many of us were assigned to the 1.10 antiaircraft gun assembly section. So there were a bunch of seventeen-and eighteen-year-old kids turning out something that was supposed to defend navy ships from aircraft. Poor sailors!"

When Japan bombed Pearl Harbor the defense effort picked up. Women began coming into the work force, and the army established an antiaircraft gun position on the roof of the building in which Jake Jones worked. The yard went on three shifts.

After working one midnight-to-8 a.m. shift in January 1942, Jones went across the river to Anacostia Naval Air station to see about enlisting in the naval aviation unit there. He could not pass the eye examination and, dejected, he returned to the Navy Yard and continued to build antiaircraft guns. But all this time he was itching to get into the service, so in October he went back to the navy and tried to enlist. The answer was again no, his eyesight was not good enough. But next door to the navy recruiting station was the army recruiting station, where he applied and was accepted for enlistment.

A few days later Jake Jones was sent to Camp Lee, Virginia for processing, classification, shots, and the rest of the enlistment procedure. He asked to be assigned to the Air Corps, and was sent to Miami Beach for basic Air Corps training.

"What a great place to get started in a war! I was assigned to a hotel at Fourteenth and Collins Avenue. Again we had shots, tests, and then we started drill and marching. We sang as we marched, so the whole area was one big noise. We were restricted to the beach, but there wasn't time to go anywhere anyway."

During the classification interviews Private Jones was asked what specialty he was interested in. He really wanted to be an aerial gunner if he could not be a pilot, but by this time he knew that his eyes would not pass the physical for flight crew. So he asked to become aircraft mechanic.

Nine days of basic training and Private Jones was put on a troop train, destination unknown. When they arrived he found he was in Amarillo, in the panhandle of Texas, at aircraft mechanics' school.

The army was really in a hurry. The school was not yet open, so for three weeks Jake Jones pulled KP and peeled potatoes. It was Thanksgiving time, so he was also put to work baking pies.

Amarillo was a big base, and they marched and marched, and sang and sang and sang, through the tumbleweeds and sagebrush and cactus, in the dry prairie wind with the sun beating down. It was a desolate place, out in the middle of nowhere. The barracks was a one-story wooden shack covered with tar paper, wired to the ground so it would not blow away in the fierce winds.

Private Jones was assigned to the 624th Technical School Squadron. Classes started on December 7, fittingly, but at midnight!—again part of the hurry-up, to use facilities to the utmost. The training area classrooms and hangars were busy, busy, busy. And uncomfortable. Some general visited and found students asleep on the night shift, ordered all chairs removed from the classrooms. After that Private Jones stood as he trained.

The school had been started to train B-17 mechanics, and there were many early B-17s scattered around, including some relics of the earliest model, the YB.

Class began with reading technical orders and learning how to fill out Air Corps forms, and proceeded to hydraulics and electronics, fuel oil, and other aspects of the aircraft. Each week they changed shifts. After class if it was day, and before class if it was night, they continued with the basic training: march, march, march, calisthenics, obstacle courses, gas mask training, lectures on health, the Articles of War, and all the soldier stuff. It was all tacked on to their class work, and it made for long days. On their one day a week off, they usually weren't allowed off base until ten or eleven in the morning and there was an 11 p.m. curfew in town, which was about an hour's bus ride from the base. This didn't give them much time to do damage, about all they would do was find a steak dinner (if they had the money) or go to a movie. As in most bases in those days, the soldiers outnumbered the civilians.

"As we progressed through our classwork we were given a session in the engine test cells to learn to diagnose and correct troubles in the engine. The control panel for the engine was directly behind it and they didn't have mufflers, so in the winter we were there it was a cold and noisy experience. To me it was one of the highlights of the whole school, because I could actually start and run an aircraft engine and even do minor repairs on it."

The school lasted four months. Private Jones graduated on April 13, 1943. The class broke up then; some men went to aerial gunnery, some were assigned to squadrons, and some were sent to the Boeing factory in Seattle. All of them were promoted to corporals, many times known sneeringly in the line as "tech school corporals."

Corporal Jones was assigned to the Boeing factory detail: "What a great war! Getting a chance to be around the really new airplanes and to be taught by the experts who really built them. A dream come true."

The Boeing course lasted until May 28, 1943. "The Boeing people really impressed us with the myth of the B-17. Even to this day I look upon the B-17 as the best airplane ever built."

The airmen were given tours of the plants and the flight line. They were told that the current B-17F was constantly being modified to meet combat conditions. They could see that this was going to be a problem, because no more than five aircraft were exactly alike.

After factory training the class was again split, some going to aerial gunnery, some to squadrons, and some to become crew chiefs on airplanes just off the assembly line.

"Another jackpot—I got a brand-new airplane, SN 42–30441. Talk about a pig in clover. The only thing that ever exceeded that moment was when my son was born.

"We were issued the sheep-lined flying gear, a parachute, and all the documents for the airplane, which we signed for. Imagine a nineteen-year-old corporal as the 'owner' of a brand-new B-17F."

Corporal Jones was told to report to the flight line one morning and make a preflight check of the airplane. They were going. Out at the airplane he realized that he did not know where the engine oil sump dipsticks were located, but luckily the pilot did. They climbed on the wing and checked all four dipsticks.

The pilots were from the Ferry Command section of the Air Transport Command. On a foggy June morning they took off from the Boeing field in Georgetown. Corporal Jones had no idea where they were going, and he was much too afraid of officers to ask. He sat in the chair in the radio compartment and watched through a small window in the fuselage as they lifted off. It was his first airplane ride!

As they climbed out over the mountains, he made a tour of the plane. Ultimately he wound up in the bombardier's nose compartment and watched for hours as the mountains moved under him.

They landed at Great Falls, Montana, a Ferry Command base for ferrying through Alaska to Soviet Russia. He saw rows and rows of C-47s and A-20 attack bombers painted with the Russian red star. For a while he thought the pilots had made a wrong turn.

For several days they flew out of Great Falls, practicing landings, before Corporal Jones realized he was participating in the training of ferry command pilots. He had been too scared to ask what they were doing.

Again they headed out, after about three weeks, and again Corporal Jones did not know where he was going. He sat in the nose compartment for the view. There were just three of them in the aircraft: the pilot, the copilot, and Crew Chief Jones.

This time on landing the pilot misjudged and nearly ran through the fence at the end of the paved runway. Sitting in the nose and watching that fence come up was a hairy experience. The pilot dragged that airplane around in a controlled ground loop at the very end, and they almost missed, but bumped a stake with a marker flag, leaving a dent in the fuselage by the tail gun compartment which remained in the aircraft for the rest of its life.

When they taxied up to the hangar, Corporal Jones discovered they were in Cheyenne, Wyoming. United Airlines had a maintenance shop there, and the B-17F was to be fitted with improvements before going into combat. It was to get a chin turret. (All the G models would come with the chin turret.)

They spent two weeks in Cheyenne. Some of the equipment being put in the aircraft was so secret that a mere crew chief was not to learn about it, and so Corporal Jones was sent to Fort Warren, an old cavalry post, to wait. For two weeks it was like being on furlough. Nobody cared what he did; he could have gone AWOL and no one would have noticed.

When the modifications were complete, Corporal Jones and the pilots went out on a test flight. He rode in the nose again to sightsee. When this new pilot landed, he ran off the runway onto the ground, which was soft mud that day. The mud spattered against the flaps and wrecked them. The plane had to be towed. The airplane then had to go to the hanger for a few more days. When it was ready it had new flaps, a whole flock of new nose guns, and more equipment.

Now, said Corporal Jones, he was going off into the wild blue yonder just like it said in the song.

"Hot Dog! [I thought.] Now that all the combat stuff is in here we're going to England with the Eighth Air Force, and maybe they'll need guys to fly as gunners, even guys with bad eyes. Now I can shoot down Nazi airplanes and get to wear one of those nifty A-2 jackets with the patches and the bombing missions painted on. Maybe I'll get promoted to staff sergeant and even win some medals.

"No kidding, that's the way I really felt.

"Well it didn't happen that way. The guys who were in combat will probably swear that I'm full of it and nobody felt that way. But I did because it was what I had dreamed of since being a little kid. I was just a bigger kid now. but still hanging on to the dreams. Maybe I was a 'war lover.'

"The reality was that this time I got into the airplane with unknown pilots again for an unknown destination. But the longer we flew the more I knew it wasn't toward England.

"This time we landed at Roswell Army Air Field, New Mexico. It was July 1943, and that's where I spent the rest of the war."

# SIX

# *Disaster at Pearl Harbor*

In the spring of 1941, President Franklin D. Roosevelt called on the U.S. Army and Navy to give him a briefing on the state of the defenses of the important American fleet and air bases at and around Pearl Harbor, in the territory of Hawaii. Army General George C. Marshall and Secretary of War Henry L. Stimson gave him an aide-mémoire which painted a rosy picture of the defenses. Oahu Island, they said, was the "strongest fortress in the world." It had 127 fixed coastal naval guns, a garrison of 35,000 men, 211 antiaircraft guns, and 3000 artillery pieces and automatic weapons. Any invasion attempt by the Japanese was doomed to failure.

As far as air defense was concerned, "Enemy carriers, naval escorts, and transports will begin to come under attack at a distance of approximately 750 miles. This attack will increase in intensity until when within 200 miles of the objective, the enemy forces will be subject to attack by all types of bombardment, closely supported by our most modern pursuit."

It sounded grand and effective. But where were those planes capable of flying out 750 miles to attack the enemy? They would have to be the B-17s, and at that moment there were not thirty-five B-17s in the islands. Indeed, at the moment of Japanese attack on December 7, 1941, there would be only twelve B-17s in Hawaii, only six of them operational.

The real danger, according to General Marshall and others in the American military high command, was sabotage. They distrusted Japanese-Americans, and fully expected them to strike out against the country that had harbored them.

In air maneuvers held in May, the defenders found and successfully attacked the invading forces from the air when they were still 250 miles at sea. But twenty-one B-17s had been specially brought to the islands for these maneuvers. The whole ambience of the war games was unreal, largely because in the games the defenders expected an attack and knew when it was coming, whereas the real thing would be a surprise. The American high command was aware of the danger, no question about that. But they could not remain alert all the time. Had they maintained a twenty-four-hour patrol system from the spring of 1941, they would have caught the Japanese in the act, but given the state of the American defenses, it was doubtful if it would have made a great deal of difference. The United States was simply not prepared for the sort of war the Japanese intended to thrust on the western world.

In July 1941, knowing that war was brewing, the Fifth Bombardment Group at Hickam Field, Hawaii, made a survey of the capability of the bombers for the defense of Oahu. A few days later the man who made the survey, Colonel William E. Farthing, was chosen to enhance it for the War Department. His finding: The Army Air Corps had the capability to defend Hawaii from attack without the help of the navy, thus releasing the navy for offensive operations. (Of course, this was just what Japan's Admiral Yamamoto feared, and was the reason for the Pearl Harbor attack, which was designed to forestall an American attack on the Japanese forces moving in Malaya, the Philippines, and the Dutch East Indies.) The Farthing Report called for daily searches, all during the daylight hours, of the area all around Hawaii, and immediate attack upon sighting a carrier, to hit it before it could launch planes.

In the report it worked out very nicely. But on the morning of December 7, there were no patrol planes in the air, there was no search pattern, there was not even an alert full crew at the key radar station. At seven o'clock in the morning, the two duty men at the Opana Mobile Radar Station near Kahuku Point on the northern tip of Oahu were shutting down their search operations, after three hours of work. Suddenly their radar screen picked up an image—probably more than fifty planes—coming in from the north. Private George E. Elliott suggested that they telephone the Combat Information Center. His partner, Private Joseph L. Lockard, first said no, their duty hours had ended. Elliott persisted: It would be a good test for the Combat Information Center—an unscheduled event. So Lockard agreed and they made the call.

By this time, the blips had moved in about twenty miles closer to Oahu.

On the morning of December 7, Washington time, which was six hours ahead of Hawaii time, army and navy intelligence officers were puzzling over intercepts of a fourteen-part Japanese message from Tokyo to the two Japanese envoys who were conducting "peace" talks with the Americans. The fourteenth part, which came in during midmorning, indicated that something important was going to happen around 1 p.m. Washington time— 7 a.m Hawaii time.

The army intelligence officers went to the office of Army Chief of Staff General George C. Marshall, and waited there until he came in at 11:25. (It was, after all, a Sunday, and he was not expecting anything in particular.) They showed him their intercepts and their conclusions. Marshall concurred and sent off a message of warning at about noon:

"Japanese are presenting at one p.m. eastern standard time today what amounts to an ultimatum. Also they are under orders to destroy their code machine immediately. Just what significance the hour set may have we do not know but be on alert accordingly. Inform naval authorities of this communication. Marshall."

When the Washington chief of communications tried to send the message to Hawaii, he ran into problems with atmospheric conditions between the West Coast and Hawaii, so he turned to commercial channels. A teletyped message was sent to Western Union in San Francisco, and then via RCA to Honolulu.

The message was received at 7:33, and was put in a pigeonhole for the Kahili area by the operator. It was not marked urgent. The delivery boy picked it up with the other Kahili area messages, got on his motorcycle, and headed for the Kahili area, which included Fort Shafter and the army communications center.

By this time the Japanese air striking force of bombers and fighters was within sight of Oahu.

The U.S. Army Air Corps Combat Information Center in Hawaii was located at Fort Shafter, east of Pearl Harbor. On the ground floor the "plotters" worked around a big table map, marking the positions of planes reported by the radar. The controller's position and that of the pursuit officer were on a balcony above. Private Joseph McDonald took the call from the radar station that morning, including the message about the sighting. Lieutenant Kermit Tyler was the pursuit officer and assistant to the controller that day. His job was to assist the controller in ordering planes into the air to intercept enemy planes. Tyler was new on his job, and had made only one tour of duty in it on December 3. Because he was new, he had pulled a most undesirable shift, starting at 4 a.m. Down below him the half dozen enlisted men who were plotters had been standing around the table. At 7 a.m. they all went off duty, and nobody showed up to replace them. So when the call from the radar station came, there was no plot.

Private McDonald was surprised by what he was hearing from the radar station, and he called to Lieutenant Tyler to take the phone. The lieutenant picked up the instrument, and the radar operator, Private Lockard, told him about the blips, where they were coming from, and where they were going. He did not tell the lieutenant that he figured there were fifty planes in the formation.

Pearl Harbor was expecting some B-17s from California. A dozen new B-17s were on their way to Hickam, the first stop on their trip to Clark Field, Philippines, to reinforce the bomber group of the Far East Air Force. Also, the carriers were out and were expected back, and it was the practice of the carriers to fly off their pilots as they reached operating distance from Pearl Harbor. So Lieutenant Tyler figured this was either a carrier group or the B-17s. He suddenly recalled a conversation with a bomber pilot who had told him they liked to home in on radio station KGMB in Honolulu, and that the station managers knew this and so played a lot of Hawaiian music by pilot request. It must be B-17s, Lieutenant Tyler said to himself. It never occurred to him that it could be anything other than American planes, because Lockard said nothing about the size of the formation. In fact the first flight of B-17s coming in from California, led by Major Richard H. Carmichael, was not very far behind the Japanese attack force that Lockard had in the radar scope.

Lieutenant Tyler told Lockard not to worry about the blips he was seeing. Tyler was sure it was the B-17s.

Just before 7:50 that morning, Aviation Machinist Mate Third Class Guy C. Avery was lying half awake in his bunk on the sun porch of a bungalow in Kaneohe on the north side of Oahu when he heard the sound of airplane engines. They did not sound quite right to him, so he went to the window. From there he saw a number of Zero fighter planes, with the big red meatball insignia on their wings, fanning out over the Kaneohe Naval Air Station. Avery did not know it, but the fleet at Pearl Harbor and the Hickam airfield would be attacked in a few moments.

Back at Pearl Harbor Lieutenant Commander Logan C. Ramsey of Patrol Wing Two was trying frantically to get the air station duty office on the phone, but without success. At the same time, the officer of the day at Kaneohe was on the telephone trying to ask nearby Bellows Field, the army base, for help, but the army men did not believe him—they thought it was some sort of joke.

On the Kaneohe base that day were thirty-six PBY patrol bombers and a few small planes. Four of the PBYs were moored in the bay, about half a mile apart. The rest were parked on the launch ramp, except four that were in the No. 1 hangar. Commander Harold M. Martin, the commanding officer of the base, hurried down to the administration building. By the time he got there, Zeros had begun strafing the PBYs in the water. In a few moments dive bombers began hitting the planes on the ramp and the service installations. Before the attack ended, six of Kaneohe's thirty-six PBYs were damaged, three which were out on patrol flights escaped the whole action, and the rest were destroyed.

Across the island at Pearl Harbor and the Hickam air base, the Japanese planes came hurtling down. Colonel Farthing, who was in command there, was in the control tower waiting for those B-17s to come in from the West Coast. Then he saw the Japanese.

The first bomb to hit at Hickam scored a direct hit on a repair hangar. Another blew up a supply building, and another hit the enlisted men's mess hall, killing thirty-five men and wounding many others. Still another smashed the base chapel. One bomb destroyed the enlisted men's brand-new beer hall. Another bomb opened up the guardhouse. The prisoners came out, looking for guns to man.

Captain Brooke Allen, acting squadron commander of a B-17 unit, jumped into a bomber and tried to start the engines. He got three started, but the fourth would not go. He taxied the B-17 away from the other parked bombers. From the seat he watched as the Japanese fighters and dive bombers worked over the B-17s, sending one after another up in flames.

At the Ford Island command center at Pearl Harbor, Lieutenant Commander Logan Ramsey saw a plane come diving down, and a moment later came the explosion of a bomb. It was a Japanese plane and a Japanese bomb, he realized.

He raced across the hall to the radio room and ordered the radio operators to send a message in plain English:

"AIR RAID. PEARL HARBOR. THIS IS NOT A DRILL."

It was 7:57 a.m. Hawaii time.

Into this attack came the B-17s from the mainland that were expected that day, manned by skeleton crews. They had no ammunition for their machine guns, because ammunition weighed too much for their fourteen-hour flight from the coast. Major Carmichael's flight of six Flying Fortresses came in during this attack. Carmichael saw all the smoke rising from Hickam and all the planes in the sky. He turned toward Bellows Field, but it, too, was under attack, so he turned north and flew his B-17 to the short fighter strip at Haleiwa and landed there. A second B-17 followed him in.

Back at Hickam Field, Lieutenant Frank Bostrom of Carmichael's flight called for landing instructions. In the tower they told him to land from east to west. The field was under attack by "unidentified" airplanes, said the controller. But as Bostrom tried to land, ground fire came up at him, so he pulled into a cloud bank.

What could he do? He could make another pass, or seek another field. His question was answered in a few moments, when he looked at his fuel gauges and saw that they were quivering on the "empty" mark. He called the Hickam tower again. The answer was negative. Stay away, said the tower, the field was under heavy attack.

Bostrom looked around. He did not have many options. Next to Hickam was the navy golf course, and he put the plane down there safely.

The other three B-17s of Carmichael's flight landed safely at Hickam in the lull between the first and second wave of Japanese attackers. As soon as they were down, they were pushed by handlers under cover.

A few minutes later the second B-17 flight from California came in, commanded by Major Truman Landon. Landon and three other pilots managed to land in that interval, too. But at 8:40 the second Japanese attack was pressed home. Lieutenant Karl T. Barthelmess landed safely, although tracked down by several small planes that he did not recognize. Captain Raymond Swenson was also escorted down, and when he hit the runway, the Zeros attacked and shot the B-17 in half. As the men tried to get out, the Zeros strafed the plane, killing Flight Surgeon William R. Schick.

Seeing this, Lieutenant Robert Richards pulled up and moved away from Hickam. Zeros came after him and began firing. Two crew members were hurt. Richards took all the evasive action he could, and landed the plane at Bellows Field.

\*      \*      \*

The lightning attack had destroyed or damaged half the aircraft at Hickam. The Japanese also bombed Wheeler Field, up on the plateau of Oahu. There, by order of General Short, the army commander in Hawaii who feared sabotage more than anything, the aircraft were positioned for destruction, all lined up neatly on the runway aprons. (Fortunately, the Wheeler Field commander knew better and had built revetments for protection.) The fighters, obsolete P-36s and modern P-40s, could not fight anyhow. Their ammunition was removed at night and placed in the hangars for safety. The hangars were bombed, they flamed, and the ammunition inside began to explode. There was not a single antiaircraft gun on the base, only machine guns. There was no real protection for planes or men on the ground. The Japanese destroyed half the base aircraft.

At Ewa Field, the U.S. Marine base at Barber's Point, the Japanese destroyed nine Wildcat fighter planes and eighteen of the thirty-two scout bombers, more than half of all the planes.

The Japanese had also bombed and torpedoed the battle fleet, sinking four battleships and a tanker, and leaving five damaged battleships and a damaged cruiser. Just after the attack, Commander H. L. Young from the *Enterprise* air group appeared over Ford Island in a dive bomber and was nearly shot down by American antiaircraft fire. He managed to land.

"What the hell goes on here?" he asked. He found out all too soon.

Right after Commander Young came eighteen more *Enterprise* airplanes. The carrier was so close to Pearl Harbor that it was very nearly a target for the Japanese enemy. But it was in the south and the enemy was in the north. As the *Enterprise* planes came in, the American antiaircraft gunners shot down one of these American planes, and Zero fighters shot down four more American aircraft.

Lieutenant Kenneth Taylor and Lieutenant George Welch, fighter pilots who were stationed at Haleiwa Field, had been playing poker all night at the Wheeler Field officers' club. When they heard the sound of bombs and firing, they jumped into Taylor's car and headed for their own field. They took off in their P-40s and were told to patrol Barber's Point, but as nothing was happening there, they went back to Wheeler Field for more ammunition and took off again. Above Wheeler Field they ran into the Japanese fighters.

Lieutenant Taylor saw them first. "I made a nice turn into them and got in a strong line of six or eight planes. I don't know how many. . . . I was on one's tail as we went over Wailua, firing at the one next to me, and there was one following firing at me, and I pulled out. . . . Lieutenant Welch, I think, shot the other man down."

Lieutenant Welch confirmed that story. "I shot one down right on Lieutenant Taylor's tail."

After that, the Japanese turned around and headed home to their carriers. It was about 10 a.m.

At San Diego Naval Air Station a bunch of young ensigns were sprawled around the lounge of the junior officers' quarters that Sunday morning, most of them nursing hangovers. They were stretched out on the rug reading the funny papers, or listening to pop music on the radio, or dozing in the leather chairs. Among them were ensigns James Shelton, Frederick Mears,* Tom Durkin, Richard Jaccard, and William Wileman.

At about 11 a.m. Pacific standard time, the music stopped abruptly.

"We interrupt this program for a news bulletin," said the announcer. "Unidentified planes have just made an attack on Pearl Harbor."

That was all.

At first no one believed it.

"Sure," said a wise guy. "Some dope dropped a smoke bomb

* Material about Frederick Mears is from *Carrier Combat* by Frederick Mears, copyright 1944 by Doubleday, a division of Bantam Doubleday Dell Publishing group, and is used by permission of the publisher.

on Waikiki Beach."

Everybody laughed.

But the announcer was back soon with more details, and it began to sink in that indeed there had been an attack on Pearl Harbor, and that it had been made by planes from Japanese carriers.

The young pilots sat around for the rest of the morning, turning dials, listening. After lunch, at 1 p.m. they were ordered to report to flight headquarters in uniform. From now on, they were told, it would be uniforms all day, every day. They were ordered to stand by.

Later that day, navy and army airmen began to count their losses. The navy had lost about a hundred planes. The army air force had lost 77 planes, and 128 had been damaged. The air installations had been hit hard, too. And for all this, plus the battleships and the other vessels, and 2400 men killed or wounded, the cost to the Japanese had been only twenty-nine aircraft, one large submarine, and five midget submarines.

The confusion engendered on Oahu by the Japanese attack was virtually complete. There would be no more talk about the "invulnerability of the islands" or the enormous effectiveness of the B-17s. As B-17 Historian Edward Jablonsky later remarked, there had been a "Maginot line" sort of thinking, that the big bombers could protect Pearl Harbor against anything. But no more.

There was one other effect of the attack, one that was to hamper the American effort very severely. On the morning of the attack, the Combat Information Center at Fort Shafter should have informed the navy that all those blips had been seen coming toward Oahu from the north. But no one told the navy. No one *ever* told the navy. Consequently, when Admiral Halsey steamed into Pearl Harbor, full of anger and dedication to "go after the goddam Japs," he went tearing off to the southeast. If someone had told him that the Japanese had come from the north, he might have gone that way and might even have caught them. On the other hand, if he had caught them it would have been like catching a tiger by the tail. One carrier task force against six? Those odds would have been tough ones even for Admiral Halsey.

In the 1920s Army Air Corps General Billy Mitchell created an enormous furor when he claimed that airplanes could sink battleships. The American admirals had scoffed. After December 7, 1941, they would scoff no more.

# SEVEN

# Philippines Air Defense

As early as November 1940 the men of the Army Air Corps in the Philippines had been making ready for a Japanese attack. The islands were defended in the air by the Fourth Composite Group, which consisted of the Third, Seventeenth, and Twentieth pursuit squadrons. They were all equipped with P-26 fighter planes, already obsolete.

In May 1941 the squadrons were reequipped with P-35 fighters. These had been diverted from a shipment sold to Sweden in a belated realization by Washington that the islands' defense needed considerable strengthening. And not only new aircraft. The fields of the Clark Field complex needed a great deal of work. That summer the Nichols Field east-west runway could not be used because the rains and bad drainage had caused dangerous conditions. Therefore the Third and Twentieth squadrons were transferred to Clark Field, and the Seventeenth Squadron was transferred to Iba Field.

The Seventeenth Squadron was given P-40B fighters, but the rest still flew the obsolete P-35s. At the same time a hundred new fighter pilots were brought in from the United States and assigned to the group for pursuit training.

In August there were more changes. Gunnery training for the fighter pilots was stepped up, and preparations were made to bring in more B-17 bombers to augment the force of the Twenty-eighth Bombardment Squadron. Yes, the United States was preparing for the defense of the Philippines.

In October another thirty-five new pilots arrived from America, which brought the fighter group's table of organization up to strength for the first time, but many of these pilots were not yet competent fighter pilots. The training continued. In November the Thirty-fourth and Twenty-first pursuit squadrons arrived from the United States. Now most of the squadrons were equipped with P-40s. Three new fields were under construction at O'Donnel, San Fernando, and Ternate.

Slowly the defenders were getting organized, but conditions were still primitive. The air raid warning system consisted of Filipino air watchers who relayed their warnings by telephone to the Fifth Intercepter Group at Neilson Field. These were then sent by teletype to the plotting board at Clark Field. Delay in time for relaying messages ran as long as twenty-five minutes, by which time the enemy could have come, struck, and left.

By November 15, the situation with Japan had become so tense that the airmen in the Philippines were expecting attack at any time. All pursuit aircraft were kept fully loaded, armed, and on constant alert, with pilots on thirty minutes' notice.

The first Japanese observation plane came over the Philippines on the night of December 2, and was sighted over Clark Field at 5:30 on the morning of December 3. Pursuit planes were sent aloft to intercept and destroy the snooper, but by the time they got into the air the snooper had vanished into cloud cover.

On the three succeeding nights enemy aircraft could be heard again, and the Filipino watchers reported the coming of observation planes. But none of the planes ventured within the range of the airfield searchlights, so there was no way to find them up there. The pursuit planes remained on the ground. By this time three radar sets had been brought into action in the islands. On the fifth morning the interloper was tracked by radar from Iba. All pursuit planes were on the alert, but no enemy aircraft were actually sighted, and the radar was so primitive that it could not be used to vector planes out. Again the pursuit planes remained on the ground.

By this time, December 6, the Japanese intentions were unmistakable, and on that day Major General Lewis H. Brereton, commander of air corps in the Philippines, held a conference at which he warned that war with Japan was imminent. Then all Air Corp units were put on alert with all personnel ready for duty.

But they were still so unready—proof that it takes months to prepare a combat unit for combat. Even the guns of the fighters and bombers were not properly adjusted, and the results of gunnery training were regarded as dismal. On the evening of December 7 (Manila time) the Thirty-fourth Pursuit Squadron received its last P-40, but it still had not checked out and made ready all of its fighter aircraft for combat on that evening.

As a part of their overall plan to achieve dominance in East Asia, the Japanese decided to attack the Philippine Islands so they could remove this base of American naval and air power. The Philippines really had little other value to Japan except as a source for timber and copper, but the strategic importance of the islands—particularly if they were in American hands—was enormous. So on December 8, 1941, the Japanese came to Cavite naval base and to the Clark Field air complex, which housed the American B-17 bombers and the fighter planes.

The Americans had been expecting an attack, and had guarded against it. But as noted, in the Clark Field complex, afraid of sabotage, the command had lined the B-17s bombers up on the aprons of the fields and then put guards around them. When the Japanese set out with 192 bombers from the Japanese Eleventh Air Fleet on Taiwan, there were the B-17s all lined up for them like pufferbellies. That morning there were thirty-five B-17s on the Clark Field airstrips. Two squadrons stayed at Clark, a total of nineteen B-17s, while two squadrons with sixteen more B-17s went down south to Del Monte, Mindanao.

Major General Brereton had a plan of sorts to carry out if hostilities should begin. He was going to make air raids on the Japanese territory of Taiwan. At 3 a.m. on December 8, Admiral Thomas Hart, commander of the U.S. Asiatic Fleet, had word, via an intercepted message from Pearl Harbor, of the Japanese attack on the Pacific Fleet base. Brereton's command scrambled a number of P-40s, but they did not find the enemy planes. Before 5 a.m. the bad news had been given to General MacArthur's headquarters in Manila. At 8:30 General Brereton's command issued a general alarm, and almost all the airplanes on the fields were scrambled, but by 10:00 the all-clear had sounded, and the American planes landed and lined up again. The air crews went off to lunch, came back, and began a leisurely study of a plan to attack Taiwan. This was a highly questionable undertaking, because the Americans did not have any charts of Takao or other Taiwanese cities and bases. General Brereton just figured that if he pointed the planes toward Taiwan, when they arrived they would find targets.

As it turned out, nothing happened.

Actually, it was not only Admiral Hart who had received notification by intercept message from Pearl Harbor. The Air Corps at Clark Field had warning too, but since the report was from a commercial channel and could not be verified by official channel, it was essentially ignored. General Brereton was informed, but no action was taken.

Half an hour later, the radar station at Iba reported an unidentified formation seventy-five miles off the coast, approaching Corregidor. The Third Pursuit Squadron was dispatched to intercept in the darkness, and the leader took them out at less than 10,000 feet. Obviously they passed beneath the incoming Japanese attack group, because although they did not find the Japanese, tracks on the plotting table showed that the fighters had intercepted the enemy.

At 9:30 that morning a large force of Japanese bombers was reported over Lingayen Gulf approaching Manila. The Seventeenth Fighter Squadron was put in the air to cover Clark Field and the Twentieth Squadron was sent to intercept over Roseales, but again they did not make contact with the enemy, who bombed Baguio and Tuguererao and then left.

All the bombers at Clark were put into the air for protection and headed south. When the danger was past, they all came back, the Twentieth Squadron covering their landing and then landing at Clark itself. Ordinarily it was a very effective system, but on this day it failed, because the Japanese were determined to destroy the American air power right off.

The Americans did have radar, but it failed, and the second wave of Japanese bombers came in, catching the Americans unaware. All but two of the American aircraft were on the ground. The Americans managed to put up several P-40s, which fought the Japanese. Second Lieutenant Randall B. Keator of the Twentieth Pursuit Squadron shot down one bomber, the first enemy plane destroyed in the Philippines.

Twelve B-17s were destroyed in that first raid, and five more were seriously damaged, while thirty P-40 fighters were wrecked or burned. In the first hours of war, about half the American air strength in the Philippines was knocked out and the Far East Air Force's striking power was destroyed.

Brereton reassessed his situation. He had about twenty bombers left, after salvaging four from the parts of seven damaged ones. On December 9, the Nineteenth Bombardment Group took to the air and made some reconnaissance missions, but it did not bomb anything. The planes were kept in the air until after dark for safety's sake.

On December 10 reconnaissance planes found a large Japanese naval convoy off Vigan and another at Aparri. That morning a number of the B-17s from Mindanao came in to augment the Clark Field force. Five B-17s set out, each with twenty 100-pound bombs aboard. They all bombed the Vigan convoy and somehow managed to sink one transport with the small bombs.

Six bombers from Mindanao showed up then at the Clark Field complex, but three of them were turned back because of an air raid alert. The planes that landed were piloted by Captain Colin P. Kelly, Lieutenant G. R. Montgomery, and Lieutenant George E. Schaetzel.

Montgomery's B-17 had just taken a 600-pound bomb aboard when a red alert interrupted the loading. Captain Kelly had three 600-pound bombs. Only Lieutenant Schaetzel had a full load of eight 600-pound bombs. They got into the air and headed for the convoys at Aparri and Vigan. Montgomery dropped his single bomb at Vigan but hit nothing. He ended up the day ditching his plane offshore after he was ordered back to Del Monte and failed to find it in the bad weather. The plane bellied in four miles offshore, but all members of the crew got out and made the land safely.

Lieutenant Schaetzel approached Aparri at 25,000 feet but ran into a flight of Zero fighters, which shot up the B-17. One engine was knocked out, and the tail section barely held together, but Schaetzel landed the plane safely at San Marcelino, south of Clark Field.

Captain Kelly went to Aparri hunting for an aircraft carrier he had heard was reported there. At 20,000 feet he thought he identified a battleship below (the cruiser *Ashigara*), and he bombed. Kelly's crew said later that one bomb fell short, a second was a near miss, and the third hit the after turret of the ship, sending up an enormous pall of smoke that then obscured vision.

After the attack, Captain Kelly's B-17 was jumped by Zeros, including one piloted by Warrant Officer Saburo Sakai, a highly experienced fighter pilot. The Zeros overtook the lone B-17 about fifty miles from Clark Field, and began pounding it with their machine guns. Waist gunner Technical Sergeant William J. Dele-hanty was decapitated by an explosive bullet. Private First Class Robert Altman was wounded. Numerous bullets hit the fuel tanks, but the tanks were self-sealing. A fire began in the bomb bay, and the cockpit was soon full of smoke. Captain Kelly ordered the crew out, and soon six parachutes could be seen drifting in the sky like white flowers, floating down not far from Clark Field. Six parachutes meant two men were still aboard, the dead Delehanty and Captain Kelly. Kelly kept the aircraft level and on course until the last man was out, and then prepared to jump himself. But just then the plane blew up and crashed. They found Captain Kelly's body, parachute on but unopened, not far from the wreckage.

When Kelly's crew was questioned, the air intelligence officers announced that they had sunk the battleship *Haruna*. At home in America, the press and people were thirsting for a victory, after days of crushing news of defeats, and this story was seized upon by an eager public, including members of Congress and the President of the United States. Captain Kelly was awarded the Distin-guished Service Cross for sinking a battleship and was hailed as the first American air hero of World War II. Arrangements were made to have his son entered at the U.S. Military Academy at West Point.

In fact, Captain Colin Kelly was every bit the hero he was claimed to be by the American media, but not for the reason given. His Japanese enemies knew the real story, and Japanese Zero pilot Saburo Sakai told the tale in his book *Samurai!*

Twenty-seven Zeros had left the field at Tainan, Taiwan, on the morning of December 10. By 10 a.m. they were over the Clark Field complex, but they did not see a single aircraft on the ground there. All the planes had been alerted and were in the air or on their way to Del Monte.

The Japanese turned north to fly cover for the amphibious landing forces going ashore at Vigan. There, one light cruiser, six destroyers, and four transports provided tempting targets for American bombers. The Zeros maintained cover for about twenty-five minutes at 18,000 feet. Suddenly Pilot Sakai saw rings on the water near the ships. Above and behind him, Sakai saw a lone B-17 bomber at 24,000 feet, speeding southward. He and his fellow pilots were chagrined and admiring: chagrined because an American bomber had avoided their screen and bombed, and admiring of the bravery of that pilot. They were also wary, because they had never heard of an unescorted single bomber in an area known to be patrolled by fighters. They looked nervously around, watching for the American fighters they expected to appear at any moment. "Unbelievable as it seemed, that B-17 had made a lone attack in the very teeth of all our planes. The pilot certainly did not lack courage."

The flight leader signaled, and all but three of a group of Zeros went after Colin Kelly's bomber. They went full throttle to catch it, and about fifty miles from Clark Field they overhauled the bomber. Three Zeros from another group crossed the path of the big plane and got in the first licks, and then seven of Sakai's group joined in. Captain Kelly and his crew tried to fight off the ten Zeros. At first the B-17 seemed to be unhurt, and its gunners fired steadily. Captain Kelly yawed the plane from side to side, to give his gunners firing room (the early B-17s did not have a tail turret), but despite his skillful defensive flying, the Zeros began to take their toll. Pieces of the starboard wing fell off. A gas tank ruptured and a spray of gasoline came back, and Sakai could see fire within the fuselage as he opened fire from close range. He fired until his ammunition was gone, and apparently he was the one to do the damage that caused the B-17 ultimately to crash.

Sakai watched Captain Kelly keep the plane on an even keel as his men bailed out, and marveled at his steadfast courage. "The bomber pilot's courage in attempting his solo bombing run was the subject of much discussion that night in our billets," he said. "We had never heard of anything like that before, a single plane risking almost certain destruction from so many fighters in order to press home its attack. The discrepancies of the surviving crew's reports in no way detracted from the act of heroism. Later in the afternoon, back in Formosa, we found the wings of two Zeros riddled with machine gun bullets which had been fired by the bomber's gunners."

So the enemy knew of Captain Colin Kelly's real heroism, and in their own way they paid him homage for it.

By December 10, the B-17s and a handful of submarines were the only offensive weapons left in the Philippines. Admiral Thomas Hart had sent Rear Admiral W. A. Glassford and the striking force of the Asiatic Fleet to the Dutch East Indies to participate in the common defense there with the British and the Dutch. The handful of submarines continued to operate out of Manila Bay, but the time of the B-17s was coming to an end. There simply were not enough planes to be effective. On December 12 a single Flying Fortress attacked the Vigan landing, in the manner of Colin Kelly, but scored no hits on the shipping below. On December 13, Lieutenant Boyd Wagner of the Seventeenth Pursuit Squadron shot down four Japanese planes near Aparri, and on December 16, one more, to become the first ace of the American Army Air Corps in World War II. But then the Japanese landed another amphibious force at Legaspi on southern Luzon Island. The nutcracker operation was about to begin, to drive north from Legaspi and south from Aparri and Vigan, and force the Americans into the Bataan Peninsula, where they would be bottled up and ultimately would have to surrender. This move made the Clark Field complex untenable.

The major base now was Del Monte, and the bombers were moved down there. On December 14, six bombers were ordered out from Del Monte to attack the Legaspi landing force. Three of them aborted (the first raid had virtually destroyed the repair and maintenance facilities of the U.S. Army Air Corps in the Philippines). The other three took off. Lieutenant Elliot Vandevanter's B-17 bombed at Legaspi, without accomplishing much, and then returned to Del Monte without incident. Lieutenant Jack Adams's plane bombed, and immediately was attacked by a swarm of Zeros. They wounded several men, one seriously, and Adams had to crash-land the plane in a rice paddy on the island of Masbate, south of Luzon. The third plane to make the attack that day was flown by Lieutenant Hewitt T. Wheless. He bombed and was attacked, and one by one his crew were wounded. They claimed to have shot down three Zeros, but the B-17 was riddled, the control cables were half shot away, the tailwheel was gone, and the oxygen system was out. Wheless decided to land at Cagayen. As he came in he saw that the field was covered with barricades to keep the Japanese from landing, but he had to go in anyhow. The plane stood on its nose and sank back on its tail, but the men walked away from it.

On December 17 General Brereton began moving his aircraft down to Australia, completing the move before Christmas. The first mission from Australia was mounted on December 22, from the new base at Batchelor Field near Darwin. Nine B-17s came in above Davao at dusk in heavy weather and bombed, sinking a tanker and setting fire to Japanese supplies on the dock. The B-17s landed at Del Monte, which was still in American hands. Next morning six of the nine planes made another mission, to Lingayen Gulf. Four planes made it all the way, and the other two aborted. The four bombers found an enormous landing force in Lingayen Gulf and bombed, but apparently they did not hit anything. The antiaircraft fire was intense, so they did not hang around to observe. On Christmas Day two bombers struck the airfield the Japanese had taken over at Davao.

General Brereton arrived at Darwin on December 29, 1941. Five days later President Roosevelt and Prime Minister Churchill announced a unified Southwest Pacific Command under General Sir Archibald Wavell. This meant the Far East Air Force came under Wavell, and so the B-17s were moved up to the Dutch East Indies. On January 5, B-17s stationed at Malang attacked shipping in Davao Bay. That same day a feisty officer, Lieutenant General George Brett, assumed command of the U.S. Army Air Forces in Australia, and on January 14 the headquarters of the Far East Air Force moved from Darwin to Java. Three days later B-17s from Malang attacked ships in Menado Bay.

At this point new B-17s were being ferried directly from Seattle down to South America, across the South Atlantic to Africa, across the Middle East to India, and then down to the Dutch East Indies. But the Japanese forward drive had so much impetus that the enemy could now interdict that route, so on January 20 General Brett put an end to it. The movement of the big planes was slowed up.

On January 22, the FEAF launched a whole series of bombing raids on the Japanese ships moving through Makassar Strait in their attack on the East Indies. The weather was very difficult, and four missions aborted altogether. Six missions were totally unsuccessful, and five missions succeeded in sinking four ships, but the losses of B-17s from Japanese fighter attacks were very high.

On January 25, 1942, Major Charles A. Sprague brought the thirteen P-40s of the Seventeenth Pursuit Squadron from Australia to Java. The remnant of the Far East Air Force left in the Philippines, fighter squadrons which had been fighting since December, moved with General Douglas MacArthur into the Bataan Peninsula, and from there attacked the Japanese at Nichols and Nielsen fields. Later in January the Japanese tried to make a number of landings on the Bataan Peninsula coast, to cut around behind the American and Filipino troops fighting there. On February 1, a number of P-40s from Bataan interdicted several of these landings, causing heavy damage and forcing the Japanese to hole up in caves. Most of these Japanese never made it back to their own lines.

In Java, the FEAF heavy bombers operated under the most trying conditions. The heavy rains prevented them from having much success with antishipping strikes. They claimed to have hit a carrier on February 4, but in fact had not. The last mission of the Far East Air Force was flown on February 4. Next day, the air force was redesignated, as part of the reorganization of the United States Army Air Forces. From this point on it would be called the Fifth Air Force.

# EIGHT

# Last Days in the Philippines

After General Brereton moved south to continue the fight from Australia, the agony of the Philippines continued. General MacArthur expected to have help from America and comported himself accordingly, calling for a last ditch defense and preparing to fight on the Bataan Peninsula until help could arrive. Steadily after December 9, the American fighter squadrons remaining in the Philippines suffered from attrition. They were very badly hampered by the disparity of performance of their P-35s and P-40s against the Japanese fighters, most of which were Zeros of the naval air forces from Taiwan. Also, communications between airfields and headquarters were very bad, with telephone lines down and confusion everywhere, and the field conditions remained uncorrected. After midnight on December 9, when telephone communications were reestablished between Nichols Field and Manila, warning came of an incoming attack force. A flight of fighters was dispatched from Del Carmen airfield, but two aircraft were demolished and one pilot killed on takeoff because of dust that swirled around the aerodrome, blinding the pilots. The four remaining planes of the flight reached Nichols Field to intercept the incoming Japanese, but failed to make contact in the dark.

In crisis, now came the cannibalization. The aircraft of the Seventeenth Squadron were transferred to Clark Field and the squadron brought up to strength with planes from the Third Squadron. The rest of the Third Squadron was sent to Nichols

Field to bring the Thirty-fourth Squadron up to strength—so exeunt Third Squadron.

When, on December 10, fighters and bombers attacked the approaching convoy in Lingayen Gulf, and all suffered losses, as indicated. The Twenty-first Squadron lost its squadron commander, a Lieutenant Sam Merritt, when a Japanese troop transport which he was attacking in his P-35 exploded in his face.

On the morning of December 10 the fighter squadrons had their greatest test. At 11:15 that morning came warnings of large enemy formations approaching the Manila area from the north. The four American fighter squadrons were sent out to Bataan and to Manila Bay, the port area, to intercept. They encountered an enormous formation of Japanese bombers, guarded by more than a hundred fighters. They tried to break through, but only the flights of lieutenants Shepherd and Mears succeeded. The remainder of the American fighters were drawn off by the Japanese fighters into dogfights over Manila, which continued until the American planes exhausted their fuel or were shot down. This was the key day in the Japanese attempt to destroy the American air force, and at the end of the day American fighter strength was reduced to thirty aircraft, eight of them obsolete P-35s.

That night headquarters issued new orders: Pursuit aircraft would be employed only on orders from headquarters. The pursuit planes would hereafter be used to replace the aircraft of the Second Reconnaissance Squadron, which had been completely wiped out in the first hours of the war.

Thus, after December 12, the reconnaissance mission was carried out by fighters, the Third and Thirty-fourth squadrons covering the southern end end of Luzon, and the Seventeenth and Twentieth squadrons covering the northern end. By this time the Japanese had installed themselves at Aparri and several other airfields, which made life even more difficult for the American defenders. But on these reconnaissance missions, the American fighter pilots did their very best. On December 13 Lieutenant Wagner strafed the Aparri airport, destroyed several planes on the ground, and then shot down four Japanese army fighters in the air. On December 16, lieutenants Wagner, Church, and

Strauss attacked the airfield at Vigan with fragmentation bombs and machine guns and claimed to destroy seventeen planes, plus supply dumps and airport installations. Lieutenant Church was killed by one of the antiaircraft guns the Japanese had brought in by this time.

Every day from December 16 to December 23 the Twenty-fourth Pursuit Group flew missions from Legaspi to Lingayen Gulf and Aparri, but the enemy strength was whittling away at the American force. On December 23 the Japanese made a new landing in San Miguel Bay. The American fighters, twelve P-40s and six P-35s, attacked using fragmentation bombs and machine guns. Two P-35s were so badly damaged that they crash-landed on returning to their field.

The situation was becoming desperate, and on December 24, orders came from headquarters for the evacuation of the air group to Bataan, where General MacArthur was moving to consolidate his defenses. It took the Air Corps two weeks to make the move. The Third Squadron was taken off air duty and moved to the mouth of the Talain River for infantry duty. The Twentieth Squadron moved to Mariveles on the Tanikan River, to become an infantry reserve. The Seventeenth Squadron moved to Kabobo Point to take up beach defenses. Altogether, eighteen P-40s and six P-35s were salvaged to operate from Bataan, and ultimately concentrated at Bataan airfield. And then came the order disbanding the Twenty-fourth Pursuit Group and creating in its place the Second Infantry Regiment of the Seventy-first Division. There were eighty-four officers and just over a thousand men, about the size of an infantry battalion. They would fight the rest of the Philippine campaign as air corps and infantry, flying when they had aircraft and fighting on the ground as the aircraft were destroyed.

As the confusion was compounded in the Manila area around Christmastime, Lieutenant Samuel C. Grashio of the Twenty-first Pursuit Squadron was wandering around Manila trying to find out what he was supposed to do. Air Corps headquarters was in complete disarray, and he did not even know where his unit was.

Grashio learned that a ship was loading on Christmas Eve—bound for where, he did not know. There was talk at that time about going to Java to continue the fight. He learned simultaneously that the Japanese had broken through the lines and were expected in Manila in a matter of hours. So he went to the port and slipped aboard the ship. Next morning the ship was off Mariveles, on the Bataan Peninsula.

Lieutenant Grashio got off the ship and drifted around for a while, not knowing to whom he should report. Then someone got the airmen together and began to give them a semblance of infantry training.

"My own previous acquaintance with even a shotgun had been pitifully limited: a bit of skeet shooting in primary flight training in order to learn how to hit a moving target. Now we practiced firing obsolete rifles and dabbling in infantry training. Most of the pilots were disgusted in varying degrees at the prospect of being turned into instant imitation infantrymen specializing in beach defense. Perhaps I too would have resented the decline in my social position had it lasted longer, but my entire career as an infantryman consisted of one reconnaissance mission, on foot, to look for places along the southwest coast of Bataan where Japanese landings might be attempted.

"In a few days I was reprieved. An order came from General George, the air commander on Bataan, to report for flying duty at Bataan field, two or three miles north of Cabcaben. A new provisional outfit was being formed composed of the more experienced pilots who had survived the disasters at Clark and Iba fields and elsewhere. As things turned out, we flew mostly reconnaissance missions until the end of the Bataan campaign. Our main concern was to keep some planes flyable, and not to risk them in combat unless presented with some exceptional opportunity to damage the enemy. . . .

"Around Manila in the first days of the year, and again on Bataan, it was brought home to us how grievously Americans had underrated both the Japanese planes and their pilots. Though the pilots were not particularly imaginative or adaptable, many of them were veterans of campaigns in China, where they had become expert at set pieces. I once saw the leader of a flight of four Japanese dive bombers drop out of formation and attack one of our antiaircraft gun batteries. He immediately drew fire from all four guns in the battery—who thereby revealed their positions. At once the other Japanese pilots peeled off, one by one, in perfect order, each picking up a different antiaircraft gun. In one graceful synchronized dive they silenced the whole battery and sped away."

The movement of the American and Filipino defenders to Bataan was almost totally unplanned. On January 8, there were about 3000 tons of canned meat and fish and some rice on the peninsula, rations for 100,000 men for thirty days. Since the Japanese controlled the rest of the Philippines, as well as the air and the sea, it was virtually impossible to get more supplies except by submarine and a group of rickety transport planes, called the Bamboo Fleet, which brought in some supplies from Cebu and other southern islands where the Japanese had not really taken control. On January 8 the Bataan force went on half rations, 2000 calories a day. In February that was cut to 1500 calories, and in March to 1000 calories.

Lieutenant Grashio recalled, "Our semi-starvation diet began to undermine my strength and energy noticeably after about four weeks. Like everyone else I tried to do something about it. I scrounged for bananas in the jungle and found quite a few. Occasionally I found a few mangoes. Now and then I was able to get on the *Canopus*, the submarine tender off Mariveles, and get a few cans of sweetened condensed milk. When it was boiled in the can and then mixed with shredded coconut the result was a rich tasty luxury.

"Many men formed hunting parties. They scoured settlements and jungle alike to kill or [sic] eat anything that moved: chickens, domestic pigs, wild pigs, deer, carabao, and cavalry horses; soon followed by dogs, cats, monkeys, iguanas, even snakes."

Because the Imperial Japanese forces had sped from victory to victory—in Hongkong, in Malaya, and in the early days, in the Philippines, as well as the shocking victory at Pearl Harbor and the sinking of the big ships *Repulse* and *Prince of Wales* off the

Malay coast—Imperial General Headquarters called for swifter action, to speed the victories even more. In Saigon the southern area commander, Field Marshal Terauchi, decided that things were going so well that General Homma, the commander in the Philippines, would not need one of the divisions he had been allocated, and that he should be able to keep to the schedule of conquest with far fewer men.

When General MacArthur opted to move out of Manila and defend the Bataan Peninsula instead, the Japanese were not ready. As a result, they did not push hard at first, and gave the Americans and Filipinos a chance to get set in what was an ideal defensive position. The Allies began inflicting heavy casualties on the Japanese, who also suffered from shortage of supply and much illness, especially malaria and dysentery. The Japanese casualty rate was eight times that of the Allies. By the end of January the Japanese offensive was stopped; seven thousand soldiers had fallen and another 10,000 were sick. Imperial General Headquarters was furious, but there was nothing to be done except to reorganize and augment the forces fighting on Bataan. It would be six weeks before the Japanese offensive could begin again.

But meanwhile the American and Filipino conditions grew worse, and morale declined steadily as the men realized that no rescue was forthcoming from America. The men of Bataan resented the navy men and army staff on Corregidor, who were living under much better conditions—temporarily. They sang a song to the tune of the "Battle Hymn of the Republic:"

*Dugout Doug MacArthur lies shaking on The Rock.*
*Safe from all the bombers, and from any sudden shock.*
*Dugout Doug is eating of the best food on Bataan.*
*And his troops go starving on.*

The air defense of Bataan staggered along, but did not falter, as Lieutenant Grashio recalled:

"Somehow our intelligence got some remarkably accurate information on February 1. That night a Japanese ship would tow thirteen barges loaded with about a thousand troops into Agla-loma Bay."

They were to come in at about 10:30 at night. When they came, the shore batteries illuminated them with searchlights, while the Bataan air force pulled out all the stops.

"The other pilots and I, singly and in two-ship formation, flew back and forth over them no higher than 200 feet, 'stitching' every barge repeatedly from end to end with .50 caliber machine gun bullets until we ran out of ammunition. Most of the barges sank."

The pilots thought they had killed or drowned all the Japanese. Actually some four hundred of them were saved, but almost all of those were run down and killed by the beach defense troops.

Although the lesson would have to be learned over again at Tulagi and Guadalcanal, because so few Americans escaped from the Philippines, the nature of the Pacific war became clear on Bataan. Lieutenant Grashio observed:

"Long before the end of the Bataan campaign, it was obvious that the Japanese were extremely brave soldiers, indeed fanatical in a sense unknown in the western world.

"If they knew where our land mines were sown they would throw themselves on the mines and detonate them to speed the passage of their comrades. If they encountered barbed, electrified fences, they acted similarly. Oftentimes they would do such things as play dead and then shoot Americans in the back, shoot at American soldiers engaged in burying Japanese dead, feign injury and then shoot American doctors who sought to administer to them, or offer to surrender and then mow down the U.S. or Filipino soldiers who went out to receive them. One of our best and most respected pilots, Lt. Marshall Anderson, bailed out of his P-40 on January 19. Japanese pilots shot him and his parachute to pieces, an act which later caused the beach defenders to fight with exceptional zeal against the Japanese on the ground.

"Japanese soldiers delighted in infiltrating our lines at night, a tactic which especially unnerved Filipino troops. On these noc-turnal excursions they would ambush patrols, murder sentries, pick off officers, and steal food and equipment. Sometimes they would don Filipino or American uniforms to confuse Filàmerican [sic] troops. Occasionally they would shoot long strings of fire-crackers over our lines in the middle of the night in an effort to induce us to fire back and thus reveal our positions. At other times they would employ sound trucks to play nostalgic songs at night, or to broadcast groans, shrieks, and other unearthly noises, all in an effort to keep us from sleeping and undermine our morale. All such actions are a part of war, of course, but to us our foes seemed unnecessarily enthusiastic about waging war by every means human ingenuity would devise.

"Much worse, it soon became apparent that many Japanese were savagely cruel. While I did not personally witness Japanese atrocities at this stage of the war, many did and there was much talk about them. Many corpses—some American, some Filipino —floated around the entrance to Manila Bay with their arms and legs tied together, riddled with bayonet stabs. It was equally com-monplace to find the bodies of one's comrades tightbound, ob-viously tortured, disemboweled, with their severed genitals stuffed in their mouths.

"The effect of such Japanese savagery on the Americans and Filipinos is not hard to imagine. The Filipinos were particularly infuriated by reports that our foes had mutilated Filipino women. Soon they began to set booby traps, to plan ambushes, and to organize anti-sniper patrols. If they managed to capture a Japa-nese they would interrogate him with 'oriental practicality.' Few Americans took Japanese prisoners at all.

". . . Only occasionally did we attempt an offensive mission. One such instance came early in February when six of us set off at night to strafe Neilson Field near Manila. Though we did not learn of it until long afterward, we came near to being killed due to one of those foul-ups which plague all armies. In this case somebody forgot to notify Corregidor that we would fly over at 8 p.m. Had not General Richard Sutherland, MacArthur's chief of staff, guessed correctly that we were Americans rather than Japanese, the whole Far Eastern Army Air Corps probably would have been shot down by The Rock's antiaircraft batteries.

"In the actual attack I flew top cover while the other pilots came in low and strafed. At the time we could only guess whether we had hit anything worthwhile. Long afterward I learned from Filipino reports that many Japanese planes had been destroyed or damaged, that Japanese casualties had been heavy, and that so much havoc had been wreaked that the enemy had changed his whole defense system around Manila."

On March 2 the Air Corps command learned that several Japanese ships had entered Subic Bay, about thirty miles northwest of Bataan. Lieutenant Ed Dyess led the planes, a 500-pound bomb attached to his P-40 fighter with a jury-rigged bomb rack. He bombed and strafed the Japanese ships and did considerable damage, then called the eight other pilots who had planes to come and help. Lieutenants Grashio, Crellin, Stinson, Burns, Fossey, Crossland, White, and Posten mounted their patched-together aircraft and flew off.

Grashio's P-40 carried three 30-pound bombs under each wing. The planes flew to Subic Bay, sighted the Japanese barges there, and attacked with bombs and machine guns. Grashio hit the bomb release handle and was disappointed that he did not see any results. When he returned to Cabcaben airfield the operations officer radioed that his flaps were down but his bombs were hung up; Grashio was instructed to bail out. But to bail out was to risk landing in a tree in the heart of the jungle or with the sharks in Manila Bay, or to be strafed by a Japanese Zero, so Grashio decided to land the plane. He did so at Mariveles, which had a longer runway.

General MacArthur left Corregidor, followed by the hoots of the men of Bataan, on March 10. They did not know that he had been ordered out by President Roosevelt, and they began calling him names more insulting than Dugout Doug. Some resented particularly the general's taking along personal servants instead of military personnel, but they were only talking about seventeen people altogether, most of them senior members of the MacArthur staff.

They had a new verse:

*Dugout Doug is ready in his Chris Craft for to flee*
*Over the billows and the wildly raging sea*
*For the Japanese are pounding on the gates of old Bataan*
*And his troops go starving on.*


Yes, the men of Bataan were bitter. "We're the battling bastards of Bataan," they sang.


*No mama, no pop, no Uncle Sam;*
*No aunts, no uncles, no nephews, no nieces,*
*No rifles, or guns, or artillery pieces . . .*
*and nobody gives a damn.*


By the end of March 1942, when General Homma renewed his offensive against Bataan with more guns and reinforcements, the American air force was down to four planes: one patched up P-40, two battered P-35s, and one nameless combination of parts from half a dozen wrecked aircraft.

On April 5, arrangements were made for a bombing raid from Australia to break the Japanese blockade of Bataan. Four fighters remained on Bataan, and four more could be brought from Mindanao to offer protection.

On April 7, two days before the surrender of American forces on Bataan, Lieutenant Grashio had a chance to escape. Previously he had turned down an offer to fly out to Mindanao and continue the struggle, along with several other pilots who did not want to abandon their comrades. He took a P-40 with a belly tank of gas, flew south looking for Japanese naval forces, saw some and noted them, and returned from the island of Culion. He came back to find the airfield under Japanese attack, and landed between attacks on the field. That afternoon the Japanese broke through the American lines and the end was near. And that night of April 7 all aircraft on Bataan were ordered to Mindanao to support the bombing mission. But the bombers did not reach Mindanao in time.

On April 8, Lieutenant I. B. Donaldson was ordered to fly a mission over the Japanese lines, drop bombs, and then fly on to

Ilo Airfield and safety. That was the last flight of a P-40 from Bataan. The next day all the Americans were captured.

Two days later the bombardment mission of B-17s arrived at Mindanao and carried out a mission, but not to Bataan. They attacked Japanese forces that had just landed at Cebu to begin the occupation of the southern Philippines. They hit the Japanese at Legaspi, Cebu, Iloilo, and Davao. They sank a light cruiser and several transports, and attacked Davao airfield and wrecked several aircraft. One B-17 and one fighter were lost.

After that, the token American air force on Mindanao kept flying missions until May 1, 1942, when the Japanese landed at three points on Mindanao and enveloped the American troops except those who escaped into the jungle and carried on the fight as guerillas. Although captured on Bataan, Lieutenant Grashio later escaped from the Japanese and survived the war, to retire as a colonel in the U.S. Air Force.

# NINE

# *Atlantic Victory*

On December 8, 1941, Admiral Karl Dönitz received permission from Adolf Hitler to send six U-boats—no more—to the American station. For the next three months those six boats, not all of them on station at any time, wreaked disaster on American and British shipping, and very nearly paralyzed the American war economy.

But by June 1942, the Americans had begun to recover, and there were signs that the tide was turning against the U-boats. The Americans were getting the knack of conducting the sea war. On July 7, 1942, Second Lieutenant Harry J. Kane of Squadron 59 took off on antisubmarine patrol from Cherry Point air station, near Cape Hatteras, North Carolina, in a Lockheed-Hudson bomber.

"After takeoff I climbed to 1500 feet altitude and then began my search pattern, flying out in a box formation. The weather was sunny, with a broken layer of cumulus clouds around Cape Hatteras.

"For an hour I saw nothing, but then I thought I saw a break in the surface of the water about ten miles away, and I headed for that position to investigate. I dropped down to about 500 feet and as I came near it became obvious that the object was a submarine. When I was about three miles away its deck was completely out of the water. No U.S. submarines had been reported in this vicinity, so it was obvious to me that it had to be an enemy. We had heard reports of Italian submarines coming to American waters, and we had already sunk two U-boats.

"I was lucky to have the sun behind me so the crew of the U-boat could not see me as I approached, but when I got to a point about two miles from the sub suddenly somebody did see me, and it started a crash-dive. Fortunately my plane had enough speed to reach them before they could get under. My first depth charge was short by twenty-five feet, but the second and third were right on target. They hit and exploded.

"I could see that the submarine was hurt. It lay half in and half under the water. In a few moments I saw two heads bob up from the stern of the submarine. Then the conning tower opened and a number of men scrambled out, and they were carrying one man.

"I circled. I saw the submarine sink. I counted fifteen heads in the water, and then another two heads a little bit inshore of those.

"I came down to about 200 feet above the surface, and when I was over the big group of survivors I dropped a portable lifeboat near the group of men in the water, and then went back several times and dropped three life rafts. Then I flew over the two men who were now about a quarter of a mile away from the others, and dropped another life raft.

"After that I went looking for help to pick up the survivors of the U-boat. I passed a freighter, and my radioman managed to make contact with her. She was a Panamanian ship. He told them we had sunk a U-boat and asked them to pick up the survivors and take them to the nearest port.

"My radio operator gave the ship the position of the survivors. Her operator acknowledged. I circled. I knew that the ship would have to turn around and inshore to find them, but as I flew away I saw no signs of change of course, and assumed that the captain had decided it was too dangerous to try to stop. There had been many reports of German submarine wolfpacks.

"I told the radio operator to keep trying to find someone to rescue the men. Finally he raised U.S. Coast Guard Cutter 472 on the emergency frequency and gave him the coordinates. I did not sight the Coast Guard cutter.

"Since that was all I could do, I continued my patrol, which was uneventful, and then before sunset I returned to base and landed at Cherry Point and reported the sinking to operations. They had no information about the U-boat or the survivors."

There had been many submarine sightings and sinkings reported by American airmen in these last few months and only two submarines actually sunk, so Lieutenant Kane's story was not entirely believed. The Coast Guard cutter radioman had misheard the coordinates and the cutter did not find the survivors. But quite by chance, two days later the airship *K-8* spotted men in the water north of the Wimble Shoals light buoy and lowered a raft. That afternoon the seven living crewmen of the U-boat were rescued by a Coast Guard seaplane and flown to the U.S. naval station at Norfolk, Virginia. They confirmed Lieutenant Kane's story of the sinking, and their U-boat was identified as *U-701*. When news of the sinking of *U-701* reached Admiral Dönitz, he pulled his U-boats away from the American station. The "Happy Time" of the U-boat commanders, when they sank ships at will, was over. The Americans had begun the convoy system, and there were too many U-boats being lost. This was the beginning of the end of the U-boat preponderance in the battle of the Atlantic. In a few more months, the U-boats were on the defensive.

# TEN

# The End of the Beginning

At the end of 1941 the American air forces in the South Pacific were thoroughly confused. Major General George H. Brett was in command of all United States forces in Australia, and Major General Brereton commanded what was left of the Far East Air Force, which had abandoned the Philippines rather than be captured. All were under command of General Sir Archibald Wavell, who headed the America-British-Dutch-Australia command that was going to try to save the Dutch East Indies from being overrun by the Japanese.

It was a forlorn hope from the beginning, however, because the whole reason for the Japanese drive south was to capture Malaya and the Indies to secure their raw materials: rubber, tin, and above all, oil for the tanks and aircraft carriers of the Japanese forces.

General Brereton was appointed to command the American air forces in Java. The force consisted of eighteen P-40 fighters, fifty-two A-24 bombers at Brisbane, and fourteen B-17s which had been evacuated from the Philippines. Ten of the fourteen Fortresses were sent to the Indies, and on January 4 from Borneo they bombed Davao in the southern Philippines, and then returned to their new base at Malang.

Soon these planes were joined by another half dozen B-17s and four of the British version of the B-24, the LB-30. And then the fighters began to come in. Five provisional fighter squadrons were organized, three of them taking the names of the fighter squadrons of the Twenty-fourth Group which had come apart in the Philippines: the Seventeenth, Twentieth, and Third. The other two squadrons were the Thirteenth and Thirty-third. The first to be organized was the new Seventeenth, made up of pilots from the Philippines, who got new P-40s that had been shipped to Australia. The sixteen planes split into two flights for the trip from Brisbane on January 16. The first stop was Rockhampton, 300 miles north of Brisbane, where one P-40 crash-landed. Then it was on to Townsville, where another P-40 was lost in an accident, to Cooncurry, to Daly Waters, and to Darwin.

The remaining fourteen planes left Darwin on January 20, and successfully flew the 540 miles over water to Koepang, Timor. On January 24, thirteen planes arrived in Surabaya, Java. The next few days were spent in pilot familiarization, adjusting themselves to working with the Dutch. Then, on February 1, the squadron set up base at Blimbing, just in time for the first Japanese bombing mission on Java, on February 3.

The early warning system on Java was not much good. By the time the Seventeenth Squadron got the word that the Japanese were coming, the enemy bombers had already arrived and bombed. But the P-40s got into the air, and Lieutenant Hennon shot down a Mitsubishi bomber, which he caught eighty-five miles out at sea. Lieutenants Roland and Coss ran into a Japanese force eighty miles south of Surabaya and attacked, but they were in turn ambushed by Zeros from a higher altitude, and Lieutenant Roland was shot down and killed. Lieutenant Coss shot down one Japanese plane and escaped the others.

On February 5 more P-40s arrived, representing the first element of the Twentieth Pursuit Squadron, and by the end of January there were twenty-four more American P-40s on their way to Java. When they reached Bali they were involved in a Japanese air raid: three of the P-40s were shot down, two were shot up on the ground, and two of a flight of seven managed to reach Surabaya. Altogether, seventeen of the twenty-four planes of Twentieth Squadron reached Java, but only twelve were still fit for combat. So the squadron was disbanded and the members taken into the Seventeenth Squadron, which operated from a new field near Surabaya. On the day that the Japanese invaded Java, February 4, four flights of fighters were put into the air to oppose eighteen Japanese bombers, and they managed to bring one of the bombers down.

Thereafter the Americans had much difficulty in resupplying planes to Java because of weather and distance. On February 11, the remnants of the Third Squadron—eight P-40s—flew from Australia, and all of them crashed en route because of weather. Finally eleven more P-40s were brought in, and the Third Squadron, too, was amalgamated with the Seventeenth, which now had thirty P-40s.

With the surrender of Singapore on February 15, 1942, the Japanese accelerated their plans to take the Dutch East Indies and secure the oil supply they needed. Two expeditionary forces were on their way, guarded by naval vessels and aircraft. On February 17, the American fighters did well against Japanese fighters, and strafed Japanese troops in landing barges. Every day there were air fights and every day the slim force of American fighters grew slimmer, although they scored many air victories. In mid-February a supply and reinforcement convoy left Darwin for the Indies, given air cover by a squadron of P-40s from Darwin. But the air cover did little good. When the convoy reached Timor it was so scattered it was sent back to Darwin without unloading.

On February 18, the Thirty-third Squadron was virtually destroyed by planes of the Japanese carrier task force of Admiral Nagumo in its celebrated attack on Darwin. Most of the P-40s were shot down or shot up on the ground. The Japanese destroyed port facilities, wrecked the port, and sank many ships in the harbor. When the day was over, all the fighting aircraft at Darwin were dead.

The destruction of Darwin port closed the Allied lifeline to Java, effectively writing "finis" to the Allied defense efforts. The fighter squadrons struggled for a while, but it was virtually impossible to resupply them with aircraft, and pilot attrition was increasing as the Japanese brought in ever more air power. By the end of February all was really lost. The British ship *Seawitch* brought in twenty-seven crated fighters to Tjilatjap, but there was no time to uncrate the planes, assemble them, and get them ready for combat. The USS *Langley*, now an air ferry, brought thirty-two P-40s from Australia on its deck, but was sunk en route to Java.

By the end of February, the Japanese invasion forces were moving fast, and the naval forces wiped out Allied sea power in the Battle of the Java Sea. Allied air power at that point consisted of six Dutch Brewster Buffaloes, six Hawker Hurricanes, a handful of P-40s, a smaller handful of B-17s, and three A-24 bombers. They were at the end of their rope, as one P-40 pilot put it:

"My plane has two tires that have huge blisters on them. It has no brakes, and no generator, and the hydraulic fluid is leaking into the cockpit."

One of the B-17s was indeed a famous aircraft, *Alexander the Swoose*, so named because it was "half swan, half goose," composed of parts of several aircraft, although basically a B-17D. After the fall of Java it became the command plane of Lieutenant General George H. Brett, commander of U.S. Army forces in Australia.

But perhaps the most celebrated of the B-17s in the southwest Pacific was the *Suzy Q*, one of the B-17Es. It was flown by Captain Felix Hardison from America to South America, to Africa, to India, and then to Java, arriving in February 1942. It had no sooner landed than it was scheduled to bomb shipping in the Makassar Strait. This was the time of trial, days of fading Empire, and desperate defense against the Japanese. The *Suzy Q* flew almost continuously in these last hours. On February 27 it dropped bombs on a Japanese convoy and then returned to the Dutch base to pick up a load of Americans and bring them to the safety of Broome, Australia. As the B-17 took off, the Dutch on the ground detonated mines under runways to destroy them and prevent the Japanese from landing.

The campaign for the Dutch East Indies was over. All the efforts of the Allied airmen had been in vain; the Japanese juggernaut was just too powerful. Nor did the Allies really understand that Sumatra and Borneo in particular were the targets of the whole southwest Pacific Japanese drive, and the main reason for the Japanese war against the Western powers: to secure oil to pursue the conquest of China.

During the spring and early summer of 1942, the Allied campaign in the southwest Pacific limped along. The decision had been made in Washington that utmost effort had to go to prosecute the European war, and fighters and bombers as well as transport planes were mostly destined for Europe. MacArthur's theater of operations took second place. The relationship between the Air Force and the MacArthur command was terrible, because General Brett and MacArthur saw eye to eye on virtually nothing. In the spring, after Lieutenant Colonel Jimmy Doolittle had led the Doolittle Raid on Japan and been promoted to major general, Washington offered him to MacArthur as replacement for General Brett, but MacArthur did not want a person as flamboyant as himself around. He declined Doolittle, and instead was given Lieutenant General George C. Kenney to be commander of the fledgling Fifth Air Force, which was officially established on August 7.

The big problem was aircraft. Kenney then had 517 aircraft at his disposal, 245 of them fighters and 62 of them heavy bombers. The Royal Australian Air Force had 70 planes. With these, Kenny set out to challenge what was then the most powerful air force in the Pacific.

Also needed were changes of equipment and tactics. Major Paul I. (Pappy) Gunn developed fragmentation bomb packages for light bombers such as the A-20. He also built a system of four .50-caliber machine guns for the nose of the A-20, making it a superb strafing attack instrument. The same idea was used for the B-25 medium bomber. And pilots began to study skip-bombing techniques and low-level bombing. In the southwest Pacific they would be operating primarily against shipping, and at that point the heavy bombers had a dismal record against shipping, because they bombed from too high an altitude to hit a moving target.

In the summer of 1942 all this was theory. What remained to be seen was how General Kenney would work it out in practice.

On August 7, 1942, Kenney staged his first demonstration. Eighteen B-17s of the Nineteenth Bombardment Group under Colonel Harold Carmichael took off to attack Rabaul's busy naval airfields, from which the Japanese Twenty-first Air Flotilla was sending aircraft that day to oppose the Americans invading Guadalcanal. Fifteen B-17s arrived over the Vunakanau Airfield, and the photos indicated that they destroyed seventy-five planes on the ground, using 500-pound instantaneous fuse bombs. The Japanese had made the same error the Americans had made earlier at Clark and Hickam airfields, and had their aircraft neatly lined up on the aprons to the runways, "wingtip to wingtip on both sides of the strip."

The bomber force encountered about twenty Japanese Zeros in the air, and claimed to have shot down eleven.

Despite the usual overclaims of airmen, in this case the results were obviously impressive. The Japanese had gotten off one big air strike against the American forces landing on Tulagi and Guadalcanal that day, but it was several days before they could pull themselves back together after the big B-17 raid. Planes had to be ferried down from Saipan and the Philippines.

General Kenney and his boys were getting started.

# ELEVEN

# Getting Ready for a War

Just after Pearl Harbor was attacked by the Japanese on December 7, 1941, Edison Vail, Jr., of Norfolk, Virginia, decided he would enlist in the United States Army Air Corps as a flight cadet in order to become a fighter pilot. He went to the Norfolk army recruiting office looking for an application, but the sergeant in charge told him he was fresh out of applications and that Vail should come back later. He went away and came back in February. This time there were plenty of applications, so he signed up. In March he was called for his examination, and in April he was sworn in as an aviation cadet.

Vail had already said goodbye to most of his friends and told his employer, the telephone company, that he was going off to war. But immediately he was informed that he had a thirty-day furlough. So he hung around home for the next month, not knowing what to do with himself. At the end of the month came another telegram: another thirty-day furlough. Edison Vail, Jr. then began to realize that there was a SNAFU (Situation Normal, All Fouled Up) somewhere.

He was quite right. The American rearmament program, begun in 1939, had received an enormous impetus with the bombing of Pearl Harbor, and the Air Corps was bogged down in paperwork and shortages. So many young men had been accepted for air training that they could not all be handled at the moment. It was going to take some time to solve the problems.

In Edison Vail's case it took half the summer. He went back to work at the telephone company. In late July he finally received orders to report to the cadet training program at Kelly Field, Texas. He went by train, arriving just about in time for his first payday, and was delighted to see that he got four months pay.

The course at Kelly Field was preflight training, which was nothing less than army basic training adapted to the Air Corps. Kelly was part of the Gulf Coast Training Command. Cadet Vail marched and learned weapons use and nomenclature, and then he marched some more to eat "square" meals. He learned to wear a uniform and to salute. He was beginning the transition from civilian to soldier.

From Kelly Field, Cadet Vail was sent to Tulsa, Oklahoma, to the Spartan Air College, a private institution enlisted by the Air Corps to train its airmen. He became one of a cadet corps of 200, and his status changed. He was no longer in primary training, where cadets were lower on the military social scale than a hound's belly. He had been dressed down by young Army Air Corps officers in the manner they had learned at the United States Military Academy at West Point. Cadet Vail and his fellows had been plebes. There was no actual hazing at Kelly, but all the rest had been there.

They had learned to salute, and they saluted everyone they saw, from the most bumbling buck private to the commanding general. Salute, salute, salute, run, run, run. If they violated any rule—and there were scores of rules to violate—they got a "gig." Seven gigs in a week meant a "tour," marching with full pack and equipment for one hour. Fourteen gigs meant two hours. Anyone with more than fourteen gigs was in real trouble, and his record would be closely examined to see if he was fit for the Air Corps.

Now that it was all over, Cadet Vail always recalled that life with relish. After he had run this gauntlet, he was prompted to basic training.

For basic flight training Cadet Vail went to Enid, Oklahoma. There he studied aeronautics, meteorology, and navigation, and he learned to fly. At the end of his basic training, Cadet Vail opted for single-engine rather than multi-engine training. He still wanted to be a fighter pilot.

He was then sent to Foster Field, at Victoria, Texas—down

south along the Mexican border, near Matagoro Island, which they used as a gunnery range. He checked out in the AT-6, the standard Army Air Corps single-engine trainer. Training ended, and he was looking forward eagerly to life as a hot fighter pilot. Just a little more time. . . .

But the air gods of Washington were having some problems.

At the end of May 1941, the Army Air Corps had created the Air Corps Ferrying Command, whose main job then was to ferry aircraft across the Atlantic Ocean to beleaguered Britain. Out of the Ferry Command that year emerged the Air Transport Command, which would have worldwide responsibility for cargo delivery.

And so, when Cadet Vail emerged from single-engine school in May 1943, with his shiny second lieutenant's bars and his hopes for a shiny P-51 to fly, he learned that almost his entire class, 43E, including Second Lieutenant Edison Vail, Jr., was assigned to multiple-engine school at Alpena, Michigan. The Air Transport Command was desperately in need of pilots.

Vail was given ten days to get from Victoria, Texas to Alpena. He went by way of Norfolk, stopping to get married to his sweetheart, another telephone company worker. Then it was on to Alpena, where he arrived with five thousand other pilots, to learn that there was but one aircraft on the base, the L-5 liaison plane of the commanding officer.

This SNAFU was sorted out by dealing out the pilots designate among the major American airlines for multi-engine training. Vail went to Miami, and there for six months he studied navigation, radio, instrument flying, and the operation of multi-engine aircraft. The checkout was a flight from Miami to Natal, Brazil, by way of Puerto Rico, Trinidad, and British Guiana. Had they been going all the way, as soon they would, they would then have flown to Ascension Island and then to North Africa.

Back in Miami it was not long before Lieutenant Vail had his sealed orders. He got aboard a C-47 at Miami along with thirty other pilots. It was two days before Thanksgiving, 1943. They ate their Thanksgiving dinner in Georgetown, British Guiana. Soon they were in Karachi, where they were SNAFUed again. They stayed on the flats of Karachi for six long weeks. Then it was up to Chabua, the headquarters of the Air Transport Command in the China-Burma-India theater. Soon Lieutenant Vail was in Misamera, twenty miles from Tezpur and his home for most of the next year. He would be flying C-46 cargo planes "over the Hump" of the Himalayas from India to China, keeping 60,000 American troops, the Fourteenth Air Force in Kunming, and nineteen Chinese armies supplied with the materials they needed to fight the Japanese.

# TWELVE

# Flying "The Hump"

By March 1942 the Japanese had swarmed over Burma, driving the Allies across the mountains into India and China, and the 650-mile-long Burma road was shut tight. The Japanese were satisfied that they had closed the door on Chiang Kaishek's Free China and that the Nationalist government would slowly starve to death in the mountains of Szechuan province without supplies from the outside world.

But the Japanese had not reckoned with President Franklin D. Roosevelt's determination to keep the flag of the Republic of China flying. Roosevelt was committed to a program to aid China, and he lived up to his commitment.

Early in 1942, a DC-3 operated by the China National Aviation Corporation had flown across the Himalaya mountain range between India and China, proving that the flight could be made. The United States Army had many such DC-3 aircraft, known in army nomenclature as C-47s.

In April the first American army air force plane flew "the Hump," and a massive airlift of supplies to keep China in the war was begun. A fleet of four C-47s was assembled at the Upper Assam Air Base of Dinjan, which lies between Chabua and Sookerating.

The Air Transport Command began to take over the supply system for China in the summer of 1942, with Major General Harold George as its commander. Commander of the India-China wing, Colonel Edward Alexander, was assigned a number of C-47 cargo planes plus a number of C-87s, which were cargo conversions of the B-24 four-engine bomber, the Liberator. That summer the ATC was ordered to raise the tonnage delivered to China to 4000 tons of goods per month.

Flying the Hump then meant going over the Santung range of the Himalayas, with its 18,000 to 20,000-foot peaks. The dangers were as much from the terrain and the weather as from the Japanese, who now controlled the skies above Burma and attacked China frequently.

Flying against the Japanese, weather, and time, the pilots continued to increase the tonnage taken into China. They were aided by the arrival of the C-46 Commando cargo plane, which had a much greater capacity than the C-47. In October 1943 there was a change of command in the ATC: Colonel Thomas Hardin became the chief of the Hump operations. In December 1943, 12,000 tons of supplies were delivered.

Colonel Hardin was very tough. He issued a dictum: "Effective immediately there will be no more weather over the Hump." No, he was not playing God. He was telling his men that missions would not be canceled anymore because of bad weather. They were going to fly above, around, or through all kinds of bad weather from now on.

The colonel also decided that the Japanese were no longer enough of a menace to prohibit flying, and said that no more flights would be canceled because of enemy fighter activity. In the month following that dictum, six ATC transports were shot down—small potatoes compared to the losses due to weather, pilot error, and mechanical failure, which cost 135 aircraft and 168 airmen in the last 6 months of 1943.

But Colonel Hardin was promoted, and for good reason. Airlifts for the six months ending on March 15, 1944 had been 33,000 tons. In the next five and a half months, the ATC delivered 85,000 tons. The change came with the drive of the Americans, British, and Chinese that pushed the Japanese out of North Burma, allowing for the rerouting of transports over the lower ranges of the Himalayas, which made for easier flights and fewer losses. By the late summer of 1944, tonnage was way up. After the battle of Myitkyina in the early spring of 1945, the Japanese retreated south to Mandalay and there were virtually no air attacks over the Himalayas. Between that time and the end of the war, 462,000 tons of supplies were flown over the Hump. After the spring of 1945, when the Burma-Ledo road was reopened, trucks carried additional thousands and thousands of tons of goods into China. But right up to the end and continuing after the Japanese surrender, the ATC pilots flew the Hump, and while it might have gotten easier, it was never, never easy.

## HITCH IN HELL
### (the lament of a "Hump" pilot)

BY BILL WISE, ONE OF THEM

*I'm sittin' here a-thinkin' of the things I left behind.*
*I hate to put on paper what is runnin' through my mind.*
*I've flown so many missions, cleared for hundreds of miles around.*
*A rougher place this side of Hell, I'm sure cannot be found.*
*But there's a certain consolation, so listen while I tell.*
*When we die we'll go to Heaven, 'cause we did our hitch in Hell.*
*We've flown so many drums of gas, Chennault should rule the land.*
*We've checked a million mags, I guess, and cleared them all by*
    *hand.*
*We've been airborne for a China flight in weather thick as ink.*
*We've fought the thunderstorms at night and ice enough to build a*
    *rink.*
*So when our work on earth is finished, our friends behind will tell:*
*These boys all went to Heaven, 'cause they did their hitch in Hell.*
*We take our Atabrine, those bitter little pills,*
*To build up our resistance to fever, aches, and chills.*
*We've seen a million Zeros zoom above us in the sky,*
*As we run like hell for cover when those yellow bastards fly.*
*Put out those lights and cigarettes, we're forced the crew to tell.*
*This isn't any picnic, it's another hitch in Hell.*
*And when the final taps are sounded and we've shed our earthly*
    *cares.*
*We'll put on our best wing parade upon the golden stairs.*
*And when the angels greet us, their harps they'll gladly play,*
*We'll draw a million beer rations, and drink it in a day.*
*We'll hear old Gabriel blow his horn, and St. Peter loudly yell:*

*"Front seats for the boys of the CBI,*
*They've done their hitch in Hell."*

In the beginning there weren't enough flying officers, so staff sergeant pilots went to fly the Hump. Staff Sergeant Monzell J. Phipps was one of a group sent over on November 23, 1942, by way of Natal.

They arrived at Chabua in Upper Assam, India, on December 20, 1942. In a few days they were flying the Hump from Chabua, Mohanbari and Sookerating. They flew C-47s in those early days.

"We would report to operations and be given our airplane number, its location on the field, and our destination in China—Kunming or Yunnanyi. Later we used Yangkai Chengkung. We would contact the tower when ready to taxi for instructions, and then after takeoff would turn off the radio as we could not reach anyone until a few miles from our destination in China. We would make several climbing circles to reach an altitude high enough to clear the first ridge. We would try to climb to 17,000 or 19,000 feet going to China. On one trip with everything forward, Richard Engel and I made it to 21,000 feet with a fully loaded C-47!"

On most trips the C-47s would climb and break out and see several other C-47s very close. This was the way, finding their own ways across the mountains, and they continued on this catch-as-catch-can basis until Phipps completed his tour of duty in December 1943. By that time he had been discharged as a staff sergeant and appointed flight officer.

From early 1942, the fleet grew steadily until January 1944, when Lieutenant Edison Vail and several hundred other pilots arrived. One was Lieutenant Dick March, who, like Edison Vail, had wanted to be a hot pursuit pilot. He was class 43B at Moore Field, but ended up at C-46 school and in Sookerating in November. The early flights were relatively short; March finished his tour of duty in a year, with 106 missions totaling 680 hours.

Another pilot was Lieutenant Jack Pope. He had enlisted in the Air Corps in June 1939. In the spring of 1942 he passed an examination for entrance to the Flying Cadet's School, and graduated as a second lieutenant a year later. His first military assignment after commercial airline school was with the Foreign Ferry Command, and his next was given in secret orders that sent him to Chabua, India. He was a duty pilot, flying the Hump. Here is his recollection:

"Flying the Hump was a task that required the sharpest kind of concentration. The slightest miscalculation could send me, my plane, passengers, and cargo down to certain death on those awful peaks and crags of the Himalayas. If I did go down and managed to survive the crash—which was unlikely—I'd either starve or freeze to death. So a mistake was something I couldn't make. If I did, I wouldn't make another. That particular task was as delicate as balancing on a cake of ice in the middle of the ocean. From my first to my last flight over the Hump, I never knew a decent night's sleep. Fear was my constant companion."

Pope would never forget his first flight over the Hump. The date was January 7, 1944. Pope and his crew got into the plane that morning and took off at 9 a.m. He climbed to 22,000 feet. Soon, the frozen pinnacles of the Himalaya were below. The wings of the plane began to ice up.

"There is a cold steel knot in my stomach that is like a lead weight. I shake my head slowly, wordlessly. My copilot looks at me strangely. What's the matter with him? I ask myself. Doesn't he know that he's as close to death as a man ever wants to be? He must be nuts not to know it. But he doesn't say anything. He just sits there breathing pure oxygen like I am. I check the instruments. . . ."

The radioman announced Check Point 2, Yunnan Yi. They were in China, on schedule and on course, compass heading 280 degrees.

But up ahead was a thunderhead, too high to fly over, too big to fly around. So Pope headed into the tall, deceptively beautiful cloud.

"Then all hell breaks loose! The Curtiss Commando [C-46] is seized as if with a giant hand. It vibrates like an air hammer running wild. My altimeter goes crazy. The uncaged gyro compass upsets and becomes useless. Then my last contact with civilization, the radio, goes dead! The ship is pivoting around like a pinwheel.

All of a sudden, the bottom drops out! Down, DOWN we go—like a rocket in reverse. I'm certain that the names of all of us on this hell flight are in the Grim Reaper's book.

"To add to the agony, the servo unit of the autopilot goes out. Now those snow-covered rocks are close—it seems as if I could reach out and touch them. But I haven't time. My copilot and I are fighting these arm-wrenching, bucking controls. We pass a ragged peak. I've already picked out the one we are going to hit. Then, almost too late, we stop falling and start up. Like a rocket shooting for altitude, we go up fast. As suddenly as it starts, it stops. We're upside down. A twist of the wheel and a kick of the rudder, and we're right side up and straight and level. Thank God those props are still turning. I must make one vital decision now.

"Should I uncage the one remaining navigational necessity? If I hit another one of those thunderheads, we will all have had it. I read the altitude: 30,000 feet. I uncage the flight indicator in the autopilot and I set my heading. I say a silent prayer. 'Dear God, let there be enough fuel remaining to make it.'

"Each hour that drags by is an eternity. In my stomach that steel knot has become a blinding pain. I regurgitate. My oxygen mask is filled. I dare not remove it. At 30,000 feet, without oxygen I'll die. I'm sick and no one can help me. Then, . . . we're over the Hump. Slowly I let the ship lose altitude. At 8000 feet I remove my oxygen mask. "Thanks, God," is all I can say. 'Thanks.' "

It was Sookerating again, on the night of January 14, 1944. The pilot was Lieutenant William J. Masters, the copilot was a Lieutenant Vansteenberg, the radio operator was Private Don Montgomery, the engineer Private First Class Ralph Divoky. At 7:30 that night they got clearance, manifest, and parachutes. It was raining. A jeep took them to the strip, where coolies were still loading the C-46, so they found a dry seat in a truck and waited there, watched the rain pelt down, and smoked. It was, the officers decided, the sort of night they told each other they would rather be with their wives at the movies than about to fly a mission.

When the plane was loaded, they got in. The tower cleared

them for takeoff, so they ran up the engines. The right magneto on the right engine cut out twice but finally behaved. Gyros checked, they took off at 8 p.m. At 5000 feet they began to hit scattered clouds, which grew thicker as they circled the field. They went on instruments. Lieutenant Masters told the crew to buckle up their parachutes. He didn't know quite why, but he had a hunch.

At 14,000 feet they started on course. At 18,500 feet they broke out of the overcast and leveled off. The windshield was covered with ice—on the inside. Vansteenberg took the controls while Masters scraped a hole in the ice and sent Divoky back for de-icing fluid. Through the tiny hole in the iced windshield Masters saw the clouds building up ahead of them.

He turned over the controls to the copilot again and told him to climb to 19,000 feet, while he advanced the propeller controls, throttles, and mixture. A few seconds later he looked at the compass and saw they were way off course.

"I pulled up my oxygen mask and asked Van what the hell was the matter and pointed to the compass. Talking was difficult at high altitude, because we had to take our masks off. He replied that he thought an engine was out."

Masters then looked at the airspeed indicator, which read 110—very slow—and took the controls. He changed gas tanks, put on carburetor heat, and trimmed the ship for single-engine flight. Engineer Divoky asked if he should start heaving cargo out.

"We haven't got time," said Masters. "Get ready to bail out."

The plane was losing altitude at the rate of 800 feet per minute, and many of the peaks around them, he knew, stood at 15,000 feet.

He told the radio operator to put the radio compass on Ledo and call out their position. It didn't work—there was too much interference. He told the crew they would bail out at 16,000 feet. That gave him about two minutes to try to start that engine.

The altimeter indicator dropped; 16,000, 15,000. . . .

At 15,000 Masters gave the order to bail out. Montgomery radioed that they were bailing out at 9:23 and then went to the back of the plane. Masters waited for Vansteenberg to get up, but he did not, so Masters got out of his seat and went aft. Divoky and Montgomery were standing by the open cargo door. Masters yelled "Let's go," and ran out the door.

All at once he saw the tail go by his nose, felt the cold air, and pulled the rip cord. Next thing he knew was absolute silence. He heard someone shouting, then stillness again. The stillness was broken by the airplane coming toward him, lights still on. It passed by, but turned around and came at him again, finally crashing almost directly beneath his swaying parachute. The plane burned and exploded, and in the light Masters saw a riverbed surrounded by mountains. Above him he saw another parachute.

Then he was crashing down through the foliage into the underbrush. He struggled out of his parachute, realized it was pitch dark, and sat. He heard a yell and yelled back. Then, realizing he was in Japanese territory, he shut up.

Masters opened his jungle kit and began stuffing the contents in his pockets. He had a bush knife, oil stone, mechanic's cap, quinine and Atabrine tablets, matches, leggings to keep leeches off, mosquito net for his head, fishing line and hooks, a morphine syringe, and chocolate. He also had a .45 caliber automatic pistol.

He wrapped himself in his parachute and tried to sleep in the rain. At 5 a.m., when it began to grow light, Lieutenant Masters headed up the mountain shouting. He found Divoky high in a tree. Divoky cut himself loose from his parachute and climbed down. He had lost both of the oxford shoes he had been wearing in the parachute jump. He and Masters cut some strips from Masters's parachute to tie around his feet. It was better than being barefoot, but not much.

They found an animal trail that led along the top of the ridge. Masters looked for landmarks but saw nothing but jungled mountain and one snowcapped peak. He and Private First Class Divoky walked, climbed, crawled, and slid through the wet, slippery jungle, panting and stopping every few yards to rest.

At about noon they came across pieces of a parachute stuffed under a log (so the Japanese would not see it) and some Phillip Morris cigarette butts. Masters knew that Vansteenberg smoked Phillip Morris, so he was sure the copilot had come down safely.

Half an hour later they heard someone on the trail. Masters grabbed his .45 and waited. But it was radio operator Montgomery, looking tired but happy to see them. Over his shoes he wore flying boots, which he gave to the lucky Divoky.

They came to a stream and rested, and Masters went fishing. He caught a five-inch fish, which they ate—all but the eyes. That afternoon they found a sandy spot and some poles, and built a tent with the parachute. They slept in it, but it rained, and the tent sagged down on them.

On January 16 the three men encountered more pieces of parachute, and knew that Vansteenberg was ahead of them. On the 17th they found him. Vansteenberg had lost one shoe and one flying boot, and the other shoe was in bad shape, so he was bumping along on one flying boot and one sick shoe. They slowed down.

Their big problem was shoes and feet. The shoes and boots got soaked, and their feet were too tender to wade streams barefoot. They were following a river, which grew steadily larger, and they saw many fish, but could not catch any more. They found a lemon tree and ate the lemons—sour, but food.

On the 18th at dusk, a B-25 medium bomber came roaring down across the jungle, but was gone before they could wave. On the 19th a low-flying transport spotted them and went away, then came back in an hour and dropped food and blankets and a note telling them to follow the river west to the Ledo road.

On January 20 the plane found them again and dropped more supplies and another note, shoes, and coveralls.

They ate the food, all of it, and on the 21st went hungry when the plane did not appear. On the 22nd they were very weak, and found it hard to keep going. But late that afternoon they came to a Naga village, and the villagers, who were not very friendly, finally agreed to guide them along their trail. That night they stayed in a village in a long hut built on stilts. When they saw a tiger come down to the river and drink, they knew why the hut was on stilts.

They came to a Kachin village, and the Kachins, who were Christians, were much more friendly to them. Finally they came to the Ledo road, flagged down an American army truck, and climbed in. They were saved.

They flew everything that was needed, these ATC pilots on the Hump run: 55-gallon drums of 100-octane gasoline for flight operations, 75mm shells in cradles of three, mortar shells, naval mines. Trucks and naval mines were always a worry because they were so heavy they could not be jettisoned to lighten a load in time of trouble.

One day early in 1944, pilot Vail was flying naval mines. When they got over the first ridge in the Naga hills at 13,000 feet, they climbed to 16,000 and one of the engines of the C-46 quit cold. Automatically Vail reached down and hit the heat control handle for the carburetors, and the engine started up again. Narrow escape? Yes, but a common one on the Hump run.

One day Vail and his crew were flying into Chanyi when the Japanese bombed the airfield. They held up and came in later. They picked up a damaged Allison engine, which they tied down in the aircraft—not much chance of pushing that out in case of trouble. Then they took off and went up to 18,000 feet as the sun was going down. The Japanese came back. The first Vail knew about it was when he saw red dots slipping by his window past the nose of the plane. Then another group. He turned to the copilot. "Did you see that?"

"Yes," said the copilot.

They redlined the airspeed indicator and put the wheel down, straight down. Over the Mekong valley they sped. The radio operator sent word that they were under attack, but the American operator at Chienyi could not understand what he was saying, so it was no help at all. Down they went, down to 11,000 feet, and then they leveled off. No more bursts of red. They climbed back to 18,000 and went on their way home.

Sometimes Lieutenant Vail and his fellow pilots in Assam Valley would make bets as to who could get over the Hump with the least altitude. Something less than 10,000 feet was the goal, and some of them did it, sometimes. Others ended up adding to the "aluminum trail" that ran across the flyways of the Himalayas.

It didn't make a lot of difference how skillful a pilot was. For a while at first, Lieutenant Vail flew with a very fine pilot named Hunt, who was regarded as top man on the base. One day they had a very rough time getting into Yunnanyi, but they made it. They came back in perfect weather the next day, Vail singing Hunt's praises. But the next time Lieutenant Hunt went out, he did not come back. No one knew where he had left his mark on the aluminum trail.

The exigencies of war obviously caused the flying schools to pass some pilots who would not have made it through a peacetime course. Lieutenant John Shaver, who arrived at Chabua early in 1944, recalled some hairy experiences with one pilot. He was flying copilot in those days.

On his second trip over the Hump, Shaver noticed that the pilot called for him to raise the landing gear when the wheels were still on the runway. He delayed raising the handle until they had cleared the runway by ten feet. Then on the trip to China he noticed that the pilot did not seem to know any more about instrument flying than he did. On the return trip, the pilot turned the aircraft over to Shaver, and he and the radio operator proceeded to go to sleep.

This was a night flight back from Kunming to Sookerating. The control tower at Kunming had been scheduling flights ten minutes apart. All aircraft were blacked out, to avoid notice by Japanese fighters.

Shaver was in the left-hand seat, monitoring the Mayday frequency, when the outline of an airplane materialized in the darkness directly in front of him. He chopped the engines and dived. They went under the other aircraft, too, too close.

The pilot of Shaver's plane had been sitting with his seatbelt loose, and he hit his head on something during the dive. He awoke and angrily demanded to know what was going on. Neither he nor the radio operator would believe that they had very nearly come to disaster. The pilot took over the plane and flew it back to Sookerating.

On Shaver's third trip, they carried a load of 100-octane gasoline for the B-29 base at Chengdu. They ran into heavy weather and were diverted to an auxiliary field, flying on instruments. Shaver offered to navigate, but the pilot said no, he knew the terrain. Ten minutes later Lieutenant Shaver looked out the window and saw a runway to their rear and mountains ahead. They were heading straight for the mountains. Shaver told the pilot, who turned, got a clearance, and went into an approach pattern. It was raining. The pilot swung around so abruptly on the final approach that they missed the runway and had to go around. On the second pass they got the wheels down onto the runway and lurched along in great bumps. They had to go around again. Shaver hoped the gear had stood up to the hard bumping. On the third try the pilot managed to get the plane down. Lieutenant Shaver blessed the people who built the C-46.

"The gear stayed on. I don't know how. My respect for the airplane grew. It must be built solid to take that, and loaded too. The lieutenant really worried me with his flying and I decided that I'd better get another pilot or make out my last will and testament."

That pilot then drew another inexperienced copilot. Again, on takeoff, he ordered the gear up when the wheels were still on the runway. The new copilot obeyed, the gear came up, and the aircraft settled down on the runway, since it did not have flying speed. Although the C-46 was loaded with drums of gasoline, it did not burn.

The last Lieutenant Shaver knew, that pilot was still grounded.

In the luck of the draw, copilot Shaver was assigned to a Lieutenant Levi, who had just suffered a close call on a Hump trip. Pilots as well as air crews were extremely nervous, and the superstition had it that trouble came in threes. So Lieutenant Levi had requested a crew change, and the new crew, with Lieutenant Shaver flying copilot, assembled and boarded the plane for Shaver's fourth Hump trip.

Once again it was a night trip to Chengdu, over the "Charlie" route, carrying high-octane aviation gas for the B-29s. They flew to Salween River, checked in over Kunming, and headed for Luliang. And then, out of Chanyi, the No. 2 engine began to misfire. The vibration grew so heavy that they shut it down. They called in to Chanyi, got a clearance as the Chanyi operations scattered a raft of stacked-up planes, and landed on instruments on one engine. Next day the engine was repaired and they set out for Chengdu again.

Out of Chanyi the engines began to ice up. They were on full instruments. Lieutenant Shaver was feeling very sluggish, and he almost let the engine die before he worked the carburetor's heating system. When they landed, Shaver asked for a check of the oxygen system and learned that his hose had come loose. He had had no oxygen on the entire trip.

After that trip, Lieutenant Shaver also found himself cut loose. Lieutenant Levi, as superstitious as the next man, had again requested a crew change because of the bad luck. So Lieutenant Levi got a new copilot. He also got a new aircraft, fresh from the factory, and a new radio operator. The bad luck seemed to have ended.

This time Levi's payload was one large GMC truck. He set off on a clear day toward the Fort Hertz valley. Somewhere on the eastern side of the valley, at 18,000 feet, Levi lost an engine in this new C-46. He tried to fly on one engine, but he could not jettison cargo—there was no way to get that GMC truck out except on the ground. The plane began to lose altitude.

Lieutenant Levi was cool and calm. He knew where they would be going down, so he called Air Rescue on the radio and told them. He picked the spot, near a village, put the airplane on automatic pilot, circling, and ordered the crew to bail out. When he himself bailed out, he was still cool and calm, and had his B-4 travel bag cradled in his arms so he would not lose anything. But when the parachute popped open, the B-4 bag got in the way of the shrouds, catching Lieutenant Levi's neck and breaking it. The body of Lieutenant Levi floated to the ground. The crew picked him up and laid him out. The C-46 spiraled gently to the ground and made a perfect belly landing on automatic pilot. Air Rescue came right on schedule and dropped supplies and instructions. The crew buried Lieutenant Levi and hiked out. It took them three weeks. The lieutenant had certainly been right: Bad luck came in threes.

Lieutenant Shaver was assigned to the crew of a Lieutenant Ralph Cunningham, an excellent pilot. He decided to remain with this crew, and flew with them for twenty-five missions during the summer of 1944. Some of them were memorable.

On one night flight to Chengdu, loaded with twenty-two drums of aviation gasoline for the B-29s and flying on instruments, they were cleared for landing. When they broke out of the murk with gear down and locked, and propellers low pitch, mixture rich, they were nearly hit by six aircraft that came at them, in formation, out of the clouds, and missed by perhaps a hundred feet. Shaver and Cunningham debated as to whether or not they should call the tower and complain about these planes' not following traffic pattern procedures. Then below them they saw flashes and heard the noise of bombs going off. They had come in just in time for a Japanese air raid. They circled and watched several B-29s burning on the ground. That night six B-29s were burned and fifty men were killed or wounded.

After the raid, the C-46 was routed to an adjacent field. They loaded off the cargo, and loaded up with fifty-five Chinese troops of the First Army, scheduled for India. Taxiing to takeoff, they were cleared for 18,000 feet. They complained that 18,000 feet was too high for human beings, and were told that their clearance was for 18,000 feet.

So they took off.

They shut the doors to the cockpit tight and began to fly. They climbed to 18,000 feet and went on instruments. Fifteen minutes later, Shaver opened the door and checked on their passengers. Half of them had already passed out. Lieutenant Cunningham said to hell with the orders, they were going to go down and give these people a chance to breathe before they all dropped dead. They went down to 10,000 feet but hit instrument weather again and had to go back to 18,000. They yo-yoed up and down all the way to Sookerating, but they arrived with a load of live passengers.

The spring and summer of 1944 marked the attempt of the Japanese to take Imphal, on the Burma-India border, and launch an invasion of India, so there was plenty of activity in the air.

One day the Cunningham crew was flying empty back from Kunming toward Sookerating, when over the Mekong River they noticed little specks in the sky off to the south. Soon, if they maintained their courses, they would pass the specks. Then the specks turned out to be six aircraft flying in formation, and a little later it appeared that they had blunt noses. Blunt noses meant Japanese Zero fighters; American P-51s, P-40s, and British Spitfires all had sharp noses.

Lieutenant Cunningham looked for a cloud. Lieutenant Shaver set up the engines: propellers low pitch, fuel mixture rich, fuel selected to center tanks, boost pump on. That was about all they could do to get ready for an attack. The Japanese fighters came on and then, as they were about two miles from the C-46, wheeled to attack. At the moment when their wings dipped, Cunningham pushed the throttle, put the nose down, and made an all-out run for a cloud. The radio operator was calling for help all the time. Cunningham got the aircraft inside a cumulus cloud as the fighters were a quarter of a mile away. It was a small cloud but a comfortable one. Each time they broke out, Cunningham turned around and reentered. After half an hour they left their cloud. The Japanese fighters had gotten bored and left.

One day in October 1944, the Cunningham crew ran into a Japanese weapon that never got much publicity during World War II—the gunship. This was a transport converted for combat, one not unlike the C-47. They had heard about it from intelligence but had never seen one. They were flying back from China at about 15,000 feet on the edge of the Fort Hertz valley when they spotted a strange plane with no markings. Cunningham and Shaver had a hunch this was a gunship, which would be lethal to them. The plane carried .50 caliber machine guns. Its technique was to come up alongside a C-46 or C-47 as if the gunship were another transport, and then slide back the cargo doors. Out would pop the .50 calibers, and the Japanese would open fire.

"Our strategy was to veer off to the north and not pass directly over. On the other hand, we wanted the gunship pilot to think we suspected nothing. If he saw our wings move in a bank, he would know we were alerted. So Cunningham held the wings level with the ailerons and skidded the nose right with the rudder, and we were able to change about 20 degrees with no perceptible wing movement. A minute or two of this and the gunship pilot must have suspected something, as he set his plane up for the coming contest. We knew something was coming when black smoke started coming out of his exhaust stacks. He probably hit the full rich on the carburetor and the water injection at the same time. As he started a left chandelle to get to our altitude and behind us, we turned to the right and down. We were already in full power, and Cunningham held the old dumbo in a power descent at 350 indicated airspeed. The red (danger) line was 280 IASD. We figured we had a 10 percent cushion on any structural failure. The radio operator, already briefed, was on the radio calling for fighter support. The gunship fell rapidly behind as we bought distance with loss of altitude in the power dive. We leveled off at about 1000 feet off the jungle and continued to let the airplane run as fast as it would as long as he followed us, which was for about twenty minutes. Then he gave up and headed south towards his home grounds. The fighters had already scrambled to cut him off, and in all probability he never made it home."

The flight over the Himalayas was considered by most airmen to be the most dangerous in the China-Burma-India area. General George Stratemeyer once said that the pilots he knew would rather fly into the heart of Japanese-held territory than take the trip over the Hump. Here is an account of one trip over the Hump, written as a letter by Staff Sergeant Charles L. Baldridge, engineer gunner on a B-24 of the 425th Squadron, 308th Bomb Group, stationed at Tezpur.

"*0455:* Charge of quarters stuck his head in the tent to wake us. Sergeant Andrew Thomas, the radio operator, and I had both been awake for the past hour—chasing mosquitos which had gotten in the net. Everything damp from the night air. Dressing by flashlight.

"*0510:* Pancakes, syrup, Spam, coffee, and grapefruit juice. Coffee now, to get fully awake.

"On our way to the ship, bouncing along a typical Indian road in the dark. It's four miles to the landing strip from our tent area. Field was built under bombing. Everything was arranged for quick, dispersed planes parked back in the trees hundreds of yards apart. We've got No. 491 again, third time in a row. Not bad, old engine that eats gas, usual amount of gas leaks.

"Preflight check completed and things ready to start engines, auxiliary power unit still inoperative.

"*0640:* Taxied out to end of runway and are going through checklist and final engine run up. Each engine has to check out right for full power or else we won't attempt to take off.

"Off to one side right in the middle runway, you can see spare parts of a sacred Indian cow, scattered all over. One of our ships hit a cow as they landed last night. Broke one of the landing gear on the B-24. With many flying hours here you collect a long list of cows, goats, vultures, Hindus, Chinese, etc. The ATC holds the most records in that respect.

"*0650:* All ready to go. Swung around the runway and lined up. Last check of all instruments. Brakes locked and the engines rev up to almost full power. The ship vibrates and strains against the brakes, nose digs down under the force—Lt. Joe Marks, the pilot, looks toward me—I nod okay. Brakes released, we're on the way, slowly picking up speed. At 70 mph Joe hollers for 20 percent flaps. As the flaps roll down, the plane staggers up a little. The end of the runway looms up, still everything okay, gradually pull up from the runway, trees flash by underneath as the gear comes up. Joe drops the nose down close to the tree tops to pick up speed. A quick check around the plane visually and we seem to be okay. No. 2 engine smoking a little. The usual leak in left rear tank.

"*0700:* We're circling around the field, trying to gain altitude. Here's where we use from 280 to 300 gallons of gas per hour, lifting so heavy a load.

*0730:* Climbing at 11,000 feet on a course of 1020, the valley seems to be coming to an end. The first series of ridges are coming up, not too high but jagged and covered solid with jungle. Looks like a pile of rocks covered with green velvet—dark green, almost black. The rice fields and low swampy land are behind us.

*0800:* We've leveled off at 16,000 feet, oxygen masks on. It appears to be a good day for the Hump—few scattered clouds above, a snowy white layer at about 14,000 feet. Both sides of us big black jagged peaks stick out of the clouds. Flying up a valley more or less. Once in a while a thundercloud rolls up and we plow right through. At first series of short hard jars, suddenly you feel like something is pushing you through the floor. The plane is being blown upward in a gust of wind several hundreds of miles per hour. Actually you can't see anything, just murk out, flight instruments show you in all attitudes of flight. Out in clear again.

"*0820:* Another periodic check through the plane. All okay. Gas leak stopped. Pilot Marks, more at ease now, lights a cigarette. Lt. Alvern Butler, the navigator, works hard every minute we're in the air. He checks and double-checks. A little bit off course, you won't fly very far before you hit solid rock. Majority of the time you fly blind all the way, just take the navigator's word there are no rocks in the dark. Radio Operator Thomas had all sets checked and is reading a book. Soon he will have a position report to radio in, weather reports from China.

"*0844:* Another check of the plane. Put three cans of grapefruit juice on the bomb bay doors. We'll have ice cold juice when we get there. Rummaged around in my A-3 bag looking for a bar of chocolate. First things I found were Bea's pink booties. I wonder how big her feet are now?"

"*0855:* I'm not sure exactly where we are headed for. We're supposed to go to Lushien, but we've got a little trick in mind that might get us a shorter destination. We took off with only 200 pounds of oxygen, not enough to take us over and back. We're going to radio to Kunming and try to land there. Lushien never had oxygen tanks before. Automatic pilot in operation, and we're breezing along over Burma. Below us, somewhere around Myitkyina, are 70,000 Japs still in the jungle. Anyone could hunt them like animals for another 50 years.

"*0955:* Clouds gathered up, and we've been plowing in the

black for ten minutes now. Everything in these clouds—snow, ice, rain, sleet. For several minutes ice accumulating along the leading edge of the wing.

"*1057:* Still in the clouds, not very rough. We're over China now. After going north for a while and northeast, we're going due east now. In an hour we should be coming into Lushien. From the looks of the weather we may have to make an instrument letdown and approach. Marks is already studying the charts.

"*1102:* Throttles and props cut back. We're virtually sinking down through the clouds, 600 feet drop per minute. Butler has done his job well. Now it's up to Marks; he's damn good on instruments. I've got work now, see if we're able to land, engines cooling off. Butler coming out of nose compartment.

"*1155:* We've been circling for an hour in this stuff, and we're now down where we can see the ground. The gear is down and locked. The final approach, skimming over a tangle of mud and sticks (the town) and down the river and in. The runway runs right beside the Yangtze River. Another trip half done.

"*1230:* Ship's all ready to go practically. All we need is oxygen. Marks and the rest went to lunch already I don't go until my work is done. When I came back from lunch we can take off quick.

"*1325:* The usual lunch of fried eggs, pork chop, and potatoes. Regardless of what meal it is, eggs are the meal—every place in China is the same way. As soon as they get through putting in the oxygen, we'll go. The rest of the crew are sitting under the wing, playing poker.

"The weather is now typical of what we usually get; the cloud ceiling is about 1000 feet above the ground. I hope the weather is open at the other end—expect some mail tonight and want to get back.

"*1415:* Copilot Boyer makes the takeoff—his first since Westover. Nothing fancy, but we got off. Everything okay except the weather.

"*1540:* We've broken away from the weather by climbing to 18,000. Can't see the ground. An occasional mountain sticks up.

"*1615:* Still clear at 18,000. Burma below us.

"Once in a while the clouds part and you get a glimpse of the land. Then you start wondering, 'How did I get here? What am I doing here?'

"Every time we go over and get a chance to see some of the terrain we wonder where Lieutenant Kleffen is and what caused his ship to blow up.

"*1725:* Weather not too bad. Trouble with No. 2 engine, using excessive fuel. Running No. 2 and No. 4 engines from No. 4's tank. Alternately draw fuel from each tank to keep No. 2 going. Airspeed pretty high, we're hurrying back—maybe they've something for supper.

"We were in the air 5 hours and 35 minutes going over. Used 1525 gallons of gas. That's what the tremendous weight does for you.

"*1735:* Butler is right on the ball. We passed over the same rocks every trip, really pinpointed.

"We're over the last ridges and back in the valley now—rivers, rice fields, etc.

"*1810:* On the ground safely. Found out we had two tanks completely dry. Luck rides again! That ship will need a checking over. Fuel gauges erratic—and a terrific loss of gas somewhere.

"I don't know who's praying for these five bums, but something does it."

# THIRTEEN

# *Gordo*

On the afternoon of December 7, 1941, in Richmond, Virginia, Gordon Cruickshanks was trying to get down to studying for this night's college classes when the word came that the Japanese had bombed Pearl Harbor. It was not much of a surprise to him; his father had been predicting the attack since 1935, and even that it would come on a Sunday.

Cruickshanks was already signed up with the U.S. Army Air Corps aviation cadet program and was waiting for the call. It came in March 1942; first Avon Park, Florida, then Sumter, South Carolina, then Craig Field at Selma, Alabama, where he got his wings and commission in the U.S. Army Air Force in March 1943.

After that, events moved more rapidly. He went to Waycross, Georgia, to join the 530th Fighter Squadron of the 311th Fighter Bomber Group. His was the first P-51 fighter group to go to China-Burma-India, to Assam province. They boarded the converted liner *Brazil* at San Francisco and forty-two days later landed at Bombay. The voyage was one long crap game for Lieutenant Cruickshanks, and a successful one. He got into the game with $20 of borrowed money and walked off the ship with $3000.

Soon the 530th Squadron was established in Assam province in the northeast corner of India, a part of the U.S. Tenth Air Force, and was fending off Japanese aerial attacks designed to further the conquest of India. It was November 1943, and the Japanese had launched a new drive to cut the Assam and Bengal railway, the lifeline of Assam and the troops holding the India-Burma border.

On Sunday morning, November 13, Lieutenant Cruickshanks took off from the squadron base at Sukerating on a routine patrol mission. Over Ledo he encountered his first Japanese aircraft, a twin-engine medium bomber, called a Sally by the Americans. In his first pass he shot the right engine off the bomber and it crashed—before the eyes of an admiring nurse of the Twentieth General Hospital.

"She didn't know it was me," said Lieutenant Cruickshanks. "She was in a slit trench and saw this fighter come on and shoot this bomber down practically on the runway next to the hospital. That night I really got a sweet reward."

Not long after this, Lieutenant Cruickshanks shot a Zero fighter off his commanding officer's tail when they got into a fight during a patrol. Then suddenly Japan's Imphal campaign to attack India ran out of gas. The Americans had invaded the Gilbert Islands, and the Japanese army had lost the southern Solomon Islands and was losing New Guinea. The war had turned around in a few short months, and Japan was on the defensive.

In December the Allied air command was integrated under Major General George E. Stratemeyer, and by January 1944 the Allies had air superiority over Burma. The Japanese were withdrawing the air units to reinforce the harried army and navy forces in the South and Central Pacific. The two quick aerial victories of Lieutenant Cruickshanks were not followed by more; the Japanese were on the decline in North Burma.

The work of the 311th turned to troop support and bombardment that spring of 1944. Lieutenant Cruickshanks was made assistant group operations officer, and as such it was his job to help plan missions, using napalm, general purpose bombs, or fragmentation bombs. The problem for the group was to keep an adequate supply of ordnance, for most of it had to come up overland across the Assam and Bengal narrow gauge railroad, which was jammed with freight for the military and civilian economies.

At one point that spring the ordnance officer reported to operations that there weren't any more bombs at all available until the next month. The reason was that three P-51 squadrons, one P-40 group, and one P-38 squadron had dropped twice as many tons of bombs in troop support as the B-25s and B-24s had dropped.

This created a serious problem, because Lieutenant General Joseph W. Stilwell was just launching the Allied counteroffensive in North Burma that spring. Merrill's Marauders, a special task force, was going in behind the Japanese lines and needed plenty of air support. Also, Stilwell's Chinese troops were running into heavy resistance near Walawbum, and the 311th was expected to furnish close air support. The Japanese had the only artillery, and so Stilwell had issued a new order:

"I want airplanes in the sky overhead during every daylight hour."

Lieutenant Colonel George Van Deusen, the 311th group operations officer, and the ordnance officer conferred:

"There's a possible answer to this, and if you'll come over to the dump and let me show you our latest shipment . . ."

So they headed for the bomb dump.

"I climbed into the jeep, and we took off for the bomb dump at Chabua. I didn't understand all the mystery that Jack was building up. He wouldn't say a word about anything until he unlocked a bamboo and thatch hut and showed us row upon row of huge stacks of the most unusual bombs I had ever laid eyes on. They were depth charges for use by the navy. They looked like ashcans—their name in the navy—300 pounds each of high explosive.

"I have an idea how we can modify those bastards so you guys can carry one on each wing and not have too much drag. I've also figured out how we can re-fuse the monsters so they'll go off on contact."

He could fit new fuses, adding another thirty pounds to each bomb, and attach bomb fins. The blunt noses could be sharpened with tips made of plaster of Paris.

So depth bombs came to the Burma jungle. Soon the P-51s were leaving on their early morning missions with a pair of the makeshift bombs under their wings.

"On early morning missions over Burma, before the hot tropical sun had a chance to burn off all the early morning mist and start the jungle steaming, you could actually see the round concussion rings of shock waves radiating from the blast point out through the mists in ever-widening rings. It was like dropping huge pebbles in a sea of jungle. We found out quickly from ground reports that if the bomb did not kill outright (and foxholes were no protection), the blast would deafen everyone within range and make them totally disoriented."

The Japanese complained. Saigon Sally, who broadcast from Indochina, called the use of depth charges in the jungle "unfair warfare."

The Tenth Air Force continued to give tactical support to the Stilwell operation all that spring as the troops closed in on Myitkyina, the central city of North Burma. A rueful Japanese company officer confided to his diary:

"Enemy aircraft are over continuously in all weather. We can do nothing but look at them. If we only had air power! Even one or two planes would be something. Superiority in the air is the decisive factor in victory."

But Japanese air power was moving ever farther eastward into Thailand, Malaya, and Sumatra. In Burma the war was turning around, as Radio Tokyo said in June:

"Our difficulty in operating on the Imphal front lies in lack of supplies and air supremacy. The enemy receives food supplies through the air route, while our men continue in battle eating a handful of barley or grain."

June and July 1944 were months of siege at Myitkyina, with the P-51s operating in such close support of the ground troops that they worked from an airstrip less than 1000 yards from the Japanese positions and dive-bombed targets only thirty-five yards from the Allied lines.

# FOURTEEN

# Carrier Strike

*Take two jiggers of Bourbon whiskey, one jigger of rum, one jigger of gin, one jigger of French vermouth, one jigger of Italian vermouth, mix in a highball glass with ice, and decorate with a slice of lemon peel.*
— Ensign Bruce Ek's K.O.-for-Tokyo cocktail

During the first week of war against Japan, feverish activity descended upon San Diego and the naval air station there. At the air station the windows of the buildings were painted black for permanent night blackout. Sailors and marines crisscrossed the base with four-foot-deep zigzag trenches, to be used as bomb shelters when the Japanese attacked. Circular antiaircraft pits housing .50 caliber machine guns were dug around the airfield. Aircraft were protected in dirt revetments, or scattered around the edges of the field 300 feet apart.

Everyone was expecting an air attack, if not an invasion attempt, at any moment. Across the channel, San Diego was warned by the Civilian Defense Council to black out at night, keep car lights off, and stay home when the street lights went out. When the air raids came, they would be announced by the sounding of the fire department's sirens.

Every time an unidentified plane came by, it set off the air raid alarms, not just in San Diego, but in Los Angeles and San Francisco as well. Everyone was very, very nervous. Merchant skippers came into coastal harbors reporting the sighting of periscopes and even attack by submarines. All Orientals were viewed with deep suspicion because the Caucasians feared sabotage from the Japanese-Americans. (This was an unreasoned fear that was totally unjustified by events. Not a single act of sabotage by Japanese-Americans or Japanese citizens was ever reported.)

The panic lasted about ten days. Then the citizens began to

realize that thousands of miles separated Japan from America. Most of the submarine sightings proved false, and there was no attack. San Diego began to return to normal.

"I guess we'll have to start buying our own drinks again," said one wag among the airmen.

After a week, the naval authorities also relaxed and authorized weekend leaves for the young officers. Enlisted men started getting passes and leaves again.

Shortly after Christmas, Ensign Frederick Mears was ordered up to Terminal Island, San Pedro, to fly antisubmarine patrols in a Kingfisher scout plane (OS2U-2). His plane was loaded with two 100-pound bombs and carried machine guns. The planes followed convoys out to sea and looked for submarines. They did not find any submarines, but they bombed several schools of fish.

Early in January 1942, Mears was sent back to San Diego and a six-week training course in Douglas dive bombers, getting ready to join the fleet. The training program meant flying six hours a day, seven days a week. They flew 150 miles out to sea, to get used to flying over water. They practiced "carrier" landings on a narrow strip marked out on the field, guided by a landing signal officer. They practiced gunnery against tow targets. They "flew" the Link trainer, simulating instrument flight. They flew night formations, following the exhaust of the plane ahead.

They practiced dive-bombing, and at the end of two weeks Mears was able to place a smoke bomb inside a fifty-foot circle. They flew in the daytime and flew hard. They played at night and played hard. They had rented a house in Coronado, and hired a cook and a bartender. Many a girl fell victim to the smoothness of the K.O.-for-Tokyo cocktail and found herself waking up in a strange bed the next morning.

In February, Ensign James Daniels came back to San Diego with the story of Admiral William F. Halsey's raid on Wotje and Maloelap in the Marshall Islands, where the Japanese had established seaplane bases. On January 25, Admiral Halsey set sail in the carrier *Enterprise*, with the cruisers *Northampton, Chester*, and *Salt Lake City* and several destroyers to conduct shore bombardment. Just after 4:30 on the morning of February 1, Halsey's planes had taken off from the carrier in moonlight to attack. Kwajalein was the main objective, Halsey had decided.

Commander Howard L. Young, the skipper of the *Enterprise* air group, led thirty-seven dive bombers to the Roi-Namur air complex, joined by a causeway, at the northern end of the Kwajalein atoll, while nine torpedo bombers went across the lagoon, looking for shipping.

The Roi attack did not go very well. Lieutenant Commander H. L. Hopping of the dive bomber squadron was shot down just after he released his bomb. Three other dive bombers were also lost to antiaircraft fire and Japanese fighter planes. Ten of the dive bombers were diverted to Kwajalein, and with the torpedo bombers they did better, sinking a transport, the *Bordeaux Maru*, and a sub-chaser. Five other ships were damaged. Eighteen Japanese planes were destroyed, and Rear Admiral Yashiro, the commander of the island base, was killed along with about ninety of his men.

Ensign Daniels participated in the Kwajalein attack in his F4F Wildcat fighter plane. He and four other pilots hit Taroa airfield on Maloelap. He dropped down to 700 feet and then released the bombs he carried, blowing up a hangar. ("It rose up and disintegrated in the air," he told his fascinated flier audience at the Coronado house over a K.O.-for-Tokyo cocktail.) Then he came back down to strafe, sending Japanese on the ground running in all directions.

On the way back to the carrier, Ensign Daniels was chased by a Japanese Zero. They sparred and shot at each other, but without result. Finally the Japanese, perhaps low on gas, turned away.

"These stories made us realize that Americans were actually fighting in the Pacific, and they whetted our zeal in training," said Ensign Mears. The airmen were all raring to go into action. Ensign Daniels had other tales to tell about the raid.

# FIFTEEN

# The Horny Maru

At the end of training, Ensign Mears was assigned to the dive bomber contingent. On March 23, 1942, he boarded the carrier *Hornet*, which was known popularly as "the Horny Maru," along with the other fliers of the new contingent of fighter pilots. They were going out for a training cruise.

They were green, green, green. Most of them did not know that they were supposed to salute the ensign (flag) aft when boarding the ship. Ensign Mears was ordered to report to the first lieutenant for a cabin assignment, and discovered that the first lieutenant was a lieutenant commander, which worried him for a while.

"Which way is the dining room?" he asked a seaman.

"The wardroom is on the first deck amidships," the seaman answered.

He walked about, barking his shins on coamings, tripping over mooring lines, being stopped by a marine from entering "captain's country."

A few hours later the *Hornet* weighed anchor and set out to sea. Soon they had their first meal, lunch. Ensign Mears was impressed by the monogrammed silver service, the spotless white linen, the black mess attendants in white uniforms. This was the way to fight a war, he decided.

Lieutenant Ray Needham, who had brought these cubs through carrier training thus far, would continue with them, get them off in their aircraft, and try to get them back aboard the *Hornet* without disaster striking.

The dive bombers went first that afternoon.

Ensign Edmondson made one good landing, but on the second he held the plane too long and floated into the island and the first wire barrier, crumpling the right wing and rearranging the aerodynamics of the propeller. Ensign Goddard landed too fast and too far to starboard. The wire caught the hook and slewed the plane off into an antiaircraft gun pod. The wheel shaft broke, and the wing crumpled.

Then the fighters took over and seemed to do better, making safe landings, until Ensign Dibb in an F4F took his cut. He hit the deck wheels first, forward of the ramp, bounced, and crashed squarely into the wire barrier, with the plane in the air and afire. The gas valve under the aircraft had been knocked loose, and flames were shooting over the nose. Dibb dived out, hit the wing, and rolled off onto the deck to be picked up by two firefighters in asbestos suits, while others dealt with the plane. First they used $CO_2$ bottles, then the hoses. The fire died down. But the water pressure in the hoses failed, the fire blazed up again, and the wooden deck caught fire. The plane buckled, a gas tank opened up, and a stream of fuel fed the fire. The carrier was now really afire, and the general fire call was sounded. Then the pressure came back in the hoses, and the fire crews got more $CO_2$. They put the fire out, and the parts of the plane were hauled onto the elevator and taken below.

That night, after dinner, the new pilots retired to their quarters—small staterooms, one or two to a room—to relax and hash over the events of the day. Next morning the qualifying began again.

Ensign Kleinman roared off the deck, but not fast enough, and disappeared off the starboard bow. There came a splash— he had gone into the drink, forgot to crack his flaps. His yellow life vest came up and he waved and splashed out of the plane. The carrier went on, leaving a destroyer to pick him up.

Ensign Mears spoke to a seaman standing next to him.

"A lot of crashes," he said.

"Oh, you guys aren't doing so bad. You should have seen the last batch."

Ensign Mears and his buddies were dubious. They watched. Ensign Eppler took the cut. He hit too far to starboard and caught a wire, but the plane went over the side and hung from the wire until the hook slipped. Then the plane disappeared below the flight deck. Splash. Ensign Eppler appeared, waving. Another destroyer was detailed to pilot pickup.

Lieutenant Needham gave his boys a little lecture. Most of them were coming in too high and too fast. Ensign Mears remembered that as he came in to land, and came in low and slow.

Lieutenant Needham gave him a wave-off. Mears speeded up and passed over the deck at just about five feet. Lieutenant Needham dropped flat on his face to avoid being run down. Mears came around again, got a cut, and landed safely. Then he made three more safe landings and was qualified.

So the cruise ended. Ensign Mears went back to the Coronado house with orders to go up to San Francisco Port of Embarkation in four days. He drove up in Ensign Jamie Dexter's car, with ensigns Jim Shelton and William Pittman. On the last night ashore, having drunk up all their money, they wrote a check for the taxi that took them to the ship. On the way someone found a dollar bill in his pocket and they tore it into four pieces. Each took a piece for good luck.

# SIXTEEN

# Jimmy Doolittle's Great Adventure

Shortly after depositing Ensign Mears and his fledgling aviator friends back at San Diego, the carrier *Hornet* headed for San Francisco and a secret mission. A plan was afoot to stage a bombing raid on the Japanese home islands.

The Japanese attack on Pearl Harbor, which brought the United States into the war against the Axis powers, had a serious negative effect on American morale, at home and in the armed services. This had been amplified by a steady string of Allied defeats in December 1941 and the first three months of 1942. Only in the Philippines, where the "Battling Bastards of Bataan" were holding out without reinforcement and with very little supply, was there any indication that the Allied powers could stand up to the Japanese juggernaut.

President Franklin D. Roosevelt, having acceded to the British request that Hitler be faced first (because without massive assistance from the United States Britain might well be forced out of the war), still worried constantly about American morale and the effects of the repeated Japanese victories in the Pacific. He and the Joint Chiefs of Staff knew that they could turn this around by application of power, but they did not have the planes, ships, and men to service both the European and Pacific theaters, and the Pacific theater would have to go on hold.

Even so, President Roosevelt kept asking General George C. Marshall, General H. H. Arnold, and Admiral Ernest J. King what could be done to strike back at the Japanese and how soon. The problem was one of distance. The Americans believed an aircraft carrier might safely approach the Japanese shores to a point about 500 miles out and launch planes which could then strike the Japanese home islands.

But what then? The navy's aircraft of 1942 could scarcely move out 300 miles from their carrier and return to the carrier safely. And once having launched planes, the carrier would have to turn about and run beyond the range of the Japanese air search and attack forces.

So in the winter of 1942 the Joint Chiefs of Staff puzzled over the problem as they planned future operations in east and west. When the Joint Chiefs considered landings in North Africa against Hitler, Admiral King suggested that army bombers might be used from carriers in such an operation. Two of Admiral King's staff members came up with the idea that the new North American B-25 medium bomber was the right plane. The B-25 had a range of 1350 miles, and this could be extended by sacrificing bomb load for gas storage. Their range also meant that in the Pacific the planes could be launched from a carrier, fly to Japan, bomb, and then fly to the safety of airfields in Free China, some of which were near the Chinese coast. (The Japanese controlled the Chinese coastline, but there were many areas into which they had not penetrated.)

Having established the feasibility of the idea, General Arnold looked for a man with the experience and leadership capability to lead such a mission. His eye fell on Lieutenant Colonel James H. Doolittle, a famous American aeronaut. Doolittle had been trained as a fighter pilot in World War I, but after thirteen years he had left the Army Air Corps to go into private aviation. He had acquired a Doctor of Science degree in aeronautical engineering from Massachusetts Institute of Technology, but most Americans knew him as a racing pilot and a stunt pilot. In 1940 Doolittle had rejoined the Army Air Corps and was serving on Arnold's staff as a manager of special projects.

Doolittle confirmed the capability of the B-25 for the task, particularly since it was the only army bomber with short enough wing span to clear the "island" of an aircraft carrier on takeoff.

When the possibility was confided to President Roosevelt, he was delighted; it was just what the American people needed.

So in February Doolittle was put in charge of the project. He assembled twenty-four five-man aircrews of volunteers for the mission, which was kept ▇ "top secret" all the way.

The simplest approach would be to fly to Japan, bomb, and then land in Soviet Russia; Doolittle suggested that the planes could then be given to the Soviet government. But the Soviets would have none of it. They had been attacked by the Japanese at Homonhon on the Manchurian-Siberian border in 1938. They half expected a resumption of those hostilities at any time, although Japan and the Soviet Union maintained a cautious neutrality because both were otherwise occupied with war.

So the point of arrival had to be Free China. The Chinese government was not notified at first, because the Americans did not trust them to keep the secret. By the time they were told, the plans were complete and immutable.

The training was carried out in the winter and early spring of 1943 at an auxiliary airfield near Eglin Field, Florida. When statistics were all in it was decided that the carrier involved would be the *Hornet*, and that its deck would accommodate only sixteen B-25s.

It was spring before the Chinese government was told about the mission. Admiral Nimitz had already assigned a sixteen-ship task force which would be led by Vice Admiral William F. Halsey in the carrier *Enterprise*. Chinese Generalissimo Chiang Kaishek was aghast; he called it a "stunt" and said it would cost the Chinese people half a million lives. Chiang knew his Japanese, and he knew that General Tojo had promised the Japanese people that the islands would never be bombed. The Japanese would rise in fury against China, he said. But the Americans were obdurate. Chiang's objections were heard, just as were the objections of a number of generals and admirals who considered the whole affair a stunt that would waste aircraft and create so many complications it should be abandoned. President Roosevelt, however, felt that the propaganda value of the raid was so great and the morale booster so badly needed by the American people that the objectors were to be ignored.

By 1942 Chiang was totally dependent on the Americans for supplies which had to come in "over the Hump." So the mission went on, and Chiang's people made the arrangements for gasoline to be supplied at the airfields near the China coast, and for Chinese forces to assist the Americans when they arrived.

On March 23, twenty-two B-25s left Eglin Field for the Sacramento air base. On April 1, sixteen planes were lashed to the decks of the *Hornet* in San Francisco Bay. And on April 2, the carrier passed under the Golden Gate Bridge and headed out into the Pacific to rendezvous with Admiral Halsey, who was sailing from Hawaii, and then steam west to arrive at a launch point 450 miles off Japan on April 19.

The plan called for Lieutenant Colonel Doolittle to lead the way in the first bomber, taking off on the afternoon of the 19th, and bombing Tokyo with incendiaries. He would then head southwest across the East China Sea and land that night at Chuchou in Hunan province. The other planes, each armed with three 500-pound general-purpose bombs and one cluster of incendiaries, were to arrive after dark and bomb, and then head for other safe fields in eastern China.

On April 13 the two task forces met at the 180th meridian. Aboard the *Hornet* Lieutenant Colonel Doolittle briefed his men twice a day. They chose targets and studied maps. He warned them to stay away from the Imperial palace, and to bomb only military targets.

"Bombing military targets is an act of strategic warfare, but hitting 'The Temple of Heaven' [palace] or other nonmilitary targets such as hospitals or schools would be interpreted as an inexcusably barbarian act. It could mean your life if you are captured."

The American fleet was enjoined to maintain strict radio silence, but it did not, and the Japanese radio monitors picked up talk between ships that gave away the mission. As of April 10 the Japanese knew the Americans were coming and were preparing to meet them. Unfortunately for the Japanese, the Combined

Fleet's major carrier striking force was otherwise occupied, on a raid of the Indian Ocean (in which they sank the British carrier *Hermes* and two British cruisers). Also, the Japanese made some miscalculations: They knew that the extreme range of American carrier planes was then about 300 miles from base, and their warning network of search planes and picket boats extended out 700 miles. So they remained secure, although expectant.

On April 14 Admiral Halsey tightened security, and there were no more leaks. The Japanese lost contact that day. They were not particularly worried; they would find the enemy in time, they presumed.

On April 15, the carriers and cruisers of the U.S. fleet fueled, and then the oilers headed for the rendezvous point at which they would be safe to await the returning warships.

On the morning of April 17, the B-25s were armed with bombs and machine gun bullets and positioned for quick takeoff. The U.S. fleet had moved faster than expected, and they anticipated taking off the next day instead of April 19. The eighty men of the B-25 air crews turned in early and tried to sleep.

Just after three o'clock on the morning of April 18, the radarman of the *Enterprise* picked up a blip and then another on the surface. They were 700 miles off the Japanese shore and, in fact, had reached the edge of the Japanese picket line. The blips were Japanese picket boats.

The fleet turned right to avoid the boats, and the alarm for general quarters—"Battle Stations"—rang out in the ships. Half an hour later the ships resumed course, and Halsey ordered out search planes and a combat air patrol. Just before six o'clock that morning the pilot of a search bomber spotted a Japanese patrol boat forty miles from the fleet and passed the word. The pilot reported that he thought he had been spotted by the Japanese.

The radiomen of the fleet monitored traffic but did not hear any messages that would indicate warning. (The Japanese had, however, seen and reported on the plane.) The matter became very clear shortly before 8 a.m., when in the squalls and heavy waves, lookouts on the *Hornet* sighted the masts of a picket boat eleven miles away. Now everyone knew that they had been sighted.

The sighting had come too soon. Lieutenant Colonel Doolittle had expected to launch from 450 miles out. Instead they were 700 miles out, which meant that every margin would be strained and at least some of the planes would not make the Chinese mainland after their attacks.

Aboard the *Enterprise* the radio room picked up a Japanese transmission, which sealed the matter. Admiral Halsey had warned Doolittle that such an emergency might occur, and now he made the decision:

"Launch planes. To Colonel Doolittle and gallant command, good luck and God bless you."

On the bridge of the *Hornet*, Jimmy Doolittle and Captain Marc Mitscher moved. Doolittle ran for his plane as the ship's squawk box warned, "Army pilots, man your planes."

At 8:15, Doolittle's plane was moved into position, the left wheel on one line that ran down the flight deck and the nose wheel on the other. The engines were started, and Doolittle ran through the pilot's checklist. At a signal he advanced the throttles to pull power. At another signal the chocks were yanked from under the tires, the brakes were released, and the B-25 began to move, wobbling a little at first and then smoothing out as it sped along the flight deck and lifted off while the flight deck rose to a wave. The B-25's wheels folded up, the plane circled over the *Hornet*, and it was off for Japan.

Doolittle's plan obviously had to be discarded; the other planes must be airborne as soon as possible so the carriers could turn around and get out of the area before the Japanese search planes found them. There would be no three hours' differential between Doolittle and his men; they would not have the bright orange fires of the incendiaries to guide them when they hit Japan. Every crew was on its own for target and survival.

One by one for the next hour the planes took off.

At noon, Lieutenant Colonel Doolittle's B-25 was in sight of Japan, and at about 12:30 Doolittle bombed. The others came along one after the other, trying to find targets and not succeeding very well. They did not manage to hit military installations, but did hit a school and a hospital, killing a number of civilians. The reaction was exactly what Doolittle had warned it would be: frustration and extreme rage on the part of the Japanese.

Fifteen of the aircraft then headed for China, as ordered. But the pilot of the sixteenth airplane said his B-25 was burning 50 percent more fuel than expected and decided to head for a nearer haven, Siberia. The plane landed safely there, but the crew and aircraft were seized. The crew was charged with violation of Soviet neutrality and interned for thirteen months until they escaped into Iran.

The other fifteen B-25s headed for east central China, through squally weather across the East China Sea. And of course the best laid plans . . .

For although the planes were virtually unmolested by fighters and antiaircraft (because the Japanese were surprised), the Doolittle Raid had to be accounted a flat military failure. They did not hit any targets of note. But the targets were not really important to the U.S. high command. As they crossed the sea toward China, the weather closed in, and the crews of ten of the aircraft, including Doolittle's, bailed out. One man was killed, but the rest of the aircrews survived. Four planes crash-landed, and crewmen sustained some injuries. Two of the aircraft came down in Japanese occupied territory and their crews were taken prisoner.

Lieutenant Colonel Doolittle was unhurt. It took him a day to round up his own crew and find a Chinese Nationalist military headquarters, which put him on the way to Chongqing, the Nationalist capital.

It was announced that American bombers had bombed Japan, and the fact was excitedly and furiously confirmed by Radio Tokyo, which called the bombing of women and children a cowardly, beastly perversion of war.

Asked about the bombing at his press conference, President Roosevelt was suave and delighted.

Where had the planes come from? a reporter demanded. What was their base of operations?

The President looked through his pince-nez and smiled. The

base? It was Shangri-La, said Mr. Roosevelt, invoking the setting of a recent popular motion picture, a mythical settlement deep in the snows of Tibet.

The press was delighted. The American public was delighted. The Japanese were shocked but quickly moved to retaliate.

From Chongqing Doolittle supervised the attempts to rescue his fliers. By May 1 all the crews were accounted for but the two that had come down in Japanese-occupied territory. Doolittle tried to persuade the Chinese to attack the Japanese and rescue his men, but General Ku Chotung, commander of the forces in the area, refused to sacrifice his people. He knew better than Doolittle what the Japanese were capable of doing.

Soon enough all China knew. The Japanese mounted an offensive in east China to close down the airfields available to the Allies there and also punish the villages which had helped the Americans. Whole villages were destroyed and the villagers killed.

The Japanese had quickly captured the crew of Lieutenant William G. Farrow. At first the Japanese combat soldiers were polite and smiling, but soon they got the official word that the raid was considered in Tokyo to be an act of piracy.

Posters were put up throughout occupied China by the Japanese, showing a picture of the captured Americans.

"Current Chinese happenings:

"The mischievous evil American fliers who bombed the homeland of Japan have been captured by the Japanese army and will be dealt with in the most severe fashion under the law.

"Moreover, they directed the attack on nonmilitary targets, such as hospitals, schools, and private houses, dropping incendiary bombs and high-explosive bombs and swooping down with machine guns, strafing elementary school children at play."

The Japanese search for the other fliers began, and became a search also for all the Chinese who had offered the Americans any assistance. Before the punitive expeditions were finished, the Japanese had killed 250,000 Chinese in retaliation for the Doolittle Raid.

Jiangsi and Chekiang provinces were hardest hit. The Japanese put fifty-three battalions of troops into the area, to make sure that the Chinese airfields did not become staging points for further raids against Japan. They destroyed airfields at Chuchou, Lishui, and Yushan. The campaign lasted two months.

A total of eight crewmen had been captured by the Japanese and sentenced to death. Three—Lieutenant Dean Hallmark, Lieutenant William G. Farrow, and Sergeant Harold A. Spatz—were executed as war criminals, but the sentences of the other five condemned fliers were commuted to life imprisonment, which turned out to be the duration of the war for four of them (one man died).

Jimmy Doolittle soon was ordered back to Washington, where he was immediately jumped to the rank of brigadier general and awarded the Medal of Honor for the exploit.

In retrospect, was the Doolittle Raid worth the effort?

As for its effect on the war, the American action was regarded as a war crime by the Japanese because of the indiscriminate bombing. But in terms of what was to come, particularly the fire raids against Japanese cities, this tiny raid on Japan was of tactical importance primarily because it showed the wave of the future. It was more important in creating a certain mind-set among the American high command relative to atrocities and war crimes; when the war ended, it became a part of the evidence in the war crimes trials of various Japanese officers and leaders.

Certainly the effect on American public and military morale was almost miraculous. The Doolittle Raid was the first "victory" of any sort by the Allies in the Pacific war, although its physical results were insignificant. The raid came just about a week after the surrender of the American troops on Bataan, which had been a morale shaker for the American people. After the raid would come more bad news—the fall of Corregidor and more Japanese landings in the South Pacific. The Battle of the Coral Sea would be perceived as a Japanese victory, and the Battle of Midway would not be immediately appreciated for its full importance in changing the military scene. Even Guadalcanal would be seen at first as a particularly desperate struggle against a powerful enemy, and it would not be until the capture of Guadalcanal that the American people would really begin to regain their confidence in victory in the Pacific.

So as propaganda, the Doolittle Raid was vitally important to American morale, and the American raiders who sacrificed so much were as gallant as Captain Colin Kelly in the Philippine campaign.

# SEVENTEEN

# *Midway*

There was a young girl from Madras
Who had a beautiful ass,
Not rounded and pink,
As you probably think,
But with long ears, a tail, and eats grass.
—from Ensign Mears' limerick notebook,
on the night before the Midway Battle

On April 8, 1942, Ensign Frederick Mears set sail for his war in a transport convoy headed for Hawaii. He worked his way across as a watch officer looking out for enemy planes and submarines. But the Japanese were not conducting submarine war against merchant shipping, there were no enemy bases between the west coast of America and the Hawaiian islands, and Japan's carrier force was far to the west. Having raided Darwin, Australia, on February 19, the Japanese carrier force had turned to the Indian Ocean, and on the day that Ensign Mears's convoy sailed, the Japanese were sinking two British cruisers and the carrier *Hermes* off Ceylon.

At Pearl Harbor, Ensign Mears was assigned to a torpedo squadron, Torpedo 3. Several of his friends, including ensigns Jamie Dexter, Jim Shelton, and Tom Durkin, were assigned to the *Yorktown* dive bomber group and went off to war. Ensign Mears began training in the TBD torpedo bomber, the Douglas. He was training during the Battle of the Coral Sea, where his friend and naval classmate Tom Durkin was shot down on a search mission and spent fourteen days on a rubber raft before being rescued.

It was the end of May. Ensign Mears was expecting to stay with Torpedo 3 and go along to a carrier when the squadron was assigned. But he got new orders assigning him to Torpedo 8, the torpedo squadron of the *Hornet*, old "Horny Maru." He reported in to Lieutenant Commander John C. Waldron, skipper of the squadron, and was taken on as a spare pilot. He would need some training, because he had never landed a torpedo plane on the deck of a carrier.

Torpedo 8 had been organized in the fall of 1941, with Waldron as commander, and had spent the autumn and early winter at Norfolk, Virginia. Commander Waldron was a very tough skipper. He flew the men six hours a day at Norfolk. He made them learn how to make engine changes on their aircraft, how to load torpedoes, how to repair the hydraulic system. He believed his pilots and crewmen should know everything possible about the weapons they used. In February 1942, the squadron was split, with half of it joining the *Hornet* and the other half remaining at Norfolk to train in the new torpedo bomber just beginning to reach the navy, the TBF. All the pilots knew that the Douglas TBD was an airplane of the past: slow, underpowered, outmoded, and no match for the Japanese Zero fighters. But everyone also knew that as of the spring of 1942 there was no alternative to the TBD in the Pacific. If there was going to be a carrier battle, it would be fought with TBDs.

No one in the U.S. Navy knew this better than Commander Waldron. His response was to try to compensate for the deficiencies of the aircraft his pilots flew by a fighting spirit that gave the men impetus to attack, no matter the odds. By the time Ensign Mears joined the squadron, this was doctrine. Attack, Attack, ATTACK!!!

One night Commander Waldron gave a big party at his home for the squadron. Almost everybody had much to drink, and the talk continued far into the night. At one point, a little unsteady, Commander Waldron stood in the middle of the floor and shouted out his slogan—ATTACK, ATTACK, ATTACK!!!!!—and everybody closed their fists in the insignia of the squadron and cheered.

At the end of May, the *Hornet* sailed out from Pearl Harbor with the *Enterprise* and a company of cruisers and destroyers. It was soon apparent that this was no ordinary voyage. They were going out to meet the Japanese, who were moving an invasion force and their Combined Fleet toward Midway Island. The men of the *Hornet* were going into battle.

As the *Hornet* moved toward Midway, Commander Waldron had a talk with his new pilots, Mears and two others who had just joined the squadron. Unless he had time on the way out to qualify them, they would not fly in the battle that was coming. But on the way he gave them a good deal of his time, familiarizing them with his methods of battle.

On June 3, the night before the battle, Waldron called his squadron to the ready room and told them what he knew.

The Japanese were descending on Midway Island, he said, and it was the job of the task force to stop them.

"The approaching battle will be the biggest of the war and may well be the turning point also," he said. "It is to be known as the Battle of Midway. It will be an historical and, I hope, a glorious event."

The torpedo planes would make their first attack early on the morning of June 4, he said, just as soon as the enemy fleet was spotted. Then they would return and launch a second attack at about ten o'clock. There would be no more briefings. They knew what to do. From this point on they should get as much "sack time" as possible and conserve their energy. He also advised them to tidy up their personal affairs and write letters home, "just in case."

Ensign Mears was so disappointed at not being allowed to participate that Waldron told him he would let him fly on the third or fourth attack, if the captain of the *Hornet* would give permission to a pilot who had never landed a TBD on the deck.

# EIGHTEEN

# "The Biggest Battle . . ."

Captain C. P. Mason had many more things on his mind than the wishes of a junior ensign to get into the fight. He called his squadron commanders to a meeting and told them what was happening, and Commander Waldron came back to the ready room and once more conferred with his squadron.

On the night of June 2, 1942, Waldron outlined the plans for the squadron's operations. The torpedo planes would make their first attack as early as possible and then return and launch a second attack. As many attacks as possible would be made during the day. Even after dark he hoped to make a surprise attack, if the command would agree. He said he figured several ships would be on fire, and that would give the pilots a beacon to lead them in.

Early next morning Waldron met them again and said he thought the squadron was ready. He told the pilots and aircrews that he thought this squadron was the best in the fleet, and he was sure they would perform nobly.

That night of June 3, Captain Mason issued an announcement over the loudspeaker system:

"The enemy are approaching for an attempt to seize the island of Midway. The attack will probably be accompanied by a feint at western Alaska. We are going to prevent them from taking Midway if possible. Be ready, and keep on the alert."

That last night the aircrews were called together and the strategy of the American force was unveiled by the senior staff.

The American task force consisted of the combined task forces of the *Hornet*, the *Enterprise*, and the *Yorktown*. They would all meet at Point Luck, 320 miles northwest of Midway.

Already on Midway was a force of army B-17 bombers, three squadrons of marine planes, and a large number of PBY patrol bombers. Also, other planes of Torpedo 8 had arrived at Midway flying the new TBF torpedo bombers, which would be operating out of Midway to join the fight.

At 3:30 on the morning of June 4, pilots and crews assembled in the ready room and began to wait. They sank down in the comfortable leather chairs and drowsed. At about five o'clock some got hungry and began drifting off to the wardroom and the chow line.

At 6:40 a.m. the keys on the large teletype machine in the front of the ready room began to move and a message printed out, informing the crews that army bombers and PBYs had attacked an enemy force west of Midway.

That news woke everybody up. They waited expectantly, but after an hour during which nothing more happened they began to settle back down to drowsiness again. Some of the men played cards. Some read. Some sat around and shot the bull. Ensign Mears found himself in a group that were telling limericks. He searched his mind and remembered the one about the young girl from Madras. Everybody laughed at the twist. Someone else told another. The skipper told a dirty one. Lieutenant H. R. Kenyon soberly wrote them all down in a little notebook. He was keeping a collection for his old age, he said. At 8:10, a message flashed on the screen.

"Many enemy planes headed for Midway. This looks like the beginning. We are about to change course to 330 degrees."

At 8:15 came another message: "8 Combat patrol pilots plus two standby pilots man planes. All fighter pilots man planes on flight deck. *Hornet* base course 240 degrees."

Over the squawk box came more: "The enemy main body is now attempting to take Midway. We are heading toward Midway to intercept and destroy them."

The picture had changed. The enemy was approaching from the northwest instead of from the west. (The Americans did not yet know that there were two Japanese forces approaching.)

The teletype went on, "Pilots of all scout bombers and torpedo planes on flight deck except squadron commanders, man your planes. Squadron commanders and group commanders remain in ready room for latest instructions. All possible instructions will be sent out by blackboard."

But then, at 8:25, "Correction. Do not man planes until directed."

From this point on, orders and informational messages streamed across the teletype screen.

"*Hornet* position latitude 31 degrees 36 minutes, longitude 176 degrees 29 minutes. Enemy bears 239 degrees."

The pilots were busy with their chart boards, working out the navigation.

"Now hear this," shouted the squawk box; "We intend to launch planes at 0900 to attack enemy while their planes are returning from Midway. We will close to about 100 miles to enemy position."

A few moments later: "Present intent to launch attack groups 0900 plus four sections, for combat air patrol. Each group attack one carrier."

Commander Waldron spoke quietly to his men. They were not to worry if they did not find the enemy at first. They would find the enemy and they must be prepared to run out all their fuel to make this attack, he told them.

What then? In that case, he laughed, they would all ditch together and have a picnic.

ATTACK ATTACK ATTACK!!!!

"I have no doubt that we'll all be back by noon," he said. But if worse comes to worst, and we find ourselves outnumbered and alone on the way to the attack, we'll keep boring in. If there is only one man left, I want that man to take his pickle in and get a hit."

Lieutenant R. A. Moore, the squadron gunnery officer, looked over at Ensign Tex Gay. "You'll never get a hit, Gay. You couldn't hit a bull in the tail with a six-foot rake."

Gay did not think that was funny. "I'll get a hit," he said solemnly.

Then came an order: "Pilots, man your planes."

The men of the squadron got up and began to move to the flight deck.

By ten o'clock all the of *Hornet* attack force was in the air. Now the men aboard the carrier had nothing to do but wait, and listen, and hope.

At 10:35 came a message:"Enemy twin float seaplane bearing 180. Fighters will investigate. Stand by combat patrol condition one."

This was a reconnaissance plane from one of the Japanese cruisers or battleships.

Next came the message: "Be prepared to repel an attack."

At 11 a.m.: "Japanese attack on Midway resulted in minimum damage. Eight enemy planes shot down."

At 1:35 p.m. the first of the *Hornet* planes returned, an SBD dive bomber. Then came the others. Most of them still carried their bombs. They had not found the enemy. The torpedo planes were still out. In three-quarters of an hour they would have exhausted their fuel. There was no word.

The squawk box spoke up: "Japanese planes approaching from astern."

But those planes were not after the *Hornet*. They had found and were attacking the *Yorktown*. They damaged the *Yorktown* seriously, but they did not bother the *Hornet* or the *Enterprise*.

Ensign Mears was standing on the starboard side of the flight deck, watching operations. Suddenly a wounded *Yorktown* fighter pilot made an emergency landing on the *Hornet*. The plane skidded, the right wheel collapsed, and the six .50 caliber machine guns began firing, spraying the deck. Mears dropped on his face. A sailor in front of him was shot in the knee. Mears dragged him back and slit his trousers. The wound was not serious. Mears looked around. Behind him lay the body of a sailor who had been hit in the face. Mears walked past him. He saw a marine sergeant on a stretcher, his arm muscles protruding from the skin. Later he learned that five men had been killed and twenty wounded in the accident.

Everybody waited for the torpedo planes, but they did not

come. At 5 p.m. the *Hornet* launched another attack on the Japanese, while *Yorktown* pilots continued to land on the *Hornet* because their carrier was inoperable and had in fact been abandoned.

The last *Hornet* air strike of dive bombers came back, and shortly afterward the captain announced that four Japanese carriers, two battleships, and two cruisers had been set afire. He was right about the carriers, but not about the battleships and cruisers; no battleships had been hit, and two cruisers had in fact collided, but had not been bombed.

That night the pilots gathered in their ready rooms and tried to put together what had happened. They did not really know much. No one knew what had become of Torpedo 8. Next morning Ensign Gay was picked up by a PBY, and then the story began to come out. Gay believed he had scored a hit on a Japanese carrier, and airmen from Midway confirmed that the Torpedo 8 bombers had scored at least two hits. But Lieutenant Moore's prediction that Gay would not score a hit had come true; in fact, no one had scored any hits. But Gay had survived, although his radioman was killed. In fact he was the single survivor; all the others had gone to death, chewed up by dozens of Zero fighters as they came lumbering in in the slow TBDs.

The whole story was not known until the end of the war, when Americans in Japan, questioning various Japanese officers in the U.S. Strategic Bombing Survey, spoke to several officers who had been present at Midway on the carriers. They told of the brave attack of the torpedo planes, which had come in low and drawn the full attention of the Japanese fighters, so that when the American dive bombers from the *Enterprise* appeared shortly afterward, the fighters were down too low to stop them, and the Americans set three of the Japanese carriers to burning: the *Kaga*, *Ikaga*, and *Soryu*. The *Hiryu*, the fourth big carrier, was bombed and set afire later in the day, and all of them sank. The Japanese invasion of Midway was called off; Admiral Yamamoto's dream of drawing the American fleet forth and smashing it with his superior force of carriers from the Combined Fleet was destroyed.

But that understanding was years away. All that was known at the time was that the Japanese had given up their attempt to take Midway. Everyone knew that a victory had been won, and that the sacrifice of Torpedo 8 had been part of it.

But Torpedo 8 was gone. Lieutenant Kenyon would never need his collection of limericks.

On the morning of June 5, the *Hornet* and the other ships of the American fleet gave chase to the Japanese who were retiring from the Midway area. Planes bombed the cruisers that had collided and ultimately sank one of them. Ensign Mears went up to the Torpedo Squadron 8 ready room. It seemed very quiet and lonely.

The facts began to come clearer. The damage to Midway had been extensive. Only five planes from three squadrons of fighters on the island remained, and two of those were out of commission.

The chase of the Japanese continued for two days and then ended. Still no one knew precisely what had happened. The *Hornet* was ordered to head for the Aleutians to contend that Japanese landing, but the order was soon rescinded and they headed for Oahu. The remainder of Torpedo 8, those beautiful new TBFs that had been left behind, had now gotten to Oahu, and they flew aboard as the carrier came toward land. The pilots were surprised to find that no one but the newcomers were left, but . . .

As Ensign Mears put it, "If there is any one trait that carrier pilots have in common, it is matter-of-factness, and I don't think those who remained in Torpedo 8 were as grief-stricken and vengeful as they have been publicized as being. In the navy and especially in wartime, you do what you are told to do, and if some of your comrades are killed in the process it is tough to take but it doesn't change you into a wrathful avenger. . . . Any time a pilot says 'Thoughts of Jack or Joe will be riding with my next torpedo,' he is just blowing or else he is emotionally unfit to be a combat aviator."

On the return trip to Pearl, Ensign Mears had the unhappy job of putting together the personal effects of the pilots and aircrewmen who did not come back, censoring their last letters home, and arranging for shipment.

When the *Hornet* reached Pearl Harbor, all flight personnel had liberty. Then began a long, long party centered around the Moana Hotel, the hotspot of Waikiki where the airmen let off steam.

Ensign Mears met his old friends from San Diego, ensigns Richard Jaccard Jamie Dexter, Bill Pittman, and Jerry Richey. They had all been on the other two carriers at Midway. Mears learned that his friend Ensign Jim Shelton did not come back from a dive-bombing attack. No one knew quite what had happened. Several other friends had been killed while flying from Midway to attack the Japanese, including Ensign Ek, the inventor of the K.O.-for-Tokyo cocktail.

# NINETEEN

# Guadalcanal

The carrier *Hornet* returned to Pearl Harbor after the Midway battle, and shortly afterward Ensign Mears was transferred to Torpedo Squadron 3, which had been at Midway aboard the carrier *Yorktown*. Torpedo 3's casualties at Midway had been almost as high as those of the *Hornet's* Torpedo 8. Only one pilot had returned to Torpedo 8, but two pilots returned to Torpedo 3.

Torpedo 3 moved to Kaneohe Naval Air Station on the north shore of Oahu and began training. The commander of the squadron was Lieutenant Commander J. M. Jett when Ensign Mears joined up. One guarantee that there would not be another failure like Midway was the arrival of the TBF, the Grumman Avenger. It was a bigger, faster, and more heavily armed plane than the old TBD, and would prove to be the best torpedo bomber of the war. It carried a pilot, a turret gunner who sat in his turret above the tail, and a bombardier radioman who sat behind the torpedo of the bomb load in the belly.

On July 15, 1942, Torpedo 3 went to war aboard the carrier *Enterprise*. There Ensign Mears rejoined his old friends from San Diego days, ensigns James Dexter and Richard Jaccard, who were both in the dive bomber squadron of the *Enterprise*. They were headed for the South Pacific.

Outside Pearl Harbor the *Enterprise* joined up with the new battleship *North Carolina*, the cruiser *Atlanta*, the cruiser *Portland*, and their destroyers.

On the way the pilots flew missions. The fighter planes guarded the fleet on combat air patrol, and the dive bombers and patrol bombers flew search missions. The torpedo planes flew out 150 to 250 miles, carrying out simulated attacks on the carrier and practicing gunnery by firing at a sled towed by the carrier or a sleeve towed by another aircraft.

Ensign Mears's crew consisted of airmen Ferrier and Deitsch. Ferrier was a veteran of the Midway battle, where he had been wounded in the head. The experience had sobered him. "I have no hankering to be an ace gunner and shoot down fifty Japs," he said. "All I want to do is put enough .50 caliber slugs in the air to keep the Zeros off our tail."

Four days after they left Pearl Harbor, Ensign Mears learned that his friend Jamie Dexter was missing. He had taken off at 3:20 p.m. about thirty miles from the equator, to tow a sleeve for the fighter planes to practice firing on. He was towing about ten miles to the starboard side of the ship. When the fighters left he was supposed to drop the sleeve, climb to 8000 feet, and then join the dive bomber squadron in an attack on the sled being towed by the carrier. But he never showed up, and was not seen again.

Commander John Crommelin, the air officer, did all possible to bring him in. The Big E broke radio silence several times to give positions, but there was no reply. So, as it was so frequently with aircraft, no one ever knew what had happened to Ensign Dexter. He might have gotten disoriented and flown along until he ran out of gas. He might have had a malfunction and spun into the water. No one knew.

The task force approached Tongatubu on July 23, and TBFs and one F4F flew to land. Ensign Mears piloted one of the TBFs, carrying Lieutenant Commander Burrough, chief of Admiral Thomas Kincaid's staff, who had official business ashore. They landed on the grass-over-clay field, occupied by a squadron of P-40s.

The navy fliers were entertained that night by the army pilots in their quarters in the jungle, a short distance from the field. The army produced Australian beer (20 percent alcohol) and talked about life on Tonga and about the native queen Salote Tabu, a 290-pound beauty. The task force, meanwhile, moved into Nukualofu. Next day the army drove the navy across the island to the port city. There they saw transports, gray ships with men in marine fatigue uniforms clustered on deck. Ensign Mears and the others then knew they were heading for a landing, but they did not know where.

On Saturday, July 24, Ensign Mears rejoined the carrier, hitting the deck just as the *Enterprise* was leaving the harbor. The task force was on its way into action. The place would be the island of Guadalcanal in the southern Solomons. There the Japanese had established a seaplane base at Tulagi, Florida Island, and across the bay on Guadalcanal had just completed an airfield that would allow them to stage planes down from the major Japanese base at Rabaul, and thus control the Australian air and sea lanes.

At noon on July 26, 400 miles south of the Fiji Islands, the *Enterprise* task force met with that of the *Wasp* and the *Saratoga*. Three American carrier task forces, with all the attendant battleships, cruisers, and destroyers, plus three Australian cruisers, made up the strongest naval force the Allies had yet mounted in the Pacific.

The next step was a dress rehearsal for an amphibious landing, conducted off the island of Koro in the Fijis. It was very successful. The marines were supposed to go ashore, but most of them never made it over the coral reef.

Ensign Mears was to serve as a tactical scout, to protect the carrier force from a Japanese attack from the rear during the exercise. He flew out with the other torpedo planes, among the islands, looking for Japanese naval craft but finding none.

The men of the *Enterprise* then geared themselves up for their war. Every day the ship issued its war bulletin, which was filled with homilies and doggerel designed to drive home lessons:

> *If you shoot him in the prop*
> *You'll make the basket flop*
> *If you shoot him in the rudder*
> *You'll only make him shudder.*

and

*A strange old bird is the wise old owl,*
*His head on a swivel and a perpetual scowl;*
*Imitate him and you're sure to find*
*No Jap will surprise you from behind.*

Every day the planes were off the ship on practice missions or on scouting jobs. One day, Ensign Mears took off for an exercise attack on the carrier, flying plane No. Tare 13. Mears was just coming in when the engine of the TBF began to cut out. It would stop for a second or two and then catch again. He circled the carrier twice, and tried to make the aircraft run properly. No luck. So he made a pass on the starboard side of the flight deck, which was the signal for a delayed forced landing.

The ship did not respond, so Mears circled again and passed down the port side, which is the signal for an immediate forced landing. The carrier then swung into the wind, and Mears came around to land. Coming up "the groove" he got a "too low" signal from the landing officer. He hit the throttle, but the engine quit again astern of the ramp. Then it caught, he got a little altitude, and the signal officer gave him the cut. He chopped back the throttle and the engine quit, but he got down without accident. Later the mechanics found a blockage in the carburetor.

On August 2, the airmen were told officially that the mission of the force was the capture and defense of the Guadalcanal-Tulagi triangle. In the next few days the specific plans were outlined for each pilot of each squadron.

On August 6, the approaching American fleet was blanketed by a large frontal area which concealed it from the long-range Kawanishi flying boats that ran reconnaissance for the Japanese from Rabaul. At sunset the force was only eighty-five miles from Guadalcanal and still had not been "spooked" by the Japanese. That evening Commander Crommelin gave the pilots a little speech:

"For eight months now we have been on the defensive. Tomorrow the tide is going to turn. Show no quarter. Don't hesitate to be absolutely ruthless. You can be sure you will receive the same treatment."

On the night of August 6, Ensign Mears heard the message on the squawk box, read by Captain Davis. Vice Admiral Richmond Kelly Turner, the commander of amphibious forces, was announcing what he intended to do the next day.

"On August 7 this force will recapture Tulagi and Guadalcanal islands, which are now in the hands of the enemy."

Two hours before sunrise on August 7, the refrain of "Boots and Saddles," the old cavalry call to action, rang throughout the carrier *Enterprise*, and the pilots hurried to dress and get to their stations. The ready room of Torpedo 3 was located in the ship's island structure, and the pilots moved in and sank down in the big chairs. They could already hear the engines of the fighter planes turning over.

An hour later the first fighter left the deck of the *Enterprise*, and soon the dive bombers were moving.

Meanwhile Torpedo 3 was getting its briefing. Eight TBFs would go out on a 200-mile search pattern north and west to see if enemy surface craft were in the area. They would be loaded with bombs, four 500s each. The other six TBFs would stand by on the flight deck loaded with torpedoes, just in case enemy warships were found.

Ensign Mears was assigned to the latter duty, but he also had a secondary duty: to be standby for search if one of the other TBFs failed. One did fail, so Ensign Mears's plane was brought up from the hangar deck on short notice and sent off with a torpedo instead of bombs. He was ordered to get rid of the torpedo somehow before he came back on board.

The fighters were already making their fighter sweeps of the airfields and the seaplane base, to destroy existing aircraft with 100-pound fragmentation bombs and then strafe with their .50 caliber machine guns. The Douglas dive bombers were striking the enemy shore batteries. The guns of the ships had started their bombardment of the shore positions and would remain on call for support fire. H hour was the moment for attack on Tulagi, and Zero hour for the attack on Guadalcanal.

At seven o'clock Ensign Mears was in the air, heading out on the first leg of his search. It was a beautiful morning in the Solomons, bright and clear. After all this time at sea, Ensign Mears could actually smell the vegetation on the land as he approached the Rossel Islands, the first landmark on his track. Thick green jungles steamed in the sun below him. Flocks of white birds fluttered from the treetops as he passed over. A few grass huts sat mutely in the jungle, and red and white plantation buildings perched along the shorelines. This had been copra country in the past.

Ensign Mears passed over the Rossels and headed across the channel toward Santa Isabel. Until now he had seen nothing, but now saw the explosion of a bomb in his wingmates' sector on the left. He flew over to investigate, and below sighted a 75-foot cargo ship. He dropped down just above the water for a look, and the people aboard the ship began firing on him with automatic weapons. He saw splashes where the bullets hit the water and ricocheted. He turned past the ship's bow and instructed his gunner to fire with the .50 caliber turret gun. Gunner Ferrier announced that his gun had jammed. Ensign Mears tried his gun and thought it, too, had jammed. (Later he discovered he had forgotten to charge it.)

He turned away from the ship then, telling his gunner to get his gun in order, and remembering to charge his own armament. Now he knew what he would do with his torpedo if he did not find a more attractive target on his search.

He flew on over the mountains of Santa Isabel Island, above Rekata Bay, and then north to Roncador Reef. He thought the Japanese might be using the lagoon there for an anchorage. But there was not even a rowboat!

Ensign Mears turned back, searching for the small ship he had seen earlier. He found it huddling under a rainsquall not far from the original sighting place. The ship opened fire as he came down low. He dropped the torpedo at close range and watched it go in. But "the pickle" had been badly aimed, and it missed the little ship. Mears then turned back and strafed.

"We came in low on the water, and they opened fire on us long before we were in range. I watched the little spurts of water creeping closer and closer to me, and when they were just under the nose I jinked over and the gunner had to pick up my range again. It was pitiful in a way, I thought, for them to be opposing an armored warplane with one small-caliber machine gun. . . . I came back to strafe. I made several runs, each time coming in low on the sea and raking the deck with my forward gun, then pulling up in a wing over and allowing my turret gunner to dump his heavier slugs downward into the structure. As I came in the second time, I saw somebody jump overboard, and then when I passed just over the mast I saw a crew member with black hair and a red shirt run and stumble under a canopy which shaded the deck. My gunner had the word by that time, and his tracers were looping into the vessel and pinking off the deck. My eyes were watering from the smell of gunpowder when we gave up the attack."

They went back to the carrier then, and Mears flew out in the afternoon on intermediate air patrol about fifty miles from the carrier.

So ended the first day of operations at Guadalcanal for the airmen. Early in the day the fighters put all the seaplanes at Tulagi out of action. On the ground the marines had an easy time of it on Guadalcanal, but a harder time on Tulagi against combat troops. And enemy bombers that came down from Rabaul that afternoon were routed by the American fighters before they could do any damage.

On the afternoon of August 8, Ensign Mears searched northward, passing over Guadalcanal and then heading out to sea. He saw a flying boat and gave chase, but it turned out to be a PBY. They waggled wings and did not fire at each other.

On the return he flew off Tulagi and saw some fires, but not much else. In the harbor the warships and transports were milling about. One transport had been hit by Japanese bombers and was burning.

That afternoon Ensign Mears got lost. He went to the place where he thought the carrier should be, but no carrier was there. It was actually thirty miles to the northeast, and the area was heavy with clouds. Sunset would come at 6:15, and by six o'clock everything was getting darker fast. Since there was no radio silence, he got on the radio, but no one replied. His gas was running low, and then he got into heavy cloud and had to go on instruments. He asked again for a vector. He had just decided to head toward Guadalcanal and land on the island, hoping there were no Japanese on the airfield, when he suddenly heard welcome words on the radio.

"Mears in eight, steer one two zero. Mears in eight, steer one two zero."

But now he looked at the gas gauge. Steer one two zero for how long? His gas was very low. But he steered one two zero and broke out of the clouds, and then there were the carriers down below. It was dark by that time. The *Enterprise* turned into the wind, and he came in at ninety miles an hour trying to get aboard. He got a wave-off for being too fast and approached again. This time he was calm and came in properly, got a cut, and landed. The gas tanks had enough for three more minutes of flight.

Ensign Mears did not know it, but that was the end of air operations over Guadalcanal—the end of American operations for awhile. Vice Admiral Frank Jack Fletcher was a timid man who had lost the carrier *Yorktown* at Midway (some said, unnecessarily), so he was not going to risk any more carriers. Thus, although the Japanese were just racking up for an all-out attack on the marines, Fletcher took the battle fleet away from Guadalcanal, leaving the marines high and dry with not even all of their initial supplies unloaded. Thus he precipitated the long, drawn-out battle of Guadalcanal.

# TWENTY

# Waste

True to his promise to stick around Guadalcanal for only forty-eight hours, Admiral Fletcher started south on the night of August 8, to take his carrier force out of danger. But he left 13,000 marines on the shores of Guadalcanal and Tulagi, as well as a covy of transports and supply ships. That night the Japanese sent a cruiser force down toward Savo Island, where they encountered an Allied cruiser force. In short order the Japanese sank three American cruisers—the *Vincennes*, the *Quincy*, and the *Astoria*—the Australian cruiser *Canberra*, and a destroyer, and they severely damaged the American cruiser *Chicago*, while suffering only a handful of casualties and no loss of ships. By morning the Japanese were long gone and the American carrier force was steaming away.

As of August 9, 1942, the Japanese had naval supremacy and air supremacy over the southern Solomons, and the whole invasion was in jeopardy. Admiral Turner had to move his transports out of Lunga Roads, half loaded still, and await some turn of events before he could return.

For two weeks the three American carrier task forces "covered the southern approaches to the Solomons," as Admiral Fletcher said, which was a pretty safe bet, considering the fact that the Japanese bases were all up north.

On August 20, nineteen marine Wildcat fighter planes and twelve Douglas Dauntless bombers landed at Henderson Field, as the Americans now called the airstrip on Guadalcanal. This was the nucleus of the Cactus Air Force (the code name for Guadalcanal was Cactus), a motley collection of American army, navy, and marine planes, Australians and New Zealanders, that would somehow manage to operate from the field while under almost constant Japanese attack for the next many weeks.

That same day Admiral Isoroku Yamamoto's striking force set sail from the Japanese base at Truk, to escort Japanese reinforcements from Rabaul and engage the American fleet in battle if they could find them.

Aboard the *Enterprise* Ensign Mears and the others could tell that some sort of action was brewing. During the next three days carrier planes made contact with enemy warships but with no carriers. Two enemy submarines were bombed. And on the morning of August 24, contact was finally made with the Japanese carriers, the *Shokaku*, the *Zuikaku*, and the *Ryujo*. Admiral Fletcher gave the advantage to the enemy by sending the carrier *Wasp*, newly arrived in the South Pacific, to safe waters in the south to fuel.

That afternoon Lieutenant Commander Charles Jett, skipper of Torpedo 3, found the enemy carrier *Ryujo* and attacked, but scored no hits. Later, planes of Bombing 6, the dive bomber squadron, claimed hits on one carrier.

Ensign Mears and his crew were flying a search that afternoon. He returned to the carrier and thought he saw something wrong—one of the accompanying cruisers was smoking.

And then he saw an antiaircraft barrage coming from the American ships which also began to maneuver to avoid attack. Looking up, he saw three Japanese dive bombers, big red circles on their wings, diving on the *Enterprise*, one after the other.

Ensign Mears saw two Japanese dive bombers and tried to go after them with his TBF. He was flying in formation with two other TBFs. One of the Japanese bombers attacked:

"As he headed toward us he opened fire and two long yellowish streamers of smoke came out of his nose. It seemed as though he were aiming straight at me, and I remember thinking, 'Jesus, I don't want him to shoot me.' "

The Japanese bomber made seven runs on the American TBFs, and they shot back at him with their turrets. "It was rather ridiculous in a way, everybody firing like mad and nobody going down."

The *Enterprise* was hit in this raid, and from above Ensign Mears watched the damage control parties struggling with the flames on the flight deck. The aircraft circled until 6:15 that evening, then were told to jettison their bombs. Mears flew out five miles, dropped his two 500-pound bombs, and returned. At first he circled the *Saratoga*, but then the *Enterprise* deck was declared ready to receive planes, so he landed on his own ship. As he came in he saw that half the flight deck aft had been blown up by a bomb hit.

In the ready room and the wardroom he learned that the *Enterprise* air group had suffered a number of casualties, including several of his friends. That night at ten the TBF Attack Group returned in the dark. One crashed on the deck, and four landed aboard the *Saratoga*.

Ensign Mears did not learn very much about this carrier battle except that the Japanese carrier *Ryujo* was set afire and many Japanese planes were shot down. That was the way it was with carrier battles: there was nothing neat or even apparently decisive. A pilot knew what happened to himself and his squadron and maybe his shipmates—at least, whether they came back or not—but that was about all.

On the morning after the battle, Ensign Mears went onto the flight deck to see the damage done to his carrier by the enemy. A bomb had exploded on the starboard side of the ship near the No. 2 elevator, but the damage had been repaired temporarily with sheets of steel.

Near the aft elevator two bombs had struck, but both had exploded on lower decks.

One bomb had exploded in an ammunition storage space below the flight deck, wiping out a gun gallery and two 5-inch antiaircraft guns on the starboard side of the carrier.

"Sailors' bodies were still in the gun gallery. Most of the men died from the concussion and then were roasted. The majority of the bodies were in one piece. They were blackened but not burned or withered, and they looked like iron statues of men, their limbs smooth and whole, their heads rounded with no hair. The faces were undistinguishable, but in almost every case the lips were drawn back in a wizened grin, giving the men the expression of rodents.

"The postures seemed either strangely normal or frankly grotesque. One gun pointer was still in his seat, leaning on his sight with one arm. He looked as though a sculptor had created him. His body was nicely proportioned, the buttocks were rounded, there was no hair anywhere. Other iron men were lying outstretched, face up or down. Two or three lying face-up were shielding themselves with their arms bent at elbows and their hands before their faces. One, who was not burned so badly, had his chest thrown out, his head way back, his hands clenched."

The *Enterprise* had been attacked by thirty dive bombers. Seventy-four men had been killed and many men wounded, but within hours the ship was again operational.

On the evening of August 26, the eight remaining pilots of Torpedo 3 were called together and told that they would fly their planes off next day with those of Bombing 6 and would remain as replacements in the South Pacific, while the *Enterprise* went back to America for repairs. Actually, only five of the planes took off, of which two went into the water on takeoff because they were too heavily laden; the other pilots stayed aboard. Ensign Mears and two others of Torpedo 3 and the bombing squadron flew to the New Hebrides and landed on a dusty airstrip. They went into town and got drunk, stole an army jeep, and charged around the back roads of the island half the night.

A few days later Ensign Mears flew north to another island to join Torpedo 8 in another jungle camp. Since the *Wasp* had been sunk in battle, Torpedo 8 was to find a new home. So Ensign Mears and Torpedo 8 headed for that new home, Henderson Field on Guadalcanal, and the "Cactus Air Force" that was about all that stood between the marines and conquest by the Japanese naval and air forces.

## TWENTY-ONE

# The Cactus Air Force

In September 1942, when Lieutenant J. G. Mears and the other pilots from the torpedo squadron of the *Enterprise* were waiting on Espiritu Santo for assignment, they learned what had been happening on Guadalcanal since the invasion. After Admiral Fletcher abandoned the marine First Division on the island, the Japanese navy had taken control of the seas around Guadalcanal, and the Japanese had been reinforcing the island. Up at Rabaul the Japanese had also been reinforcing their naval air arm, stepping it up from Air Flotilla to Air Fleet and bringing in many more aircraft.

Admiral Turner had done his best to bring planes to Guadalcanal to protect the marines. A marine fighter squadron and a dive bomber squadron had come, and a number of carrier planes, some army planes, and some Australian planes had been flown in. They constituted the backbone of the Cactus Air Force.

In the daylight hours, the American fighters and bombers had a very good position. The Japanese sent air raids nearly every day to bomb the airfield, but they had to travel hundreds of miles from Rabaul, across islands which held dozens of Australian coast-watchers. And so Guadalcanal was almost always alerted to the Japanese coming; and a few minutes before time, the fighters came up from the field, usually succeeding in breaking up the Japanese attack. But it was tiring work. The pilots were on call constantly, the attrition of aircraft was high, and the pilots and planes were wearing down.

After dark at Henderson Field the ground crews did not dare

turn the field lights on to allow planes to take off, because "the Tokyo Express" arrived nearly every night. This Japanese force might consist of destroyers or cruisers or even battleships, and they would bombard the field with hundreds of shells, wrecking more planes, putting holes in the runway, and destroying caches of aviation fuel. Day and night the Japanese troops on the island, with plenty of machine guns and mortars and some field pieces, would fire at the American aircraft as they entered the landing circle.

The life of a pilot on Guadalcanal, as described to Lieutenant Mears by his fellows, consisted of flying eight or ten hours a day, then undergoing bombardment to keep sleep away at night, and living on very little food, catching malaria, and probably getting dysentery.

In late September Mears and five of his fellow torpedo pilots were assigned to deliver torpedoes to Guadalcanal. They flew their torpedo planes in, arriving shortly before sunset.

That night it rained. At about midnight came the air raid alert. Mears and two companions who were sleeping in the same tent stumbled out and looked for a foxhole. Most of the holes were already occupied by old hands who started out the night sleeping there. Finally they found an empty narrow trench and crouched there while shells were lobbed at the airfield. It was a Japanese submarine attacking this time.

Next day Mears and the other two pilots flew back to Espiritu Santo, and he told acquaintances that things on Guadalcanal weren't so bad—just overrated in terms of danger.

On October 1, Mears and another pilot were flown to Guadalcanal for duty, arriving in a B-17. When they arrived he learned that five of the torpedo planes were on a mission to attack four Japanese destroyers. Three of the planes did not come back. That night, late, Mears dove into a foxhole when a lone Japanese bomber hit the airfield. Sleep was hard to come by. He was beginning to learn what life on Guadalcanal was all about.

On the second day, after sunrise, Mears took off on a search mission to try to find the three missing torpedo planes. He spotted a number of newly wrecked Japanese planes on the beach. When he got back to Henderson he was told that the three pilots of the American torpedo planes and their crews had been rescued, although the aircraft were lost.

He was back on Henderson Field in mid-morning, lounging in his tent, waiting for a call. At 12:15 came the daily air raid, and he stood beside a foxhole and watched the American fighters and the Japanese Zeros shoot at each other. One Zero was shot down.

On October 3, Mears went on his first attack from Guadalcanal. Three torpedo planes and four dive bombers headed for a cruiser and two destroyers reported 150 miles west of "the slot."

In late afternoon they found the cruiser and destroyers, a destroyer leading. Mears's bomber was carrying four 500-pound bombs. The dive bombers went first and scored some near misses, but no direct hits. Then the torpedo bombers went in. Mears dropped two bombs and hit the cruiser, and his gunner shot down a Japanese float plane that came up at them. Then Mears made another pass, and his gunner told him that his bombardier had been hit. Mears headed back to Guadalcanal, flying low over the water for forty minutes, and landed. An ambulance came up and rushed the bombardier to the hospital with three pieces of shrapnel in his brain but still alive.

They examined the aircraft. It had been hit by a 20mm shell from a destroyer which made a 12-inch hole in the fuselage. The shrapnel had wounded the bombardier and very nearly cut the control cables. There were twenty other holes in the plane, but it had held together.

Mears then settled in to the life of Henderson Field as it was lived in October 1942. The marine and navy Grumman Wildcat fighters and the Douglas Dauntless dive bombers were the core of the Cactus Air Force. The handful of torpedo planes were the "heavy bombers." The army had a few P-39s on the island, which were mostly useful for strafing missions against ground troops. They were no match for the enemy Zeros, however, so they stayed away. The B-17s staged in from Espiritu Santo on missions against the northern Solomons.

The big problem from the beginning, and growing worse in

October, was the shortage of aviation fuel. Because the Japanese controlled the sea, the American transports could not deliver gas in quantity. It came in by barge, by air, and by submarine.

Early every morning a scouting flight went out from Henderson. Usually all the pilots saw was the Japanese cruiser or destroyer force heading back to base after the nightly bombardments or reinforcement of the Japanese infantry on the island.

At about noon the daily air raid arrived: silver-winged Japanese navy bombers, perhaps thirty of them. If there was time, the Americans fighters were scrambled and went after the bombers, but the Japanese Zeros tangled with the fighters, trying to keep them away. Sometimes the Japanese bombed unmolested.

In the afternoon the Americans sent out another scouting flight, which usually discovered the Tokyo Express coming down from the north for the nightly routine of reinforcement and bombardment. As soon as the scouting group reported, the attack group took off and tried to find the enemy ships. Sometimes they did. Sometimes they did not. They came home after dark, and then the air and waters were Japanese again.

Almost every night, sometime after 8:30 p.m., "Washing Machine Charlie" came overhead. The plane was one of a number of Japanese float planes so named for the tinny quality of their engine noise. "Washing Machine Charlie" dropped flares to light up the area for the approaching Japanese warships, and bombs to harass the Americans. Thus, every night Mears found himself occupying his foxhole.

On October 5, Mears went on a mission to Rekata Bay to try to destroy the Japanese seaplane base there. The mission began at 1:30 in the morning, for it was to be a long flight north to the north side of Santa Isabel Island. The primary purpose was to keep the seaplanes from taking off that morning and possibly discovering the carrier *Hornet* and its task force, which was going to raid Bougainville. There would be five torpedo bombers laden with bombs, fifteen dive bombers, and a handful of B-17s coming up from the south.

The Guadalcanal contingent took off at 3 a.m., the dive bombers out front and the torpedo bombers behind. They had very bad weather, and the torpedo bombers first lost contact with the dive bombers, and then with each other. Off the coast of Santa Isabel, Mears found that the clouds went right down to the water. He kept intermittent contact with the other torpedo bombers until they reached the island. Then he lost sight of the exhausts, and circled and waited for daylight to attack. When day came, he found the target, and as he came down on the base he saw a burning plane on the water. Then he saw an American dive bomber make a run and come out of it with a float plane on his tail. Mears was attacked by that same float plane as he prepared to go into the bombing run, and his gunner began firing and drove the plane off. At the same time two other float planes were attacking from port and starboard, and a Zero was coming up underneath.

Mears pressed the bomb release but did not see any bombs. He did see the Japanese antiaircraft positions below, so he circled and pressed the emergency bomb release to try to get them. Meanwhile his gunners were both shooting, and the tunnel gunner-bombardier shot down the Zero. The other gunner shot down one of the float planes.

When Mears returned to Henderson Field, he discovered that none of his bombs had released; the release mechanism had jammed. It was not a very successful mission. Only nine of the navy planes had arrived on target, and none of the B-17s got there. Still, they did keep the Japanese occupied and prevent them from mounting patrols in the direction of the carrier force.

Unfortunately, this mission was all too typical of the attack missions of the American planes from Guadalcanal. The problem was aircraft parts and maintenance. The Cactus Air Force got most of its spare parts from wrecked aircraft, and the ground crews were kept so busy just keeping the planes flying that they had little opportunity to keep them finely tuned.

On October 8 the coast watchers in the northern Solomons announced the coming of the Tokyo Express—a cruiser and five destroyers—and the Cactus Air Force moved to intercept. That afternoon four torpedo planes, seven dive bombers, and eight fighter planes were launched from Henderson Field. They found the five destroyers and cruiser, with the destroyers in a horseshoe formation about the bigger ship.

They moved to attack with the sun low on the horizon, from 10,000 feet. The ships were still just streaks on the water, the open end of the horsehoe out in front.

Mears and the other torpedo pilots circled, while the dive bombers streaked down. The torpedo pilots then started their bomb runs. Mears came in at the port quarter of the cruiser, running a gauntlet of fire from two of the destroyers. By the time he neared the cruiser, that ship had already taken at least one bomb hit and was smoking. Mears headed in, dropped, ran another gauntlet of fire, and ran out. The air intelligence officers back at Henderson gave the four torpedo planes credit for one hit on the cruiser, but the Japanese records indicate only that the air attack was so sever that the Tokyo Express turned back that night—not that a cruiser was hard hit.

The battle for Guadalcanal was approaching its crisis in mid-October, and the Japanese pulled out all the stops on their air attack to help the Imperial army infantry try to capture the airfield. The Imperial navy had been performing brilliantly, but the army had never grasped the true situation on Guadalcanal. The army general staff consistently underestimated the number of American troops on the island and what it would take to dislodge them. In October a marine officer suggested that it would take 65,000 enemy troops to capture the island from the 20,000 marines, because of the realities of defense and offense. Yet the Japanese never had more than 25,000 troops on the island, and these were undersupplied and worse fed then the Americans.

Lieutenant Mears, who lived in the transient area of the field complex, was hungry all the time, living on vegetables, Japanese rice, and very little meat. But the Japanese, even in October, were so short of food they were subsisting on local plants.

Still the Japanese were planning major air-sea, land offensives to retake the island, and the air activity early in October reflected it.

On October 13, just after noon, twenty-seven Japanese bombers raided Henderson Field and bombed the plane parking area effectively. They had made a detour approach and had not been observed by the coastwatchers, so the raid came as a complete surprise and was very damaging to the parked aircraft.

That same afternoon a second bomber raid hit Henderson Field, and at the end of the day only two torpedo planes were still in flying condition. That night the Japanese began the most serious preparations yet for their expected land assault on the airfield. The infantry and artillery were firing on the airfield with big howitzers that had been brought in with the reinforcing troops of a new division, and very early on October 14, battleships joined the fight, bombarding Henderson Field with 16-inch high-explosive shells that created huge craters and destroyed buildings completely. This was the heaviest bombardment of the campaign so far, and it made a shambles of Henderson Field. The shelling continued through the night.

In the morning, the pilots looked out on the field. None of the torpedo bombers, and only a dozen planes of any sort, were flyable. That day the Japanese hit the airfield again, and the airmen moved down to the beach for safety. But now the tide turned. More American fighters and bombers were staged in. The Japanese air raids were countered. The Japanese on the ground attacked and attacked again, but somehow the marines held on and Henderson Field was kept limping along in the face of this determined drive. The Japanese who hurtled toward Henderson Field were thrown back with enormous losses. At one point a Japanese unit did break through almost to the field and triumphantly announced the capture. But that unit was bottled up and destroyed, and soon the major attempt at capture was known to have failed. And so there came a respite in the last week of October.

On October 27, Lieutenant Mears and the rest of his squadron were evacuated to New Hebrides, exhausted. From there Mears was sent home on a transport, and on December 7, 1942 the transport reached San Francisco. For a little while, Lieutenant Mears's war could be forgotten.

Mears was given leave that winter, and then he was reassigned to the San Diego naval station. He was scheduled to join one of the escort carriers being sent to the Pacific to participate in the Central Pacific amphibious landings, and was training at San Diego for sea duty in that spring of 1943 when something happened on a training flight and Mears failed to return. Posthumously he was awarded the Distinguished Flying Cross for his exploits in early October against the Japanese cruisers.

# TWENTY-TWO

# The Professional

Thomas Jeffrey was born in the slate mining community of Arvonia, Virginia to a Welsh-American family that had been associated with the quarries since the nineteenth century. He grew up there, and worked in the quarry each summer until he went to Virginia Military Institute in 1934.

In his third year at VMI Jeffrey went to Reserve Officers Training Corps camp at Fort Hoyle, Maryland, for six weeks of field artillery training, since that was the branch of the service he had preselected at VMI. One day at Fort Hoyle he saw an airplane on a field and went over to inspect it. The pilot came up, carrying his helmet and goggles, and looked the cadet up and down.

"Do you like airplanes?" he asked. "Do you want to go up?"

And so Tom Jeffrey had his first ride.

Before they took off, the pilot showed Jeffrey how to put on his parachute and how to pull the rip cord. He showed him how to use the stick and the rudder pedals ("in case something happens to me"), and he told Jeffrey what they were going to do. His mission was to drop smoke on troops maneuvering at Fort Mead. This they did, coming in low at 180 miles per hour, and leaving a field covered with a smokescreen.

"This is the place to be," said Tom Jeffrey.

The excitement of flying slowly died out in Tom Jeffrey's consciousness as he went back to his last year at VMI and his specialty of electrical engineering, which was applicable to the civilian environment in which he expected to live. Before graduation he was offered a job with General Electric, and he tentatively decided to take it. But shortly before graduation an Army Air Corps Examining Board came to VMI from Randolph Field, Texas, looking for candidates for flying school. Someone suggested that Tom Jeffrey take the examination. He passed, and was offered a trip to Texas.

"What shall I do?" he asked his father.

His father said the trip would be a nice vacation for him before he faced the real world. So Jeffrey went to Kelly Field, Texas, and soon was flying the same type of airplane in which he had gone up on that first flight in Maryland.

Very shortly thereafter the world in which Tom Jeffrey was living as a flying cadet became the real world, with the call-up of American army reservists. Cadet Jeffrey became Second Lieutenant Jeffrey of the U.S. Army Air Corps, and was assigned to Langley Field, Virginia.

At about the same time, Lieutenant Jeffrey got a telegram from the War Department calling him to duty as second lieutenant in the field artillery. He ignored it, since he was already on active duty with the Air Corps. The telegram was followed by other messages, each more strident than the last. Finally, Lieutenant Jeffrey had to get his commanding officer to call Washington and arrange the cancellation of his field artillery commission—because he was about to be charged AWOL.

In 1939 the American army air force was divided into four basic sections: pursuit, attack, observation, and bombardment. He chose bombardment and soon was flying the B-18, the military version of the Douglas DC-3, like the army's C-47.

Lieutenant Jeffrey was a part of the Twenty-first Reconnaissance Squadron at Langley. Almost every day they flew out on a mission. Each time they carried sealed orders which they opened on schedule. The orders always stipulated that they carry out the mission and then return to base. That occurred week after week during the summer.

One day in the fall they took off as usual. They read the sealed orders.

"You will proceed to Miami, Florida," said the orders. And

they did, without personal possessions or change of uniform. Lieutenant Jeffrey had even left his car.

For several months the Twenty-first Reconnaissance Squadron photographed the Caribbean, the Florida Keys, Cuba, and the Yucatan peninsula. Then Lieutenant Jeffrey was reassigned to the Twenty-seventh Reconnaissance Squadron at Borinquen, Puerto Rico, and to get there he flew a brand-new aircraft by way of Cuba.

From Borinquen the Twenty-seventh flew almost daily, improving their photo capability, bombing, and aerial navigation by working over almost all of the Caribbean and Central America. They overflew Jamaica, Trinidad, the Guianas. They landed on little airstrips and went into the jungle, learning to subsist on iguana—to live off the land.

In April 1940 the girl Tom Jeffrey had met in Texas came by fruit boat from New Orleans, and they were married in San Juan.

In December 1941, Lieutenant Jeffrey and his wife, planning a leave to visit the Jeffrey family in Arvania, Virginia, made reservations on one of the ships out of San Juan. They went to the port on the day of sailing, only to be told that their ship had sailed the previous day. So Helen Jeffrey stayed home at the officers quarters in Borinquen, and Jeffrey went to Virginia alone. He went to Arvania and then drove to Washington. When Pearl Harbor was bombed and war was declared, he checked in with the Air Corps and was told to report to the nearest base, which was Langley Field. From there he was sent to Miami and then back to Puerto Rico. When he got home to the base he learned that no more dependents were to be allowed on "foreign" bases. If his wife had caught that ship, she could not have come back to Puerto Rico. But as it was, she stayed.

After war was declared, what had seemed to be all games before, now became deadly earnest. Jeffrey flew 106 hours a month on antisubmarine patrol. It was tedious, unrewarding flying, hours and hours above the sea, finding nothing. There were German U-boats in the Caribbean all this while, but Pilot Jeffrey did not encounter them.

The air base at Puerto Rico was a big one, but soon it was deserted. From now on the war was on for real. Helen Jeffrey flew back to America for the duration, and Jeffrey was sent to Panama with the Fortieth Bombardment Group to protect the canal. For a time they were stationed at Guatemala City, and flew south to the Galapagos Islands daily on patrol. This schedule demanded very careful airmanship, because although the Galapagos Islands are only twenty-three miles south of the equator, the Antarctic current passes by, resulting in queer weather conditions. The field at the Galapagos was almost always fogged in at night by the cold wet air hitting the heat rising from the runway. The next day, when they flew back to Guatemala City, they had to contend with the airfield atop a 5000-foot cliff.

There wasn't much excitement for Lieutenant Jeffrey except that he made captain in this period. One day, flying a B-18, he did spot a submarine on the surface and went down to identify it. He overflew at low altitude. The submarine was obviously charging batteries, but there was no one on deck. He came back, firing his .50 caliber machine guns near the submarine. No response. Then he came back again. This time the bombardier opened the bomb bay doors. Men appeared on the deck of the submarine frantically waving American flags.

In 1942, when the first B-17 equipped with antisubmarine radar appeared, Captain Jeffrey was sent up to San Antonio to bring one down as copilot. He first spent some time at Boca Raton, going to radar school, before going on to get the B-17. He had never been checked out in a B-17, although he had flown a half dozen types of aircraft, but he now began flying B-17s.

Jeffrey received orders to take a new B-17 back to Guatemala from Marsden Field, Tampa. He also was told he had to carry sixteen passengers who were going to duty there. Nobody mentioned the oxygen supply when they cut the orders, and of course on the day in question there was not enough oxygen in the aircraft to accommodate the passengers. Some ground pounder had not realized that B-17s are not passenger planes.

Captain Jeffrey took off for Guatemala, knowing that he could not fly over the weather without oxygen for everyone. Instead, he flew under it, Yucatan, Cuba, at 100 feet above the sea. When he hit Porto Barrio, Guatemala, he climbed to 15,000 feet, but the passengers immediately began to suffer, so he had to come down.

In the weather he could not find Guatemala City, but he knew it was 8000 feet in altitude.

Suddenly one of his engines began to heat up, and before he could feather the propeller it began windmilling. The drag cost altitude, and as he headed for the Pacific side of Central America he started coming down. Somehow he managed to fly between peaks that towered over him, flew for forty minutes, and finally reached the Pacific side. He was low on fuel, one engine was a mess, and he could not find San Jose air field. Was he north or south of it? He flew south ten minutes and did not find it. He flew north twenty minutes and then did find it. As he made his landing approach one more engine cut out, but he landed safely. He spent the night there while the plane was repaired and gassed up, and next day he flew to Guatemala City.

Two days after that hairy experience, Captain Jeffrey was scheduled to fly to the Galapagos Islands. The plane was loaded up and took off toward the sea. They had just reached lift-off and were at maximum power when the copilot reported the oil pressure in the No. 3 engine had dropped to zero.

"Shall I feather?"

Jeffrey thought for half a second. That engine would hold together for thirty seconds, and he needed twenty seconds to get altitude.

"Hell, no!" he said, and took off. The engine quit, but they came around on three engines and landed safely.

The aircraft was repaired, and then it was back to the routine of antisubmarine patrols in the South Atlantic.

# TWENTY-THREE

# *The Coming of the Eighth Air Force*

The summer of 1942 in Europe was a time of trial for the United States Army Air Force in the war against Nazi Germany. No one, friend or foe, knew much about the Air Force's capabilities. The American heavy bombers, the B-17s and B-24s, were untried, and the British, with three years of war behind them, had a very strong tendency to underrate their American allies in matters of skill and equipment. A writer in the *Times* of London gave this assessment:

> "American heavy bombers—the latest Fortresses and Liberators—are fine flying machines, but not suited for bombing Europe. Their bombs and bomb loads are small, their armour and armament are low. They are really more suitable for flying patrol missions over the Atlantic submarine lanes."

There was a real lack of confidence in the Flying Fortress. Its performance in the Far East had been anything but brilliant. The Japanese were contemptuous of the B-17s, and the British were not at all sure about them. The British still looked upon the United States as "the arsenal of democracy," a magnificent producing machine but an untried military machine. "Give us the tools," they were fond of quoting their prime minister, "and we will finish the job."

But Americans were not willing simply to give their ally the tools, nor, probably, could the British have finished the job with tools alone. At least that is not how it turned out.

In any event, in the summer of 1942 all this was just beginning.

On June 9, just after the Battle of Midway, the cadre of the Eighth U.S. Army Air Force began to arrive in the United Kingdom. Soon the ground contingents also came along, many of the men aboard the *Queen Elizabeth*. This included the Ninety-seventh Bomb Wing and the First and Thirty-first fighter groups. On June 15, General Carl Spaatz, the commander of the Eighth Air Force, arrived in the United Kingdom. Immediately he established the the First Bombardment Wing at Brampton Grange.

In Washington, General George C. Marshall instructed Major General General Dwight D. Eisenhower to integrate all American air units into the Eighth Air Force. The job would be to secure air supremacy over Europe in preparation for the ultimate invasion of Fortress Europe. Soon Eisenhower was talking about achieving air dominance over Europe by April 1, 1943.

All this was a bit premature and based on the American hope of invading the European continent across the English Channel in 1942. Wiser heads prevailed, however, recognizing the enormous need for landing craft and equipment that was not yet ready.

On June 25, Eighth Air Force headquarters was established in Bushey Park, a suburb of London. A day later air echelons of the Thirty-first Fighter Group were established at Atcham and High Ercall. June 29, 1942 saw two "firsts": Captain Charles C. Kegelman, the commanding officer of the Fifteenth Bombardment Squadron, became the first American officially to drop a bomb on enemy-occupied Europe on a mission with the Royal Air Force, and First Lieutenant Alfred W. Giacomini of the Thirty-first Fighter Group was the first American pilot fatality when he crashed a Spitfire while landing at Atcham. Not a very glorious beginning.

It was July 1 when the first B-17 landed at Prestwick, Scotland, but there were still no American units in regular operation. On the Fourth of July the Fifteenth Bombardment Squadron, flying six Boston bombers, joined RAF planes in low-level attack on four airfields in the Netherlands. Many people thought it was a stunt, particularly since all the aircraft belonged to the RAF. Captain Kegelman was involved again; his plane was damaged, but he flew it home to the base at Swanton Moley. Stunt or no stunt, the

Americans were in the air war against the Germans in northern Europe. A few days later Kegelman got a medal, the Distinguished Service Cross, "for extraordinary gallantry"—perhaps a little overkill, but when General Spaatz pinned on the medal he was, in a sense, emphasizing the American commitment.

The B-17s began to arrive in numbers in July. So did P-38 fighter interceptors. But the Americans were not yet ready to operate purely with their own equipment and personnel. On July 26, Lieutenant Colonel Albert P. Clark, executive officer of the Thirty-first Fighter Group, went with the RAF on a sweep over France. He was shot down flying an RAF fighter, and thus became the first fighter pilot to be shot down in the European Theater of Operations and the first official American Air Force prisoner of war.

By August 5, 1942, the Americans were ready to begin. That day eleven aircraft of the Thirty-first Fighter Group made a dry run over France and came back safely. A week later the Thirty-first Fighter Group was declared by the British to be ready to go into action—under RAF supervision until it gained a little experience.

Then came August 17, 1942.

A first American bombing mission had been planned earlier but had been scratched because of weather. Another mission was planned for August 1, against the Sotteville railroad marshaling yards in Rouen, one of the key transportation centers in northern France. At that time the yard held 2000 rail cars and was considered the focal point for rail traffic to channel ports.

Twelve B-17s would make the mission. Colonel Armstrong of the Ninety-seventh Bomb Group would lead, and his copilot would be Major Paul Tibbetts. Carrying forty-five 600-pound bombs and nine 1100-pound bombs, these planes would bomb Rouen while six other B-17s made a diversionary sweep along the coast. Four squadrons of RAF Spitfires would cover the B-17s on the way out, and five more squadrons would meet them and bring them home. Two other Spitfire squadrons would cover the diversion.

General Eaker was going along to see for himself just what his boys would be facing over Europe. He would ride in the lead plane of the second flight, the *Yankee Doodle*, piloted by Lieutenant John P. Dowswell.

The mission began in mid-afternoon, with the first B-17 airborne at 3:36 p.m.

The Germans weren't quite sure what to make of this formation of odd aircraft crossing the French coast, and reported it as "twelve Lancasters [British heavy bombers] heading inland."

When the flight reached St. Valery, greasy bursts of flak began to appear. They were flying at 23,000 feet in clear, bright weather. It was so clear that they spotted the target ten minutes before the bomb run.

When the bomb runs began, some of the bombs hit a mile short of the target, and one burst in the woods a mile to the west. But most of the bombs fell in the target area, and General Eaker expressed himself as pleased.

On the turn away from the target, they ran into flak and two B-17s were damaged. When they reached the Ypreville area, German fighters began to appear, but the Spitfires arrived just in time.

One Messerschmitt moved into the B-17s' formation, and the waist and turret gunners began firing on it. A Focke-Wulf 190 made a climbing turn into the formation, and came under the guns of ball turret gunner Sergeant Kent R. West of the airplane known as *Birmingham Blitzkrieg*. He shot the plane down, thus becoming the first gunner to shoot down a German fighter in the ETO. Two German planes were destroyed in the fight and others damaged, while two Spitfires were lost.

At the air base the ground personnel were learning the new experience of "sweating out" a mission. The busiest man in the air base squadron was the cook, answering calls for more coffee. Just before eleven o'clock little specks were sighted off in the distance, but no one could count more than eleven Flying Fortresses out there. Then up came a straggler, and the formation was complete. A cheer went up from the ground.

In total disregard of air discipline, three of the B-17s peeled off, zoomed down, and buzzed the tower. No one minded.

So the planes were home safely. The only damage that day came to one of the diversionary flight. A pigeon crashed through the Plexiglas of the nose compartment, and the flying plastic splinters cut the bombardier and the navigator slightly.

The aircrews came down talking a mile a minute. It was the next day before the air intelligence officers could sort out the picture.

General Eaker was satisfied, although he said he felt the formation should be tightened. General Spaatz was elated.

"I think the crews behaved like veterans," he said. "Everything went according to plan."

The youngest man on the mission, seventeen-year-old Sergeant Frank Christensen, spoke with the air of a fifty-mission veteran: "It's all in the day's work."

One pilot had this to say:

"When I was a little kid, I had a cousin who used to tell me about the last war. I used to think if it was me I'd have been scared. And so in this show I expected to be scared too.

"Well, sir, it was a funny thing. When we sighted the French coast I kept thinking: 'Well, here it starts,' but nothing happened—just a little flak. Then as we got to the target I thought 'All right, this is where it starts.' But it didn't. We just dropped our load and headed home without being bothered by a single fighter. Some of the ships were hit, but ours wasn't."

Everyone on the base agreed that it had been a most successful beginning.

Then messages began coming in, as if this were—and indeed it was—an historic occasion.

Air Marshal Sir Arthur Harris said this:

"Congratulations from all ranks of Bomber Command on the highly successful completion of the first all-American raid by the big fellows on German-occupied territory in Europe. Yankee Doodle certainly went to town and can stick yet another well-deserved feather in his cap." Certainly somebody over there was familiar with American history.

There was nothing fabricated about the congratulatory spirit of the British. They knew that America was now in the war and that from now on these bomber crews would be sharing the real danger, death, and fear of the RAF. This mission might have been a "piece of cake," but those in the future would not be. The British knew this far better than the Americans.

There remained considerable skepticism about the American claim to precision bombing from high altitude. When these first American crews were used up and replacements came along, some of the British airmen predicted, the whole system might fall apart. They believed that these crews were "professionals," when the fact was that only two of 200 officers of the group were West Point-trained.

When word of this first mission arrived in Washington, the Air Force staff was jubilant and crowed a little. Under General Arnold's signature a message was sent to the Joint Chiefs of Staff:

"This mission again verifies the soundness of our policy of precision bombing of strategic objectives rather than mass (blitz) bombing of large city-size areas."

That was one claim the British never believed. Ultimately the Americans came around to another view. Not particularly in Europe, but until the end of the war, investigation showed how relatively little had been accomplished on such targets as the German submarine pens by hundreds of thousands of tons of bombs. In the spring of 1945 General Curtis LeMay inaugurated the B-29 fire bombing of Japan to destroy the cities with incendiaries dropped from low altitude in saturation volume.

On August 19, the Ninety-seventh Bomb Group was aloft again over occupied France. This time it was participating in a mission against the Abbeville-Drucat airdrome, to occupy German fighters and keep them from working over the Canadian troops making a raid on Dieppe. Twenty-two of the twenty-four Fortresses bombed the target, in a combined raid with the British. Lieutenant Samuel F. Junkins, Jr., of the 309th Fighter Squadron, flying a

Spitfire, shot down a German fighter, thus becoming the first Eighth Air Force fighter pilot to score an aerial victory out of the United Kingdom.

America was now in the European air war with both wings, full of self-confidence and gusto. Both qualities would be sorely needed in the coming months.

# TWENTY-FOUR

# "The Boeing Is Most Terrifying . . ."*

The airman's war was fast and furious, with no time to double-check results, and consequently the results obtained were always exaggerated. This was true of every air force in the world. In the Pacific the Japanese airmen were prone to "see" carriers. If every carrier reported hit by a Japanese bomb had been sunk, the United States would have run out of carriers by 1944.

One case of exaggerated results that persisted in myth until after the war, when Japanese records became available, was the story of the Battle of the Bismarck Sea, which involved an important Japanese convoy and aircraft of the United States Fifth Air Force.

In January 1943, knowing that Guadalcanal was gone, the Imperial General Headquarters ordered a new major offensive against New Guinea. General Imamura at Rabaul and Admiral Yamamoto were to combine forces and complete the subjugation of New Guinea. They already held Dutch New Guinea, but Papua, near Australia, was still largely in Allied hands despite the Japanese landings at Lae and Salamaua and an attempt to move overland and capture Port Moresby after the original Port Moresby invasion plan had failed in the spring of 1942. The Japanese army, in particular, had always regarded New Guinea as the most important target in the area, the springboard from which they would eventually invade Australia.

General Imamura and Admiral Kusaka, the commander of the

*Statement of a Japanese survivor of the Battle of the Bismarck sea.

Eighth Fleet, decided, with the concurrence of higher commands, that they would reinforce the garrison at Lae with another 7000 troops. In January the Japanese reinforced the Lae garrison with considerable success, losing two of five transports, and in February they sent another three ships in safely.

By the end of February the Japanese were ready to try again with a bigger convoy: eight transports and eight destroyers, carrying nearly 7000 men. Rear Admiral Masatomi Kimura supervised the amphibious operation, and two high-ranking generals, Lieutenant General Hatazo Adachi of the Eighteenth Army and Lieutenant General Nakano of the Fifty-first Division, were in charge of land operations. It was unusual to have so much authority clustered in one spot, an indication of the importance which Imperial General Headquarters attached to the capture of New Guinea.

The convoy sailed on the last night of February, and the next day it moved through the Bismarck Sea towards Dampier Strait. On the afternoon of March 1, the convoy was spotted by a B-24 reconnaissance bomber. Those aboard the ships did not see this as too much of a problem, because the weather was very bad for flying, and they did not expect air attacks. Besides, the army and the navy together had promised the convoy a cover of at least 200 planes if necessary.

The admiral and the generals did not have much respect for the Allied air forces in Australia. They had not been bothered too much in the past by these planes. But they did not know that Lieutenant General George F. Kenney, the new commander of the Fifth U.S. Air Force, was now ready to make a play for control of the skies above New Guinea. For the effort he had 207 bombers and 129 fighter planes and, equally important, a new philosophy of attack.

The B-25 medium bombers had been modified. Instead of a bombardier in the nose bubble, they now carried eight .50 caliber machine guns for strafing. They were also equipped with delayed-action bombs, so that they could come in low, skip bomb, and not be blown up by their own bomb blasts. They had been practicing low-level bombing techniques for weeks.

The huge B-17 Flying Fortresses, which the Japanese tended to regard with contempt ("they never hit anything"), were also using low-level techniques, which had increased their effectiveness remarkably against shipping.

On the afternoon of March 1, contact was made by Allied scout planes with the convoy, but it was lost that night. In the morning of March 2, the contact was resumed by another B-24.

Very shortly thereafter eleven B-17s of the Sixty-fourth Bombardment Squadron took off from Jackson Field and made rendezvous with seventeen other heavy bombers and some fighter planes. They headed for Cape Gloucester, ran into heavy clouds forty miles south of the cape, and went on instruments. They flew on, came out of the clouds, and sighted the convoy just east of Sakar Island. At ten that morning they began their attacks. These attacks were made at 4700 to 5600 feet, in three-ship V formations or individually. They aimed to cross the ships at right angles and then drop, pulling up in a climbing turn to right or left, and then seeking cloud cover from the ships' antiaircraft fire. This one squadron registered one direct hit and three major near misses with 1000-pound instantaneous demolition bombs, and shot down two Zeros and a Japanese army fighter. There was no strafing by the bombers, because of the bad weather. By noon, after the assaults of the heavy bombers, one Japanese transport had sunk and two were damaged. The second heavy bomber attack on the convoy was made that afternoon, and the B-17s claimed one more transport sunk. One B-17 was damaged but managed to make its base.

On the morning of March 3 seven B-17s took off from Jackson Field, picked up fighter escort, and again attacked the convoy, which was then about sixty miles off Lae. Japanese Zeros attacked, of which the Americans later claimed to have shot down seven. The B-17s also claimed to have "probably" sunk one more transport and damaged another.

That afternoon eight B-17s picked up fighters and hit the convoy again. They claimed to have sunk another transport and damaged a destroyer on this mission. Three of the B-17s went down to strafe burning ships, the men in the water, and small boats full of troops.

On both sides it was a no-quarter merciless battle. One B-17 attacked by Zeros lost a wing, and seven men parachuted out of the wreck. All were machine-gunned by the Zeros. Three P-38s which went to their rescue were shot down by the Zeros too, but five Zeros were also shot down.

On March 3 the attack on the convoy was joined by A-20 attack bombers and B-25 medium bombers, whose crews had been practicing skip bombing.

At 8:30 in the morning Captain W. S. Royalty of the Seventy-first Bombardment Squadron of B-25s took off in No. 7 in a seven-plane flight. They were to bomb from medium altitude, about 5000 feet. Here is Royalty's report:

"We knew from past experience that there would be Zeros protecting the ships, but we also knew that we were to have some P-38s for top cover. After the way these P-38s had shown themselves for the past two or three months, it made us feel fairly safe from the Zeros.

"Our planes were the first flight over the rendezvous point, which was some distance from the convoy's last reported position south of Finschshafen. We circled around waiting for the rest of the planes in the coordinated attack. As we made the first circle we could see, coming over the mountain, an almost unbelievable number of planes.

"Eight B-17s were getting into formation slightly above us. Below us three separate flights of B-25s were already in formation and beginning to circle. Below also were a great number of Beaufighters, A-20s, and P-40s all in formation more or less.

"We were at 5300 feet, and a few thousand feet above I counted twenty-three P-38s in formations of twos, threes, and fours. It was the most concentrated flight of aircraft that any of us had ever seen. After we had circled twice, all the planes started for the convoy at once. Our flight followed two flights of three B-17s each.

"About thirty miles out we saw some ships of the convoy. Nearest to us, as we came closer, were what seemed to be two cruisers and three destroyers. These ships were making violent maneuvers, and wakes were streaming out ten or twelve times their lengths. I counted six transports and cargo vessels on the other side of these warships and at least two more warships further on. The warships were moving fast, but the cargo ships seemed to be almost at a standstill.

"We followed along behind the B-17s as they flew parallel to the line of warships, and the nearest cruiser threw three broadsides at us. It looked like the whole ship was lit up. As we got opposite this ship, the B-17s turned to go over the convoy.

"Our flight went on for a minute or more and then turned in also. As we turned, another broadside left the cruiser, and immediately afterward one of the bombs from a B-17 hit that ship dead center and a huge cloud of brown smoke billowed out.

"I didn't have time to watch it any more. Below I saw an almost endless stream of planes strafing and skip bombing every ship in the convoy. A B-25 scored a direct hit by skip bombing on a large transport, and the whole stern blew up and burned fiercely.

"We lined up on three transports, started a bombing run, and then I saw seven or eight Zeros at about twelve o'clock, a long way off. Almost at the same time several P-38s came down on them. They started some good dogfights, but other things were attracting my attention.

"We were just dropping our bombs at the middle transport of three. Pictures showed later that we made a direct hit and some near misses on the ship. As we turned to leave for home, I saw at least five ships smoking, and three of these were flaming. A-20s, Beaufighters, B-25s, and B-17s were still strafing and skip bombing all the ships I could see.

"During the approach to the convoy and during the attack, I was riding in the nose behind the bombardier, and after we left I crawled back through the tunnel and watched through the navigation dome.

"When we were about thirty miles away I saw one ship explode with a tremendous volume of smoke and fire. It seemed to spread over half the ocean. At the same time huge columns of black smoke came up from three more vessels, and bombs were still exploding around in different parts of the convoy.

"On our return trip planes passed us going both ways. I didn't see any planes shot down during all of this time, but how the broadsides missed us I will never know. It seemed that with so many planes over the target at the same time and at so many altitudes, the Japs didn't know which to shoot at, so their fire was never concentrated on a single flight or ship. They didn't even come close to hitting us."

Captain John P. Henebry's Ninetieth Bombardment Squadron was assigned to skip bombing, a different technique altogether.

"We flew at our assigned altitude (5000 feet) until we sighted our target. We then started to let down. Our squadron had three or four flights of B-25C-1s. We were supposed to follow the Beaufighters in on our target. They swung to the right of the convoy, made a left turn under the B-17s and medium-altitude B-25s. Their attack was in a southwesterly direction. The Beaufighters went in ahead of the other low-altitude B-25s and A-20s, after the first wave of B-17s had dropped their bombs. They strafed the decks of all the ships that they came in contact with.

"Five of our planes, of which I was one, saw some very good targets to our left, so we did not follow the other planes in. We turned left in front of the convoy, which was heading southeast at this time. We were at about 500 feet. Major Larner gave the order, and we split our formation. Each plane was to pick his own target and attack singly.

"We were encountering some heavy ack-ack fire from the five warships leading the convoy. Because of this I dived and turned continuously until I came close enough to get a shot with my eight .50 caliber guns. I started for a large transport but was cut out by one of our own planes, who had the same thing in mind. It was just as well, because there was another Jap transport directly to my right. I started my run on him in a slight dive. It was a broadside attack. We were indicating about 260 mph when we passed over the target. I fired in as close as I could, as the decks were covered with troops and supplies. Just before I pulled up to clear the mast, my copilot released two of our three 500-pound bombs. One fell short and the other scored a direct hit on the side of the ship, at the waterline.

"We had one more bomb, so we pulled up to about 300 feet and made a quarterly attack on a freighter that was sighted slightly to our left.

"This time my forward guns started a fire on the stern of the target. The bomb scored a near miss, and I am sure it did some damage.

"That afternoon, we returned to the convoy as part of a co-ordinated attack to finish off what was left. I got a direct hit with a 500-pound bomb on a damaged destroyer. I strafed a couple of sinking ships, starting a fire on one, and then made about fifteen strafing passes at small craft and survivors in the water.

"We were attacked by six Zeros when we were flat out on the water. My rear gunner shot down one of them, and for some reason the other five failed to press the attack home."

Also from the Ninetieth Squadron, in came Lieutenant J. B. Criswell's plane at 220 miles per hour, against a Japanese destroyer that had been traveling at about eight knots until the skipper saw what Criswell was up to and suddenly put on speed.

The B-25 attacked at mast height, and the captain of the destroyer made the error of making a 90-degree turn just before the plane bombed, presenting a broadside target. The bomb hit amidships, and the B-25 then swung off in a 90-degree left turn, as the bomb blew off and smoke and debris rose to 300 feet.

"Considering this to be a sinking condition, I then proceeded to the center of the battle area to bring my forward machine guns to bear on personnel in the water. The effect of this strafing could not be accurately determined, because of the confusion and the debris in the water. The runs began from about 200 feet and continued until water and debris, caused by the bullets hitting the target, piled up and made it necessary to pull up. Four of these runs were made before I directed my attention to a cargo ship which was burning at the south of the area.

"This approach was made at 220 mph at mast height, broadside. She [the ship] was about 5000 tons. Personnel were visible on the deck in spite of fire and the possibility of explosion. The ship's visible protection was a three- to five-inch gun mounted on the afterdeck, pointed aft, with no attendance. I fired several bursts from the forward guns as we drew in range, and a marked effect was noted among the troops on deck. Two bombs were dropped. They fell long and would be considered effective near misses. The rest of the time was spent strafing the personnel in the sea."

In another low-level attack, Lieutenant E. W. Atkins was the pilot of B-25 No. 899. As he approached the convoy he saw smoke from four burning ships rising to the cloud base at 2000 feet. Three or four miles past the burning ships, a destroyer was seen traveling at high speed. In the area beyond the burning ships and the destroyer, large quantities of wreckage and many men were in the water.

Flying at 500 feet, Lieutenant Atkins saw a B-25 start a run on the destroyer. Seconds later he saw an explosion amidships which must have been caused by a bomb dropped from an airplane much higher up. Then he saw gun flashes from the destroyer and tracer bullets directed toward his aircraft. He made his bomb run, beside another plane, against the bow of the destroyer. As he passed over and dropped his bomb, his plane was rocked by an explosion which he thought must have been caused by bombs dropped from another B-25.

Then Atkins's tail gunner reported that his bomb scored a hit on the forward deck of the destroyer. The tail gunner also observed splashes from bombs in the water near the destroyer. Lieutenant Atkins turned to the left and saw smoke belching from the destroyer, and the tail gunner saw explosions aboard the ship.

Atkins's plane then made a strafing run on the men in the water and the wreckage in the area. They went after one lifeboat, and the turret gunner strafed and saw men jumping out of the boat. The boat capsized.

Atkins then made another bomb run on a transport believed to be 9000 tons, and another pilot reported near misses. On leaving the area, Lieutenant Atkins reported a dense column of white smoke rising over the target area.

Captain Royalty also went back against the convoy on that afternoon of March 3:

"We took off on the afternoon attack with much more confidence than we had on the morning mission. There were two flights—one three-plane and one four-plane formation. The assembly point was the same as before, but we didn't get together very well and there was some confusion when we finally reached the target.

"We made our run on either a destroyer or a cruiser, and just as we got lined up for a run the Zeros hit us. There were between eight and fourteen of them, and they made passes at the entire formation from above and at four o'clock and eight o'clock. The attacks were not pressed, and we were able to make a good run at 4800 feet. We weren't attacked after dropping our bombs.

"Our bombs hit on and around the cruiser in such a close pattern that the ship was lost to view as a result of the explosion. We got some good photographs that show three direct hits and at least six near misses. The ship was burning fiercely, and as we pulled away it exploded. The smoke and flames were so bad that the ship was never visible again."

The Japanese convoy was sorely wounded by the evening of March 3, but the bombers and fighters came again on March 4. Captain Henebry's plane and eight others from his squadron made a sweep of the battle area on the afternoon of March 4 to finish off cripples. They sank one damaged destroyer (Captain Henebry's plane hit it with a 500-pound bomb that proved to be a dud), and they strafed many lifeboats and rafts full of Japanese.

The Lae convoy then was a total failure. Of the 7000 reinforcements scheduled for New Guinea, only a few hundred were delivered. Most of these were without supplies or weapons, so they become a liability rather than an asset in the battle for New Guinea.

So many Allied aircraft had been involved in this battle that the facts were hard to sort out. The MacArthur command claimed that twenty destroyers and transports were sunk. Actually, after PT boats had searched the area, sinking crippled ships and destroying small craft, the score stood at four of eight destroyers and eight of eight transports sunk. But more than the numbers, the consequent policy of the Japanese in reinforcing New Guinea tells the story: Never again did the Japanese send a convoy to New Guinea. Thereafter the reinforcement was done by barge and boat. The new technique of mast-high bombing and skip bombing was, as the Japanese recognized, devastating.

# TWENTY-FIVE

# *Assassination*

Early in April 1943, Admiral Isoroku Yamamoto moved down from Truk to Rabaul. He wanted to take personal direction of an air offensive, named Operation I-Go, which was designed to break the back of Allied air power in the Solomons and New Guinea. A few days later he decided to make a tour of the frontline naval air bases for the purpose of raising the morale of the troops.

Word of the admiral's coming was sent to the forward Japanese bases in an itinerary prepared by Yamamoto's staff and broadcast in the naval code on April 14. In essence, the coded message said that on April 18 the Commander in Chief of the Combined Fleet would travel to Ballale, Buin, and several other forward bases to visit aircrews and hospitals. He would leave Rabaul at 6 A.M., then fly or travel by minesweeper to the other naval air bases. He would be flying into Ballale at 9:35 in the morning with his chief of staff, Vice Admiral Matome Ugaki, in two Betty bombers, because for security's sake Yamamoto and his chief of staff never traveled together.

The Americans had broken the Japanese naval code before Midway, and such was the arrogance of the generals and admirals at Imperial Headquarters that they had never changed the code. So the American radio intelligence teams also received the message intended for the Japanese frontline units.

Admiral Nimitz was notified, and his intelligence officer, Commander Edwin T. Layton, was eager to "get Yamamoto." Admiral Nimitz was less eager. Certainly the assassination of Yamamoto would be a plus for the Americans. He was the greatest hero of the Japanese navy and the Japanese public since Admiral Togo led the navy in the Russo-Japanese War, and there was no other who could take his place. The death of Yamamoto would be a great blow to Japan.

But what if the Japanese discovered the breach of their naval code and changed it? Without access to that code the Americans probably would have lost the Battle of Midway. Before and since they had relied on that code for word of Japanese military movements. Admiral Charles Lockwood's Pacific Fleet submarines needed it to intercept news of Japanese shipping movements. To lose the code would be to lose the greatest single naval weapon the Americans possessed.

Commander Layton was eager to see the assassination. "There was no doubt in my mind that shooting down Yamamoto would be a vital and serious blow to the Japanese," he later recalled. He proposed that the navy issue an ex post facto statement that the interception came from word received from coastwatchers.

But Nimitz was a careful man. He also asked the advice of Admiral Halsey and Admiral King on this matter. Halsey raised the question of the effect on the breach of the Japanese codes, and King recognized political as well as military overtones to the projected assassination. He informed President Roosevelt, who was extremely conscious of public relations. In spite of Admiral Halsey's suspicion that the Japanese would know what had really happened, the decision was finally made to try the interception.

Not long before the Yamamoto affair began, the 339th Army Air Force fighter squadron had been brought to Guadalcanal. The pilots flew P-38 twin-engine fighters. The distance to Ballale was over 400 miles, far beyond the range of naval (or any other) fighters. But by employing belly tanks to carry extra gasoline, the P-38s could make the round trip to Ballale with about ten minutes on the target.

Major John Mitchell was selected to lead this mission of sixteen P-38 fighters. Twelve of them would fly cover, and four were designated as trigger men to shoot down the two bombers that would be coming in, no matter how many Zeros covered them.

Captain Thomas Lanphier, Lieutenant Rex Barber, Lieutenant Joseph Moore, and Lieutenant James McLanahan would go after the bombers. Under Major Mitchell's plan they would try to make the interception thirty-five miles up the Bougainville coast from Kahili. This would give them a chance to hit and run before the Japanese fields on Bougainville could be alerted and the whole area became as deadly as a wasps' nest.

On the morning of April 18 the sixteen P-38s taxied to the Henderson Field runway. On takeoff Lieutenant McLanahan blew a tire. Fifteen P-38s took off.

On forming up for the trip, one of Lieutenant Moore's engines began to misfire. Fourteen P-38s formed up for the air trip, and Lieutenant Besby Holmes and Lieutenant Raymond K. Hine took the places of the two missing pilots in the trigger formation.

They flew for two hours and nine minutes until they approached the rendezvous point. There, right on schedule, came the formation of two twin-engine bombers flying at 4500 feet and six Zero fighters in two V sections 1500 feet above them.

The P-38s were down on the deck, flying about thirty feet above the water to avoid detection. Up went ten, unseen, to 15,000 feet, while the four attack planes climbed to the level of the twin-engine Japanese bombers two miles away. Captain Tom Lanphier ordered them all to drop their belly tanks and attack. He and Barber dropped theirs, but Lieutenant Holmes's tank would not readily drop off, so Lieutenant Hine stuck with Holmes while the other two attacked.

The P-38s reached a point only a mile away from the bombers when the Zeros saw them and peeled off, and the bombers dove down for the deck. Lanphier turned into a Zero and shot it down at 6000 feet; then he drove after the bombers.

Lieutenant Barber went straight for a bomber and made some hits, but overshot and came around. Lanphier made a pass at one bomber and said he saw a wing fly off and the bomber crash into the jungle. Holmes, who had managed to get rid of his belly tank, engaged the Zeros, as did Hines. Holmes then noticed one bomber flying just above the water. He and Hines went after it, but Barber got there first and began firing. The bomber crashed in the sea. They all engaged Zeros and Hine was hit. He headed for home and was last seen, engines smoking, near the Russell Islands.

Lieutenant Holmes ran low on fuel and had to land in the Russell Islands. The others went back to Guadalcanal, where Captain Lanphier claimed that he had shot down Yamamoto. Lieutenant Barber thought *he* had shot down Yamamoto, but the only ones who could back the stories were Hine and Holmes, who had seen the action up close. Hine was down at sea, and Holmes did not get back to base until the next day to speak for Barber. By then it was too late; Lanphier had already been given credit for the assassination.

The glory, however, was very short-lived. Immediately the scuttlebutt on Guadalcanal was overflowing with the story of the killing of Yamamoto, and Admiral Halsey panicked. He had raised the question of the danger that the move would pose if the Japanese discovered that the naval code was responsible for the mission. Now the talk was all over Guadalcanal, and the island was crawling with journalists and photographers. Halsey ordered an absolute ban on publicity and cautioned the men involved in the assassination that they must observe secrecy or face court-martial. Censorship was invoked on the news correspondents, and newsreel film was seized and destroyed.

All seemed to be going well for several days. Then an Australian newsreel cameraman, returning to Sydney, blew the whistle and gave an interview to a newspaper. The scoop was international and was picked up by neutral newspapers in Buenos Aires and Stockholm, which were carefully read by agents of Japanese naval intelligence in those countries.

The South Pacific command began to sweat. All the pilots involved were immediately shipped back to America and scattered around the country, with threats of instant court-martial if they so much as mentioned the Yamamoto mission. It was many, many months before the argument as to "who got Yamamoto" could be continued, and by the end of the war nobody really cared except the participants. In fact it was President Franklin D. Roosevelt who "got" him, for he made the decision to assassinate. The fliers were simply his instruments.

Admiral Halsey and many other high-ranking navy officials had many sleepless nights, contemplating the effects of the mission on the Japanese codes.

Vice Admiral Ugaki, Yamamoto's chief of staff, was injured when his plane was shot down and fell into the sea. He was in no condition to discuss the matter immediately, but he suspected that the code had been broken.

Captain Yasuji Watanabe, Yamamoto's gunnery officer, who had planned the itinerary and handled communications, discovered that the Japanese army had also sent word of Yamamoto's movement through its own code system, and he charged that it was the army's messages that had tipped off the Americans. There was no love lost between Japanese army and navy, and so the admirals were pleased to believe that the army was responsible.

All this became a smokescreen that prevented Imperial General Headquarters from coming to the proper conclusions, and the arrogance of the general staff precluded belief that the stupid Americans could break the Imperial codes. So the Americans, despite their brash action, were very lucky. The code breach was maintained, and American submarines went right on sinking Japanese convoys.

# TWENTY-SIX

# *Air Drop*

On November 5, 1942, the Allies prepared for the American invasion of French North Africa. Six B-17 bombers of the Ninety-seventh Bombardment Group brought General Dwight D. Eisenhower and staff from Britain to Gibraltar for the operation. In one of those B-17s rode Major General James H. Doolittle, newly appointed commander of the Twelfth Air Force, which would operate in the Mediterranean.

The B-17s had been stripped down for the long flight. The only guns in Doolittle's B-17 were the fixed guns, the top turret, the ball turret, and the tail gun—no waist guns. John C. Summers was Doolittle's pilot and Thomas F. Lohr was copilot.

Summers got into trouble on takeoff; the hydraulic system failed and they barely made it back to the field. The other staff-laden B-17s flew on to Gibraltar; the Doolittle B-17 would have to make the long trip alone across German-occupied territory, with no fighter cover and insufficient armament.

They took off again on November 6 and headed for Gibraltar. Off Cape Finisterre in Spain, the pilot sighted four black specks and had the sinking feeling that these were German fighters. They were, in fact, twin-engine JU-88s, on a reconnaissance flight over the South Atlantic, looking for Allied shipping to attack. The German fighters were virtually at the end of their patrol and low on fuel, but they still decided to investigate this single plane. They broke into two elements of two planes each and dived on the B-17. These pilots obviously had not seen many B-17s, and for a while they flew alongside the bomber, looking but not attacking.

Then the fighters pulled ahead and turned to make a frontal attack on the bomber in approved textbook fashion.

Pilot Summers jinked and took other evasive actions, manipulating rudder and throttles to confuse the enemy. They fired but missed, and then they closed. One 20mm shell exploded inside the cockpit, shattering the windshield and instrument panel and wounding Copilot Lohr. Another shell hit the No. 3 engine, and its propeller began to windmill, creating enormous drag and cutting the speed of the aircraft. Pilot Summers took the plane down onto the deck, just above the water. The Germans made a few more passes, but their leader must have looked at his gas gauge, because they pulled up and away and headed for home base. Copilot Lohr stayed in his seat. They got the No. 3 engine feathered at last, and the vibration stopped. Lohr then went down into the navigator's compartment to get his wound dressed, and General Doolittle took over as copilot, although he had never flown a B-17 in his life. They landed safely at Gibraltar, and two days later the invasion of North Africa began.

The Twelfth Air Force flew many planes, including British Spitfire fighters, in the North Africa campaign. On November 9, General Doolittle arrived in Algeria in his B-17, this time escorted by twelve Spitfires. C-47s of the Sixtieth Troop Carrier Group made the air drops at La Senia, carried troops to Algiers, and were also dropping British paratroops. The Air Force's B-17s and P-38 fighters were also in action. Lieutenant General Carl Spaatz was made deputy commander in chief of the Allied expeditionary force for air. More and more heavy bombers were diverted from the Eighth Air Force to the Twelfth to participate in the North African fighting, which moved into Tunisia.

By January, planes of the Twelfth Air Force were seeking targets in the Straits of Sicily, and eyes were pointing to that Italian island as a point of attack. In February General Doolittle took over Twelfth Bomber Command and General Spaatz took over the Twelfth Air Force, which was downgraded to be an arm of the bigger North African Air Force.

The American and British air forces operated with close cooperation until the end of the North African campaign.

\*        \*        \*

And then the Allies got ready for the next big step, the invasion of Sicily, for which they brought in the Sixty-first Troops Carrier Group, with four squadrons.

Joseph J. Yuhasz was a staff sergeant in the Fifteenth Squadron, and assistant crew chief of the C-47 named *Down and Go*. The pilot was Lieutenant Anthony J. Halas, the copilot was Lieutenant Douglas Moore, the radio operator was Herbert Triick, and the crew chief was Lloyd D. York.

As Sergeant Yuhasz recalled, "Our airplanes were C-47s, which were the DC-3s made by Douglas Aircraft for the airlines. The airplanes did not have any armor, arms, or self-sealing gasoline tanks. . . . Our airplane was named *Down and Go* by the pilot, after the phrase used in poker games."

The airplanes of the Fifteenth Squadron were flown to Africa from Pope Field, Fort Bragg, North Carolina, by the South American route via Ascension Island.

The ground crew went to Camp Shanks outside New York City and boarded the liner *America*, now called the USS *West Point*, which sailed alone to Casablanca by way of Nova Scotia. It was an easy trip, and the men landed at Casablanca in the third week of May 1943. They lived in pup tents outside town for a few days and then made their way in stages to Tunisia, where they bedded down on a dry lake bed outside the town of Kairouan. The airstrip had been bulldozed out of the desert.

They spent part of their time chasing centipedes with hammers and flying supplies to Kairouan from Casablanca, Oran, or Algiers. They brought in the Eighty-second Airborne Division, and they waited.

It was hot.

"To give you an idea of how hot it was there in Tunisia—when we would land at our base with a load of paratroopers and they would get of the airplanes, they would put up their hands to shield their faces from the heat and they would say, 'Boy, the engines are throwing off a lot of heat.' "

But it was just as hot everywhere.

"At noon I would stand under the shower with my clothes on,

wet myself down, and by the time I had walked 150 feet toward the line I would be dry. It was so hot during the day that we were ordered not to work from 11 a.m. until 4 p.m. when our tools became so hot they were too hot to hold. At night the ground would have frost on it."

The paratroops of the Eighty-second Airborne were bivouacked about two miles from the field, to be nearby for the mission to come.

The tents of the airmen were fifty yards apart, so that if they were strafed not many would be hit in one pass. The planes were also placed on both sides of the airstrip. A week before the Sicilian invasion, the planes were sent off to small fields in the area for the night, to prevent large losses in case of a major air attack. Such an attack was expected, because enemy planes came over nightly to drop flares.

As they got ready for the paradrop, six para racks were bolted to the bottom of each airplane. The paratroopers would put their equipment into bags and put the bags in the racks. The bags would be dropped like bombs from a bomber before the troops were dropped.

The paratroops set up long tables on the strip to pack their own parachutes.

The first mission to Sicily was on the night of July 11. Sergeant Yuhasz volunteered for it, but the crew chief went that night. Yuhasz would go on the second drop, on the night of July 12. As they waited in the airplanes, they tuned in to Axis Sally.

She said in her most confiding voice that she was talking to the Eighty-second Airborne Division. She knew they were at Ouidja but that they had just moved to Kairouan. "I understand that the Eighty-second is going to drop in on us tonight near Gela."

Whang! That was a shock, for Gela was indeed the drop point.

"We will have a big welcoming party for you, with lots for fireworks, racket, noisemakers, and we will give you a host welcome."

Paratroopers in Yuhasz's aircraft jumped up, ran out of the plane, and yelled to their buddies:

"They know we are coming and exactly where!"

It was not the happiest moment.

Yuhasz and the other crew members tried to jolly up the paratroops. One of them told Yuhasz he was afraid this jump would be his last, and he was not ready to die.

"I felt sorry for him but there wasn't anything I could do. After all, he had volunteered for the Airborne, and now there was no way to back out.

"Actually we had several paratroops aboard who had failed to jump on the first mission. When they got to the door, they fell down on the floor and the rest went by them. They were brought back to the field and told by their officers they could go on the next mission or get shot! So they went on the second mission."

Sergeant Yuhasz got ready to go:

"Once we got into the air we could see planes taking off all over that part of Africa. . . . I did not realize that there were so many airfields in our part of Tunisia. It seemed to me there must be a thousand airplanes that took off and were milling around and working into the formation to go to Sicily."

They flew east over Tunisia, carrying their paratroops, and then out over the Mediterranean Sea, at about 100 feet above the water, until they came to Malta. Then they followed the south coast of Malta and turned north along the east coast toward Sicily.

The formation was uncertain, flying without lights, and it was difficult to see the other planes.

"The only way we could tell where they were was to look at the water. The planes would blot out the light of the moon's reflection on the waves, and in this way we could see the outlines of the planes ahead and to the side of us. It was very scary, because we were not sure of the other planes' positions. Planes were jockeying to the right and to the left, up and down, trying to avoid each other, and once in a while one plane would have to go down under another as he was being boxed in. This would bring the lower plane very close to the water, but luckily no one collided."

Suddenly, ahead of the *Down and Go* a light flashed the color code of the day. A destroyer wanted to see if they were friend or foe. This was a surprise, and they were not ready. The pilot told

Sergeant Yuhasz to break out the signaling lantern, but by the time he did, they were past the ship. Luckily the destroyer did not fire on them.

Pilot Halas had been told at the briefing to enter Sicily at the southeast point of the island and then turn left and fly over land northwest, paralleling the south coast. He would come to a lake with a road leading from the interior of the island, and he was to fly for several minutes until he reached the drop zone.

As they neared the coast of Sicily they saw mountains ahead extending right down to the coast. They had to climb to go over. This had not been in the briefing. Climbing, the *Down and Go* lost contact with the formation, but they knew the other planes were nearby because from some source they began to get flak, which fascinated Sergeant Yuhasz:

"I was standing between the pilot and the copilot. I would look out the window, and suddenly out of the blackness down there would appear three or four red balls like the charges from a Roman candle, coming up as a group into the sky. At first they seemed to rise slowly towards a point way ahead of us, and as we went by they seemed to curve towards us. When they got close to our altitude they really zipped by. They always came up ahead of our plane. Whoever was shooting at us thought we were going faster than we really were. We could see these balls coming up, so we turned the plane to the right and then to the left, trying to keep from getting hit.

"Tony asked me for some water, and I gave him the canteen. Then Doug Moore, the copilot, asked and I gave him the canteen. Tony bent forward and told me to feel his back, and I felt that his shirt was all wet. That surprised me, because I wasn't too frightened yet. I then realized that they were under great tension."

To the right, a big ball of flame appeared in the sky, and Yuhasz realized it was a C-47, hit and on fire. It went down, down and hit the ground. That is when Sergeant Yuhasz started to get frightened. His legs began to shake.

They flew up the coast, with flak coming up all the time. They dropped down and hedgehopped, and the flak stopped. But they could not find the lake and the drop zone. Pilot Halas turned around and made a second run. He still could not find the drop zone.

The paratroops were sitting in their bucket seats in the back of the C-47, looking out the window at the flak. Halas told Yuhasz to tell the jumpmaster of the paratroops that they were lost. What did he want to do—continue to look, or find a spot and jump? He said to keep looking, but soon the heavily laden jumpmaster squeezed into the cockpit and said that the pilot should pick a spot and they would jump. By this time the paratroops were lying on the floor on the principle that they made lesser targets that way. Then they came to a lake with a road coming down from inland. They really did not know where they were, but the pilot turned inland along the road, and there was no flak, so the pilot told the jumpmaster to get ready. They hooked up to their static lines, which ran along a line to the hatch, and faced the rear of the plane. The 15-foot static lines pulled the parachute packs loose and opened the chutes.

Sergeant Yuhasz stood by the door, watching the lights. The green light came on, so he released the parapacks below the plane. Then the paratroopers came, and they moved out the door. One of them grabbed Yuhasz and tried to take him out with him, but Yuhasz held onto the bars on the side of the plane and escaped the clutch.

When the last trooper was out, the sergeant looked out the door. He could see them floating down, having jumped from 600 feet above the ground. There was no flak.

Yuhasz grabbed the static lines and pulled them back into the aircraft. Then he went up front and reported to pilot Halas that the paratroops had jumped. Now their task was to retrace their steps to Tunisia.

Pilot Halas turned the plane around and headed back toward the coast. He flew in the direction of Gela, where they were supposed to exit from the island air space. They encountered a great deal of flak. Sergeant Yuhasz suggested that it was nice and quiet out over the ocean, and it would be nice to be out there insted of inland with all the antiaircraft fire coming up.

The pilot thought this over. Instructions were to follow a path,

Corporal Jake Jones, U.S. Army Air Corps (1942–1946). *(S. Kann Sons Co.)*

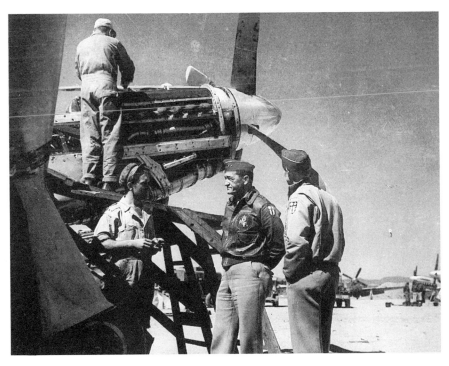

Major General Claire Chennault and some of his Flying Tigers on the Kunming airfield in China. *(National Archives)*

Flying Tigers over the Chinese countryside.   *(National Archives)*

Edison Vail in training.

The wreckage of one of the Doolittle B-52 bombers that came down in China after the raid on Japan.  *(National Archives)*

One of Jimmy Doolittle's B-25s takes off from the carrier *Hornet* for the first raid on Japan.  *(National Archives)*

A bomber takes off from the deck of an American carrier in the Battle of Midway.  *(National Archives)*

U.S. Navy dive-bombers hit one of the Japanese carriers in the Battle of Midway. Four Japanese carriers were sunk in this battle. *(National Archives)*

The twin-engined bomber, one of the most effective Japanese air weapons in the Pacific war. *(National Archives)*

The sinking of the U.S. carrier *Yorktown*, lost in the Battle of Midway. *(National Archives)*

An SBD on the deck of the carrier *Enterprise*. *(National Archives)*

On the left, pods of antiaircraft guns protect a carrier during the raid on Tulagi in May 1942. On the right, some airplane handlers, or "airedales," move a plane on deck while others hurry to handle another. *(National Archives)*

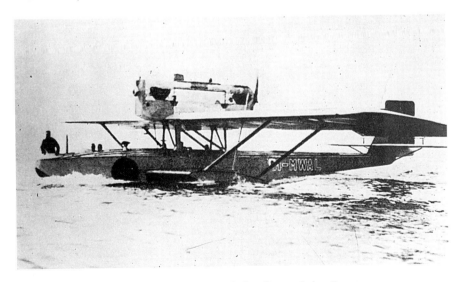

The Dornier-Wahl seaplane, one of the first of the Japanese seaplanes. *(National Archives)*

A pilot looks over
his P-51 wing rockets
before taking off
on a strafing mission
in China.
(*National Archives*)

P-51 fighters on the
field at Nanning,
China. Widely used
by the Fourteenth
Air Force, this was
the most effective
fighter plane in the
Chinese theater.
(*National Archives*)

B-25s in the Battle of
the Bismarck Sea.
*(Smithsonian Institution
Photo No. D23285AC)*

B-17s of the 571st Squadron on an English airfield. *(National Archives)*

Lieutenant Colonel Thomas Jeffrey *(facing camera)* makes a preflight check on one of his group's air crews.

Lieutenant Colonel Jeffrey is decorated with the Distinguished Flying Cross.

Major General Curtis LeMay, division commander, with Lieutenant Colonel Jeffrey.

The ME-109, a major
enemy of the B-17s.
*(National Archives)*

A truck convoy of P-47 fighters moves up to an airfield through a
British town.  *(National Archives)*

The German port of Danzig—one of the reasons Germany went to war with Poland—was vital to the German war effort. The B-17s hit the city several times.

Adolf Hitler presents a medal to one of his most effective fighter pilots, Captain Raumback. *(National Archives)*

German Ace Adolf Galland was the leading German fighter pilot and ultimately became commander of fighters. *(National Archives)*

A PBM in flight. This is the type of plane flown by Joe Layer.
(*National Archives*)

An airman proudly shows off with his aircraft. The bombs
and swastikas are symbols of raids and air victories.

Keeping tight formation was one of the secrets of a successful mission with minimal losses.

Contrails, formed by exhausts in the thin air, mark the passage of the big bombers on a mission.

but he deviated and headed out to sea, flying low over the ground, following the land contour. What he did not know was that an invasion fleet of Allied warships was out there, and that by not following orders, he was putting himself outside the protection zone. Or so it was said—in fact, there was no protection zone.

The pilot made a left turn and headed for the coast, going down to 200 feet above the ground. They started to get flak again, and this time Sergeant Yuhasz saw that the red balls were going through the aircraft.

"I looked out the window and saw that we were flying alongside of a ship. We were flying so low that I would look up and see the sailors and the guns and the tracers coming down at us. The pilot turned on the lights on the bottom of the plane, which were the color of the day, and he banked to right and left to show them. The only effect that this had was to give away our position, and the fire increased. I looked back into the cargo section and could see the red balls flying through the airplane. The sound was similar to that made by a punch press. The shells would come in one side of the plane and go out the other. The pattern was that the shells would work forward, so that the final shells went through the airplane in the cockpit right above our heads. It was very much like in the movies when you see the holes appear one after the other in the side of the airplane.

"The shells were coming through all the time. As we left one ship, the next one would pick us up."

The radio operator was sitting upright in his chair and shells were going all around him, even through the radios. He did not move.

Sergeant Yuhasz was standing in back of the pilots, looking out the window. The pilots were slumped in their seats so that their eyes were just above the dash, and they could just see out the window.

Suddenly the copilot cried out, "Up-up-up!" and motioned with his hands.

The pilot yanked back on the wheel, and they missed the ship that had loomed up in front of them by feet.

There was a loud explosion.

That must have been the ship that got them. Something had hit the left engine. Sergeant Yuhasz could hear the pilot and copilot shouting, but he could not understand what they were saying. He thought he was the only one left intact. He headed back to the rest of the plane because he had heard that the tail section sometimes survived a crash, and he was sure they would crash at any moment.

The door from pilot compartment to cargo compartment had been jammed by a flak burst, but he bent the door and got through it somehow. The floor of the plane was strewn with Plexiglas from the windows broken by the flak. He lay down on the floor and held onto a panel that held the bucket seat above him and waited. More shells came through the fuselage just above his head.

The pilot was blown out of his seat into the aisle by a flak burst in the cockpit. The copilot took the wheel and held the plane steady. The pilot got up and cut the magneto switches, and the copilot landed the plane in the water.

As the plane hit the water, Sergeant Yuhasz was catapulted along the floor and hit the bulkhead that separated cabin and cockpit. In an instant he was buried beneath life rafts, cranks, seats, and all kinds of gear torn loose from its fastenings by the impact.

The plane hit and skipped six times. Each time copilot Moore was able to right it, but the left engine was on fire. Finally they hit hard, the engine went under, and the fire went out.

When the aircraft stopped, Sergeant Yuhasz dug his way out of the mountain of debris and began to run for the door. Then radio operator Triick called to him, and for the first time Yuhasz realized that he was not the only one left alive in the aircraft. Triick said they should launch a life raft.

They pulled some life rafts out of the rubble. Sergeant Yuhasz inflated his Mae West and jumped into the water to hold the raft so it would not be carried away from the door. Triick opened the raft bag, pulled out the raft, and pushed it half out the door. Then he pulled the cord to inflate it.

Instead of inflating, the raft made a loud noise, "Razzzzoooo," and that was all. They realized that the raft had been shot up and would not hold the gas. Triick found another raft, but it too was destroyed by flak. Finally, a third raft held together and inflated properly in all sections. Triick then pushed the raft into the water, only to find that it was upside down. He jumped into the water to try to right it, and he and Yuhasz looked at it dumbly. Just then copilot Moore appeared at the door screaming, and jumped into the raft.

"We gave up trying to turn the raft over because he was lying on the raft, screaming. We saw that his head was all bloody. He had hit it against the windshield when the plane stopped. He had cuts all over him and was bleeding badly."

The copilot was lying on the overturned raft, and it was beginning to drift away from the door. Triick and Yuhasz were in the water. The pilot was still in the cockpit, and the tail of the plane was rising, which meant the nose was going down. Triick got aboard the overturned raft and began to paddle back toward the door.

Yuhasz was in the water holding the raft with his left hand. He could just reach the floor of the plane, but when he tried to pull himself up his fingers slipped off, because the floor was beveled downward to accept the loading ramps. He decided to get up on the raft and climb into the plane, but just then the pilot appeared in the doorway, having pulled himself along the floor from the cockpit.

"I asked him if he could get himself onto the raft, and he said he could not. So I asked him if he could fall into the water—I would grab him and Triick and I would roll him onto the raft. That is what he did. He just rolled forward and fell three or four feet into the water. When he hit the water, I grabbed him and held him so that his head was above water. Herb pulled him and I pushed him up onto the raft."

As soon as the others were safely aboard the overturned raft, Sergeant Yuhasz climbed on. They immediately started to paddle away from the aircraft, because the tail had risen more and they were worried about the suction of the aircraft when it went down.

By the time they were past the wingtip, the plane had assumed a 30-degree angle. And then very quietly and smoothly the plane slid down and forward without even a ripple, and it was gone.

So there they were, the four of them, in the middle of the Mediterranean on an overturned raft. Around them they could see the ships firing at other aircraft. A C-47 flew over them low, throttles wide open, roaring as it went.

They began to take stock. Pilot Halas had been wounded in the left hand and left leg and hip. The leg wounds looked like craters, about three inches in diameter, and he could not sit up or move about.

Yuhasz and radioman Triick sat on the edge of the raft, with the two wounded pilots stretched out in the middle. Yuhasz threw away his shoes as useless and sat with his feet in the water. Then he remembered a movie in which Edward G. Robinson had trailed his hand in the sea from a small boat and a shark had bitten off the hand. Sergeant Yuhasz took his feet out of the water.

They looked around. The shoreline came up in the distance. (They had been shot down ten miles off the coast of Scoglitti.) They were drifting slowly out to sea. Nearby they saw the two leaky rafts and realized these were valuable because they contained emergency provisions and water. They gathered up the rafts and lashed them to their own raft.

They decided that they must have been shot down by the Italian navy, but they still had to take the chance of capture to attract attention and get help for the wounded pilots. Radio operator Triick got a Very pistol out of one of the rafts, and Yuhasz fired a flare.

"The flare shot up into the sky, made a loop, and started down. As it started down the ships around us opened up on us, and the tracers were racing at us from several different directions. The shells zipped over at about ten feet above us and we were all screaming again. Instead of getting help with our distress signal, we were being fired upon. [But] the firing did not last long, and soon we were floating around again in the quiet, black night."

Later that night they saw a large ship heading for them. They talked about firing another flare, but were afraid that the ship would begin shooting at them, so they did not. The ship came up, and they stared at the two big guns in the turret. The ship kept coming on toward them. It stopped about 100 yards away. "Hello there!" shouted Sergeant Yuhasz.

"Who are you?" demanded a voice from the ship.

"Americans."

Yuhasz could hear the people on the ship talking to each other and he thought they were speaking Italian.

Nonetheless they needed help for the wounded.

"Come on," shouted Yuhasz, "take us aboard. We have wounded men here and we need help."

Someone with an English accent told them to come alongside the vessel. So they paddled to the ship and the men aboard the vessel threw them a line.

The ship was the HMS *Abercrombie*, a very old-fashioned monitor with antitorpedo plating on its sides. With difficulty they managed to get alongside, and then sailors came down and helped get the pilot and copilot up onto the deck. They treated the wounded and wrapped the two unwounded men in blankets and told them to sleep, which they did.

The crew of the *Down and Go* had jumped their troops at 11:30 p.m. on July 11, and were picked up by the *Abercrombie* at 3 a.m. on July 12.

The next day they were taken to the USS *Ancon*, the command ship for the area, and they learned that General Mark Clark and several other high-ranking officers were aboard. They also learned that they had been shot down by American ships!

Here is the story told to them by the officers of the *Ancon*:

On the night of July 11, when the C-47s were scheduled to fly over the fleet, the *Ancon* had signaled to other ships that friendly planes would be flying over around midnight and that they should not fire on them. But shortly before midnight, some ships were attacked by a handful of German bombers, so the gunners began firing at everything they saw.

When the American planes began coming in at 11:30 the *Ancon* again signaled a warning that these were American aircraft, but the tyro gunners of this untried American fleet were paying no attention. The *Ancon* ordered the ships to stop firing, but they would not stop. That night the American navy shot down fifty-four American C-47s, in one of the most disgraceful incidents of lack of discipline and "friendly fire" of the entire war.

Lieutenant Moore, Sergeant Yuhasz, and radioman Triick went ashore at Oran and returned to the unit, while Pilot Halas was repatriated to an American hospital. Sergeant Yuhasz returned to the base and went back to duty. His squadron mates had thought he was dead, and had begun to parcel out his belongings.

A few weeks later Sergeant Yuhasz was sent to a rest camp at Ain Taya, a village on the Mediterranean coast five miles east of Algiers. There he swam in the sea, ate three good meals a day, and spent much of his time sleeping.

At the rest camp Sergeant Yuhasz met one of the Eighty-second Airborne troopers who had jumped into Sicily from his airplane. They had landed in a plowed field along the road, he said, and they all got down safely. They were about five miles from the drop zone, and luckily so, said the trooper. If they had been dropped in the drop zone they probably would have been killed, because the Germans were zeroed in on the area with tanks and field pieces and many machine guns. He had come back after the Sicily fighting to discover that almost all of the men of his unit had been killed.

And so ended the misadventure of the Sicily invasion, the product of troop carrier command's lack of experience and the poor fire discipline of the American naval units, which were seeing their first action in World War II. Everybody was going to have to learn.

# TWENTY-SEVEN

# *Regensburg*

In October 1942, when the Eighth Bomber Command in England had turned to making raids on the German U-boat pens around Lorient and the Cactus Air Force on Guadalcanal was turning the tide in the air battles around Henderson Field, Captain Tom Jeffrey was ordered up from Guatemala to the Air Force Bombardier School at Fort George E. Wright, near Spokane, Washington. In two weeks he was given a nine-month course as pilot-bombardier, and after that he was ordered to nearby Geiger Field. There the Air Force was building cadres for the fledgling Eighth Air Force, at the rate of one cadre per month, and shipping each one out with four aircraft.

At Geiger Field they were delighted to see Captain Jeffrey, who had far more experience in multi-engine aircraft than most officers. He was assigned to the 391st Squadron of the Thirty-fourth Bomb Group, and four days later he was made squadron leader.

The training program was fast and furious. They flew to Blythe, California, without maps, and only made it because they squeezed their way across the Rockies and then managed to find Las Vegas.

At Blythe the training continued. But again the exigencies of war made affairs move fast. On February 16, 1943, Lieutenant Colonel Irvine Rendle of the Thirty-fourth Bomb Group learned that he had been instructed to activate the 390th Bombardment Group. He asked Major Jeffrey, commander of the 391st Bomb Squadron, to become his deputy.

"Man, that's great," said Major Jeffrey.

And so, it seemed, it was settled.

But it wasn't. Rendle and Jeffrey had just completed the organization of the 390th and were preparing to go overseas when Rendle was reassigned as commander of a B-24 bombardment group. His old friend Lieutenant Colonel Ed Wittan became the new group commander. The 390th were ordered to Orlando, Florida, for tactical training and then back to Geiger Field for more training. Then the squadrons were assigned to their own fields. They flew to Great Falls, Montana, and then Cutbank and Lewistown and Glasgow. They were ordered across the country. Major Jeffrey led forty-eight planes on that trip. Again, half the time they were not sure where they were going. Flying across America's wheat belt, one little town with its grain elevators looked very much like another. Major Jeffrey finally discovered that they were at Salina, Kansas, by swooping down to read the lettering on the grain elevator.

They stopped off at Kansas City, where he had a few hours with his wife Helen, but then it was on to Langley Field. On the way, Major Jeffrey took a slight detour, and buzzed the house and slate works at Arvonia. He also made another slight detour because of bad weather, and found himself suddenly looking at the Washington Monument and the Capitol. Flying over Washington was forbidden—if the government could have made it a capital offense, it probably would have. Jeffrey gulped, ducked into the clouds, and did not emerge until he was over Annapolis. When he landed, a very suspicious field commander asked where he had been.

Flying in to duty, said Major Jeffrey.

"Where did you fly coming in here?"

"Off the coast of Ocean City."

"Did you fly over Washington?"

"Why sir, you know that is practically a capital offense . . ."

"Well, goddamit, somebody did, and the Pentagon is raising hell."

But the Pentagon never discovered the number of the airplane or the name of the miscreant.

More flights, up to Bangor, Maine, and then across to Prestwick, Scotland. The real war was coming nearer.

At Prestwick they were told they could not possibly make England without an escort, and an Air Transport Command pilot was assigned to escort them to East Anglia. But the ATC pilot got lost, and instead of going to Ipswich, they ended up on the other side of England, near Liverpool.

Here, in the summer of 1943 the Eighth Air Force was still on "hold" while the major action was in the Mediterranean. But Major Jeffrey swiftly learned what their mission was going to be. Together the Eighth and Fifteenth air forces were dedicated to the strategic bombardment of the German empire, and particularly to the destruction of the German Luftwaffe.

The new boys had to have some seasoning, and the old boys who had been flying missions for a year were there to give it to them. Major Jeffrey's first mission was with the Ninety-fifth Bombardment Group, as an observer. Lieutenant Colonel John Gearhart, the group commander, took them to Rostock.

The 390th's first mission was flown on August 12, 1943.

The target was a synthetic oil plant at Wesseling in the Ruhr valley. At the briefing Lieutenant R. Rowland, pilot of the 570th Squadron's *Virgin Sturgeon*, listened as the briefing officers talked about flak. They should remember that the black smoke of the bursting flak shells was primarily a psychological weapon. They should also remember that they would have Spitfire escorts as far as the English Channel. Why not beyond? Because the Spitfires did not have the range to fly farther.

After the briefing, the B-17s began to take off. They crossed the Channel, said goodbye to the Spitfires and flew toward the Ruhr Valley. As they approached the Ruhr, the antiaircraft guns opened up. Lieutenant Rowland was scared:

"I was completely demoralized at the sight of the black smoke of the shell bursts. As we entered the valley I received a shell burst just under my left wing which knocked me out of formation. I lost about a thousand feet of altitude before I recovered.

"Scared as I was, my only thought was to get back to my position in the formation. So, with a lot of maneuvering and fighting prop wash, I was able to get back to position."

When the 243 planes were in the air, the weather suddenly worsened in the Ruhr Valley and they attacked a secondary target, an optical instrument plant at Bonn. It was not a very good mission. They bombed and broke a bridge across the Rhine and put some bombs into the railroad yards, but most of the bombs went into the residential district and nearby fields.

Lieutenant Rowland reported, "I was so scared I never realized we had completed our bomb run and [had] started to return to base."

For him, the first was the worst.

Of all the targets of the 390th, three stood out in Tom Jeffrey's memory: Regensburg, Muenster, and Schweinfurt.

Regensburg was the site of a major production facility that was making two-hundred ME-109 fighters every month. It was a long flight from England, and those up above decided that it would be a shuttle mission, with the B-17s going on to land in Africa after bombing. The leader of this mission was Lieutenant Colonel Wittan, not flying his own plane, but standing between the pilot and copilot in the lead bomber, *Cabin in the Sky.*

The mission began before dawn. Almost immediately there was excitement. The aircraft flying on the right wing of the *Cocaine Bill* suddenly spewed out parachutes over England. Apparently the bailout bell had somehow been triggered in their flight, and the men in the rear of the aircraft thought they were supposed to bail out. One waist gunner hooked up his chest pack and went to jettison the waist door. The other waist gunner was right behind him. Below they saw houses of a village too close below, and the first man hesitated. The second gunner thought he was afraid to jump and kicked him out. They were both lucky that their parachutes had time to open.

The plane went on, minus its waist door and two gunners.

Aboard the *Cocaine Bill,* radio operator Wilbert H. Richarz had watched the two gunners jump. Now he concentrated on the work at hand. The ground station went into a silent period about an hour before target time. Pilot Jack Bouton broke the silence:

"You'd better man the waist gun, Rich. We're under fighter attack."

Gunner operator Richarz hurried back to the waist. He had some trouble connecting the oxygen line, electric suit plug, and radio connection. When he had done so, the chatter of the other machine guns in the plane was clearly audible. The interphone squawked as each gunner called out what he was seeing. Mostly what they were seeing just then was a major attack by German fighters on the squadron just below them. The orange flashes from the 20mm cannon brightened the sky.

"With each pass that they made, bombers would tumble out, as many as three at a time, and go spinning end over end belching flame and black smoke. Some few turned out of formation, afire and streaming flame, and fell out behind to die a slower death. A fortress pilot once wrote a story about his ship called 'Queens Die Proudly,' and I thought of that as I watched those ships go down." After three or four passes, that squadron below them had been completely wiped out (though one B-17 did make it back to England), and then the German fighters moved up to attack the 570th Squadron. Richarz searched the sky for fighter escort, but there was none. The fighters were having their own troubles up in the front of the formation, where they were beset by dozens of German fighters.

"The fighters came in on us like so many angry bees—diving at our formation from the rear and then breaking away to circle and try again. Dixie Anderson (tail), Hap Hallek (ball) and Snake Myers (upper turret) were all talking on the interphone at once, calling out attacking ships and remarking about the ships they could see going down.

"Then Dixie would break in with a shout: 'Get off the interphone—here they come!' And then, since Dixie was in the best position to call out the tail attacks, there would be momentary silence while Dixie gave us the poop.

"Suddenly he called out, 'Here come three at four o'clock high.'

"That being my side, I strained against the Plexiglas to see if I could pick them up. I saw this one joker at three o'clock about 400 yards out, a sleek-looking dull-colored FW-190, his blunt nose swinging in toward us fast. I picked up my lead and opened fire at about 300 yards, just as his ship swung into position to fire on us. . . . I fired in long bursts, and I could see flashes of flame on the wings and engine cowling where strikes were scored. [But] though I kept firing and seemed to be hitting him, he kept boring in.

"His ship wavered, the gap of distance closed between us rapidly, and I realized he was practically flying formation with us.

"He came in high, and the nose of his ship was no longer pointed at us, so he was not in position to fire on us. I found myself looking at a gunner's dream, a no-deflection shot, the legendary sitting duck, and that a mere fifty yards or so away. . . . I centered my sight on him and cut loose. . . . The 190, now clearly defined against the sky, wobbled and wavered. Smoke streamed out from around the engine in a dense cloud, and over the sight of my bucking gun I could see the pilot fumbling desperately to unfasten his canopy cover.

"As I aligned the sights on him he looked down at me, and our eyes locked. His look was one of fear and pleading. He was begging me not to shoot. . . ."

"From a practical viewpoint I knew I *should* shoot. The Germans had few pilots but plenty of planes. If I let him go, he could come back tomorrow and shoot down who knows how many B-17s. Besides, how many B-17s had he accounted for already?

"But I could not pull the trigger—I held off. The next split second the canopy blew, and out he went. In the instant that he seemed to hang there in midair I could see clearly the details of his flying suit. Then he was whisked away below our tail.

"I stopped firing and yelled into the interphone, 'I got him! I got him!' only to find to my surprise that Snake was doing the same thing from the top turret. We had both tacked the same ship in and fired on it.

"Hap was calling out from the lower ball that he had just shot another one down, and the bombardier was saying something about the bomb bay doors opening. Dixie's guns were still hammering away. At 'Bombs Away' and just before I made my way back to the radio room to check the bomb bays, I remember I could still see the fighters queuing up. Right after 'Bombs Away' Dixie got a kill, a twin-engine job."

The attacks dwindled, and shortly afterward radio operator Richarz was back at the radio copying code and wondering if it had all been a dream.

After the bombing, the surviving planes headed for North Africa, because the target was too far from home for a round-trip on one load of gas. It was the first shuttle mission.

From North Africa Colonel Curtis LeMay, who had led the mission overall, radioed a message to headquarters:

"Mission flown as planned. Fighter support poor. Wing under constant attack from Antwerp for thirty minutes after leaving target. Objective believed to be totally destroyed. . . . Airplanes have landed at a number of fields other than those scheduled, due to battle damage and gas shortage."

The mission began with 146 planes. Of the 127 that attacked, 24 were lost. The 390th lost two planes in the target area. A third lost two engines but landed safely in Switzerland, and a fourth plane, also in trouble, headed for Spain but landed at Toulon in southern France, and the crew were made prisoner. Two other 390th planes ran out of gas and ditched in the Mediterranean, and the crews were picked up by the Air Sea Rescue Service.

The group's planes collected at Telergma, North Africa, and camped for several days under the wings of their aircraft, living on K rations. Then they went home.

Back at the base in England, radio operator Richarz learned what had happened to that other plane which had lost the two waist gunners before the mission really began. When the German fighters began to hit the formation, the lower ball gunner shot off all his ammunition and then manned the waist guns one by one. He shot down three German fighters, and the plane completed the mission.

# TWENTY-EIGHT

# Quixotic Mission

Sometimes the missions of the 390th Bombardment Group were led by Colonel Wittan or Lieutenant Colonel Tom Jeffrey, who was now air executive of the group. Usually the war itself was pretty grim, but once in a while what the British call a "cockup" occurred, affording some mild amusement.

One morning, after briefing the crews for the day's mission, Colonel Wittan, the group operations officer, and Lieutenant Colonel Jeffrey adjourned to the control tower at Framlingham and waited for takeoff. It was dark—it seemed always to be dark when the planes began to take off for a mission.

At a signal, the planes started taxiing toward the runway. The planes would taxi in order of takeoff to the end, and wait in a staggered formation, with six planes on the runway and others stretched out along the perimeter taxi strip.

Just before the moment of takeoff the engineering officer came to the tower and told Colonel Wittan that the group leader for the mission was still back on the hardstand with a flat tailwheel tire.

The radio was blacked out, so there was no easy way to tell the No. 2 wingman that he would have to lead the formation up and assemble at 18,000 feet. Colonel Wittan knew only one way to pass the word. He turned to Lieutenant Colonel Jeffrey:

"Take my staff car and ride around to the end of the runway and tell the pilot of No. 2 to take the group up to the assembly altitude."

Jeffrey went out to the car and sped down the runway. He pulled the car off the runway opposite the lead airplane, left the lights on and the engine running, and jumped into the back door of the B-17. He had on a summer flight suit, but not the altitude gear.

Just as Jeffrey stepped into the plane, the pilot pushed the throttles forward for takeoff. Jeffrey yelled, but with four engines roaring nobody heard him. He worked his way up through the waist gun compartment, the radio room, the bomb bay, and up through the top turret. By the time he reached the cockpit the plane was traveling at 60 mph down the runway and it was too late to cut the engines, because the next plane in line would start moving in fifteen seconds.

Jeffrey moved to a position behind the two pilots' seats and stood there. When the gear came up and the plane was under control, he reached over and tapped the pilot on the shoulder. The pilot turned around.

"What the hell are you doing up here?"

"It's a long story. But let's keep going until we get organized."

So they started to climb and circled around, getting the formation pulled together. Jeffrey began to get cold in his summer flying suit. He had no jacket, parachute, or oxygen mask, yet it looked as though he was about to go to Germany.

There were only two ways to get Jeffrey back to the ground. One was to abort the mission—at least this plane's mission. The other was for Jeffrey to bail out.

Neither was attractive. Aborting was a very serious matter in the 390th Group. Anyone who aborted had to report immediately to Lieutenant Colonel Jeffrey, who almost always could find some reason to read the pilot off for error. If Jeffrey were now to cause the aircraft to abort, his credibility as a tough flight boss would be seriously eroded.

As for bailout, that was quickly resolved when they discovered there was no extra parachute on the aircraft.

The aircraft continued to circle around the assembly point at 18,000 feet, and a shivering Lieutenant Colonel Jeffrey gulped at the emergency oxygen bottle. Soon the group leader showed up and took over, his tailwheel tire fixed. They pulled off on the wing.

Now what to do?

Would Jeffrey go to Germany and freeze half to death on the way? And what if the aircraft was a casualty? How would he get out? Was he going to abort the mission? There was no way he could take a parachute from a crew member on his way to enemy territory.

Fortunately, just then fate intervened. The radio came on, and operations announced that the mission had been canceled. Heavy weather over the target would make bombing very iffy. The group leader got on the radio.

"Mission canceled. Heavy weather over target."

The men of the 390th gave little silent cheers, none of them more fervent than Jeffrey's.

They carried a full load of bombs and a full load of fuel, so they had to circle for four more hours to lose fuel before it was safe to come in for landing.

When they reached the hardstand, Lieutenant Colonel Jeffrey got out of the aircraft and went to the quarters he shared with Colonel Wittan. The colonel was just waking up from a nap, since he had gotten up at 2 a.m. for the briefing. He looked at his air executive.

"Jeff, will you please tell me where the hell you have been? And why did you leave my car at the end of the runway with the engine running and the lights on?"

Lieutenant Colonel Jeffrey looked at the colonel.

"Well," he said, "I'll tell you, it was like this . . ."

# TWENTY-NINE

# Twenty-Sixth Fighter Squadron

Lieutenant Ray B. Stone began his military career as an aviation cadet, became a flight instructor, trained in dive bombers, and then was moved to B-17s as copilot and then pilot. He ended up in 1943 as a fighter pilot in the Fourteenth Air Force in China, Fifty-First Fighter Group, Twenty-Sixth Squadron.

After flying many missions, Lieutenant Stone concluded that the most dangerous aspect of flying the P-51 was rifle and small-arms fire from the ground. Most of his squadron's losses were from being hit by ground fire during low-level strafing.

"A hit in the coolant system anywhere in a P-51 meant you had exactly eight minutes to head for the hills away from Japanese-occupied territory before you had to bail out or belly in."

Here is Stone's account of a fighter strike on Kukiang on the Yangtze River:

"Six P-51-Ds. You are a P-51 pilot leader. Ray Stone. Known as the Green Hornet. Price on head $50,000 gold. Mission: seek out shipping.

"Armament: two 500-pound demolition bombs—ten-second delay—under wings with 3200 pounds of fragmentation bombs slung over each demolition bomb; 2400 rounds of .50 caliber ammunition for the machine guns, designed to converge at 3000 yards, every sixth round was tracer. Armor piercing.

"Objective: eight large freighters in the harbor. Seek and destroy.

"Technique: Take off from Kunming airfield in flights of two.

Join up over airfield at 10,000 feet. Fly loft echelon stacked down. Fly heading 90 degrees for one hour, head 180 degrees to Kukiang, approximately one hour and twenty minutes with throttle leaned back. Maintain alert.

"When target is sighted, snap on gun sight. Note to others: 'Do not fire until I fire first.'

"Arm bombs selectively. Will drop left bomb first.

"Full throttle while over target (approximately thirty minutes).

"Start shooting at 300 yards. Fire spasmodically to prevent gun overheating and jamming. Maintain maximum speed at all times.

"Stay in two-ship flights. Guard your tail.

"Drop bomb with ten-second delays; time to get the hell out of the way.

"I will take the first ship to the right; my wing man takes the second. After passing over the target, check instruments to determine if you are hit. Execute maximum performance climbing turn to left. We will go into Lufbery circle to left and come around again. Stay stacked down from plane ahead so empty shell casings do not hit you.

"Maintain radio silence except in dire emergency.

"Keep proper spacing to protect each other's tails.

"Look out for Zeros!

"If a Zero is spotted, be calm! Tell his exact location: ten o'clock high, or eight o'clock low, or level, or whatever. Nothing is as disturbing as for someone to shout: 'There's a Zero!' He could be at 360 degrees on the compass and coming at you out of the sun.

"As you come around for a second time, determine whether to hit the same ship again or go for another. Remember, a near miss [bomb] is more damaging than a direct hit on shipping.

"Keep guns firing intermittently. There will be less firing back at you.

"Maintain Lufbery circle.

"After about a half hour on target, I will waggle my wings. We'll make one more pass to allow all to get rid of bombs, then we will join up at 4000 feet and ten miles north form up in V formation, flights of two. Look out for Oscars [Japanese army fighters] out of sun.

"We head for home. I want a signal from each element leader if all is okay. We climb to 10,000 feet with sharp lookout for enemy fighters.

"Throttle back to maximum lean. Guard your oxygen; use only as needed.

"Set or reset 'little airplane' for level flight if we have to go into clouds.

"Carefully read all instruments, fuel level.

"Set course for home, prearranged map plan, course 290 degrees. Start looking for landmarks. Check watch. Fly by time and distance. Pray.

"Once Kunming is sighted, check ones low on fuel; lowest goes in first. 360-degree overhead approach for landing.

"Meet friends on revetment at alert shack.

"Time to resume poker game with Chennault."

# THIRTY

# Hankow

August 21, 1943: The target was the great Chinese river port city of Hankow on the Yangtze River, one of the central operations and supply ports of the Japanese, and also a base of the Japanese army air force for fighter pilot training. There were so many Japanese airfields in the area that it was regarded as a suicide target.

But the mission was assigned, and that was that. Before it could be carried out, the weather took a turn for the worse. The pilots and crews of the 374th and 375th bombardment squadrons of the Fourteenth Air Force's 308th Bomb Group had been sitting and waiting, as they did so often in China. They were waiting for a weather change. For three days a frontal system with low clouds, rain, and fog had hung over Chengkung and most of southwestern China, extending to the eastern slope of the Himalayas.

This mission called for fourteen B-24s to assemble over Chengkung and fly to Hengyang, where they would pick up fighter cover from the fighters stationed there, and then go on to bomb the warehouses and docks at Hankow.

The fourth day dawned bright and sunny, and the planes had their weather clearance. They taxied up to take off like a herd of elephants, one by one. The lead aircraft was flown by Major Bruce Beat, the commander of the 374th Squadron, with Captain George Bell, his A flight commander, as copilot. The second flight was led by Major Phil Adler, the 374th operations officer.

The 375th Squadron contingent was led by Major Henry G. Brady, Jr., the commanding officer of the squadron.

They flew to Hengyang, but found no fighters there to meet them. They looked down at the Hengyang airfield and saw that it had just recently been shot up by the Japanese, and the fighters were either wrecked or hidden. They were used to this sort of action, because Japanese spies were very active in China, and the Japanese had obviously gotten wind of the mission. There would be no fighter protection, and they could expect the enemy to be alert at Hankow. They might also expect Japanese fighters to meet them there.

They had three options:

1. Land at Guilin or Hengyang and wait for fighter support that might or might not materialize.
2. Abort the mission and return to the base at Chengkung.
3. Fly to Hankow and bomb without escort.

Mission Leader Beat opted for the third course, and so they stopped circling and headed for Hankow.

Suddenly, before Hankow was sighted, Beat's B-24 went into a steep dive, followed by most of the 374th aircraft, who apparently thought he was executing a combat maneuver. But it soon became apparent that Beat's aircraft was on fire. He had been jumped by a swarm of Zero fighters that suddenly appeared. And in just a moment, the B-24 blew up.

The Japanese had indeed known they were coming, and more than fifty enemy fighters were attacking.

The Zeros concentrated on the planes of the 374th Squadron, and soon that formation was in shambles, with Zeros attacking B-24s all over the sky. But now P-40 fighters appeared to challenge the Zeros too. In the confusion Major Brady pulled away, and the planes of the 375th followed him and left the melee. One of their number was shot down and the pilot was killed. The other crew members parachuted and were picked up by Chinese guerillas and eventually returned to Chengkung.

One plane of the 374th tagged onto the 375th formation and stuck with them during the rest of the mission. They reached Hankow and bombed the target and then began the long journey home.

They would have to make their way through the enemy cordon, so Major Brady led them down to a much lower level, hoping to evade the Zeros on the way back and give the top gunners of the B-24s the best view for shooting. The Zeros came, mostly with frontal attack. The B-24s damaged some Zeros; together with the fighters and a flight of B-25s that were also attacking Hankow that day, they claimed to have shot down twenty Japanese fighters. Major Brady could not attest to that. He was too busy evading and maneuvering to keep any count. Finally they reached Hengyang and landed. The 374th, or what was left of it, did the same.

When they surveyed the damage, they discovered that of the fourteen B-24s that had set out, only five were left in shape for combat. Major Beat was lost, so Brady became senior officer, and was ordered to be prepared to return to Hankow the next day. But when he reported only five aircraft ready for the mission, Fourteenth Air Force Headquarters scrubbed the assignment. Instead of going to Hankow, Brady was ordered to Kunming to report to General Claire Chennault, commanding officer of the Fourteenth Air Force, and explain.

This was Brady's first meeting with "the old man." Colonel John Neal, Fourteenth Air Force operations officer, met Brady at the airstrip and warned him that the general was very deaf, so he must speak up.

The general greeted them with a smile and listened attentively as Brady told his story, cupping his hand behind his ear to catch the words.

When the major had finished the tale, the general asked him why they had proceeded with the mission when they discovered at Hengyang that they had no fighter cover.

The major said that the decision had been Major Beat's as mission leader, but that if he had been in charge he would have done the same.

Chennault smiled and said no more. Major Brady flew back to Chengkung.

The next afternoon the mission pictures were up. Colonel Beebe, commander of the bombardment group, announced that they showed direct hits on the Hankow target, where fires were still burning, and destruction of many Zero fighters.

The success of the raid had put the Japanese on full alert. On August 24th the 373rd Heavy Bombardment Squadron and the 425th were ordered to repeat the raid on Hankow. The 373rd had to abort for weather reasons, but the 425th, with fighter cover of twenty-two P-40s and P-38s and six B-25s, did bomb Hankow again. This time four B-24s were lost, while the 425th claimed to have shot down twenty-four enemy fighters. That day the group lost its operations officer and the commander of the 425th Squadron, Major Ellsworth.

# THIRTY-ONE

# *Sunk!*

Chester W. Driest was working for General Electric in aircraft electronics in Bridgeport, Connecticut when the Japanese struck Pearl Harbor. At the end of 1942 he was drafted and entered the Army Air Force. Because of his job experience he was sent to radio school at Camp Crowder, Missouri. He was so far ahead of his class that the Signal Corps borrowed him as an instructor, until the Air Force demanded him. He was sent to the First Fighter Control Squadron, then at March Field, California, to find that the squadron was on alert for shipment overseas.

No passes.

Driest's wife had been following him from one place to another (once she even worked picking grapes), but now she realized that he was shipping out, so she decided to go home to Michigan for the duration. Her train would be passing through Los Angeles and would stop briefly there.

Driest asked his commanding officer for a few hours' leave but was turned down.

"Tell it to the chaplain," his buddies said when he complained.

So he did, and the chaplain got him the leave and lent him $10 to make the trip to L.A.

He hitched a ride on the highway, but arrived too late at the station. His wife's train had come and gone.

"There I was in Los Angeles with that sick feeling starting in the pit of my stomach. I asked, 'Why do these things happen the way they do?' I decided to make it back to the highway. Soon a car came by which was going right to the base. This fellow who picked me up was also stationed at March Field, so during the trip we told each other about how this war was screwing up everyone and everything, but like it or not . . ."

Driest's job was with air-to-ground and point-to-point communications, which meant aircraft control.

In September the squadron got a new CO, Captain Irwin C. McBride. In October they shipped to Camp Stoneman, and on October 27, embarked on the Army transport *Cape San Juan.* Spirits were high at first, until they sailed and discovered that they were not part of a convoy, as they had expected to be, but were "going it alone."

How small the ship seemed: 417 feet and 6700 tons, with a speed of fourteen knots. She was a new ship, operated by the Hawaii America line. She had been designed as a freighter but altered to be a Victory ship. This was her second voyage; she had first made a trip to Espiritu Santo and Noumea. Now she was carrying troops destined for Townsville, Australia, to augment General Douglas MacArthur's Southwest Pacific Command. All went well on this second voyage of the *Cape San Juan* until November 11, Armistice Day. There was no armistice in this war against the Japan, and that morning at 5:30 a Japanese torpedo slammed into the side of the *Cape San Juan* near the Fiji Islands.

Airman Driest and his fellows of the First Fighter Control Squadron were in No. 1 hold, and the torpedo hit in No. 2 hold just below the waterline. Driest made his way up to the deck. The gunners were firing their deck guns to keep the submarine down if it was still in the area. Crewmen were lowering the lifeboats. Driest went to the rail and looked over. The "Abandon Ship" order had been given and men were already in the water, but they were soaked with oil. The No. 2 hold was an oil bunker, and fuel oil had spilled all around the ship.

Confusion seemed to reign. The lifeboats were overboard, but they were drifting away from the ship with very few men aboard. Other men were throwing life rafts over the side, and some were throwing hatch covers and planks. Driest lent a hand.

"Is there any way we can help?" Driest asked a ship's officer.

"You'd better abandon ship immediately," was the reply.

"But all the rafts and lifeboats are gone."

"Then you'd better jump over the side."

By this time the ship had a 20-degree list. Driest and two friends decided it would be better to go off the low side of the ship, so they crossed the deck. They picked out life jackets, Driest taking a cork jacket instead of kapok. He wondered, would it hold him up, and for how long? But there was no time to be wasted, so the three went over the side.

"The fall into the water from that height was not too bad. The oil was going to be a problem, however. I had already felt some splash into one eye. I quickly closed it, thinking that would help, but it didn't. Now it felt like sandpaper grinding into my eye. I kept my eye closed as I tried to swim away from the ship.

"I called out to my buddies: 'Let's get the hell away from this ship before it blows up or this oil starts to burn.'

"I wondered why we were down here in the water, when the ship was still afloat. At least there were no sharks up there on deck.

"By this time the three of us figured our life jackets would hold us up.

"Off in the distance we could see a raft, as the waves would lift us high above the trough. We knew our only hope was to get to a raft or with some other men. As we began to swim toward the raft we soon understood that it was moving away from us faster than we could swim.

"I realized then that it was just the three of us. . .

"We kept close tabs on each other as the big waves rolled under us. I turned to check our position with respect to our ship. It was nowhere to be seen. My buddies and I figured it must have gone down. Later we learned we had drifted in the strong current some thirty miles from the ship.

"We had been in the water about five hours when I heard the sound of an aircraft. Soon a plane with New Zealand markings flew over at about 1000 feet. The aircraft kept turning in a wide circle, and I could see that they were sending a message by signal light. The guys asked, 'Hey, Driest, what are they saying?'

"My radio code now paid off. The message said, 'Help is on the way.'

"The salt water I had swallowed was giving me a fit. I was very sick. One eye hurting, sick to my stomach, and very weak. I turned to check on my buddies and they were nowhere to be seen. I called out. No answer. The waves by this time were fifteen or eighteen feet in height. As I drifted I thought that maybe the sharks had found them and that they were now dead. Where is everyone? I kept asking myself. Why don't I see a lifeboat or a raft? I began to panic. I was alone. I also remembered seeing sharks earlier in the day."

Airman Driest began to pray.

"I passed out. I remember coming to and hearing the drone of an aircraft. As I scanned the sky with my one good eye, I could see a flying boat making a wide sweeping turn and flying very low. He passed right over me."

The aircraft was a navy PBM. It landed on the water, about a quarter of a mile from Airman Driest. He watched but could not figure out what they were doing, revving the engines and then stopping. Then he saw that the PBM was picking up survivors, and he wondered if they would see him.

They did not see him. After several attempts, the PBM got into the air and flew away.

Driest felt completely alone.

He prayed that night. When day broke, he heard voices and looked around. There, a few yards from him, was a raft. He tried to swim and eventually attracted the attention of the men on the raft. Two men swam over to him and took him to the raft. It was overloaded, and men were clinging to the sides, but one of his squadron mates gave up his position and Driest was hoisted aboard the raft. He passed out. When he came to he went into the water so another man could go aboard the raft. He figured it had been twenty-eight hours since the torpedoing of their ship.

After thirty hours, a ship came up, minesweeper *YMS 241*. Driest wondered why they were shooting from the bow into the water. When a seaman swam up, put a rope under his arms, and hoisted him aboard the minesweeper, he found out. He leaned over on a white canvas bundle, and when he touched it realized it was a body—part of a body. Some of the men in the water had been killed by sharks.

Someone gave Driest a drink of whisky, and two men started to clean the oil off him. Someone gave him clean clothes. He found a space on deck aft of the stacks which was warm, and he curled up there while the ship continued to search for survivors. Soon they were on their way to a hospital at Suva, Fiji. There the survivors were treated for shock and immersion and the injuries caused by the heavy fuel oil.

For a while Driest heard that the squadron had been so decimated that it would be broken up, and he was sent to the Fifth Replacement depot at Camp Ascot, in Brisbane. But the squadron remained and was filled up by replacements.

# THIRTY-TWO

# October Crisis

The second week of October 1943 was a week of crisis for the United States Eighth Air Force, and for the German Luftwaffe. The Eighth Air Force was beginning a major program to reduce German fighting capacity; the Luftwaffe was responding with great vigor and many fighters. It was a week that anyone who lived through would never forget.

On the 390th Group base, the week began on October 8, 1943, with a planned raid on the big German port of Bremen. Everyone knew it would be a tough raid, for the Germans had massed heavy antiaircraft installations around the port, which was in the heart of the airfields that could put up the cream of the German fighter force. Therefore 350 bombers were scheduled to attack Bremen and the U-boat construction facilities at Vegesack. No one in the Eighth Air Force made light of the mission; but the success of the Regensburg mission in virtually eliminating the aircraft plant there had shown how big a job could be done, and Eighth Air Force headquarters said that the results had more than compensated for the losses involved. So here was another such mission.

In the usual morning briefing something new was announced: Forty B-17s from the Third Division would use airborne transmitters to jam German radar. That ought to help.

Lieutenant Colonel Jeffrey led the twenty B-17s of the 390th. The 100th Bombardment Group was also involved, as well as the 388th and the 96th, and B-24s of the Second Division, which would strike Vegesack. The First Division would fly across Holland.

The 100th Bomb Group's Twenty-one aircraft would create a legend this day as they set off from Thorpe Abbots. They were led by Major John Kidd, who had also led the 100th's planes on the Regensburg raid, at 9000 feet. Combat Wing set off that day with six planes in the lead, six low, and nine high. They carried 500-pound bombs.

The 100th Group had a bad reputation, earned in the Regensburg Raid by the plane of Captain R. Knox. The B-17s had run into serious fighter trouble, as noted in the account of the 390th Group's raid, and Knox's plane lost two engines and lagged behind the formation. It was surrounded by German fighters, and Knox lowered the wheels of the B-17. In those days lowering wheels meant the plane was surrendering, and the German fighters, according to the Code of the Air, stopped their attacks. But the engines started up again, and apparently Captain Knox changed his mind about surrendering. His gunners began blasting the German planes that were escorting them and knocked several down. The wheels went up, and the plane made a dash for England. It did not get there. The furious German fighter pilots came in by fives and sixes, and in less than a minute shot the bomber down. Thus the Germans called the 100th Bombardment Squadron "the Bloody 100th," and the Luftwaffe made a pledge to destroy the bombardment group. Whenever the 100th Group flew, the German fighters would concentrate on those planes to the exclusion of other B-17 bomber groups.

Pilot of the plane *Just-a-Snappin'* was Captain Everett E. Blakely, commander of the 418th Squadron. The usual copilot, Lieutenant Charles A. Via, rode in the tail gunner's compartment, serving as formation control officer.

The 100th planes formed up and passed over Framlingham, where the 390th and the Ninety-fifth group planes joined up. This, then, was the Thirteenth Combat Wing. The planes passed over Spalding in perfect formation just after 1 p.m., and less than half an hour later the whole Fourth Air Division was in formation, traveling toward Germany.

The unit passed over Emden, which had been bombed on September 27 and October 2. Down below, the Germans were ready this time and sent up a dense smokescreen. The German fighters also seemed to concentrate on the P-47 fighter escort rather than the bombers.

By about 3:30 the division had passed Emden. The ground haze had cleared away, and ahead a dense black cloud marked the city of Bremen, the result of the flak the German gunners were throwing up at the first heavy bombers to reach the city that day. Lieutenant Harry Crosby, the navigator of the lead B-17, realized suddenly that they had been wrongly briefed—to fly at virtually the same altitude for attack as the group that had gone in before them. The Germans were primed for this division.

Two minutes before Crosby's plane reached target, it was hit by the first burst of *flieger-abwehr-kanonen* fire. A burst struck the ball turret, and although it did not penetrate, it hurt something, for thereafter the turret operated in a jerky manner.

They estimated that 300 antiaircraft guns were down there, perhaps all firing at them!

Half a minute before it was time to drop bombs, a burst struck the nose compartment, shattering the window to the right of the bombardier's head. One fragment ripped through Bombardier James R. Douglass's clothing and flak suit but did not break the lieutenant's skin. He continued to work, and at 3:25 he dropped his bombs on target.

A few seconds later a burst of flak struck the No. 4 engine squarely and knocked it out and shattered the control wires. The left elevator was hit at the same time, and the plane went into a spin, out of control.

Lieutenant Crosby, who was keeping a log of the action, wrote: "We were plunging down in a helpless, careening dive. Flames were blazing from our No. 4 engine. Our control surfaces were all cut and torn."

Other planes saw the *Just-a-Snappin'* fall and observed three parachutes opening below the plane.

Captain Blakely and Major Kidd fought the controls. The major told the radio operator to tell the deputy leader of the 100th Bomb Group to take over. But the plane of the deputy leader of the 100th Bomb Group had been shot down, and so many flight leaders had also been shot down that there was nothing to do but tell the 100th pilots to tag on to the 390th Group for protection.

For 3000 feet the pilots fought the controls, and it was only because the B-17 was a "very forgiving airplane" (as Lieutenant Colonel Jeffrey put it) that they were able to regain control. They leveled off at 19,000 feet and started back for England. As they went they were subjected to constant attack by German fighters, which always singled out the cripples. The crew of the plane claimed to have shot down twelve or thirteen fighters on this mission, but they got official credit for only seven.

Ahead they saw a lone B-17 limping along toward England. It was being harassed by three Messerschmitt fighters, which made pass after pass until the ship burst into flames and went down.

The three Messerschmitts then turned to Blakely's plane, but they soon found that they had bitten off a lot. On the first attack Technical Sergeant Monroe B. Thornton shot the propeller off the first fighter when it came in on the right. The pilot bailed out. Then a second ME-110 came in on the right, high. Thornton began firing, the right engine of the fighter caught fire, and both men bailed out.

flipped up, and exposed its belly. Douglass shot off the whole tail assembly, and the plane went into a spin.

A few minutes later another JU-88 came in from ten o'clock, and Lieutenant Crosby began firing. He must have hit the plane; it did not go down, but it did not make any further attacks, either.

While they were over the bombing target, Lieutenant Via was wounded by flak, but he continued to man the tail gun. Via shot down two ME-210s that came toward the tail, even though he was wounded again by one of them. The two waist gunners, Staff Sergeant Edward Yevich and Staff Sergeant Lester Saunders, each shot down fighters; Saunders was mortally wounded and died in a hospital a week later.

Top turret gunner Staff Sergeant William McClelland was wounded three times, but he continued to man his gun. When the turret was destroyed, he climbed into the waist compartment, and then over the Dutch coast he was hit by flak again.

At 4:20 in the afternoon they reached the Zuider Zee. To avoid

German fighter fields, they turned to cross the West Frisian Islands. They were now at 7000 feet and flying only 120 miles per hour. The shore batteries attacked, knocking out the No. 3 engine and putting many holes in the aircraft. The pilot got through the barrage by jinking, but dropped to 4000 feet. It seemed certain that they would have to ditch the aircraft, but then a survey of the crew's wounds indicated that they couldn't ditch. Technical Sergeant Edmund Forkner, the radio operator, had treated all the wounded, staunched the flow of blood from their wounds, and calmed them with morphine. But he said they could not be moved. Lieutenant Via, Sargeant Thornton, and the other wounded were too badly hurt to get out if the plane ditched.

Lieutenant Crosby recalled: "Our next out was to lighten the load of the plane. We threw everything away. Our guns went first, and the ammunition with them. I threw away my flying equipment, my GEE box, my radio, anything with even an ounce of weight. Now comes an amazing fact. Although our airspeed still remained at 115 to 120 miles per hour, a very small number of miles above the stalling speed of our plane, Captain Blakely not only managed to keep the plane level, but actually gained three hundred feet of altitude."

They hit England near the Ludham airport and saw planes on the ground parked around the field. The moment the aircraft touched the ground, the brake cables snapped. The elevator was useless, the airplane would not steer, and the plane plowed down the runway at 100 miles per hour, heading for a big tree. They hit the tree between the No. 2 engine and the pilot's compartment, going 50 miles per hour. The plane slewed around to the left in a ground loop. The nose compartment was destroyed, but that did not make much difference because the B-17 was riddled with holes from bullets and cannon and flak. The salvage crew counted 800 holes from the tail to the rear of the cabin and then stopped counting.

Their troubles were not over. They had a plane full of wounded, and they discovered that the planes they had seen parked were dummies—it was a disused field. But as they came over the coast they had fired distress rockets, and Sergeant Forkner had somehow managed to send distress signals on the radio. Soon some RAF medical officers arrived with two ambulances and took the wounded to Norwich and to Norfolk General Hospital.

The wounded, except for Sergeant Saunders, who had a cannon hole clear through his body, survived their wounds. Back at the base, Major Kidd learned of the cost. Of the thirty-eight Air Force bombers shot down that day, seven had been planes of the 100th Group. That meant seventy-two combat crewmen either killed or prisoners of war. The Germans were maintaining their vendetta—the 390th, which mounted just one less plane than the 100th that day, lost only three planes to the enemy.

That night at the 100th base, the Century Bombers played dance music and the airmen partied at the Old Officers' Club. There was plenty of food and beer, and the English girls came in by truck and were taken out at midnight. Late that night the Luftwaffe sent an especially heavy raid to London.

Black October had begun for the 100th with a heavy loss.

Other hard days were still to come.

On October 9, the Third Bomb Division went to bomb the Focke-Wulf factory in Marienburg, which was producing about half of the Luftwaffe's FW-190s. The 390th sent twenty-one planes on this mission, and the 100th Bombardment Group sent thirteen. It was an easy mission, if a long and wearying one; neither group lost any planes, because the antiaircraft batteries were very few. But other groups bombing that day lost twenty-eight bombers, mostly to fighters, over Anklam and Danzig. The Thirteenth Combat Wing was just lucky.

October 10 came, and another mission for the Third Division. This one was to Münster, and it was another one the Third Division would remember.

The problem was rail transport in the Ruhr Valley. Most of the rail workers in the valley were billeted in Münster, and so this mission, unashamedly aimed at the city itself and its civilian population, was scheduled in the hope of creating such confusion in housing that the effectiveness of the rail system would be affected sharply. When this was brought out at the briefing, it created some mixed reactions among the airmen. Some of them did not like the idea of going outright against civilians, including captives of the Germans who were working under durance. Some objected to hitting the center of the city, which meant churches and hospitals. This Sunday was going to be full of fireworks, because it was anticipated that the Germans could put up 250 single-engine and 290 twin-engine fighters in this area.

There was a good deal of moaning, but the mission was scheduled, and they had to go.

The Ninety-fifth Group led with twenty planes, the 100th had the low position with twenty planes, and the 390th was flying high this day with nineteen. Six of the 100th's planes aborted over the North Sea or Holland, but the remainder went on. They were escorted by P-47s, which had to turn back about nine minutes flying time from Münster. The replacement fighters somehow got lost and did not show up.

Just then, the Germans began putting up fighters by the score. Soon there were about 250 of them in the air, pursuing the B-17s.

First the Germans flew through the 390th Squadron to get at their particular enemy, the Bloody 100th. The attack was at 23,000 feet, with pairs of FWs in quick succession coming in to within seventy-five yards, attacking and then breaking away. The group leader, *Mademoiselle Zig Zag*, piloted by Lieutenant John Brady, was one of the first to fall. The Luftwaffe had new weapons, rockets, and apparently the B-17 was hit by one in the belly; it trailed a long plume of smoke and began a slow descent. One, two, and three engines quit, and No. 4 started to run away. Waist gunner Harold Clanton had been killed by flak, and ball turret gunner Roland Gangwer was wounded. Bombardier Howard Hamilton was hit in the back by a 20mm shell. But there were still ten survivors, all captured by the Germans.

After this first attack, the B-17s began to fall, one by one. Pilot Winton MacCarter's plane was next. Oberleutnant Heinz Knoke recalled watching from his ME-109: "Feldwebel [Sergeants] Barran and Führmann were flying with me. We all watched as the ME-110s launched their rockets in salvos and could see the dark smoke trails left by the rockets as they streaked in toward the bombers from behind. The sky seemed full of rockets, and we saw two of the fortresses going down."

When B-17 42-30090, piloted by Lieutenant MacCarter, was attacked by two ME-110s, MacCarter noticed that they were firing "long narrow shells." These turned out to be the rockets. Mac-Carter evaded the first ones, but thirty seconds later a rocket struck the left wing, igniting that main gas tank and the No. 1 engine. MacCarter banked to the right to try to sideslip and put out the flames, but he could not. He held the plane steady and rang the bailout bell, while the engineer salvoed the bombs. All ten of the crew parachuted to safety.

Lieutenant Maurice Beatty's B-17 exploded, and only copilot James Dabney and waist gunner Edward Karamol survived.

Lieutenant Robert Kramer's plane was hit over the Dutch-German border. The controls were shot away and the right wing was aflame. Then cockpit exploded and three men were caught, but seven bailed out to safety.

The plane *Forever Yours* flamed and went into a dive. Eight men got out of that one.

Lietenant Charles Walts's B-17 exploded, also destroying the FW-190 that was attacking it, and six men got out. Charles Thompson's Fortress spiraled down in flames, and seven men bailed out.

After the bombing, the B-17 piloted by William Beddow was struck by an ME-109. It exploded, and only four men got out. The engineer, Sergeant Dan James, had the seat of his flying suit blown away, but he survived.

That same collision also involved the plane piloted by Richard Atchison. He got out with five other members of the crew.

And so the Germans worked over "the Bloody 100th," also shooting down the planes of Captain Charles Cruikshank (with eight survivors) and Lieutenant John Stephens, who almost made it to the Channel but belly-landed at Aalten, Holland (all ten men survived.)

After bombing, the crew of *Pasadena Nena* found themselves alone in the air. They dived to find protection with another formation five miles away, but this group was under attack, and

*Pasadena Nena* was hit and damaged. The No. 4 engine went out, and the plane went into a spin. After a struggle with the controls, Pilot John Justice and copilot John Shields gained control—under 1000 feet—and leveled off. There was no sound from the rear, so they assumed that everyone else had bailed out. Then the plane was sprayed with 20mm shells by a single German fighter, wounding copilot Shields, who was manning the top turret. The plane was going down, so the pilots parachuted. Justice was found by the Dutch Resistance and made his way through Holland, Belgium, France, and Spain to Gibraltar. From there he was taken back to London, where he was arrested and held until he could be identified. Lieutenant Shields died of his wounds, and the tail gunner was apparently killed in action, but the other seven crew members had bailed out and were captured.

So the Bloody 100th had all but been wiped out that day. Thirteen of the group's planes reached the target, and twelve of them were shot down. The one 100th plane to return was the *Royal Flush*, piloted by Lieutenant Robert Rosenthal, and this plane had been subjected to a whole series of concentrated attacks by the Germans, again particularly because it bore the insignia of the hated 100th Bombardment Group.

During the bomb run, an aggressive ME-109 came in off the right wing, and the pilot positioned it to start firing. Lieutenant Rosenthal was busy flying the plane and did not see it, but copilot Lieutenant Lewis pushed the control column. This forced the bomber into a shallow dive and put the German out of firing position. Lieutenant Rosenthal did not bat an eye but kept flying the airplane.

Lieutenant Rosenthal put the airplane on automatic pilot and Lieutenant Clifford Millburn, the bombardier, took over. He sighted through the telescope of the Norden bombsight, lined up the target, and dropped the bombs in the target area.

The target area was the main city center. At first the people down below could not believe what was happening. Previous bombings had been directed only at military targets. This was the first all-out raid on a civilian target by the Americans.

A teenager, Hildegard Kosters, looked out the windows of her home in the city center and saw target smoke markers above the railroad station. She and her family ran out into the street and headed for an air raid shelter, a concrete bunker 150 yards away, built below the station platforms. People were trampled in the hurry to get into the shelter. Then the bombs began to explode. The bunker shook with the impact above, and suddenly all the lights went out.

Others could see the action in the clear air above Münster. One man ran toward the shelter, but when the bombs began to fall he ducked down beside the railway's station management building. There he found a window leading to the basement, kicked it in, and dove through. From his hideaway he could hear the bombs and the people screaming as they were trapped beneath houses and rubble. When it was over, half the city had been flattened, and the railway station was a mess. Wherever he looked he saw people dead and injured.

Up above, the last 100th plane, the *Royal Flush*, was heading for home with its No. 1 engine knocked out. Now that it was a cripple, the *Royal Flush* became the object of a series of concentrated attacks by German fighters. Soon the No. 3 engine was hit and the propeller had to be feathered. The oxygen system went next, destroyed by a rocket, and then a rocket went through the right wing, narrowly missing a gas tank.

By that time the two waist gunners, Loren Darling and John Shaffer, had both been seriously wounded. The tail gunner was hit in the hip, and the top turret gunner, Clarence Hall, had a small nick in his forehead. But Hall had shot down two enemy fighters, or so he believed, and Radio Operator Michael Bocuzzi had shot down another. (These claims were later shown to be exuberant by the German records. The 390th claimed to have destroyed sixty-two enemy fighters, but the official German records showed that only twenty-six fighters were shot down that day, and another seven severely damaged.)

Eventually the Germans ran low on fuel and stopped the assaults. But the *Royal Flush* was losing altitude, so all the extra equipment, guns, and ammunition were jettisoned. This done,

Lieutenant Rosenthal was able to bring the airplane back safely to England.

Pilot Rosenthal then accompanied his wounded gunners to the hospital. In the control tower, Colonel Harding waited for word of the rest of his group. When, after Rosenthal had rushed to the hospital, Captain Keith Harris landed his 390th B-17 *Stork Club* at Thorpe Abbotts, the colonel asked what had happened. All shot down, said Harris, all shot down. But the colonel would not believe him, until his story was confirmed by the commander of the Ninety-fifth Group.

The Germans were definitely concentrating that day on the Bloody 100th, the planes with the square D on their tails. They flew through the lead group without attacking, to get at the 100th. After they had disposed of the 100th, they turned to the 390th and then the Ninety-fifth Group. It had taken them only seven minutes to shoot down the planes of the 100th.

The men of the 390th were amazed at the new tactics employed by the Luftwaffe. As they saw it, "While the FW-190s and ME-109s were slipping through the formation, twin-engine fighters stayed out of range and fired explosive cannon shells from 1200 to 1500 yards. JU-88s attacked with rockets from 800 to 1000 yards. One feature was the use of Dornier bombers, which flew parallel to the formation and fired rockets from a 1500-yard range."

One rocket fell inside the fuselage of a B-17, and a waist gunner picked it up and threw it overboard. He said it was a one-pound dry cell battery with one end of tin like a stove pipe.

As the pilots of the Third Bombardment Division wended their way homeward, those of the Thirteenth Combat Wing knew they had been in a very difficult fight. The Bloody 100th was all but wiped out, the 95th had lost five of twenty planes, and the 390th had lost eight of twenty.

As the historian of the 390th Group wrote, "It was the blackest day in the group's history. And to make it worse, on the return to the field heavy haze covered Framlingham. B-17s were full of holes and made as many as three approaches to land. Some landed crossrunway style. One, with seven hundred holes in it, limped to another base with half a crew. Another pilot of one of the Fortresses, with a leg shattered by a cannon shell, stayed in a propped up position directing his copilot to the field."

After Captain Harris, several other pilots of the 390th also landed their aircraft at Thorpe Abbotts. They found it a very dismal place that evening. Lieutenant Rosenthal and some others went to the officers club to try to relax, but the atmosphere was very glum. The 100th had lost twenty-one aircraft and two hundred men in a single week, and the aircrews were talking about the vendetta of the Germans against their air group.

In the debriefing that followed the mission, Lieutenant Rosenthal was the only one who could speak for the 100th. At 10:30 on the morning of October 11, the senior officers of the Third Bombardment Division were debriefed at their headquarters at Elveden Hall, near Thetford. Lieutenant Rosenthal went to tell his sorry tale of what he had seen. He explained how the flak had hit them first and the how they had been torn apart in minutes by enemy fighters. When he finished the room was completely silent.

It was a dismal story he had to tell. As his ball gunner, Sergeant Ray Robinson, put it privately, "The first night, after Bremen, we were too scared to sleep; the second night, after Marienburg (a very long mission), we were too tired, and the third night, after Münster, we were just through—finished."

Lieutenant Colonel Jeffrey, who attended the debriefing of the 390th, said, "This raid had been the worst to date as far as losses of the 390th were concerned. They were felt very heavily by Colonel Wittan and I (sic) who had known each missing crew member since his assignment to the group."

After writing a narrative of the Münster raid, the operations officer of the 306th Bomb Group recommended that missions should not be flown on three consecutive days, since it led to undue fatigue.

Although missions had been scheduled for the next fews days by higher authority, they did not come about because of the weather. On October 12, the groups of the Thirteenth Wing were briefed for Emden, but heavy ground fog caused the scrubbing of the mission. On October 13, the groups were again briefed for Emden and managed to take off, but they were recalled by radio because of weather over the target.

But then, on October 14, a Thursday, the decision was made to attack the ball bearing plants at Schweinfurt.

General Anderson, the commander of Eighth Bomber Command, sent the usual Air Force analysis:

"This air operation today is the most important air operation yet conducted in this war. The target must be destroyed. It is of vital importance to the enemy."

But not many of the men of the 100th were listening. There were not so many of them to listen. They could only manage to put eight airplanes in the air for this one, and the morale of the air crews was about as low as it could get.

Captain Everett Blakely was appointed commander of the 418th Squadron in place of Major John Egan, who had been shot down on the Bremen raid. Captain Albert Elton was appointed commander of the 350th in place of Major Cleven, who had been shot down on the Münster raid.

The officers and men were despondent. They had figured that the life expectancy of a B-17 that autumn was eleven missions. The commander of the Ninety-fifth Bomb Group sent two crew members over to Thorpe Abbotts just after they had finished their twenty-fifth mission and were about to head home, to show that people really could make twenty-five alive, but nobody was much impressed.

On the morning of October 14, about 230 heavy bombers set out to attack the five ball bearing plants at Schweinfurt. The 100th's eight planes were split, four flying with the 390th and four flying with the Ninety-fifth Group. Lieutenant Colonel Jeffrey of the 390th led the Thirteenth Combat Wing planes that day.

The heavy bombers had made an earlier attack on Schweinfurt in August, and consequently the Germans had prepared. They had ringed the town with smoke-making apparatus, put in forty-four heavy antiaircraft guns, and built up airfields around the area with twin-engined fighters. They had also camouflaged the ball bearing works.

Two hundred and ninety-one planes were dispatched to the target by bomber command, but more than sixty aborted or were shot down by fighters before they got there. So 228 planes attacked the target.

Leading the Thirteenth Wing, Lieutenant Colonel Jeffrey took fifteen of the 390th planes over the target area. One plane was shot down by a combination of flak and fighters. But the big problem at Schweinfurt was that the fighter planes that were to have escorted the bombers on their way home were disoriented by bad weather and did not make the rendezvous, so some groups of bombers were harried all the way across the continent.

The planes of the 100th Group all came back, but the 100th was the only unit to lose no planes, and some other groups on the mission were hard hit by fighters and flak. The Eighth Air Force lost sixty heavy bombers that day; the 390th lost eight. Five planes crashed on their return, twelve more were written off after crash landings, and 121 required repairs. Six hundred men were missing or dead, and five dead and fifty wounded were taken from the aircraft that returned.

After Schweinfurt and the two big raids that had gone before in Black October, questions were raised in America and especially in Congress. (The events of Black October became celebrated in the motion picture *Command Decision*, starring Clark Gable.)

At the end of the raid, the Schweinfurt area's ball bearing manufacturing capacity was estimated to have been seventy-five percent destroyed. The Germans did not rebuild above ground but moved production into underground factories.

For its part in this raid the 390th Bombardment Group received the third Presidential Unit Citation granted to the U.S. Air Force:

"Sixty aircraft of the United States Army Air Forces were lost that day. At the time of the mission, the ball and roller bearing plant at Schweinfurt was designated as the most important target in Germany. The three plants comprising the objective account for over 50 percent of Germany's entire supply of ball and roller bearings, which are essential to all makes of aircraft, tanks, and other military equipment. The operation involved a flight of seven hours and ten minutes duration, and covered a total flying distance of 923 miles. Over 370 of these miles were flown without friendly fighter support.

"Carefully planned and savagely executed German fighter attacks persisted from the time the group reached Luxembourg until it was over the channel on the return trip. The 390th Bombardment Group (H) encountered as many as 100 hostile aircraft, both single- and twin-engined fighters, attacking singly, in pairs, and five abreast, simultaneously from all directions. The twin-engined fighters, screened by ME-109s and Focke-Wulf 190s, attacked with cannon and rocket projectiles. Fourteen enemy aircraft were destroyed and an additional five were damaged.

"Antiaircraft fire ripped a hole in the wing of the lead airplane, damaged the windshield of the pilot's compartment, and put the automatic pilot out of commission, effectively preventing its use as an aid on the bombing run. The excellence of the bombing pattern, set under these difficult conditions, and the precision with which it was followed by the other aircraft of this unit, testify to the skill and gallantry displayed. All aircraft bombed on target. Of the 94,000 pounds of bombs dropped by this unit, 36,000 pounds landed within a thousand-foot target area, and 79,000 pounds landed within a two-thousand-foot target area. It is a conservative estimate that it would take from six to nine months for the enemy to restore the factory normal rate of production and the intervening lost production could never be made up. Despite the difficulties and dangers of the enemy defenses, this organization succeeded in attacking and seriously damaging a vital war industry. The aggressiveness, courage, and heroic determination and skill of the officers and enlisted men of the 390th Bombardment Group (H) on this occasion were largely responsible for the success of the mission with a minimum of loss. By the serious damage of the vital industrial plants at Schweinfurt, Germany, this unit rendered an invaluable contribution to the war effort of the United States."

*        *        *

A mission to Duren, a metal industry center, scheduled for October 17 and then October 18, was scrubbed because of weather, but on October 20 the mission was flown. The 100th Bomb Group still had only eight aircraft available for action, and they all went on the mission. A hundred and fourteen planes bombed, but the results were not very effective, because of cloud cover.

That was the end of missions for the Thirteenth Combat Wing for the month of October 1943. The cost to the Americans had been very high, but the cost to the Germans had been much higher. A progress report by the joint British-American air command noted that nineteen important German towns and cities had been destroyed, nineteen severely damaged, and nine more effectively damaged. Another report noted that 10 percent of the total war potential of Germany had been destroyed in strategic bombing raids.

# THIRTY-THREE

# *Escape*

The American effort in the air war was increasing in intensity, and in December 1943 for the first time Americans dropped more bomb tonnage on the enemy than the Royal Air Force.

On the day before Christmas, the Eighth Air Force announced that twenty-six heavy bomber groups were operating from Britain. That day 670 big bombers attacked German missile-launching sites in the Pas de Calais area for the first time. The sites were not yet that heavily defended, and no aircraft were lost.

Among the B-17 groups was the 351st Heavy Bombardment Group. The men had a respite from Christmas Eve until December 30, and then they hit the German synthetic oil plant at Ludwigshafen. There the flak and fighters were intense, and the Eighth lost 123 of the 658 bombers that started on the mission.

On the 31st, another five hundred bombers of the Eighth Air Force took off to hit targets in France. Sergeant F. E. Anderson was all snugged down in his bunk. Having flown the Ludwigshafen mission—his fifth—the day before, he did not expect to be called for a couple of days at least.

But at 2 a.m. on New Year's Day the operations sergeant suddenly appeared in the barracks and got Anderson out of bed with bad news: His crew was flying the day's mission.

Sergeant Anderson got up, dressed, and went to the mess hall and to the briefing. The target was an airfield at Bordeaux.

The course of the 351st would be a wide detour around the Brest peninsula, which bristled with enemy airfields and antiaircraft installations, and then into France across the Bay of Biscay.

The B-17s arrived over the French coast; so did the German fighters, and the Germans had also protected the airfield area with plenty of ack-ack. The fighters were halfhearted in their attacks, but the flak was very heavy and very accurate. Anderson could hear the sound of the antiaircraft shells exploding above the roar of the four engines. Then came a loud noise and a shudder. The B-17 had been hit in the right wing, between engines. The wing began to burn, the engines quit, and the plane dropped out of formation.

"Bail out," the pilot ordered, and the ten men of the crew began to jump.

Sergeant Anderson saw the seacoast below as he bailed out over open farmland. He floated down seeing no other chutes and no one on the ground. There was no reception committee.

On the ground he opened his escape kit and studied the maps. He figured he was 300 miles from the border of neutral Spain. If he could make the border, then he was safe. He began walking south.

Night fell and it grew very cold. The temperature was below freezing. It was too cold to stop and lie down, so Anderson kept walking. From time to time he passed a farm, which he always knew by the sounds of the barking dogs. It made him nervous and he dared not stop.

Before dawn he came to the village of Saujon. He had been told at the briefing that the Germans had imposed a 10 p.m. curfew and that anyone shot down should stay out of civilized areas at night. So he found a place that he thought was safe and holed up there until daybreak. It was very, very cold, so he marched in place and did other exercises to keep from getting chilled.

As morning came, he passed through Saujon seeing no one, and continued to travel south along the road.

By mid-morning he was feeling nervous in his obviously foreign clothing and felt the need to get some civilian clothes. He decided to risk an encounter and stopped at a farmhouse. Using sign language, he identified himself to the farmer, who seemed sympathetic, and told him he needed food and clothing. He was offered milk and bread, which he took, and he exchanged his uniform for a civilian coat and trousers. Then, feeling safer, he headed south again.

Suddenly as he came around a turn in the road he saw a man on a bicycle approaching from the other direction. As the cyclist came up, Anderson recognized the pale blue of the Luftwaffe uniform. The man was a corporal, he saw. What to do? The man had seen him. If he panicked and got off the road, the corporal would get the wind up and Anderson would probably be hunted down. The only thing to do was to brazen out the encounter.

As if he had not a care in the world, Anderson continued walking down the road. The other man approached, and Anderson hoped he would pass by with a nod. But the corporal wanted something, and crossed over to Anderson's side of the road and dismounted. He then spoke to Anderson, in what language Anderson did not know, and paused, waiting for a reply.

Anderson sensed that he was seeking information, and without speaking he stretched out one arm and pointed in the direction from which he had come. The corporal said something, got back on his bicycle, and rode away.

Anderson had been having visions of life in a prison camp, but he heaved several sighs of relief and started again on his trek.

After a while he came to another village. Here he sensed that the people were unfriendly and suspicious. Housewives stared at him as he passed by and did not give a greeting of any sort.

Suddenly, out of nowhere, that German corporal on the bicycle appeared again. This time he did not seem friendly but very suspicious. He got down from his bicycle and confronted Anderson, who was petrified. The German spoke. Anderson gesticulated that he could not understand.

Before the Luftwaffe corporal could react, he was accosted by a young Frenchman, who spoke to him in what Anderson recognized as German. Apparently he told the German what he wanted to know, but Anderson could not be sure, for he was walking as fast as he could to get away from the scene.

He looked back and saw the German get on his bicycle and ride away.

Anderson held his ground then, and soon the young French-man came up. In halting English they held a conversation. Anderson admitted that he was an American airman who had parachuted from his damaged aircraft near Cognac, and said he was trying to get to Spain. The young man wished him well, they shook hands, and Anderson set off again.

In eight days, avoiding villages, Anderson walked two hundred miles. Finally he stopped at one house and was told that the people would help him. He was hidden, fed, and turned over to the local Maquis organization, which passed him from one place to another in short journeys, until he crossed the mountains and arrived in Spain on January 19, 1944.

When he got back to England he learned that two others of the crew had also escaped, going different ways. Later he learned that seven crewmen had been captured and were prisoners of war.

# THIRTY-FOUR

# *Control*

There were rough days ahead in the program of preparation for the amphibious assault on Fortress Europe. A new Eighth Air Force report averred that the daylight strategic bombing program was under threat: too many enemy fighters.

Something had to be done, because the Germans were raising their fighter production and transferring more fighters to the western front.

The year 1944 opened with a reorganization of the United States Army Air Force operations in the European Theater. Lieutenant General Carl Spaatz was appointed commander of the United States Strategic Air Forces in Europe, Major General James Doolittle replaced General Ira Eaker as commander of the Eighth Air Force, and Eaker took Doolittle's old command in the Mediterranean. The emphasis on daylight strategic bombing was stepped up.

The warning about German fighters was underscored on January 11, when 570 B-17s and B-24s bombed industrial targets at Halberstadt and in the Brunswick area. Five hundred German fighters came up to meet them, and the sky was one great melee. In the end sixty U.S. bombers were lost.

The loss ratio was simply too high, so until other arrangements could be made, the bombing of Germany was to be stopped for a while. But by the end of January the insistence on the bombing program from on high made it necessary to resume heavy raids and heavy losses.

January 29, 1943 was the day that Captain Robert Sellers became senior flying control officer of the 458th Bomb Group.

The mission of January 29 was another rough one. For the first time, more than 760 heavy bombers struck at heavy industry in the area of Frankfurt-am-Main. Nearly fifty of the bombers got lost and bombed Ludwigshafen. Over the main target the fighter opposition was fierce, and twenty-nine planes were lost. One of the big problems for cripples coming home was an inability to find the base, partly due to the weather.

Captain Sellers was well aware of this problem and felt a heavy responsibility to do what he could to solve it.

"We felt that if pilots were to place their aircraft in our hands in time of emergency we should do things that told them, 'We really know what you are facing, so have confidence in our instructions.' "

Just after the Second Air Division was put on a "maximum effort" basis, the 458th was ordered to fly a mission to interdict German fighters and fighter production. They were to hit airfields in western Germany and aircraft factories in the Brunswick area.

Looking at the operations board, Captain Sellers noted that Lieutenant Bud Walker's airplane was scratched from the mission and learned that one crewman was sick that day. So Captain Sellers offered to take his place, a suggestion that was welcomed by the lieutenant and the others because they were sweating out the last few of their fifty missions. Sellers did not have to fly any missions. He was a control officer, not an aircrew member. But he wanted to go.

Captain Sellers was assigned to man the nose gun turret and to help the navigator from that forward position. As they flew into Germany, Sellers noted that the group leader was taking them on a course that would put them directly over a heavy flak area. He passed the word to Lieutenant Walker, and Walker radioed the group leader.

"I'll check it out," said the group leader. But if he did check it out, he did not get accurate information, because they kept straight on course for trouble.

As Sellers recalls, "we were flying at 22,000 feet, and the sky was so clear that we could look straight down at the ground."

Of course it was just as clear for the Germans down below.

"We soon learned that the Germans had been using their time to track the first flight on its course, checking height and speed and fine-tuning their sights. They let them go by. Then, as we came along, they let loose.

"One antiaircraft battery fired four bursts. The first went off in front of me; the second literally tore the No. 3 engine off the wing; the third tore off the bomb bay doors and our bombs went tumbling out; and the fourth burst went off just outside the left waist gunner's window."

The B-17 slid to the left and raced toward the ground as the two pilots struggled to straighten it out. Lieutenant Walker sent an alert through the intercom.

"Prepare to bail out."

In a few seconds the aircraft dropped 8000 feet, spinning out of control. Fortunately the dive had taken them out of the range of the flak batteries and there was no more firing. Still, the aircraft was badly hit and shuddered so violently that Captain Sellers feared it would come apart.

"I came out of the nose turret and saw holes all around in the fuselage, but I was not even scratched. Sergeant Bugs Bayuzik came out of the upper turret and joined me in making a quick damage assessment. Through the hatch to the bomb bay we could see the damage, or some of it. The doors to the bomb bay were completely gone, and we had a hole 10 by 15 feet in the airframe. Control cables were hanging loose, and something—either gasoline or hydraulic fluid—was spraying all over."

The rear hatch of the bomb bay was open, but they could not see anyone in the rear of the aircraft.

Captain Sellers went to the cockpit and told the pilots not to use the intercom because of the danger. They talked for a minute about bailing out, but first Lieutenant Walker wanted to know what had happened aft. What about the belly turret gunner, the rear turret gunner, and the two waist gunners?

Captain Sellers signaled the flight engineer to follow him and moved to the open hatch, intending to cross the catwalk of the bomb bay. He picked up a portable oxygen bottle and disconnected it from the ship's system. He put his legs through the hatch onto the walkway; his parachute was blocking his way, so he took it off.

"The wind was howling all around me and pulling at me as I stood up; and as I turned to move across the catwalk, I noticed one of the waist gunners lying on the floor of the plane. He raised his arm. So at least someone was alive back there. Then the wind caught me. My foot slipped in the liquid spraying out (which was hydraulic fluid) and I went down, straddling the catwalk and hanging on for dear life.

"Bugs grabbed me by the arm and pulled me back. I looked down. It was a long way to the ground. My God, I thought, and I'm out here without my chute!"

Sergeant Bayuzik helped him back into the forward compartment. Then they looked at the oxygen bottle. The gauge read zero.

Captain Sellers then went back to the cockpit and told them that at least one man was alive, though wounded. So Lieutenant Walker decided to stick with the aircraft, and the copilot, Sellers, and the flight engineer did too. They would try to get the B-17 home.

The flight engineer went back up into the top turret to keep a watch for enemy fighters. Lieutenant Walker did a little tentative experimenting and found that by reducing speed he could reduce the vibration. But with the No. 3 engine out they had no brakes or flaps, and the copilot did not think they would be able to crank the landing gear down by hand.

Full of trepidation, they limped along back toward the English Channel. Lieutenant Ted Joiner, the navigator, studied his maps and came up with a shorter route to Manston, the closest field, where they would shoot for an emergency landing.

Captain Sellers stood in back of the pilots, leaning on the seat backs, and watched the English coast come up. Soon he spotted Manston. He told Lieutenant Walker to head for the field.

" 'Don't call them,' I said. 'We might catch fire. We'll shoot flares. That will tell them we've been hit.' We all watched the fuel gauges on the working engines. The indicators were very near the empty mark.

'Lieutenant Walker and the copilot were having a real struggle to keep the aircraft on an even keel. We lost altitude constantly, because every time Walker tried to gun the engines, the vibration started again, and the plane shuddered violently."

Ahead of them was the emergency runaway: 3000 feet of grass undershoot area, 9000 feet of pavement, and then another 3000 feet of grass overshoot area.

"We headed straight in. I saw several fighters preparing to land, but they were not a problem. They would be using a different runway."

Then came the green light from the tower, giving them clearance to go straight in.

Lieutenant Walker headed in, but he was too low. It looked like they would land on the undershoot grass, but he managed to get the plane up a little. They hit the macadam at 150 mph and bounced. Captain Sellers could sense that either they had blown the tires on impact or the tires had been shot up. The B-17 skidded down the runway, and the nose wheel collapsed. The plane ground-looped off to one side of the runway, and then came to a stop.

Up front they got out of the aircraft in a hurry, worried about fire. The crash crew was there, firefighters and all the rest, and they got the wounded out of the back of the plane. Nobody was dead.

As the ambulances took away the wounded, Captain Sellers looked over the aircraft. It was lying on its side, one engine gone, the wing peeled back, and full of holes (later the mechanics counted 700).

Flying control's weapons carrier picked them up and took them to Operations, where the flight surgeon presented them with their combat ration: a shot of whisky each. They needed it.

Captain Sellers then called their home base and was told that they had already been reported as missing in action.

"Hey," he said, "please send the chaplain to our quarters to tell them that we are okay. I don't want to lose my Short Coat."

So the chaplain was dispatched and got to the BOQ in time to save their personal belongings from the "He won't need these anymore" syndrome.

Then the crew of Walker's bombers, minus the wounded gunners, made arrangements for transportation back to the base. Another day's work was done.

# THIRTY-FIVE

# *Kinsinger*

Kenneth Kinsinger was an agronomist on the staff of the University of Illinois, and in 1941 it appeared that he had a nice deferment from the service because of the need for farm experts. But very shortly Ken Kinsinger's draft board informed him that he did not have such a deferment and that he was soon to be amalgamated into the Army of the United States.

So Ken Kinsinger joined the U.S. Army Air Corps pilot training program.

His training followed the familiar pattern: George Field near Terre Haute, Indiana, assigned to multi-engines and B-24s; Tonopaugh, Nevada; Salt Lake City; San Francisco Port of Embarkation and Palm Beach; Dakar and Tunis; and finally Italy, where he arrived in April as a replacement in the 716th Squadron of the 449th Bombardment Group.

The 449th had been activated at Tucson, Arizona on May 1, 1943. After training, the 449th moved via Topeka, Kansas, to Morrison Field, Florida, and then to Trinidad, Puerto Rico, Brazil, Dakar, and the North African airfields recently captured. The airplane was the B-24, the unlovely and unloved (at first) poor cousin to the spectacular B-17 Flying Fortress.

On the way to war, the first B-24 cracked up in Puerto Rico. No one was hurt. Then a B-24 piloted by Captain David Council, squadron commander of the 719th Squadron, ran into a mountain in the Atlas range of North Africa, and fourteen men were killed. Another plane piloted by the operations officer of the 719th also crashed, but all the crew survived except Captain Hiero Hays, the pilot. He got his crew to parachute out but lost his own life.

Not a happy beginning, but not unusual for these green crews rushing into battle in 1943. Most of them made it successfully.

The ground crews of the original group had it tougher than most of the aircrews. In December 1943 they set sail from Hampton Roads, Virginia. As the group historian remembered it:

"A haze prevented the men from seeing the shore, and they realized their last view of America had been the previous night when they had watched the lights of Hampton Roads from the decks of their ships. All day the convoy jockeyed about as the ships took their positions and the convoy assumed a definite shape, with its ships arranged in straight lines, horizontally and vertically. In addition to their loads of men, the ships carried tanks, trucks, and jeeps on their decks and explosives in their holds.

Men were stacked five deep in the holds. Fresh hot water was nonexistent. Two meals were served each day to the officers and men, who ate the same poor food and stood in the same line to be served."

There was no excitement.

"So quiet was the passage that it was hard to believe the waters were submarine-infested. Only the occasional zigzagging of the convoy or the sight of corvettes racing between the ships indicated danger."

The transports separated at Gibraltar, and the squadrons went different ways. The 716th Squadron disembarked at Palermo, Sicily, and then moved to Naples. Ultimately the four squadrons traveled the long road from Avellino to Ariano, Foggia, and Bari, then to Taranto, and finally to Grottaglie, which would be their base.

They were a part of the Fifteenth U.S. Army Air Force, which was created to do to the southern part of the Axis empire what the Eighth Air Force was to do to the northern part. Hungary, Rumania, Yugoslavia, Bulgaria, Albania, Greece, southern France, Austria, Poland—southern and eastern Europe were too far from English bases. So when southern Italy was captured, it provided an important ready base for strategic air operations.

Headquarters was set up at Bari, and the Foggia area became the center of air activity. The heel of the Italian boot became the hub of operations of the Forty-seventh Wing of the Fifteenth Air Force, to which the 449th Group was assigned.

From the outset, the war of the 449th Bombardment Group was a soggy war. Grottaglie, the site of the base, was an ancient town twelve miles from Taranto, the big Italian naval base. It boasted two dirigible hangars and a sea of mud. Bombing attacks from North Africa had destroyed most of the buildings. When the men arrived, this is what they found:

"Debris lay everywhere about the field. Some booby traps could still be found, although the area in which the group was living had been cleared of these menaces. Gaping holes marked most of the buildings, while every structure had been scarred above the ground level by bullet holes and bomb fragments. Bomb craters had been filled in, but the recency of destruction filled the air.

"Drinking water was scarce, while water for washing, bathing, and shaving was nonexistent. It was learned that baths could be had in Taranto, but in the first days baths were far from the thoughts of the men. . . . Solution to immediate problems such as eating and sleeping had to be improvised. A four-hole latrine had been dug, and men stood in line. . . .

"The entire group—close to 2000 men—was quartered in or about two stone buildings, the headquarters of the former Italian air base. From five to ten men slept on the floor of each small room, while the surplus stretched out in the windy hallways or outside. Some men bought oil lamps in Grottaglie so that there was light. Ingenious men rigged up primitive can heaters in which gasoline could be burned to heat water. Some of the rooms contained wash basins into which cold water flowed, but a bomb burst had damaged the water line and water was not safe for drinking. In most rooms it did not flow at all."

On the night of January 7, 1944, the 449th got orders for its first mission, an easy one against an enemy fighter field at Mostar, Yugoslavia.

On the morning of January 8, eighteen bombers took off from the base field and flew to Yugoslavia, returning to buzz the field. In debriefing, the crews bragged about how well they had done —they demolished the target, they said. But the mission photographs showed that not a single bomb had struck the airfield or the dispersal area which had been the primary target. That month the 98th and 376th heavy bombardment groups refitted and trained, while the 449th and 450th took over bombing operations.

At first they were singularly unsuccessful. A second bombing strike, at shipping at Zara, Yugoslavia, also produced no results. On the third attack, on railroad marshaling yards at Skopje, Yugoslavia, a few hits were seen—improvement. On the fourth mission they aimed at an airfield near Perugia, Italy, and again failed. Not a bomb hit in the target area. The fifth raid, a return to Mostar, was marked by a foul-up which cost an aircraft and crew. The squadrons had very poor flight discipline, and as the bomb run started several planes were out of position. At the moment of drop, one B-24 flew directly under another, and the bombs blew it up. Nine men died and two men parachuted to safety but became prisoners of war. In the bombing plane the concussion of the nearby explosion was so great that five men bailed out without orders. The plane plummeted 2000 feet before the pilot regained control. He flew it back to base without a copilot, without rudder control, and with only one aileron.

The group continued to do an incompetent job. A raid on January 15 near Florence cost another aircraft and yielded no results. By this time the men of the 449th were beginning to feel that they were picked on by wing and Air Force headquarters. They griped that their living conditions were terrible, and that they did not have adequate tools to repair their aircraft. The group seemed to be becoming a problem.

But on January 16 the bombers bombed an airfield and managed to hit the center of the field. Flak caught one bomber and forced it to ditch in the Adriatic.

On January 17 the group bombed rail yards at Arezzo, Italy, and made some hits. Then on January 18 came the first really successful mission, against the rail yards at Pisa. Thereafter the skill of the group continued to increase.

On January 22 the group attacked a highway on the side of a cliff at Terracina. The mission, to cause a landslide to make the highway unusable, was successful. The men of the 449th did not then know it, but their mission was in support of the Anzio landings, to prevent the Germans from rushing reinforcements to the coast areas.

Colonel Darr H. Alkire, the commander of the group, was shot down in an attack on the Aviano airfield at the north end of the Adriatic. He was replaced by Lieutenant Colonel Thomas J. Gent, Jr., a 1935 graduate of the Military Academy at West Point.

In February the missions slowed down as the weather grew foggy and cold. Missions were flown in support of the Anzio beachhead, but the weather did not permit many. It was a quiet, cold, miserable time for the men, with more casualties from gasoline stoves than from enemy action until Colonel Gent prohibited the use of the stoves in the headquarters building.

For recreation, such as it was, the officers and men went to Taranto, where there was a British-American officers club and a theater, there were women, and the men could have hot baths. There still were no bathing facilities on the base.

February was the month when the 449th began to be a part of the Strategic Bombing operations, with raids on the ball bearing plant at Steyr, Austria. They also joined with heavy bombers from the Eighth Air Force in England to hit the Messerschmitt factory at Regensburg.

In the Regensburg attack the B-24s ran into heavy fighter defense. The plane named *Pistol Packin' Mama* was jumped by a dozen fighters, and soon two engines were shot out before they reached the target. The pilot, Lieutenant Gilbert Bradley, kept the ship on course and it bombed, but after the bombing it was jumped again by fighters. Sergeant Paul Biggart, a gunner, shot down four enemy planes, his comrades said, but was then killed by an enemy bullet. Altogether the crew claimed fifteen enemy fighters.

The crew parachuted and brought Sergeant Biggart's body down in a parachute, too, and then buried it. They were in Yugoslav territory, and they made their way to the lines of Marshal Tito's partisans.

Early in March the 449th returned to support the Anzio beachhead, but attacks in March were few and far between. April was a better month. On April 2 the group once again hit the ball bearing works at Steyr, a raid marked by a dreadful accident. One plane veered to avoid flak and collided with another. The two burst into flames and brought down a third B-24. Nine parachutes were seen.

Next day the 449th flew against Budapest, and the day after that they attacked Bucharest. Altogether 450 bombers and 119 P-38s flying cover attacked the marshaling yards at Bucharest. Called the 4-4-44 mission, it was by far the most spectacular the group had yet carried out. The 449th was lead group for the Forty-seventh Wing. Shortly after hitting the rendezvous point the groups ran into heavy weather and separated. The 449th went to the target alone and without fighter escort. Lieutenant Colonel Gent led twenty-eight B-24s in this attack.

Thirty miles northwest of Bucharest the group encountered its first enemy fighters. Then for an hour and a half the B-24s fought off fighters—ME-109s, FW-190s, ME-110s. The enemy used aerial cannon, machine guns, rockets, and bombs. They bombed six B-24s on the left wing of the formation and knocked three of them down. The rest of the 449th planes reached the target and bombed, came out of the bomb run, and fought Germans for a hundred miles on the way home. When the first wave of enemy fighters pulled away, they were replaced by a new group which shot down four more B-24s. In all, twenty-one of the twenty-eight bombers of the group survived the mission, although most of them were badly shot up by the time they got back to base. The gunners of the 449th claimed forty German fighters that day.

The next signal attack came the following day on the Rumanian oil fields at Ploesti. The area had been hit before, by Russian planes early in the war and by B-24s in August 1943. But these attacks had not even slowed enemy oil production and had resulted in heavy losses (one-third from North African bases).

The attack of April 5, 1944 was against the marshaling yards which were filled with oil cars. The B-24s met heavy flak and fighter opposition again, but after this attack was over it was learned that the Rumanians buried seventy fighter pilots. The back of the Rumanian fighter force was destroyed, but the Germans moved Luftwaffe forces into the Bucharest and Ploesti regions in strength to safeguard their oil lifelines.

Bombing was suspended for a week, and then the 449th hit the Messerschmitt factory at Weiner-Neustadt, south of Vienna. Next day came another raid, on the Vecses aerodrome at Budapest, and another of those accidents involving breach of air discipline. One B-24 flew directly under another and was bombed, and the bombed plane disintegrated in midair.

During the spring, P-51 fighter planes began to arrive in the Mediterranean theater. One that was on a mission to Rumania was shot down by a B-24 whose crew did not recognize the plane and thought it was an ME-109. Arrangements were made for a flyover of the Grottaglie base by P-51s for recognition purposes. One pilot came down to buzz the field. No one had warned him about the two big dirigible hangars at Grottaglie, and he crashed into one of them. The pilot was killed, and the engine of the plane was thrown 500 feet from the scene.

April was the month when Lieutenant Kenneth Kinsinger arrived by way of North Africa to join the 716th Squadron. Almost immediately he was flying missions.

On April 23, the group attacked the Schwechat aircraft factory near Vienna. Next day it was Ploesti. On April 29 they hit the big naval base at Toulon.

For Lieutenant Kinsinger, recreation was infrequent and not very satisfactory. In April Taranto was declared off limits because of a smallpox epidemic, so then it was recreation on the base. If you did not play poker fiercely, as Lieutenant Kinsinger did not, then the possibilities were limited. There was a base officers' club, but it was not much. There were entertainments, but the competition for the company of Red Cross girls and army nurses was furious. Lieutenant Kinsinger took his war seriously, flew nearly every day, and kept his mind on the missions.

In May the 449th flew some missions in support of the Allied summer offensive in Italy. After Cassino fell on May 17, the Americans speeded up the attack on Anzio and moved toward Rome. The 449th and the other heavy bombers resumed their strategic bombing campaign.

By June 1, all the aircrews of the original squadrons of the 449th had completed their assigned fifty missions* and headed home on rotation. Lieutenant Kinsinger was soon an old hand with the 716th Squadron.

---

*Fifty missions were the norm, but such missions as the dangerous one to Ploesti counted double toward rotation points. Ploesti was the third most heavily defended German target in Europe, after Berlin and Vienna.

# THIRTY-SIX

# POW

On February 22, 1944, the 449th celebrated Washington's Birthday with a raid on Regensburg. Lieutenant Carl Browning's crew was dispossessed of their B-24 that day by the mechanics who were working on some hydraulic problems, so they scrounged another plane named *Stinky B.T.O.* They would have been far better off if they had stayed grounded. The mission was a failure due to weather, and they were shot down, along with three other planes from their group, on the way home. Sergeant Lloyd Lewis, the engineer and top turret gunner of the crew, was wounded in the attack. Lieutenant Harold Quisno, the navigator, fastened up the sergeant's parachute and dumped him out the forward bomb bay. When Lewis regained consciousness he was in a hospital in Graz and a POW.

The Germans were very responsive to Allied bombing. British bombers made several night raids on Graz, and antiaircraft guns close to the hospital fired on them, keeping the patients very much awake. One night German guards came storming into the hospital and rousted all the able-bodied patients out of bed, marched them to the railroad station, and sent them off to prison camp—Stalag 17A, Wiener-Neustadt, Austria. There the prisoners were interrogated by German officers, who threatened them, and tried to shame them with talk of Allied bombing of women and children.

Soon Sergeant Lewis was transferred to Krems to Stalag 17B.

Life in prison camp was grim. Here is a typical day's menu:

Breakfast:    one cupful of warm water
 Lunch:    two small potatoes
 Dinner:    soup made from dehydrated rutabagas
            and their worms

The Geneva Convention called for meat rations, but when they got meat it was horse blood sausage. What kept them going were the Red Cross packages, but these were withheld by the Germans as punishment, not just for prison misdemeanors, but for Allied victories and bombings as well.

Usually the American Red Cross packages were issued on Fridays. The guards punctured all the cans in the packages with bayonets, because they did not want any cans stored up for escape attempts.

If there was a bombing nearby around the end of the week, the guards would withold the packages. One time the packages were withheld for six weeks. The Germans announced that the Americans had bombed the trains carrying the packages.

Soon the Allies knew of the POW camp, and one day a squadron of P-51s put on a show for the POWs. They flew down on Krems, bombing and strafing, and buzzed the POW camp, giving the thumbs-up sign.

One day a large group of B-24s bombed the Krems marshaling yards and hit the funeral train of an important official on its way to Vienna. The Germans were furious and took it out on the POWs for several weeks.

By early April 1945, the Soviet army was only thirty miles from Stalag 17B, and the Germans decided to move. On April 8 they assembled the POWS and marched them out in groups of five hundred. Sergeant Lewis was marched for seventeen days and covered 280 miles. At night they slept in open fields or barnyards, and ended up in a large pine forest which the Germans had designated as the new camp. The POWs had to build their own shelters from pine boughs.

Sergeant Lewis and the others remained there, under German guard, from April 25 to May 3, when they were liberated by General George Patton's Third U.S. Army.

# THIRTY-SEVEN

# Szablinski

One of the most remarkable escapes from enemy territory was made by Sergeant John Szablinski of the 716th Squadron. Szablinski was a photographer-gunner who enlisted in the air corps in November 1942 and ended up in 1944 with the 449th Heavy Bombardment Group. On June 9, 1944, he took off on his twenty-third mission, against Oberhoffenpofen Airfield at Munich, where the Germans were supposed to be experimenting with jet aircraft. As they flew into Germany the weather grew worse steadily, and by the time they neared the target it was apparent that the mission had to be scrapped. The group turned back to attack a secondary target, the Port Marghera oil installation in Italy. The aircraft in which Szablinski was riding was hit by flak, and the No. 3 and No. 4 engines were in trouble. Szablinski was the first to bail out. The others rode the plane for a while, but then had to bail out and were captured by the Germans in Austria.

Sergeant Szablinski landed south of Munich, deep in Bavaria, and decided he would walk out. He began walking, keeping to the countryside and away from farms and houses. His food was mostly berries and the leaves of grape vines and blueberries. He started south, passing by Garmisch-Partenkirchen and Innsbruck, and then headed east, skirting around Spittal and Villach, toward Klagenfurt. He encountered a band of gypsies who befriended him, and he stayed with them for a week. They took him to a siding near Salzburg where a southbound train was sitting. Just as the train started up he jumped aboard. The train ended up in the Alps in the area where Austria, Italy, and Yugoslavia meet.

From there he headed east, crossed back into Austria and moved toward Klagenfurt. He crossed over from Austria into Yugoslavia between Klagenfurt and Maribor.

Szablinski approached one farmhouse which seemed to be unoccupied at the moment, and watched for an hour. When no one appeared, he entered the house and ransacked the kitchen for food. He had gotten quite a cache when he heard the front door slam, so he went hurriedly out the back with his food into the woods. That night he set out again.

He came to another farmhouse, where he approached a farmer. At first the Yugoslav farmer was suspicious, but Szablinski showed him his American dogtags, some American currency, and a small American flag from his escape kit. Convinced that Szablinski was not a German, the farmer hid him and got in touch with the partisans in the area. A day later they came to get Szablinski.

He spent some time with the partisans, fielding political questions (they were Communists) and eventually winding up at Marshal Tito's headquarters. He met Tito there, and they exchanged a few words. Then he was taken by couriers to American intelligence agents operating in Yugoslavia. They got him to Bihac, where he was flown out to Italy. Szablinski rejoined the 449th to make three more missions, after which he returned to the United States on rotation.

# THIRTY-EIGHT

# Photo Mission

William H. Watkins enlisted in the United States Army Air Corps in the summer of 1941. He was soon assigned to the First Photo Squadron, which was located at Army Air Corps Headquarters at Bolling Field in Washington, D.C. After a few months he was sent to the Fifth Photo Mapping Squadron at Bradley Field, Connecticut.

The Fifth was trained in aerial mapping and then sent to Peterson Field at Colorado Springs, Colorado, and redesignated as the Eleventh Mapping Squadron. They flew B-17s.

At Peterson, Private Watkins trained as an aerial photographer and also as a laboratory technician. He began using the then-new trimetrogon mapping system, which involved the use of three overlapping Fairchild K-17 cameras. Soon he made sergeant (he would eventually be advanced to technical sergeant).

In October 1942 Sergeant Watkins was shipped out to Norfolk Naval Air Station as a replacement. In November he boarded the converted Cunard liner *Empress of Scotland* and, with many other replacement troops for the army air forces, he traveled to Casablanca, Morocco. It was a harrowing journey: six days across the South Atlantic, where the German U-boats were then very active, and then through the Straits of Gibraltar into the narrow confines of the Meditteranean.

At Casablanca the replacements enjoyed a few days of rest and recreation, but were then taken to the railroad station and stuffed aboard a train made up of several dozen of the old *40 hommes ou 8 chevaux* ("forty men or eight horses") boxcars of World War I vintage. Each boxcar was equipped with a Lister bag filled with chlorinated water and mounted on a tripod. Each time the train lurched to a start or jerked to a stop, the Lister bag would swing and sway, and the precious rationed water would slop out. Each car also had several cases of C rations stacked in a corner. The floor was covered with straw that was changed occasionally. There were twenty men in Sergeant Watkins's car.

The train set out for a thousand-mile journey from Casablanca to Bizerte in Tunisia. The bouncing and twisting of the cars, along with the assorted clinks and clanks of movement, made it very difficult to sleep on the ancient train. When the train stopped the men opened C rations and wolfed them down. They used the outdoors as a latrine, and the unlucky had to rush to get the train as it started to move again. The French trainmen signaled starting and stopping with small, shrill silver whistles that soon became items of sale. The trainmen seemed to have an inexhaustible supply, which they sold to the airmen for 100 francs ($20) each.

Occasionally the train would stop long enough that they could build fires and heat the C rations. When they stopped at a station or a village, the men bargained and traded for fresh fruit, mostly with French and Arab children.

And so they lurched across North Africa, with a spectacular view of the mountain scenery from their open boxcar door. It was winter, so the heat was not bad in the daytime, but at night the cold was severe. They put on their fleece-lined flight jackets and shivered.

The journey consumed the better part of two months. They stopped for other trains carrying fighting ground troops. They stopped for supply trains. Occasionally they stopped for cleanup, showers, rest on a cot, and a real hot meal. They stopped because . . . they just stopped, and sometimes nobody knew why.

Finally, in January, they reached Bizerte. A few days more and they were on their way to Italy. By this time North Africa had been conquered by the Allies, and Field Marshal Rommel's Afrika Korps had been destroyed, although Rommel himself had escaped to fight again. The Allies had landed in Sicily, the Italian government had fallen, and the Germans had rushed reinforcements down to Italy to hold the line. Then in September came the invasion of the Italian boot at Salerno. By the time Sergeant Watkins arrived on the scene early in 1943, the Allies were well ensconced on the European mainland. He was sent to a replacement depot at Naples and then on until he was assigned to the Ninety-ninth Heavy Bombardment Group 1, a B-17 unit, based at Tortorella Airdrome, near Foggia. He began flying photo missions.

Watkins's job was to photograph the bomb strikes as they occurred. His photos were then taken to the photo intelligence unit and examined for patterns. From the bomb patterns the photo-interpreters could estimate the degree of accuracy and probable damage of a strike. The bombed areas were also photographed after the fact, and these photos were compared to the others for target information.

On February 15, 1944, Sergeant Watkins's group bombed Montecassino Benedictine Abbey, an historic landmark. It was one of the more controversial targets of World War II.

Watkins also participated in raids on the ME-109 factory at Wiener-Neustadt, Austria, the Ploesti oil fields, Rumanian factories and oil installations, the Brenner Pass and the Po River valley, submarine pens near Athens, and the port of Marseilles.

On April 17, 1944, the group bombed the railroad marshaling yards at Sofia, Bulgaria. Coming off the target the B-17 took a flak hit directly under the right inboard engine and into the gas tank. White gasoline fumes spewed out from under the wing. The pilot feathered the engine and told the crew there was to be no more smoking, and weapons were not to be fired unless they were attacked, to avoid fire. When the B-17 got back to its base, the crew inspected the damage. There was a hole the size of a softball in the gas tank—but the self-sealing lining in the tank had expanded to fill this enormous gap.

On June 2, 1944, Sergeant Watkins embarked on his great adventure of the war. Operation FRANTIC, the shuttle bombing of German targets by B-17s escorted by P-51 fighter planes. It was, said General Eaker, to be a "maximum effort" operation, and all the planes of the Ninety-ninth Bomb Group were to go.

Group called all aircrews to a meeting in the briefing hall. In case of a crash landing in Soviet territory, the men were given American flags to sew onto their flight jackets, hastily prepared lists of Russian phrases, plus the usual escape packets. They were told that the aircraft would carry only half the normal bomb load because of the long distance involved. The engineering crew installed extra gas tanks, called "Tokyo tanks," in half the bomb bay areas. The flight, from the Foggia base to Poltava in the Ukraine, would take all day.

Sergeant Watkins's aircraft left at dawn and hit the marshaling yards at Debrecen, Hungary. The raid was a surprise, and no enemy air opposition appeared. They flew on to Poltava and made a bumpy landing on steel mats laid in a wheat field near by. Russian officers flocked around to see the B-17s, the likes of which they had never seen before.

The atmosphere was very friendly. The crews remained based in Poltava for about ten days. They went on several missions taking Soviet officers along.

Finally it was time to return to Italy. On the day they were to leave, the aircraft's right waist gunner was taken ill and had to be left behind. The pilot asked Watkins to take over the right waist gun as soon as he was finished photographing. Sergeant Watkins said he would. The pilot did not ask if he knew how to operate a .50 caliber machine gun, and Watkins did not volunteer the fact that he had never fired one.

On this strike they attacked the rail marshaling yards at Sofia. This was regarded as one of the most heavily defended areas in Europe, and Sergeant Watkins found the description was no exaggeration.

Suddenly they were in the middle of a firefight with a flock of ME-109s. Sergeant Watkins had discovered how to charge the gun and how to safety it. When one of the ME-109s made a pass at the plane on his side, he let loose a long burst—and the gun jammed. The left waist gunner came over and explained that long bursts jammed guns. He showed him how to unjam it and "hose" the target while watching the tracer rounds. Watkins began to get the idea, but just barely. Perhaps his wild firing had an effect on the enemy. Anyhow, the plane was not shot down, and made it back to Foggia safely.

Not all the B-17s made it back. About ten days after the Ninety-ninth left the Russian base at Poltava, a group from England made the shuttle trip. As was their habit in England, they parked their B-17s in nice neat rows. The Russians did not say anything to them, perhaps out of politeness, but Germans were watching, and a reconnaissance plane noted the neat formation. Then at night along came a flight of German light bombers, and by flarelight they bombed and strafed the neat formations. They destroyed forty-seven bombers, a story that was concealed from press and public for a long time.

Watkins went back to his aerial photography, and in all flew forty missions before he was rotated back to America. He remained in the service until after VJ-day and was mustered out in October 1945.

# THIRTY-NINE

*4-4-44*

To the old hands of the 449th Bombardment Group, one mission would always stand out: the mission of April 4, 1944, against Bucharest.

The Fifteenth Air Force was sending 350 bombers against the Bucharest marshaling yards, with 119 P-38 fighters to protect them. The 449th Group was the lead group of the Forty-seventh Wing that day.

Takeoff was supposed to be at 7 a.m., but the weather was terrible and delayed it for three hours. They finally took off through low cloud cover. Up on top aircraft milled around, searching for their assigned positions. When the planes did find their units, several of them ended up in unfamiliar positions.

On the way to the target the B-24s ran into heavy weather. The groups got separated and lost their fighter cover. The 449th went on, unescorted and alone, a Lieutenant Colonel Gent leading twenty-eight B-24s. The rest of the American bombers were about a half hour behind.

Crossing the Adriatic, Colonel Gent was leading with a flight of twelve planes, and behind and on the left was Lieutenant Polink's flight of B-24s.

The formation:

Polink
16

Kendall                              McCormick
13                                    11

Garrison
8

Geisel                    Olson
14                        10

Soon Lieutenant Geisel turned back for some reason or other, leaving 5 planes in Polink's low box.

The enemy fighters appeared when the group's planes were thirty miles northwest of Bucharest. The first attack was by ME-109s, FW-190s, JU-88s, and ME-110s. They attacked from all levels and came to within fifty yards of the group's planes. Concentrating on the left wing of the 449th, they hit with rockets, machine guns, and bombs. That first attack knocked down three B-24s in forty-five minutes. Lieutenant John McCormick said he saw 200 fighters in the air that day, mostly ME-109s and FW-190s.

In the second wave, which struck immediately after the bombing, the enemy knocked down four more B-24s.

Lieutenant McCormick was flying plane No. 11:

"Right after we hit the target, my tail gunner called in to say that the sky was full of enemy fighters. We had seen them earlier at a distance, but they looked like a group of B-17s. The air battle started with the squadron that was the least protected, and for the next thirty minutes they attacked in waves of six planes flying abreast of each other.

"The 20mm shells began exploding out front of us, so that at first I thought it was flak that we were running into. Soon after the fight began, Lieutenant Olson's plane left our low box and closed in the diamond in the low box of the lead unit headed by Colonel Gent. This left our flight in the following position:

Polink
16

Kendall                                    McCormick
13                                         11

Garrison
8

"The first plane that I saw go down in our flight was Lieutenant Garrison's. . . . The entire plane was afire, and through the flames I saw the girl's poster that was painted on the side, and the words *Paper Doll.*

"After Garrison's plane went down there was a short break in the fighting, but it soon began again, with planes coming in at us from all angles. The next plane to go down was Lieutenant Kendall's plane. His copilot was Lieutenant Rhoades. Kendall's plane went out of control, and Lieutenant Polink and I had a hard time keeping away from a collision with his plane."

Here is Lieutenant Rhoades's recollection of the loss of Kendall's unfortunate aircraft *The Dixie Belle*:

"We were all under attack and badly hurt. Our plane had three engines feathered and burning with the control cables shot out, and we were slewing all over the sky. Dick Kendall yelled at me to to get on the pedals and the wheel and hold it while we got the crew out, and he rang the 'Bail Out' alarm to signal the crew in the rear to get the hell out. . . .

"One incident that I recall was an intercom call from waist gunner Sergeant Hollingsworth stating that he had two badly wounded or dead men in the waist and he wanted to try to get chutes on them and drop them out before bailing out himself. Apparently he never accomplished this heroic effort, because the fighters came in sideways and probably cut him to mincemeat.

"The rest of us went out of that doomed plane any way that we could. I had always made it a habit to keep a pair of GI shoes behind my seat, in case I crash-landed and had to walk out of enemy territory, flying in a pair of newly issued English high fleece-lined boots instead. However, by the time I got my oxygen mask, throat mike, flak vest, steel helmet, and seat belt off and my chest chute pack on, I had no time or desire to change into those GI shoes. I dove through the bomb bay from the navigator's deck just to get the hell out of there in one piece. The whole probably took one minute, but it seemed like hours until that parachute opened with a most painful but welcome jerk. (I remember thinking that I would never be a father again after that jerk.)"

Lieutenant McCormick took evasive action to avoid the flaming wreckage of plane No. 13:

"Tony Polink's plane next flamed and pulled out below and to the left of me, where I presume he went down. It now appeared that my plane was the last of the flight in the low box, and as I maneuvered to see if I could attach myself to another flight, our plane was attacked by two ME-109s coming in from the front."

"Ball turret Gunner Dow reported over the intercom that he was out of ammunition but that he would stay in the ball turret and track the gun to try to discourage fighters from coming in."

The tail turret gunner Sergeant Elsrod was also out of ammunition, and he came back into the waist of the plane. The top turret gunner Engineer Van Arkel and the nose turret Gunner Radioman Thompson had ammunition, and Lieutenant McCormick told them to watch the two ME-109s that were maneuvering to attack the plane. On the first pass, one of the fighters was shot down but the other turned away to get a different angle on the bomber. For a moment Lieutenant McCormick thought the German had given up on them, but then he saw orange spurts coming out of the fighter's wing guns. The next thing he knew, the plane received a hard blow which sounded like somebody scraping metal on a washboard. The No. 2 and No. 3 engines flamed. The plane's nose was aflame, and two balls of flame came through, one between McCormick's legs and one between copilot Lynch's. Gunner Dow was killed in his turret.

Lieutenant McCormick could not control the plane, so he rang the bail-out bell. The plane pulled up in a climb, and the G force trapped the pilot, copilot, engineer, and navigator on the floor of the flight deck. Then the plane winged over, and the G force ended. Copilot Lynch crawled back to the control pedestal and pulled the bomb bay door release.

Navigator Stagman had been half in and half out of the flight deck. When the doors opened, he turned and jumped out the left side of the bomb bay. Engineer Van Arkel then pushed Lynch out the right side and McCormick pushed Van Arkel out the left side.

Pilot McCormick crawled out, noting that there was a chute caught on the back compartment of the bomb bay. He could hardly see because the flight deck was filled with smoke and flames. He jumped into the slipstream and then pulled the rip cord. The parachute opened with such force that one of the panels was ripped open.

McCormick's lungs were full of smoke and he was coughing. He saw an ME-109 heading straight for him and thought this was the end, but as the plane came up, the pilot waved at him and pulled to one side. McCormick was then hypnotized by looking at the ground, and suddenly it came up and hit him. The soft flying boots did not offer any support, and he sprained his ankle.

McCormick was captured immediately and taken to a village near the Danube. He thought he had been picked up by the partisans, but when he heard a man scream and turned to look, he was hit on the side of the head. McCormick was kept prisoner in a small room in the town hall until copilot Lynch, waist gunner Schattler, waist Gunner Lowe, and tail gunner Elsrod were brought in about an hour later. That night they were picked up by a truck that already had parts of Kendall's and Polink's crews aboard. They were taken to Alexandria, Rumania, and then moved to Bucharest. There they encountered the remnants of several other crews, as well as more of Lieutenant Kendall's.

As Lieutenant Rhoades related, he had drifted down in his parachute, looking around him.

"It looked like a paratroop invasion, with white American and colored enemy chutes by the dozens either in the sky or on the ground. In addition, the horizon was dotted with the fires of burning planes, both American and enemy. Like McCormick, I was so engrossed that I hit the ground sideways without warning and hurt my good right ankle.

"Sergeant Gerald Danison, our flight engineer, hit the ground close by me, and after discussing the situation we decided to abandon our chutes. We could see soldiers with dogs, trucks, and peasant carts in the distance, but we had not been discovered and escape seemed possible."

They crawled to a hedgerow several hundred yards from their landing place and hid until dark. Then, with Sergeant Danison suporting Lieutenant Rhoades, they followed Rhoades's escape-packet compass and moved several miles to the west before dawn. That day they slept in a corn shuck pile.

Next day Rhoades made a crutch from a forked stick. He sent Danison on westward, and moved at his own pace. They both ate the concentrated food bars, which tasted like sawdust-covered molasses. Lieutenant Rhoades was very thirsty. When he finally came to a ditch full of slimy green water, he filled his canteen and added four Halazone purification tablets (the usual dose is one per canteen) and drank the stuff down thirstily.

After the third day, Rhoades's wounded ankle was badly swollen and the inflammation had run up his leg to the knee. He had a fever. He realized that it would be impossible for him to escape, and he felt relieved when he was found by a peasant, loaded into a cart (along with Danison), and taken to the German garrison in a little town, Giurgiu.

The German soldiers treated them very well. That night they ate thick vegetable soup and pork chops. After a few days they were loaded into an old Chevrolet sedan and, accompanied by a German captain, were taken to a local cemetery. Shown a dozen newly dug graves, they were asked to identify the remains of several fliers. Rhoades had a hard time—most of them were badly burned—but he did identify Lieutenant Garrison by the name stenciled on the parachute harness.

Funeral services were held, followed by the burial, and local peasant women placed flowers on the graves. Rhoades then thanked the German officer for the kindness. The German shrugged; "They were soldiers," he said.

*        *        *

In Bucharest, McCormick began to sort out what had happened. Of the ten members of his crew, five were killed in action. The parachute hanging from the plane had been Lieutenant Stagman's. It had caught and ripped loose, and his body was found with three feet of parachute shroud attached. Radio operator Thompson and bombardier Ornstein were never seen—they must have been killed by the first headlong rush. The other five members of the crew had survived and were prisoners of war.

It had been a hard fight all the way. When the next echelons of bombers arrived, the enemy fighters were all gone, and they reported a routine mission! But for the men of the 449th it had been anything but routine. They lost heavily, but they claimed forty fighters shot down, thirteen probables, and six damaged. Later it was a decided that this was the battle that broke the back of the Rumanian air force.

# FORTY

# *Partisans*

On February 24, 1944, the Americans began a coordinated series of attacks on European targets with the Eighth Air Force. On February 25 the 449th sent planes against marshaling yards at Fiume and Graz. More than thirty American planes were shot down that day, but the Eighth claimed ninety German fighters. Here is the story told by Ball Turret Gunner F. A. Grudaugh of the B-24 called *Pistol Packin' Mama.*

The formation was crossing the Alps on the way to the target when it was hit by German fighters. What followed was a running fight that lasted two hours, until the American planes turned back toward Italy. Over the target the Grudaugh's B-24 had been damaged by flak and a 20mm shell from a fighter. One engine burned out, so they crossed the Alps on three engines. But they were attacked again by fighters; now gunner Prescher was hit in the legs and was out of action. Soon all but Grudaugh's ball turret were also out. Grudaugh saw two planes he was firing at explode, and pilots bailed out of two others.

The oil lines on two of the working engines seized up. Gunner Biggart had been killed, but the other nine men all got out of the plane, bailing out at 2:15 in the afternoon. They were soon picked up by Marshal Tito's partisans and taken to a house near the advanced partisan base, where they remained for three days. On Sunday, February 27, they were taken by horsedrawn sleigh to another camp. There they met four men from the 350th Bomb Group, and the thirteen men traveled together.

On February 29 Sergeant Grudaugh was taken to see Owen Reed, a British major who was with the partisans. They stayed for four days at this camp, where they met seven men who had bailed out of a B-17 on January 31. These seven had had a rough time, and they all had body lice. They got baths, and the barber gave them shaves.

On March 4 Major Reed told them that a plane was coming to drop food and clothing. The 449th men hoped to get out by plane from an airstrip near the camp. But they had to wait for the snow to melt.

The airmen were sleeping on straw pallets, two men to a bed. They met lice, bed bugs, fleas, and cockroaches in bed. That morning they staged a louse hunt, one of them finding nineteen lice in his clothes. They had to pick the straw out of their bread. Major Reed told them they were stuck in this place for at least thirty days. So it went. Snow. Broth for breakfast, stew for lunch, and sauerkraut for dinner. More snow. By March 6 the snow reached a depth of four feet around the camp. It stopped snowing on March 7; Grudaugh went for a hike, but the snow was so deep he didn't get anywhere. It snowed again on March 10 and was very cold all day. They stayed in the hut, close to the stove.

Major Reed had sent some British battle dress uniforms, underwear, and socks, which were gratefully received.

The days went by slowly. Other airmen came in.

On March 14, at nine in the morning, they left the area, walking for five miles and then traveling in sleds. That night they had a meal of ham, eggs, and tuna fish, the best meal they had eaten since bailing out.

On March 15 the sun came out and they traveled again. This time it was a long journey, twenty miles, and they marched until midnight. Most of them had sore feet from their flying boots. That night they slept on boards with no blankets.

On March 16 they traveled only one hour, and then came upon a road held by the Germans. They stopped here for the rest of the day and waited. They crossed the road on the night of March 17.

By March 20 they had marched across another mountain range

5000 feet high, and that day they met Marshal Tito and a party of Englishmen. At Tito's headquarters they all had hot showers, their first since landing.

On March 26 more than a dozen other Allied refugees showed up, creating a feeding problem. There were only enough plates, chairs, and silverware for fifteen, so they had to establish a system of sittings. Several of the Americans were moved to a private home, where they were treated very well.

They were waiting for planes, but the weather and the Germans made it very hard. Several times German planes flew over the area, apparently knowing what was down there even if they could not see it.

On March 29 twenty men went to the little airfield. While they were waiting there for a plane, the Germans came and strafed them.

On Sunday, April 2, thirty-six men were flown out, and a little later in April Sergeant Grudaugh got out.

# FORTY-ONE

# Training Command

They also served who only flew around.

That was more or less the description of Corporal Jake Jones's war. When he and his two pilots landed their B-17 at Roswell, New Mexico in the summer of 1943, he did not know, of course, what was coming next. What did come was most disappointing.

Corporal Jones accompanied his airplane to the hangar and heard the order that all the special equipment added to the plane up north was now to be removed.

"Why?"

"Because there's a war on, corporal. Ever heard of it?"

Roswell was just then switching over from being a bombardier and two-engine advanced training school to being a B-17 training base. Corporal Jones was immediately assigned to the 965th Two-Engine Flying Training Squadron. The squadron was a maintenance unit with fifteen B-17s in a pool arrangement.

When Corporal Jones first reported in to the master sergeant in charge of maintenance, he asked, "Will I be able to keep my airplane?"

The answer was swift and to the point. "Son," said the grizzled master sergeant, "we would not even let you be responsible for the parachutes in that airplane."

What a blow! "There have been a few lower moments in my life, but not many," Corporal Jones recalled later. But he was an amenable young man, and he did not fret.

The squadron was organized so that each airplane had a ground crew chief and a helper. The squadron also had a radio repair, supply, and refueling section, administration, oxygen, clerks, and the like. It could have been a combat unit, but it was part of the U.S. Army Air Force Training Command. While Lieutenant Rosenthal and Lieutenant Colonel Jeffrey were shooting at Germans, being shot at, and winning medals, Corporal Jones was helping to train the young men who would come to fill the depleted ranks of the "Bloody 100th." It was pretty dull work.

"The saving part for me was that each airplane had to have an enlisted crewman aboard. Sometimes he was crew chief. Sometimes he was flight engineer. Whatever the title, we did the same job. We flew three shifts a day, which meant that each airplane had three enlisted men assigned to fly with it. If we were lucky we got to fly in the same airplane most of the time. Staying with the same airplane helped us to know a little of what to expect if something went wrong."

After Corporal Jones's deflation by the master sergeant, he switched to airplane No. 42-3053 and rarely flew in his old airplane. If their assigned airplane was not flying, it was usually because of maintenance problems. He stood by, because most of the time at least one of the other crewmen was off on some other duty.

The day shift flew from 6 a.m. to 1 p.m., the afternoon shift from noon to 7 p.m., and the the night shift from 6 p.m. to 2 a.m. The pilots were trained in takeoffs and landing with one or two engines not operating, in instrument flight, navigation, and high-altitude missions, formation flying, emergency procedures, and long-distance navigation. Once in a while they had bombing practice with 100-pound practice bombs on a desert range.

Every day when Corporal Jones went out to the airplane, he had to take the items that had been removed on the previous shift: a first aid kit (because the morphine would be stolen out of it if it was left aboard for even a couple of hours), crash axes, a signal lamp (removed for testing between shifts), a large thermos of coffee, a large thermos of water, paper cups, and his own parachute harness and oxygen mask.

Once he got all the stuff aboard, he checked the aircraft status forms, noting what was inoperative that day. Then he looked over the aircraft for flat tires, missing covers, and inspection plates, and checked the fuel and the hydraulic fluid. Then, even if the plane had just come in from a flight, he started and ran all engines and checked them. When he was sure the airplane was operating as well as possible, he cleaned the windshield inside and out, disposed of the trash left aboard by the previous crew, and stowed the coffee, water, and so forth.

When the pilots arrived, they were so busy with their checklists that they had no time to tell Corporal Jones where they were going or what they were going to do.

When the pilots were ready, Corporal Jones and a ground crewman turned over the three-bladed propellers, nine turns for each engine. By the time thirty-six turns were made, Corporal Jones was panting. Then the pilots went aboard the aircraft through the main door—none of this up-through-the-nose-hatch business shown in the movies. Corporal Jones stayed on the ground in front of the aircraft, with a fire extinguisher in hand, as the engines were started one by one, from left to right. (If the engines were not started properly, they could catch fire and burn up the aircraft.)

After the engines were running, the pilot gave the signal to pull wheel chocks. Corporal Jones ran around the aircraft, pulled the wheel chocks, loaded himself aboard, and slammed the door as the pilot began to taxi. As they moved, the instructor read off the checklist. Corporal Jones positioned himself behind the pilot and watched the instrument panel for problems.

At the top of the runway the pilot stopped the aircraft and ran one engine at a time up to full power, checking magnetos, propellers, and superchargers. Corporal Jones and the instructor stood silent, each saying a private prayer that the pilot would get the plane off the ground safely.

"Some guys would cross themselves, and I think I saw a few St. Christopher medals being rubbed."

When the aircraft was off the ground, the landing gear was retracted, and then Corporal Jones's real job started. First he had to squeeze back through the bomb bay catwalk to the tail of the aircraft to see if the tailwheel had retracted. Then he went back to the cockpit to report "tailwheel up, sir."

If the mission was to practice landings and takeoffs, they worked from a nearby landing strip to reduce the traffic at the base. Because they were always only 2000 feet above the ground, the flights were turbulent. Often there were other aircraft in the landing patterns, and then the student pilots were fighting ground turbulence and prop wash. To make things exciting the instructor might pull back on the throttles of one or two engines, making it even tougher; sometimes then it took both pilots to hold the rudder pedals.

As soon as the aircraft touched the ground, the flaps were retracted and another takeoff started. The instructor usually pulled one or more throttles back, making the airplane turn into the dead engines. These were the times when Corporal Jones began to sweat.

This would go on, and on, and on. A typical mission might involve thirty-eight takeoffs and landings and last as long as six hours. For Corporal Jones it was hours of boredom interspersed with moments of terror.

Each circuit involved retracting and lowering the landing gear. Every time the gear changed, Corporal Jones had to make his trip aft through the bomb bay and report on the tailwheel.

One night at the enlisted men's club, the corporal told his buddies, "We've got a real gravy train. Our job consists of running back and forth through the aircraft saying 'Tailwheel down, sir' —and we get paid for this."

They thought that was pretty funny. He became known as "Tailwheel Jones."

At the end of the run they usually came in with forty or fifty other B-17s in the landing pattern, which was sometimes a hairy experience in itself. Once they were finally down, the plane was taken to the squadron parking area. The pilots got off, and Corporal Jones took over again. He chocked the wheels and waited for the fuel truck. When the truck arrived, one hose went over each wing, and Corporal Jones scurried back and forth to see that neither hose overflowed. After the gas tanks were full, there were forms to fill out, and then Corporal Jones could call it a day.

They flew six days a week, and on the seventh day usually headed for Roswell if they had any money. As usual with small towns and big bases, there were more soldiers than civilians. If it was payday they went to a bar called The Bank, looking for girls, but usually there were many GIs and no women, so they ended up getting as drunk as they could as fast as they could. Then it was back to the base to sleep it off until it was time to fly again.

Sometimes the mission was instrument flight, and then the pilot's seat was curtained off, while the instructor sat in the co-pilot's seat and waited for trouble. Corporal Jones stood in back of the curtain with his eye glued to the left window looking for aircraft, in case the pilot wanted to turn left. On instruments, a student who failed to set his directional gyro properly might think he was going in the right direction, while he actually was going full blast off to one side or the other of the runway, maybe pointing at the hangar or the tower. There were many dry throats on these flights.

At a certain point in the training schedule, the two student pilots were told to solo, and dropped off the instructor—but not Corporal Jones. Almost always as the instructor left the aircraft, he gave Corporal Jones a sick look, as if to say, "You poor slob, you have my sympathy." Sometimes he even wished Jones luck!

One of the solo missions was a long nonstop flight from Roswell to Amarillo, Lubbock, and Carlsbad, and back to Roswell. Usually at some point the pilots were so bored they asked Corporal Jones if he wanted to fly the aircraft, and of course he always did. He might spend four hours flying, while one student pilot sat in the copilot's seat and the other went back aft to sleep.

Where was the war?

Corporal Jones didn't know. Nothing changed at Roswell but the faces of the students. He flew mission after mission with no end in sight. He just kept flying, while following the news reports and hoping to get overseas. As the months passed, he even gave up on that.

He was destined to be a corporal forever, it seemed. Those enlisted men at the base on flight pay could not be promoted above corporal, since the Army Air Force was saving promotions for combat personnel. Anyhow, there were no promotions at Roswell for any enlisted personnel.

And so the very dull war of Corporal Jones went on.

# FORTY-TWO

# Paradrop

The 441st Troop Carrier Group was formed at Sedalia, Missouri, in the summer of 1943. It was trained in Missouri and the Carolinas and later in England for the big battle of D-day and for subsequent air drops over the Low Countries.

On the night of June 5, 1944, the C-47s were warmed up at the troop carriers squadrons across England and prepared to drop some 17,000 paratroops inside Fortress Europe, on the Normandy peninsula. The 441st Troop Carrier Group flew Mission Albany, which took off at 11:51 p.m. An hour later the C-47 pilots were over the Channel Islands, getting their first taste of German antiaircraft fire. They moved in on the west coast of Normandy and looked for their drop zones. Clouds and flak made it very difficult for the plane crews, most of whom had no combat experience. Some did not drop their paratroops at all but flew back to England.

Most of the planes, however, did make their drops, although many were wide of the mark because of searchlights and ground fires. In a way this helped the invasion, because the dropping of paratroops higgledy-piggledy, far from the their destinations, kept the Germans from coming to grips immediately with the problem of meeting the paratroops invasion.

By D-day the Eighth and Ninth air forces had played havoc with the Luftwaffe, to the extent that the anticipated strong air defense of Fortress Europe did not develop. Hermann Göring was saving his Luftwaffe for the expected invasion of the Pas de

Calais area, highly advertised by the Allies as the real invasion that was yet to come. But three of the group's planes were shot down by German antiaircraft guns, two of them after they had dropped their troops. Lieutenant Harvey W. Doering's plane crash-landed and bounced over a stone wall, and the crew walked away unhurt. Three weeks later American GIs moving toward Cherbourg found them safe and sound.

Lieutenant Richard H. Worl's plane was shot up by flak but managed to drop its paratroopers and then returned to England. Staff Sergeant Charles Bortzfield, the crew chief, had been wounded by flak in the arm and ankle.

Major Lloyd Neblett's plane flew under another C-47 just as it was dropping a supply pack. Before the chute could open it struck the plane, knocking off the right wing tip. Major Neblett nearly lost control of the aircraft, but he recovered and took the plane home.

Colonel William H. Parkhill, deputy commander of the 441st Troop Carrier Group, was leading the second serial of that group on the flight. The plan called for the troop carriers to assemble over England in a 1200-plane train, with serials of forty-five aircraft each, and fly at low altitude to a point west of the Cherbourg peninsula. Then they would turn east, climb to 1500 feet, and descend to drop altitude just before reaching the target.

But Colonel Parkhill wanted to check the time they hit the coast, for navigational purposes, so he delayed his climb to 1500 feet. There was no flak near the coast. When he started to climb, the colonel discovered a cloud deck which began at 800 feet and extended to 2500 feet over the land. When he hit the cloud deck, he nosed over and brought the formation down below the clouds. They stayed below the clouds until he reached the target area, dropped their paratroopers on target, and went home. By flying so low they sustained flak damage to 90 percent of the planes, but it was mostly light damage.

Most of the troop carrier aircraft followed their orders, and when they got over the Cherbourg peninsula they found themselves up in the clouds, or over them, unable to see the land. Then came the great period of confusion, in which formation broke down and many pilots could not find their drop zones.

And so the troop carrier pilots got a bad reputation with the airborne troops because of the quality of the air drops, while the troop carrier commanders blamed the weathermen for not warning them about the clouds that covered the land.

On June 7, 1944, the 441st Troop Carrier Group brought gliders full of airborne troops and their equipment to join the paratroops and the soldiers fighting on the Normandy beaches. The gliders and their tow planes were covered by P-47s and Spitfires as they crossed the Channel, but again there was no air opposition. The real problems were putting the gliders down through flak, and landing in the small fields assigned, where the Germans had erected *Rommelspargel* (Rommel's Asparagus)—tall poles, some of them with mines attached to stop and blow up gliders. One glider pilot was killed and one was seriously hurt in the landings. It was easier than they had anticipated.

# FORTY-THREE

# The Bloody 100th

In the winter of 1943–44 the Allied air forces (with not inconsiderable help from the Russians on the eastern front) were still pursuing their mission of destroying the Luftwaffe. The Thirteenth Bombardment Wing had a big part in this effort. After the Münster raid the 100th had considerable morale problems and did not seem to be very highly regarded at Eighth Air Force headquarters, but morale was helped a lot by the finishing up of tours by a number of officers and men in February 1944.

On February 19, General Orville Anderson of the Eighth Bomber Command was informed by meteorologists that for the next three days the weather over Germany would be clear and ideal for precision bombing. So the general decided the time had come to launch a series of attacks against German aircraft plants. Thus came about Big Week, which began on February 20, when a thousand bombers were dispatched to twelve targets.

The Third Division was to fly without escort after the First and Second divisions had left base. They were, in effect, to be bait, to lure the Luftwaffe away from north Germany.

That day the 100th's target was the Focke-Wulf assembly plant at Posan, Poland. Beside the rockets, they ran into a new threat from the Germans: a plane dangling a bomb from a cable and trying to swing it into a B-17.

On February 21, the Third Division was assigned to Brunswick, but weather at the assembly point ruined the formation and the planes bombed targets of opportunity. On the third day of Big Week, high winds and overcast skies made for a very poor mission.

The division headed for Schweinfurt, but General LeMay abandoned the mission before they hit the coast.

On the fourth day the bombers were grounded, but on the fifth day, February 24, the Third Division, headed for north German aviation plants, dropped on Rostock and other targets of opportunity. On the sixth day Colonel Harding, the CO, led a mission to Regensburg. Two planes were lost as Big Week came to an end, not having been very "big."

At the end of February, the Eighth Air Force announced it had dropped more bombs on the enemy in that last week than in the entire first year of operations. But morale among the men of the 100th remained low, as indicated by a training exercise held by the group's Ground Defense Team that weekend. To signal the beginning of the movement, Lieutenant "Hardrock" Caverly drew his Very pistol dramatically and fired a flare. The flare sputtered, rose slowly five feet in the air, and collapsed.

"Symbolic of the Hundredth," said Sergeant Vernon Sheedy, who kept the official log.

On March 3, 1944, 750 planes of the Eighth Air Force were assigned to the first daylight raid on Berlin. Because of weather the First Division canceled and the Third was told to cancel, but two squadrons from the Ninety-fifth Group and one squadron from the 100th pushed on toward the target. Fourteen minutes from Berlin the planes were intercepted by German fighters. Top turret gunner Harold Stearns of the *Rubber Check* hit the first German plane downed by an American over Berlin, and ME-109 that went down in flames.

The bombing was through cloud cover by radar, and the return trip was through cloud and with much fighter opposition. Two planes of the Ninety-fifth and one of the 100th were shot down.

Reichsmarschall Hermann Göring, the chief of the Luftwaffe, had boasted that the Americans would never reach Berlin, and the bombing of March 3 by thirty-one planes was regarded as an anomaly. But on March 5 the word came down from the Third

Division that the next day's target would be Berlin, and it would be a major air force effort.

That evening, Lieutenant Ralph Cotter, bombardier of the plane called *Terry and the Pirates*, went to the officers' club and, sitting there in the twilight, wrote a letter to his mother:

"Well, today is Sunday, and I am sitting in the club. We did not have a raid today, but it was such a nice day we went up and practiced bombing all afternoon. I had a very good day, I guess that is why I feel so well. Oh. Mom, I want you to look carefully in the *Gazette* and the Boston papers, because they gave our crew a write-up over the St. Omer raid. It starts off about Lieutenant William Terry, my pilot, and all our names are mentioned. Enclosed you will find a clipping on my sixteenth raid. Just think, only nine more raids and then I will be home. It will take about a month or more after I finish my twenty-five missions, but there is nothing to worry about. Well, Mom, everything is fine and I will say good night until tomorrow. Love, Ralph."

This time 658 bombers went with 800 fighters in a column that stretched for eighty miles.

The first interceptions occurred near Dummer Lake, where the German fighters had concentrated. The German ground controllers had quickly spotted a weakness: the thirteenth Wing, flying in the middle of the bomber column and in the center of the Third Division, had no escort. The Germans sent interceptors immediately to attack the Allied fighters at the head and tail of the wing, and then a very large force of fighters to hit the unshielded groups, the ninety-fifth and the 100th. With their first sweep, they set fire to six of the high squadron's planes, and for a few seconds they flew blazing, in formation—all this within seconds.

The high squadron was led by Captain David Miner and copiloted by Lieutenant George Kinsella. Their plane was hit by the first fighter, which came out of the sun and killed both pilots with its fire burst through the windshield. Several members of the crew parachuted to become prisoners.

The plane called *Terry and the Pirates* may have been the next one hit. The shells exploded all over the nose area and broke a big hole in the Plexiglas nose of the bombardier's compartment. Lieutenant Cotter just sat still in his seat, and he did not put on his parachute. Perhaps he was immobilized by concussion.

The plane went into a spin and fell thousands of feet, and the wings came off. The navigator, Lieutenant Robert Schremser, headed for the hole in the nose. Lieutenant Cotter, without a parachute, headed for the escape hatch—that was the last seen of him. The tail broke off, the wreckage crashed, and the bombs exploded. Three survivors were captured by the Germans.

Ten B-17s of the 100th were shot down from the low box of the Thirteenth Combat Wing. The rest of the formation went on Berlin and bombed, in spite of heavy flak. There was no further pretense of differentiating between military and civilian targets these days. The bombs fell in a five-mile area of the Berlin suburbs in largely residential districts, destroying the public gas, electric, and telephone services and wrecking hundreds of houses.

When the B-17 called *Rubber Check* was hit, its No 4. engine was knocked out, and the aircraft fell out of formation. Pilot Lieutenant Frank Granack asked the flight leader, Major Bucky Elton, if he could slow down five miles per hour so the plane could get back into formation, but the answer was no. The greatest good for greatest number.

"Good luck," said Major Elton.

Gradually, the *Rubber Check* fell behind and below the formation, until it was all alone. Lieutenant Granack had control of the aircraft, although they had to lose altitude to maintain a safe airspeed; copilot Lieutenant Bob Dunham was monitoring the damage, and navigator Lieutenant Murray Geisler gave a course for Sweden. Pilot Granack gave this account:

"We weren't alone for long. 'Fighters at three o'clock' crackled over the interphone. ME-109s and FW-190s were attacking from several different directions, and we were raked the length of our plane by heavy gunfire; a fierce running battle ensued. All the gunners in our valiant crew fought back with all the .50 caliber power they could muster.

"Several enemy fighters were hit; two or three may have been downed. Sergeant Harold Stearns [who had shot down the first German plane over Berlin] was sure he got one with his top turret guns. However, the additional damage inflicted on our plane was considerable. Our No. 2 engine was having problems, and No. 3 was damaged and out of commission. Both 3 and 4 were smoking, and now fire was a serious threat. Our intercom was shot out, and therefore it was impossible to get a rapid assessment of the extent of our damage and casualties.

"However, it turned out that the greatest and most painful losses were in the crew. Sergeant Grant Scott, radio operator, and Sergeant Glenn Brown, waist gunner, were both killed by the fighters. Sergeant Ed Harrell, the other waist gunner, was wounded in the leg.

"About this time the enemy fighter attacks slackened, at least for the moment. We had to ease up on our good engine, No. 1, when it appeared to be developing trouble. We were now losing altitude rapidly to maintain airspeed to keep basic control of the plane. Cockpit adjustments to maintain control were steadily getting more difficult. Our position was getting more perilous by the moment, and to preclude the possibility of a total disaster, I decided to order the plane abandoned. Because the intercom was out, I instructed copilot Dunham to go through the plane and see that each surviving crew member was aware of my orders to bail out immediately.

"He was to provide assistance to anyone who needed it. Sergeant Lloyd Rodgers, ball turret gunner, and Sergeant George Christian, tail gunner, were to be freed of their confining positions as soon as possible to prevent their being trapped in case of a sudden control emergency. Lieutenant Dunham was to report back to me; knowing the urgency of the situation, he left quickly to carry out orders. Meanwhile the bomb bay doors, an important exit, would not open; fortunately, later they suddenly dropped open.

"Lieutenant Dunham returned shortly and told me he had carried out all my orders. I thanked him and ordered him to bail out with the crew. We shouted a few brief words of farewell as he took off for the bomb bay. From the cockpit I looked back toward the bomb bay and watched as crewmen tumbled out one after the other, until they were all gone.

"*Rubber Check* was virtually without power; the No. 3 and 4 engines were smoking, another was making death sounds. I turned the trim tabs to put the plane in a steeper glide to reduce the chances of a stall or other sudden negative violent movement by the plane as I was trying to get out. I then slipped out of my pilot's seat and held control of the plane as long as I could; I let go and ran down the passageway to the bomb bay, where I made a running head-first dive into space as I bailed out."

All eight crew members who bailed out survived and were taken prisoner.

This all happened at about 1:15 p.m. Twenty-five minutes later, after a lull, the Luftwaffe returned to the formation, but this time P-38s intervened and the formation neared the North Sea. The last of the 100th Group's planes to go down was the *Kind a Ruff*.

On their return to Thorpe Abbotts, Colonel John Bennett, the deputy group commander, noted that fifteen planes with 150 men came straggling back. Just half their number had been shot down that day. It was a really rough mission. The Eighth Air Force lost sixty-nine bombers, the highest number to that date, and 347 were damaged. The 100th had again suffered the highest loss of any group.

That day, Colonel Harding, the CO of the 100th, gave up after weeks of pain and admitted he could not go on, because he was suffering from gallstones. For weeks he had refused to see the medics, but there came a time . . .

Colonel Bennett took over as temporary group commanding officer. He later recalled, "We were a sad group of men that evening. I'm afraid I didn't appear too confident."

The weather next day gave them a respite, but only for one day. As Colonel Bennett said, "Thank God we had a day off to lick our wounds."

But it was one day only; at ten o'clock on the night of March 7 the colonel knew the target for the next day was going to be

Berlin, over the same route that had cost the 100th 50 percent of its force two days earlier.

The group operations officer was furious: "What are they trying to do, kill all of us?"

The intelligence officer simply shook his head in disbelief.

Colonel Bennett was worried. Group morale was so low that he was afraid most of the pilots would abort rather than return to Berlin. He went into another room and called wing headquarters and leveled with them. He asked permission to lead the wing although it was not the turn of the 100th, and he wanted to lead personally.

The request was granted.

Next morning at the briefing Colonel Bennett waited for reaction. When the group had an easy mission, everybody cheered as the curtain was pulled back and the map exposed. This day, when the Berlin mission was announced, there was dead silence in the room.

The target, the intelligence men announced, would be the Erkner ball bearing plant in Berlin. They showed pictures. The operations officer then explained that the Forty-fifth Combat Wing would lead the Eighth Air Force this day, and the 100th would lead the Thirteenth Wing, which would be the second wing on the target.

Colonel Bennett then got up. He did not know what to say to raise morale. He reminded them of the second Regensburg mission, a week earlier, when he had led forty-two planes in and they had lost only one.

Today the 100th could muster only fifteen aircraft, and as they flew toward the target, Colonel Bennett kept checking to see how many he still had with him.

"No abortions" was the report.

He checked again as they left England and began the flight over the sea. Still "no abortions."

The flight over the North Sea and Holland was made at 24,000 feet. At the Dutch coastline they picked up a fighter escort of P-47s. They reached Dummer Lake, where the slaughter had begun two days earlier. The P-47s left them there, but the P-51s that were supposed to replace them did not show up.

As they passed Dummer Lake they saw fighters coming up high and behind them.

Was it the escort?

No, it was Germans, and they flew directly at the B-17s, picked the wing ahead of Bennett's 100th, and attacked fifteen abreast.

B-17s began to fall.

"There must have been 150 planes in this first bunch of fighters that jumped us. They knocked the leader of the wing out on their second pass, and the third attack got the deputy leader. Most of the German planes passed under the 100th as they dived away from the attack."

Now there was not much left of the Forty-fifth Combat Wing, and Bennett brought the 100th to take the lead of the air force. Although they were then under attack for the rest of trip to Berlin, they fought off the attacks. One plane was damaged, but it dropped down from the high formation and stuck with the low formation all the way.

Still no aborts.

They came to Berlin, the big sprawling city laid out for them in the clear air. Colonel Bennett looked back. Behind he could see hundreds of bombers—and the welcome sight of the P-51 fighters that had finally caught up.

The B-17s bored in and bombed, the fighters held back the enemy, and the mission continued. After that the mission was uneventful for all except Lieutenant Norman Chapman's crew. Chapman's plane was the one that had been damaged and dropped down with the low formation. He insisted on bombing, and then his plane began to fail. The crew bailed out, to become prisoners of war.

Fourteen of the fifteen 100th Group bombers returned that day, and morale inched up.

One thing had been proved: If there had been a vendetta by the Germans against the 100th Bombardment Group, it was now finished. The German fighters had concentrated all right, but on breaking up the leading Forty-fifth Group.

Morale went up another inch when nine 100th bombers returned to bomb Berlin a few hours later and there were no losses. It rose a bit more when the critique of the Berlin operations held at Framlingham singled out the 100th for good performance.

There were no operations for nearly a week. Thirteen new crews arrived. General Spaatz, the chief in Europe, General Doolittle, the commander of the Eighth Air Force, and General LeMay seemed belatedly to recognize that there was something wrong at the 100th for which they might have some responsibility, so they visited the base, all medals and good fellowship, and held court at the officers' club. The result was salutary.

The next missions were Brunswick and air installations in southern Germany and France. There were losses—two B-17s collided after one mission was aborted and the leader broke up the formation—but they were bearable losses. There was another Berlin mission on March 22 and no losses. But the morale of the 100th Group remained relatively low.

The food was improved: eggs and hot cakes for breakfast. The morale officer rigged up benefits and raffles for the men and parties at the officers' club. The men of the 100th still felt defeated and alone. The 390th and the ninety-fifth groups of the thirteenth Combat Wing had both been given the Presidential Unit citation, but Doolittle had turned it down for the 100th.

Easter came, with a big dinner like at Christmas, and then the weather socked in so that more missions were canceled than flown, but still group morale hovered at quite a low level.

On April 13 the 100th Group flew its 100th mission, to Augsburg to hit the Messerschmitt plant. All the planes returned, though some were shot up.

Higher headquarters decided that what the 100th needed was a new commanding officer. On April 19 Colonel Robert H. Kelly, a West Pointer, arrived, and Colonel Bennett reverted to deputy group commander.

Bombing results were not very good, so Colonel Kelly announced on April 27 that in the next day's raid on Sottevast, a V-weapons site on the Cherbourg peninsula, the pilots would not take evasive action even if they ran into flak on the bomb run. That would give better bombing results, said Colonel Kelly.

"Yeah, and more dead men," said the aircrews.

Sottevast was regarded as just a milk run. Colonel Kelly did not make himself popular when he announced that he personally would lead the raid. Captain Jack Swartout was to have flown the lead with lead pilot William Lakin, who was making his last mission. Major Robert Elton, Lakin's roommate, had arranged for a bucket of champagne to be at the hardstand on return. But Swartout was bounced and the colonel took over.

"Picked himself a milk run for his first official mission, didn't he?"

The colonel became even less popular on the mission when they moved over the target and the bombardiers were ready to loose their bombs.

"Hold it," he said over the intercom. "We're going around again."

A waist gunner of one of the other aircraft recalled what happened next:

"We must have made the longest 360-degree turn in recorded history. Kelly took us far out over the water, and it took forever. We came back in on the bomb run at the same speed, same altitude, and same course, flying in rigid formation."

The formation was an antiaircraft gunner's dream.

"The Kraut guns got us good."

On the first run the flak had been light and well below the bombers. But on this second run, the German gunners got Colonel Kelly's plane first off; two direct hits caused the plane to disintegrate immediately. Colonel Kelly and Captain Lakin were killed, as were four other members of the crew. The others bailed out and became prisoners of war.

So Colonel Bennett again took temporary command of the 100th Bombardment Group.

\*         \*         \*

In late April 1944 there were mixed signals about the luck of the 100th. It seemed to have changed—or had it? On April 29 they flew to Berlin again with no losses, although that day the Eighth Air Force lost sixty-eight bombers. And finally the War Department approved the 100th's citation for the Regensburg mission, but the 100th's citation for the first Berlin mission bounced at Eighth Air Force.

"Somebody doesn't like us, maybe" was the comment at Thorpe Abbotts.

They had just flown eleven missions in twelve days.

# FORTY-FOUR

# *One Plane Did Not Return*

On the Schweinfurt raid of October 14, 1943, only one B-17 of the 390th Bombardment Group was lost: *Patches*, piloted by Lieutenant F. F. McEwin. Here is the story of that crew's mission and the aftermath, which was a fate suffered by many thousands of American airmen in World War II.

Staff Sergeant George Jahnke was the left waist gunner aboard the *Patches*, officially designated as aircraft No. 991 of the 571st Squadron. On the morning of October 14, he was awakened before dawn for the mission of the day, and he went to the mess hall for a breakfast of eggs, toast, and hot coffee.

After breakfast they headed for the briefing room, where they were told the target of the day would be Schweinfurt. The men of the 390th Bomb Group had been there before. This morning the debate was warm: Would it be a milk run, or would it be a ballbreaker? Jahnke had mixed emotions. Possibly it would be a milk run, but he could not forget that on the last three missions the Eighth Air Force had lost eighty-eight aircraft.

The air intelligence officers were not very heartening. They told the crews they could expect plenty of single-engine and twin-engine fighters and very heavy flak. German aircraft production, they announced, was on the rise in spite of round-the-clock bombing by Allied air forces. Schweinfurt was in the Rhine Valley, and the Rhine Valley was known as Flak-Happy Valley.

Still, Sergeant Jahnke was not too worried, and his worries were alleviated by thinking of the score. He had completed twelve missions, with thirteen to go before his tour would be over and he would get back to the United States.

This feeling of confidence was in turn replaced by another worry, however. There were now only four of the original crews left in his squadron, their old pilot was not with them anymore, and their bombardier had been shot down in another plane on another mission. The feeling of comradeship with which he had begun his missions was no longer there.

The sense of being alone was intensified when the flight surgeon took a look at their radio operator and grounded him for sick call. In the briefing they were assigned Sergeant Al Widman as radio operator and Lieutenant L. A. Bennett as bombardier.

At the gunners' briefing Sergeant Jahnke was told that he should expect heavy fighter presence and intense antiaircraft fire all the way in the Ruhr Valley.

They were flying No. 2 position in the squadron, and the squadron was leading the group and the wing.

There was some fighter opposition before they hit the target, but Sergeant Jahnke remembered the pilot turning the aircraft over to the bombardier. Then Jahnke was called to the bomb bay to help release a cluster of hung-up incendiary bombs. That meant venturing out on a six-inch catwalk four miles above ground and lugging a portable oxygen bottle. Somehow they got the bombs loose. Then Staff Sergeant E. A. Pearce, the other waist gunner, shouted that smoke was coming from engine No. 2. Sergeant Jahnke took a look. Sure enough, they had smoke, and they were also losing fuel from a six-inch slash in the wing. As Sergeant Jahnke went back to his left waist gun he saw an ME-109 coming in at three o'clock high. He opened fire, and the German fighter exploded. A piece of the wreckage hit the horizontal stabilizer, and engine No. 2 stopped, feathered.

Jahnke noticed that his plane had dropped back from the formation, but he was so busy firing at fighters that he had no time to consider the matter.

Then Sergeant Widman came out of the radio room and Staff Sergeant Cecil Holladay came out of the ball turret. Sergeant

Pearce motioned to him to get to the back of the ship—that meant bailout. Sergeant Jahnke snapped on his parachute. Before he got to the escape door it was kicked off. When he went back to be sure that the wing was really burning, he saw a fighter coming in. He manned the gun and heard an explosion that he believed was the fighter, and then he went back aft. Four of the crewmen were there. Sergeant Jahnke had been off oxygen for a while during his movements, and now he squatted in front of the escape hatch and fell out. When he awoke his chute was open and he felt as if he were suspended in midair.

Below he saw the plane making wide circles, burning. He saw only one other parachute.

As Sergeant Jahnke swung in his parachute, his mind raced, "I wondered how my family would take the news that I was missing in action. Would I be able to escape capture and get back to England? Would the Germans shoot me when I reached the ground? I prayed as I'd never prayed before. My prayer and thoughts were interrupted when a Jerry ME-110 came at me while I was suspended in the air. I knew I was an easy target drifting toward the earth and had heard that many had been killed in this situation. I hung very limp, hoping he would think I was already dead. Instead of shooting me he circled me, and as I peeked overhead I could see the pilot waving at me. I figured he was telling the ground troops where I might land. I waved back, and he flew away.

"The last 150 feet or so I was conscious of falling very fast, swaying in the wind. I looked down and noticed two men running to where I might land. They appeared to be older men, maybe farmers. The one in the lead was holding a hay fork up at me. As I got nearly on top of him I put my right foot out to protect myself from the tines of the fork. My foot struck him in the upturned face. He fell one way and I the other. Hitting him with my foot caused my right shoulder to hit the ground first. It caused a severe dislocation of my shoulder. My arm was about an inch out of my shoulder socket. . . .

"I raised myself as best I could and noticed the fellow I had landed on was lying on the ground. His whole body was shaking, and his head seemed to be under his back. I feared I had killed him.

"While I was attempting to raise [myself] enough to get a better look, the other man began to beat me with a post. I was very weak. I couldn't defend myself with my dislocated shoulder, a wounded knee, and the added complication of being tangled in my chute. All I could do was lie there and receive the beating I was getting.

"After several blows to all parts of my body I heard a gunshot. The man stopped beating me as soldiers approached in an army command car. The soldiers picked me up and helped me into the back seat of the topless car. I was concerned about the man I had landed on, but they paid no attention to him. They just drove off with me and my chute.

". . . We neared a group of people along a street in a small town. I was made to sit up on the top of the back seat. The vehicle was slowed down, and the soldiers yelled "Luft-gangster" over and over again. People threw whatever they could get their hands on at me. I was struck several times on the body and the head. I don't know if I passed out from being struck by something or from the pain of my injuries, but when I regained consciousness I was being carried into a jailhouse."

In the jail he found all the other members of the crew. They were searched by the guards, who took their watches and rings. Jahnke kept his watch by stuffing it up his rectum.

Then all ten of them were taken to an interrogation center outside Frankfurt and put into separate small cells. Next morning Sergeant Jahnke was taken for interrogation. The officer asked him to sign a paper, but he would give only his name, rank, and serial number.

The officer grew angry.

"You are in Germany now, and you will do as we ask."

"I'm sorry, I can't," said Sergeant Jahnke.

The officer continued to ask questions, but Sergeant Jahnke did not answer.

He was taken back to his cell and flung in. Later in the day he was given a cup of water and a piece of dark bread two inches thick.

Time stood still. Sometimes he slept. Sometimes he was awake. He heard lots of noise, shouting followed by gunshots. He thought he was going to be shot.

The interrogation officer had him in again, and again Sergeant Jahnke refused to sign any forms.

"He yelled something in German, and another intelligence officer came in carrying a device that looked like a wooden shoe with a handscrew on the front of it.

'Take off your right shoe,' the new officer said in English.

Jahnke would not take off his shoe, but he was too weak to resist as two German soldiers put his foot in the device and began to squeeze his foot. They kept tightening the boot until he passed out.

When Sergeant Jahnke came to, he was in a compound with his crewmates. They were fed and put onto a streetcar. On the streetcar people shook their fists and shouted at them. They were taken off the streetcar and walked to a prison camp. Over the gate the sign said Dulag Luft #13. There they found people of their own squadron who had been shot down on previous missions.

At the prison camp they were issued clothing, their pictures were taken, and they were fed decent food. A few days later the enlisted men were marched to a train and put into boxcars. Then they began moving; with intermittent stops on sidings, they moved for a week. They then arrived at a big prison camp, Stalag 17B, which Jahnke later learned was near Krems, Austria. He could tell they were in the mountains.

"As we marched into the American sector of the camp, a sign above the gate greeted us. 'Für Sie ist der Krieg fertig'—For you the war is over."

# FORTY-FIVE

# Stalag 17B

The crew of aircraft No. 991 stuck together once they arrived at Stalag 17B in the Austrian mountains. They were assigned to a tarpaper shack called Barracks 34. It had two sections, A and their B section, separated by a washroom. The latter consisted of long wooden sinks and cold water taps that were turned on for an hour in the morning and an hour in the evening.

The toilets were outside in a long privy shed with wooden seats and twenty holes. They were cleaned by Russian and Polish prisoners, who were used as slave labor.

Inside the B section the men found their beds in a heap on the floor, waiting to be assembled. Put together, these turned out to be two bunks across and 3 bunks high. The prisoners did not use the lowest level but piled the straw mattresses on the board slats, and the Red Cross single woollen blanket over that.

The barracks were heated with brick chimneys, which had cleanout traps; those they used to make coffee and heat Red Cross food. A single row of wires hung down the middle of the barracks, with light bulbs hanging here and there.

Staff Sergeant Jahnke recalled their first meal:

"It came in something resembling a 50-gallon wooden barrel cut in half with a place to put a pole through so two men could carry it on their shoulders. The meal consisted of mashed potatoes with pieces of salmon to give it a pink look and a little flavor. The salmon was from the American Red Cross."

Along the outer edge of the camp were two rows of tall fences. Coiled barbed wire was strung between, and guard towers eighteen feet high were fixed with machine guns and searchlights, with guards on duty twenty-four hours a day. In the daytime the prisoners could wander as they wished inside the camp, but at night they were confined to barracks.

After Jahnke had been in camp for about a month he got his first Red Cross package. One package was shared by two men. It consisted of cans of corned beef, salmon, liver pate, margarine, powdered milk, fruit drink, dried prunes, lump sugar, chocolate, biscuits, instant coffee, soap, and five packages of cigarettes.

As winter came, it got cold in the mountains, and many of the prisoners did not get out of bed all day except to eat and make their toilet and answer roll call. Jahnke would lie with his head under the covers so that his breath would warm his body. The water in the washroom was sometimes frozen for a week or more. The prisoners got drinking water by melting ice.

Worst was the boredom. They had no news of the war, no newspapers, and very few books to read.

Physically they had little attention from the Germans as long as nothing went wrong. Jahnke never did get medical treatment for his dislocated shoulder. There was a German field hospital not far away, but Jahnke noticed that the prisoners who went there did not ever seem to come back. Several of the other "kriegies" helped; they held him down, and one who had been a medical student yanked his arm and popped it back into the socket. Then came weeks of homemade physical therapy. They rigged up a pulley for him to use as traction, and he exercised until he began to have the use of his arm again.

Occasionally there were attempts to escape, but not many.

"One night we were awakened by shots from the guard towers. I rushed to the door to see one of our men running back to the barracks area. Searchlights were all over, and I saw him jump into the air raid trench behind the toilet. Everything went quiet, and soon several soldiers came running through our compound toward the air raid ditch. One of them took out his pistol and pointed it toward the air raid ditch. I heard the GI shout, 'I give up. Kamerad! Kamerad! I give up!' "

"I saw his hand raised from the ditch, and I saw the German

smile as he shot three times at point-blank range into the GI's body and killed him. In unison a cry went up from those of us watching from the barracks as we shouted obscenities at the soldier. I felt sick and cried and prayed for the man who had been killed. He had no weapon and he had surrendered. I don't think anyone slept much that night. The next morning the place was swarming with Gestapo troops. We were headed out to roll call at daylight that day, and we were kept in formation in a cold rain. We were forced to watch as a soldier picked up the body and dragged it out of the compound on a cloth. Then we were matched against our prison pictures before we could return to the barracks. Before I got back inside, 4.5 hours had passed. I was freezing cold and soaked to the bone. After that we never did return the 'Guten Morgen' when the commandant greeted us at rollcall."

Word of the Normandy invasion reached the camp shortly after it occurred, and the prisoners went wild with joy. The Germans became very worried, and doubled the guard against a mass escape attempt. The POWs began to get news through secret radio sets, and the Germans began giving them propaganda news reports. At the time of the Battle of the Bulge the prisoners became very worried about the apparent success of the counterattack, but soon American fighters began to appear over the camp, waggling their wings and then going in to strafe the town of Krems.

The war was obviously growing worse for the Germans. The younger guards started to disappear; if the prisoners asked an old guard about them, he would say "Russkie front."

The prisoners grew cocky with the intimation of Allied victory, and the Germans grew more worried. At the end of the first week of April 1945, the camp was disbanded and the prisoners marched off to avoid the bombings, to Mauthausen, Linz, and then across the Danube River. They marched until April 25, when they came to the Inn River and were put inside a stockade with 4000 others. There they built lean-tos.

The guards gew lax, and one day while going to the river for water, Jahnke and five others decided to make a break, and marched upstream. They found a road and followed it until they came to farmhouses, where farm women fed them. Marching on, they hid in the woods near the road while a German armored column and infantry passed. Close behind was the American infantry, from whom they got weapons. A day later they came to a farm where the farmer gave them his car, a 1937 Ford with a charcoal burner to run it. They gave him a letter of commendation for the gift, signing "Thomas Jefferson, George Washington, Harry Truman," and went off in the car. They went into a town and looted the jewelry store for souvenirs. Next, they stopped at a tavern, pushed open the door, demanded beer, and liberated a small keg.

They headed for Paris. At night they commandeered houses, and what there was to drink, and local girls.

"We traveled this way for several days. Each day supplied its own joys and surprises. With our guns we took what we wanted. One day when we had a nice place to stay we stayed over to allow stomachs and headaches to straighten up and catch up with our fast minds. We came upon a military police checkpoint along the road near the French border. The MPs told us we could not travel any farther in our German car. We weren't disappointed. We all wanted to get back to the States, and our present mode of transportation had too many interruptions. The beer supply had disappeared several days before."

So they caught a ride in the back of an army truck. The MPs told them they would have to leave the souvenirs—and as the truck pulled away, they saw the MPs splitting up the bags of souvenirs!

Finally the six arrived in Paris. At the supply dump they were all outfitted in full OD uniform, including stripes. They were put on a C-47 and flown to Le Havre, to Camp Lucky Strike, a POW processing center, where they were hospitalized, given physical examinations, and then taken aboard the Liberty ship *John B. Hood* and shipped home to New York City. At New York they were taken by bus to McGuire Army Air Base in New Jersey, and then were given partial payment (their records were in limbo) and Pullman rail tickets home. This time it was true, their war was over.

# FORTY-SIX

# New Broom

On May 6, 1944, Colonel Thomas Jeffrey was assigned to go in and straighten out the 100th Bombardment Group. He had shown at the 390th that he could maintain discipline, get combat results, and still remain popular with the officers and men. Something new was definitely needed at the 100th, and because of his long service and proximity it did not seem likely that Lieutenant Colonel Bennett could provide what was needed. So Bennett was moved up to Wing, soon to go to Third Division headquarters on the staff of General LeMay, and Colonel Jeffrey came to Thorpe Abbotts.

"Wonder how long he'll last," they speculated in the barracks.

But there were soon no more bets, because Colonel Jeffrey knew what he was about. He had flown so many missions, it was inconceivable that he could make the sort of mistakes that caused Colonel Kelly's death. And he did not choose milk runs to lead. He led raids to Berlin and against vital and highly protected German factories. On May 12, the Third Division bombed the largest synthetic oil plant in the Third Reich, at Brüx, Czechoslovakia, and that night General LeMay called Colonel Jeffrey to congratulate the 100th on hitting the mean point of impact dead center and virtually wiping out the factory.

This was the sort of word that raised morale, this and minimal losses. On that raid the 100th lost only two airplanes.

On May 19 Colonel Jeffrey led a mission to Berlin, with Captain Robert Rosenthal flying in the No. 2 position. They bombed Berlin, but three planes were lost.

Then came May 24 and another mission to Berlin. This one was a disaster, and the cause was in the United States, where someone had decided to move officers with long stateside service into the Eighth Air Force. Some of these officers had rank, and that meant they would be given positions of leadership although they had no combat experience. At the 100th one such officer was Major Maurice Fitzgerald. He was to be appointed 350th Squadron commander because the current CO, Captain Jack Swartout, was finishing his tour of duty this day, leading the A group. Because of Major Fitzgerald's rank and his stateside experience, he was chosen to lead the B group of the 100th on this mission. There was some concern about his experience, so Colonel Jeffrey made sure there were plenty of experienced people around him. Captain Jim Geary was to be lead pilot. Lieutenant Frank Malooly and his crew had already finished their twenty-five missions, but Swartout needed people who were familiar with the Berlin run, so Malooly agreed to go along on this, his Twenty-seventh mission, because he had more missions to Berlin than anyone in the group. He would lead the squadron and also act as deputy group leader.

After takeoff, Malooly watched as Fitzgerald fumbled. The B group leader had difficulty in forming up with the wing, and the 100th started off across the North Sea behind the wing formation, hurrying to catch up. They entered enemy territory all strung out, and with the low squadron behind by several hundred feet. This was "meat for the Luftwaffe," and fighters swiftly attacked the low squadron. Squadron leader Mark Wilson escaped and got back to England by flying down on the deck, but the rest of the squadron was all broken up.

The remains of the group straggled on to Berlin and bombed, and then pilot Malooly saw group leader Fitzgerald's plane turn to the right, which was the wrong way, and begin to lose altitude. He got on the radio but could not get a response from the group leader. He saw the Fitzgerald plane going down and told the group to re-form on his plane. This whole action caused the group to lose place in the wing formation, and they were suddenly alone. Just then they were bounced by a large group of FW-190s firing 20mm cannon.

Fitzgerald's plane was hit with a shower of lead. The intercom system and probably the radio were knocked out, and soon the crew parachuted.

Pilot Malooly's plane was shot down by the second group of FW-190s. The plane on his left wing, piloted by Lieutenant Lindley Williamson, was also shot down, and the copilot and radio operator were killed.

That day a total of nine of the 100ths bombers were shot down, largely because of poor leadership. That night Captain Robert Rosenthal was appointed commanding officer of the 350th Squadron.

Colonel Jeffrey led the mission on June 5 to Abbeyville, France, in a softening-up process before the D-day invasion. It was a rough mission, and the 100th lost two planes to antiaircraft fire. On the way home, Colonel Jeffrey was ordered to Third Division headquarters, where he was informed of the D-day operation. Next day the 100th attacked in three waves, and Colonel Jeffrey led one of them. In all, the group flew seventy-eight sorties that day with no aborts; they flew until they ran out of bombs.

After D-day the group's missions were mostly airfields, roads, and bridges held by enemy troops, but soon enough they were back over Germany. By September Colonel Jeffrey was able to hold a "lecture" in which he reported that the 100th had flown more missions in July than any other group, had dropped 1300 tons of bombs, and had been commended by the Eighth Air Force top brass. Morale had picked up remarkably, and it was not damaged even by the compulsory attendance at the illustrated VD lecture that followed the colonel. Life was loosening up a bit.

On September 10, 1944, the target was Nuremberg. On the way home after plastering the target, a tank factory, Major Rosenthal's plane was badly hit by flak that they had not been warned about in the briefing. He managed to stay in the air until they got to Belgium, and then he crash-landed. The crew, which could have bailed out over enemy territory but chose to stick with the plane and the major, were badly shaken up in the crash landing, and the bombardier had a broken leg. But they were brought out safely by Free French and quickly taken to a British hospital. Two days later Major Rosenthal was in a hospital at Oxford with a broken arm, but otherwise intact.

The war went on. With his broken arm Major Rosenthal was assigned to Third Division headquarters, but there he complained so loudly about ground duty that he was reassigned to the 100th once more.

At Christmastime 1944, the 100th sat on the ground and bit lips while the Germans unleashed their Ardennes offensive in skies too dark to fly. Not until Christmas Eve had the weather cleared enough for a mission. That day the Eighth Air Force announced that everything that could fly would fly, and more than 2000 heavy bombers dropped more than 5000 tons of bombs on airfields and other German concentrations.

Then on New Year's Eve came a raid on Hamburg which turned out to be a disaster. The 100th was hard hit by flak and fighters and lost twelve planes that day. The entire Eighth Air Force lost only 14 of more than 1200.

# FORTY-SEVEN

# Chick's Crew

They met at Salt Lake City, four of the ten members of the crew of a B-17. The pilot was Lieutenant Anthony J. Cecchini, who was known as "Chick." The copilot was Lieutenant Stanley Fisher. The radio operator was Ben Smith, Jr. One of the waist gunners, and an armorer, was Sergeant Robert J. O'Hearn.

Soon they were loaded aboard a troop train and sent to Alexandria, Louisiana, to train for an overseas assignment. On the way, O'Hearn and Smith were caught out of uniform. They were just the couple of suckers the mess sergeant was searching for, and they drew KP for the duration of the train trip. But that was not so bad for a couple of enterprising soldiers. They made up bologna sandwiches, dressed them up in waxed paper, and sold them to the officers. So the trip passed pleasantly for these two enlisted men, and a lot of money passed into their hands, unbeknownst to the mess sergeant.

At Alexandria Air Base the crew got its navigator, Lieutenant Edward Veigel. They started to train in a B-17F which had been retired from combat. It was great training for trouble, since almost every flight meant a malfunction of some sort for the tired old airplane. One night on a cross-country flight two engines caught fire, but by that time the crew was so expert that most of them, asleep in the waist, did not even know there was a fire.

They learned many things, about half of them useless in combat, including how to repair radios in flight, radios which did not work at high altitude in subzero temperatures. They were taught to receive code at high speed, although when in combat they would take it at low speed. They learned how to fire machine guns, but not the deflection shooting they would use in combat. They were trained in night missions, but all their combat missions would be by day. In training they lost their ball turret gunner and picked up Sergeant George Kepics. Ultimately they graduated, were deemed ready for combat, and were sent off on home leave, the enlisted men with good conduct medals that several of them did not deserve, and with sergeant's stripes.

Next stop was Grand Island, Nebraska, getting equipment and a new B-17G right out of the factory.

Where were they headed? Nobody knew, but they were issued machetes, mosquito nets, and jungle kits.

One March day in 1944, they took off for Presque Isle, Maine—hardly the way to the jungle. It was not, of course, but rather the way to Goose Bay, Labrador, and points European. They made the passage with fifty-four other bombers, flying through snow. Two planes were lost on the trip to Iceland, then Stornoway on the Isle of Lewis in the Outer Hebrides.

On March 15 Chick and his crew took off from Stornoway and flew to Prestwick. There, to their shock, they lost their airplane —it was simply whisked away from them. At least the crew stayed together, but they were sent to the Combat Crew Replacement Center at Bovingdon, close to London. Here they began to learn the hard facts of the war, including the tales of the losses. Up above they could see planes coming home with pieces out of their wings, props feathered, some trailing smoke, others missing parts of their horizontal stabilizers.

Soon Lieutenant Cecchini's crew was sent from Bovingdon to Molesworth. They were going to join the 303rd Bombardment Group, known as Hell's Angels, which was under the command of Colonel Kermit D. Stevens. The group had gotten its name from one of the original American aircraft to arrive in England, now long gone, which had been the first Flying Fortress to make twenty-five missions. Hell's Angels was a name in the "wild blue yonder" tradition of the American air force; in conversation the 303rd was known as the Molesworth group.

The officers of the new crew moved into the bachelor officers' quarters. The enlisted men were assigned to a barracks shared by two other crews. The six empty bunks that were waiting for them had been occupied twenty-four hours earlier by another crew, but that crew had not come home from a mission.

The new crew hardly got the time of day from the old hands. When they first came in, a nonstop poker game was in progress and no one looked up. They got a few nods from airmen lying on their sacks reading. Not much else. Then the door flew open and a handful of noisy drunks came in. The men who now called themselves Chick's Crew were dismayed. They sensed something hysterical about the behavior pattern and soon discovered that these were veterans of Schweinfurt and the Oschersleben raids. The war, Chick's Crew suddenly learned, was not as it had been painted back home, but a compendium of anxieties. They began to learn the ropes. They were part of the First Air Division, Forty-first Combat Wing. The bomb group consisted of four squadrons: the 358th, 359th, 360th, and 427th. Theirs was the 360th, commanded by Colonel Walter K. Shayler.

Chick's Crew was something of an anomaly. There was no discipline in the crew except air discipline, and they called each other by first names and buddied together. They were often in trouble with the commandant of crews.

Chick, the pilot, a 200-pound New York State policeman, was an Italian cop who looked like an Irishman. He was another of those who had wanted to be a fighter pilot, and he still liked to play games with his aircraft. On the way over, he had flown over his home town of Poughkeepsie, New York, and buzzed his own house. Now in England he liked nothing better than to buzz farmhouses.

Lieutenant Stan Fisher, the copilot, was the Beau Brummel of the crew. He wore a tailored Eisenhower jacket, a fur parka from Goose Bay, and English buckle shoes.

Lieutenant Edward Veigel, the navigator, was called Jasper because of a monumental goof in navigation in the States, when he mistook Beaumont, Texas, for Jasper and started to take the crew out over the Gulf of Mexico. He reformed after that escapade and showed great competence.

Lieutenant Theodore McDevitt, the bombardier, was a dapper young man whose preoccupation in the air was to get rid of his bombs.

Sergeant Clarence Cogdell, waist gunner, was a Tennessean and a lover of bluegrass music. He was known as Alvin York in the crew. Staff sergeant Ben Smith, Jr., was called Snuffy after a comic strip character. Sergeant Cliff Bachman, a German from Grand Rapids, was the flight engineer and the bravest man of the crew. Sergeant Robert J. O'Hearn was an Irishman from Massachusetts who loved to drink. Sergeant Ward Hudson, the tail gunner, was a Scotsman from Chicago. Sergeant George Kepics, a Hungarian from New Jersey, was the crew wise guy and a card shark.

As Staff Sergeant Smith summed it up "We were descended from Irish, Italian, English, Scotch, Hungarian, Jewish, and German immigrants. We were typical."

Chick's Crew arrived in Molesworth in March 1944. Elsewhere in the world, American airmen were bombing the Germans in the Anzio area of Italy; Lieutenant Cruickshanks's P-51 squadron was flying close support missions in Burma for General Orde Wingate's special forces behind the Japanese lines; and fighters were striking Rabaul, the big Japanese base on New Britain Island.

Chick's Crew was green, green, green. And a good thing, too. They did not know that the Eighth Air Force was just then suffering its heaviest losses of the war. On March 6, 658 heavy bombers hit Berlin, and the German fighters took a heavy toll: 69 bombers, the highest number lost by the Eighth in a single day, failed to returned to base.

At first the new boys flew dry runs over the Wash, an inlet on the north coast of East Anglia, where they were unlikely to be disturbed by German fighters.

Then on April 17 they were alerted with the rest of the squadron to be prepared to fly a mission the next morning.

Very early on the 18th, before dawn, the door of the barracks flew open. The charge of quarters blew in and shouted, "Cecchini's Crew."

That was the word for the enlisted men. They were going. Later, when they got to know the CQ, he would give more information.

"Twenty-seven hundred gallons and ten five hundreds," he would say—which meant a long mission, probably Germany.

The six enlisted men dressed in flying coveralls, heated boots, and suits. Then they went to the mess hall for a mission breakfast: They could have anything they wanted to eat within reason— pancakes, eggs any way. To Sergeant Smith it was akin to the last meal of a condemned man.

Then the mission crews were briefed all together, officers and noncoms. The mission was Berlin!

Sergeant Smith was briefed again with other radio operators by an intelligence officer. "He had a hearty manner, for a good reason: he didn't have to go." The air intelligence officer peeled the cover from the mission map. The men groaned as they saw the red lines that led deep into Germany. The target was the Heinkel Oranienburg plant in Berlin's suburbs. There would be heavy fighter opposition, and "intense" flak at the target.

Chick's crew would be flying No. 3 position in the high squadron (as opposed to the lead squadron and the low squadron).

That was it. The Catholics began to receive the Sacrament from the priest, Father Skopner. Then they all climbed into trucks and headed for the hardstands where the B-17s were lined up. The ground crews were swarming over the planes, and the armorers were putting in the bombs. It was still dark.

The enlisted crew got aboard. They put machine guns in their casings and attached the gun belts. Then they left the bombers and went to the dispersal tent. There they sacked out on the cots, listening to the coughs of the aircraft engines as they wheezed and finally started up.

Then it was time to board for sure. The Fortresses taxied out and lined up. Every thirty seconds one B-17 pilot would gun the engines and rush down the runway. This was one of the critical moments, taking off with a heavy bomb and gas load.

At 10,000 feet Chick told the boys to go on oxygen. First the squadron formed up on the leader, who directed them with flares; then the combat group formed, and finally the wing. Then— Mission Berlin—they headed toward the North Sea.

The lords of the sky had chosen a fine, bright day for this first mission of Chick's Crew. As far as they could see, the sky was filled with B-17s, the olive drab B-17s and the silver B-17Gs. Overhead was a formation of P-38 fighters. The crew relaxed and made wisecracks over the intercom until Chick shut them up. Then the flak came. Sergeant Smith heard it first. Wham-whoosh, wham-whoosh. Bombardier McDevitt was the first to shout:

"Flak twelve o'clock. Christ, look at it!"

They were almost on target and turning into the bomb run. The bomb bay doors opened, and a blast of cold air rushed into the fuselage. The plane reeled from the shock of almost continuous nearby explosions. The bursts filled the sky all around the B-17 formation.

Radioman Smith's task at this point was to throw out "window" or "chaff"—shredded tinfoil—to confuse the enemy radar. Then it was "Bombs Away," as bombardier McDevitt pressed his switches. Sergeant Smith stood in the door to the bomb bay to see that all the bombs had cleared. They had, but as he stood there he was hit in the chest by a piece of shrapnel that also cut the command radio in two. Smith's flak vest saved his life, but a small bit of shrapnel struck him in the neck. He was bleeding but not seriously hurt, not even enough to get a Purple Heart.

Chick headed toward the coast, and German antiaircraft batteries shot at them until they hit the island of Helgoland and then passed out of German territory. Over the North Sea, they let down below 10,000 feet and took off the oxygen masks. They had been on oxygen for eight hours.

They reached Molesworth, and gingerly Pilot Cecchini let the plane down. He knew the hydraulic system had been hit, and he wondered if the landing gear would hold up. But the gear held and the B-17 rolled to safety, moving off the runway and turning slowly to the right until it stopped. The crew got out and looked at the aircraft. It was full of holes, but it had come home. One ship from their squadron did not. It was shot down over the target, but the crew bailed out and was saved. That crew had been on its last mission.

If one had to be in a war, life at Molesworth base was good duty. The Americans there lived in permanent stucco barracks, not metal huts. The discipline was easy, and the administrative officers left the flight crews pretty much to themselves.

The barracks were reasonably comfortable, with heat from potbellied stoves. The men lazed around in flight clothes and played cards or read for recreation. A poker game went on almost incessantly. The big winner was ball turret gunner Kepics, who sent home about a thousand dollars a month. He warned the crew not to play with him, but some of them did anyhow. They learned.

The men listened to the BBC ("dry as dust") and mooned over popular ballads on the Armed Forces Radio Network. Sometimes they listened to Axis Sally telling them all about their future—or lack of it. One of her favorite ploys was to call out the name of some American soldier (gotten from a POW interrogation) and tell him that his wife was going out with other men in America. Chick's Crew thought these were pretty funny stories.

The walls of the barracks were covered with pinups, most of them clipped from the pages of *Yank*, the soldier's magazine. Betty Grable and Rita Hayworth were the squadron favorites.

The second mission of Chick's Crew was to Cherbourg, the French Norman port. The third was to Hamm in the Ruhr Valley; on that one German fighters followed them home and attacked the bombers as they went into the landing pattern. They played particular havoc with the group's B-24s.

On the crew's fourth mission they had a colonel aboard, because they were being looked over as a potential "lead crew." On the bomb run, it was the radio operator's job after the bombing to report on whether all the bombs had gotten away. On this mission the flak was very heavy, so Sergeant Smith shouted, "Bomb bay clear," without looking, and the door closed. But as they came over the English Channel he started through the cat-walk and saw that fully half the bombs had not cleared and were still hanging there—fully armed.

What to do? They were very close to the English coast, so Chick and the colonel decided to land with the bombs. Chick made a perfect landing, but the crew did not become lead crew.

Nobody said anything to Sergeant Smith except Chick.

"For Chrissakes, Smitty!" he said ruefully. And that was all.

After their fifth mission they got air medals and leave to go to London, where they saw the sights and spent most of their time in pubs. Then it was back to the war, and to Berlin again, and Rouen.

On May 11, Chick's Crew flew their eighth mission. The target was Saarbrucken, in the heart of the German industrial district. The flak grew heavy as they approached the target, led by a "fearless leader." Most aircrews were not very high on fearless leaders, who they felt had very slight respect for the lives of the crews. This fearless leader led them through the flak, then announced that they were off the target and were going around again. He made a wide circle and started in. By this time Chick's Crew figured every gun in the Ruhr was shooting at them, and several of the B-17s were trailing smoke and had feathered engines. Some had left the formation and headed for Switzerland. Staff Sergeant Smith recollected:

"The bomb bay doors came open again, and this time we dropped. Captain Long's aircraft was burning. I could clearly see the waist gunners, looking at us through the waist windows. . . . These fellows were our friends and lived in our barracks. They stayed in formation until 'Bombs Away' and then started down out of control. Our tail gunner saw them blow up. There were no survivors."

It was that crew's final mission. If they had made it, they would have gone home.

Chick's crew had no time to worry about their friends, however. Flak knocked out their two outboard engines and blew off one bomb bay door. The plane began to lose altitude, and it was obvious that they could not stay with the formation. That was worrisome, for the German fighters were clustering around, looking for cripples. Chick considered heading for Switzerland, but that meant internment for the duration of the war. He decided to try to make it home.

The plane kept dropping until they were down to 11,000 feet. They crossed over a German airfield, and the flak began coming, fast and accurate. Chick put the plane into an almost vertical dive to escape the flak, pulling out just above the treetops. Then he ordered the crew to jettison anything that could be thrown overboard. Ammunition, machine guns, radios, even clothing began to go out. The crew assembled in the radio room and solemnly shook hands. They thought they were goners.

Chick ordered them into the nose for balance, except for Sergeant Smith, who stayed at his post in the radio room.

By this time the B-17 was over Belgium and so low that they were dodging church steeples. They were on war emergency power and making 140 mph, which was too much. The two working engines overheated, turned cherry red, and threatened to explode. Chick reduced manifold pressure and rpms, and the engines cooled down as the airspeed dropped to 125 mph.

Down on the deck, they approached the coast, and the defenders began firing at them. Sergeant Smith watched the tracers coming up. The crew could not shoot back because they had jettisoned their machine guns.

Shells began to explode inside the aircraft. Chick was hit, and so were the navigator and the tail gunner. Smith received a crease wound from a machine gun bullet.

Chick bobbed the plane and weaved, jinking to avoid the flak. He was in pain from a piece of shrapnel sticking into his thigh.

And then they crossed the coast and were over the Channel. Staff Sergeant Smith tuned in the distress frequency on the liaison set, and the DF station answered and began tracking them. It appeared that they would have to ditch. But they neared the English coast and then were directed to a fighter field by the DF station.

Suddenly they realized they had no brakes and no flaps. The

whole hydraulic system was a shambles. They would have to crash-land on this small field at Southend-on-Sea on the Thames estuary.

It was going to be a one-shot landing. They came in fast and almost immediately began to run out of field. The bomber was heading toward a big concrete building. Chick unlocked the tail wheel, kicked the right rudder, and goosed the left engine. The plane careened to the right and missed the building by a few feet. They hit a barbed wire barrier and went through it as if it were paper. They hit a stump, the landing gear collapsed, and the plane dropped onto its belly. Finally they hit a ditch, and the plane ground-looped and stopped.

The unwounded crewmen got the wounded out. The navigator was unconscious. Chick was in great pain. The "meat wagon" and the RAF firetrucks hurried up and picked them up, with loud congratulations for a splendid landing.

In a few minutes they were in the RAF sergeants' mess, being plied with whisky and quickly becoming lightheaded.

Chick's crew stayed at Southend for a few days. Chick, navi-gator Veigel, and gunner Hudson went to the hospital and stayed for several days. When the unwounded got back to Molesworth, they discovered that they had been reported missing, and all their gear had been picked over by their friends. It took Staff Sergeant Smith a week to round up his bicycle and other treasures.

# FORTY-EIGHT

# High Priority

October 1944 was a slow month for the 449th Group. On October 4, bombers attacked the rail line through the Brenner pass. On October 7 they flew a mission in support of the Russian armies attacking Budapest. On October 11 they attacked oil facilities in the Vienna area, but overcast skies prevented them from bombing.

The weather held up attacks for most of the rest of the month, but on October 29 they hit the west rail yards of Munich.

Winter began in November, and with it, the big event of the month, the fire at the 716th barracks. These barracks had been built by the Germans and taken over by the Americans. A fire started in one of the gasoline stoves when a guard went off to breakfast, and in less than an hour four barracks went up in smoke.

November was also notable for the news that German fighter production was actually increasing, despite all the attacks by the strategic air force on plants, and had hit 1500 per month. The Germans' big problem was fuel. The 449th helped exacerbate that problem with strikes on the Moosbierbaum oil refinery and the refinery at Florisdorf. Still, more fighters than ever were noted at Udine and Aviano, including some new jet fighters.

In December the 449th was again supporting the Russian drive in Hungary and the Allied drive in northern Italy.

Only five missions were flown in January. In February several missions were flown against oil resources and several against German jet airplane factories and airfields. The group's 200th mission was set against the Moosbierbaum oil refinery, but it was an almost complete bust. The big event of the month was a 6000-plane mission flown by the British and by the U.S. Eighth, Ninth, Twelfth, and Fifteenth air forces on German targets on February 22. The 449th's target was the rail yards at Spittal, Austria.

The war had changed greatly in the last few months. In 1944 the 449th had flown missions from Marseilles to the Black Sea, but now the attack area was restricted to Austria, Northern Italy, and Bavaria. In order to bomb anywhere else in German Europe, a group had to have specific clearance from higher headquarters. And the airmen of the Fifteenth Air Force had some disquieting news: Men were being transferred from the air forces to the infantry.

By March the high priority target was Moosbierbaum.

If March was a slow month, April was even slower. It was obvious that the war was winding down. Some of the 449th missions were designed to harry the retreating Germans, and several missions were flow against the rail line through the Brenner Pass which the Germans struggled to keep open.

Lieutenant General Ira Eaker returned to the United States, and command of the Mediterranean Allied Air Force went to Major General Joseph Cannon.

The major mission of April was the Apple mission.

It was begun on April 9 by the British eighth Army against the Gothic Line toward the town of Argenta, entry to the Po Valley. The 449th bombed concentrations near Lugo. For the rest of the month the group attacked largely in support of troop operations. As the last week of the month began, the Russians were only five miles from Berlin, and the Fifth and Eighth armies were moving forward in northern Italy. On April 21 the Fifth Army captured Bologna. The 449th attacked targets, mostly German communications, ahead of the advancing infantry.

On April 26, thirty-two B-24s took off on a mission to attack enemy ammunition stores at Casarsa della Delizia, Italy, but the weather was so bad they did not bomb. No one knew it at the time, but this mission, the group's 254th, was its last mission of World War II.

# FORTY-NINE

# On Patrol

Joe Layer was a student at Manhattan College in New York City when the Japanese hit Pearl Harbor. Soon he had the itch to volunteer for flight service with the navy. They put him in the V-5 program. They called him to duty in 1942 and sent him to Rutgers University in New Jersey for civilian pilot training. Soon he soloed and then got his private pilot's license.

After that he was sent to the University of North Carolina at Chapel Hill for preflight training—which meant a lot of physical training and marching. When the cadets weren't moving about, they were learning the rudiments of navigation and meteorology and something about aeronautics.

Norman, Oklahoma, was the next stop, for primary training. Then it was Corpus Christi, Texas, where Cadet Layer and his classmates had flight training and emerged as ensigns in the United States Navy.

But when they were ready for the naval air service, the naval air service was not ready for them. Cadet Layer had opted for fighters, but the navy had all the fighter pilots it could use just then. There was no room in the fleet. The cadets who had graduated with the highest math grades were sent to navigation school.

"Uh-oh," said Cadet Layer. "Bye-bye blue yonder, here comes the briny."

But it was not so. After eight weeks of stiff aerial navigation training at Hollywood, Florida, Joe Layer was assigned to multi-engine flying boats and trained more in PBYs at Norfolk naval air station and in PBMs on the Banana River in Florida. The patrol plane commander was Lieutenant John Carr, and the other pilot was Ensign Bob Wolff.

After the Banana River training, while waiting for his commission as ensign, Cadet Layer and two other young pilots and one mechanic took a PBY up for a check flight before it could be returned to the line for training following engine changes. They started out on what was usually a five-hour flight. It was a very hot day, so they decided to land on the Gulf of Mexico and go for a swim. They were swimming happily when cadet Layer looked around suddenly. No airplane!! The anchor with which they thought they had secured the plane had dragged, and the aircraft was drifting rapidly downwind. The swimmers all became sprinters, caught their aircraft, and anchored it down—securely this time. "It would have been very embarrassing to swim ashore naked and report the loss of a PBY."

In the spring of 1944 Cadet Layer became Ensign Layer. He ended up at Alameda Naval Air Station in San Francisco, and from there, with with his new squadron, VP-16, he was sent to Kaneohe Naval Air Station in Hawaii. He was third pilot. Besides the copilot and the patrol plane commander, the PBM medium patrol bomber carried a crew chief, two mechanics, three radio and radar operators, and four gunners.

And how did they get to Kaneohe? They flew. Kaneohe was fourteen hours flying time, and the PBM had a range of around fifteen hours depending on headwinds. So they flew, a little bit hesitant, but they flew.

Hawaii meant more training and very little time for the fleshpots. April passed all too quickly, and May passed more quickly. Guadalcanal was now a quiet base. The once-bloodstained beach at Tarawa in the Gilberts was a place to swim.

In June, VP-16 headed out to sea from Oahu—south to Palmyra first, then to Canton Island, Tarawa, and Eniwetok in the Marshalls, where not so long ago there had been fighting, and then to Saipan.

On June 11, Vice Admiral Marc Mitscher had led fifteen aircraft carriers of the U.S. Fifth Fleet in strikes on the islands of

Saipan, Tinian, Guam, and Rota. This was a softening-up process for the invasion of Saipan, which the army air forces wanted as a base for their B-29 heavy bombers that were already flying against Japan from bases in western China.

So the invasion of the Mariana Islands began.

On June 16 Admiral Mitscher flew from his carrier flagship to Aslito Airfield on Saipan for a meeting with Admiral Raymond Spruance, commander of the Fifth Fleet, and Vice Admiral Richmond Kelly Turner, commander of the amphibious forces. They talked about the success of their invasion and the need to knock out the Japanese fleet, which was approaching and looking for battle. The marines and army troops going ashore on Saipan, the first part of the inner Japanese empire to be breached were beginning to encounter very stiff resistance there. So Admiral Mitscher went back to his carrier and soon had orders to "go out and get 'em," to find and fight Vice Admiral Jisaburo Ozawa and his Combined Fleet.

Meanwhile Ensign Joe Layer and his friends had left Eniwetok, bound for Saipan, under the impression that the fighting would be all over by the time they arrived. They were told to land on the east side of the island and take possession of the former Japanese seaplane base there.

Before dawn on June 18, Admiral Mitscher was routed out of his bunk aboard the flagship by his chief of staff, Captain Arleigh Burke. They had a message from Pearl Harbor: A submarine had found the Japanese fleet. Admiral Mitscher figured the enemy would reach a launch point 660 miles from Saipan by dawn. If they steamed toward the enemy at flank speed, they could reach a launch point by late afternoon—in time to make at least one strike against the enemy on June 18. But Mitscher was overruled by the ultraconservative Admiral Spruance. The battle was delayed, and the Japanese were given the opportunity to make the first strike.

While this maneuvering occurred, the American marines and army troops were landing on Saipan and encountering increasingly strong resistance. The Japanese intended to fight for every foot of this island stronghold, as Ensign Layer learned when his squadron of PBMs approached the east side of Saipan later in the day. They spotted the seaplane base and headed toward it, but asthey approached they saw below them a number of aircraft in the water, all bearing the red ~~circle~~ DISC of the Rising Sun of Japan. Somebody had made an error of presumption: the Japanese were still firmly in control of the seaplane base.

So around they came in a 90-degree turn and headed north. Then they flew around the north side of the island over to the west side near Aslito Airfield, which was in American hands. But Aslito was not a base for float planes, so they had to put down in the open sea adjacent to the invasion fleet—not a very comfortable place for a patrol squadron to rest.

They were offered sanctuary by a freighter in the roadstead, and they tied up to it. When they went aboard the ship for chow and a movie, they were informed that the freighter was an ammunition ship. Ensign Layer and his friends blanched visibly, but the ammunition ship people were used to that.

"Don't worry," they said. "If the Japs come, we will cut you loose."

Comforting thought: they would either be blown up or cut loose to float around the harbor as the target of the guns of Zeros.

But in a few hours the old four-stack destroyer USS *Ballard* showed up and took the squadron in tow. It was their tender for the next few days of June 1944. Then, finally, in came the USS *Pocomoke,* a real seaplane tender.

Because they were under combat conditions, half the crew stayed aboard the PBM while the other half went aboard the tender. That evening, life became a little rocky for the men aboard the flying boats moored in the roadstead. The Japanese had planned a shuttle bombing system at Saipan to move their fighter planes from the incoming carriers to the land bases and back again. Thus the Zero fighters arrived at Saipan looking for targets, and attacked the invasion fleet. The plan was to bomb and strafe the Americans, then put down at one of the airfields, refuel, rearm, hit the Americans again on the shore and at sea, and then land aboard the Japanese carriers and repeat the process.

In theory the shuttle system increased the effectiveness of the Japanese air fleet by at least half, but in fact it did not work that way. The Japanese were just getting organized, and the passes they made at the PBMs on the water were halfhearted. They did not hit anything. Many of the Japanese planes were shot down by the air patrols of the escort carriers or by the fighter sweeps made by the offshore big carriers. Several Zeros swooped down on the PBMs that were sitting off the invasion beach like sitting ducks. Each Zero was carrying three bombs, but the bombs all missed.

That night Ensign Layer's crew flew their first wartime mission, a search for the Japanese fleet 600 miles from Saipan. The search sector was divided into pie-shaped wedges, one of which was assigned to Ensign Layer's aircraft. The next night one of the PBMs of the squadron sighted the Japanese fleet but its radio failed so it could not report the sighting until it returned. By then the battle known to the American carrier pilots as "the Marianas Turkey Shoot"—because it was much like a sport in which riflemen fire at captive turkey targets for prizes—was under way, and the Japanese fleet was taking a terrible beating. Ensign Layer's aircraft was on the night shift; they flew by night and slept away the daylight hours. The missions lasted fourteen hours. Sometimes the crew picked up flocks of blips on their radar—aircraft ferried in from Yap and other islands by the Japanese to try to continue the battle. They reported these, but the enemy were usually long gone before intercepters got up after them.

The major job was to look for submarines by radar. Since the sinking of an escort carrier by a submarine during the Gilberts invasion, the Pacific Fleet had been very careful to double its submarine watch. There were plenty of Japanese submarines around the Marianas this summer, but they were leery.

So the PBMs went out day after day and night after night down on the deck and flying at under 1000 feet altitude for the most part, and they saw very little for several days. They did make some contacts and dropped many depth charges, but there were no definitive results. The Japanese were making serious efforts to rescue their own airmen, most of them navy fliers who were in very short supply, as the fighting on Saipan turned steadily to the side of the Americans. Several I-boats were sunk in these night-time rescue efforts.

One day in late July came the turn of Ensign Layer's aircraft. They were on patrol north of Saipan when they had a radar contact with an underwater object, and they were pretty sure it was not a whale. They attacked through cloud cover and dropped four sonar buoys, which soon gave off definite sounds of underwater engines. They called in the surface navy and dropped depth charges. Next day the destroyers found debris, and the men of Ensign Layer's PBM got credit for an assist in sinking an enemy submarine. That was all they ever knew about it.

After that things became dull. Ensign Layer's crew set out at six o'clock each night and flew until eight in the morning. Going and coming, they flew low over the Japanese lines on Saipan,— since one of their tasks was to keep track of Japanese troop movements on the island.

Some of the missions were hairy because of weather and the behavior of their Wright Cyclone engines, which swallowed valves the way a monkey swallows peanuts. A long night flight was often followed by a long day of work by the mechanics on those unbeloved engines.

During the daylight hours, when the crew woke up, there was the wardroom of the tender, with its phonograph and the running acey-deucey games and poker. In VP-16 there were two excellent poker players who always won. One night they got the commander of the base into the game and cleaned him out. Next day he issued an order forbidding card playing on his base.

They did have some beer parties, following the navy pattern; liberty boats took officers and men to a little island, where they swam and played cards and drank beer. Late in afternoon they came back. On one of these expeditions they found an island that had been a Japanese base of some sort, underwoven with caves. Ensign Layer and Ensign Jules Lemoine went down to explore the caves, and stayed for an hour poking around with flashlights. When they came back up they discovered the rest of the liberty party had abandoned them. That was a scary feeling. Lost at sea in the harbor! They took off their shirts and began to signal. Ultimately they attracted the attention of a traveling workboat and were rescued. They had another problem: All the ships in the harbor looked pretty much alike to these airlubbers, and they did not know where their tender was. So the workboat crisscrossed the harbor, hailing one vessel after another until they finally lucked out and saw the tender with the PBMs bobbing around like corks.

After one search mission in which the plane was shot up by ground fire, the skipper decided the plane should come out of the water for repairs. This was accomplished at a small seaplane ramp. But the area was not yet secured from enemy action, so the marines were detailed to guard the plane overnight on its ramp. At about midnight, people were awakened by a lot of noise on the tin roof of a destroyed building near the ramp. The marines opened up with automatic weapons. In the morning they found two slaughtered hogs on the roof.

After Saipan was secured at the end of August, the squadron was ordered back to Eniwetok to restage for a new assignment.

They went to the seaplane base at Ebeye. The Wright Cyclones were played out and had to be replaced, so from August 27 until September 12, 1944 they waited for new engines.

At Ebeye, recreation was pretty limited. One day Ensign Max Jones and Ensign Layer decided to go out on the beach looking for necklace shells. They crossed the lagoon through knee-deep water and spent several hours shell hunting and swimming in the surf. Then they returned, or tried to. When they reached the gap between the islands, they found the knee-deep water had become eight feet deep with the changing tide, and the flow was very fast going out to sea. The two men were getting ready to bed down for the night when a landing craft happened by, took pity on them, and delivered them to their own island.

By the time they had the new engines, the war had moved on. Preparations were being made for the the invasion of the Philippines, but first would come the invasion of the Palau Islands. Here was the spot to which the Japanese had moved the sorry remnants of their Combined Fleet after the Battle of the Philippine Sea, and here was the naval bastion of the Japanese Pacific that Admiral Nimitz termed the "cojones" of the enemy.

The Americans did not know it, but the war had gone so badly for the Japanese by this time that Palau had been abandoned as fleet base for the Singapore area and Borneo. The reason was unavailability of fuel. The need for conservation was so great that training and gunnery exercises had been suspended. The Japanese were still counting on one last desperate sortie against the Americans, to try to win a major fleet victory. The Combined Fleet was waiting for that last great push, the Sho or Victory operation, which was scheduled to begin with the American invasion, whether in the Philippines, Taiwan, or the China coast.

So in September the Americans invaded Palau, to find virtually no Japanese in situ. Palau was to be the new base of operations of VP-16. Their new seaplane tender was the USS *Pocomoke*; a converted banana boat.

Again there were long and arduous patrols over mile after mile of deserted sea, searching for the enemy. They were out every night. For the most part they patrolled for submarines, flying at 800 feet or less. The PBM carried two full fuselage tanks as it started out each day, plus an extra tank in the bomb bay for the long-distance patrols.

On September 20 they got into trouble. Flying at 800 feet, at the halfway point of the patrol, they lost one of the Wright Cyclones. The PBM could be trimmed to fly on a single engine, but it did not help a lot to start the procedure at 800 feet. They managed to jettison the depth charges (each about 330 pounds), and drop some gasoline, and stabilized the flight home. The tender had a string of lights out for them for landing in the dark, but whoever had rigged them had done it backwards, and they were pointed to a landing downwind. They came in losing altitude and slowing, and then the patrol plane commander suddenly saw the bulk of the ship looming up directly in front of them. Simultaneously the radio opened up to the da-dit of danger. The commander yanked back on the wheel, the plane began to lift by the inch, and they cleared the bright lights and the ship by running between the masts!

Now they knew the danger, at least, but they still had to land downwind in the dark with one engine. They came around again and somehow made it down, slopping a lot of water but not breaking anything.

On October 18 the invasion of Leyte got under way, and by November 29 the area was fairly secure. There was no Japanese air force left in the islands except kamikazes. Most of the Japanese surface ships were down deep in the briny, and Admiral John Hoover, the panjandrum of landbased naval air, declared the area secure. There were Japanese submarines lurking about (one later sank the cruiser *Indianapolis*), but the threat did not seem severe, so VP-16's tour of duty was over and the squadron went home to the United States for relief, recreation, rehabilitation, and reassignment.

# FIFTY

# *Joint Raid*

On D-day at Normandy, as the Allied troops were scurrying toward the beaches, the 449th was bombing Ploesti again. Many planes straggled home with extensive flak damage, but none were lost.

The Germans increased their air-to-air bombing, and more planes were lost, but the Allied attacks were stepped up in vigor. Trieste, Constanza in Rumania, and Munich were now targets. So was Bratislava in Slovakia, where the bombers burned an oil refinery.

Morale grew better and better, particularly as more amenities appeared at the air base. A new outdoor theater was built to accommodate over a thousand men. The seats were bomb fins; the movies changed three times a week.

The 449th also had its favorite dog, Doc, who had attached himself to one of the pilots. He slept on the pilot's cot, accompanied him to the mess and the officers' club, and went to the plane. He was even known to have flown on a few missions. But one day Doc's pilot did not return from a mission. Doc searched the field and the airplanes but could not find him. He stuck around the air base visiting one mess hall or another, but never allowing himself to become attached to one person. As long as the 449th remained at Grottaglie, so did Doc.

Hollywood's motion picture makers were doing their best to contribute to the American war spirit, and they made a lot of movies about what was going on in Europe and the Pacific. One

of these was *Bombardier*, a tribute to the bombers and their personnel. But to the men of the 449th it was the funniest movie of
the year, full of technical errors. The high point was the scene
where the bombardier leaned out the camera hatch until he almost
plummeted, and placed a single bomb in the center of a raft at
sea from an altitude of 20,000 feet. That scene broke up the
audience, for the reality of the war was something quite different
from the romance.

Regensburg and Ploesti were names to conjure with. Sometimes a mission went awry, as on February 22, 1944, when the
Eighth Air Force from England and the Fifteenth from Italy
raided Regensburg. The 449th was deeply involved, but with
about half the planes, something happened.

Here is the story as told by Lieutenant Don Lapham, copilot
of the B-24 called *Patches*:

"It was just one of those days when everything went wrong.
There were clouds on group forming. Altitude was five thousand
feet. There were ten ships of a briefed eighteen-ship section. We
couldn't find the other section. The section that we thought was
ours fired red-green flares instead of the yellow-yellow of the
449th.

"I took over the controls for a stretch. . . .

"The engines droned on. I could see formations far below us.
We went through the oxygen check more often; altitude was
25,000 feet, temperature about −45°F. The snow of the Alps
below was a glossy white.

Our formation had dwindled to eight ships—high, alone, and
afraid in the sky.

" 'This is navigator. We are off course to Regensburg. We are
heading to the Graz-Klagenfurt area.'

"I glanced out of the side blister. Out at about 2000 yards was
a tight formation of planes. B-24s, I said to myself. One of the
planes banked up sharply as seven of them peeled off. My eyes
bulged; they had two engines.

" 'Seven ME-110s at two o'clock low. This is ball. Six JU-88s at
nine o'clock low. Are entrail over.'

" 'Roger, ball.'

" 'Tail turret. There are about six or seven ME-110s following us entrail.'

"At three o'clock low was a lone JU-88. He pulled up until he just about stalled. A large ball of fire seemed to sail from beneath his wings.

"It was a rocket, and a devil of a big one. He missed the group that he was firing at by about half a mile.

"Here we are over Austria, without a target and with about thirty enemy fighters following us, waiting to attack.

" 'This is nose. A lone ME-109 just blew up at eleven o'clock low. Guess that group ahead must have gotten him.'

" 'This is waist. That group way down at four o'clock, I think one of their planes just blew up.'

"Pilot; 'If we get out of here alive, it will be altitude that saved us.'

"Out of range, the ME-110s to our right passed under us and in front of us. I saw them bank as they came in for an attack at twelve o'clock low.

" 'Nose turret. 110s coming at twelve o'clock low.'

"At about 600 yards, Derwin Eggleton, nose gunner and radio operator, fired a short burst and another short burst and then a longer burst.

" 'This is nose. Have hit 110. Is on fire. There he goes. Flying into pieces. There goes a wing.'

"I glanced out the window and saw a ball of fire. Then a remarkable thing happened . . . the other planes that were coming in turned. The rest of their passes were timid. We got in a few long shots, but that was all. They attempted to lob 20 mm's into the formation, but didn't do too well. Guess they were a group of green pilots.

" 'There's a city. It's Graz. We are making a run on the airdrome, I think,' said the pilot. We were using a new bombardier and he was on interphone, so we just dumped our bombs on a snowcapped peak. We landed that night, and we were disgusted. We missed the target, endangered the lives of all concerned. We had failed to meet the other ships, and detracted 180 guns from their fire power. They had lost four ships; we had lost none. We just didn't make sense that day. Eggy's plane was confirmed by myself and another ball gunner who hadn't fired a shot. With over thirty enemy planes following us and one pass, one of the bombers in our formation reported "no enemy action."

Here is another tale of Regensburg, this one from bombadier Lieutenant Dean Manning of the Sixteenth Squadron. The pilot was Lieutenant Bob Bird. Their own aircraft, *Sophisticated Lady*, was up for repairs after a raid on the Anzio beach head area, so they borrowed plane No. 498, *Pistol Packin' Mama*, and they also borrowed a copilot and a navigator for the mission.

"It was one of those days—this was in the days before radar. We hadn't seen the ground for five hours because of solid clouds below, we could not see the target, our fighter escort couldn't find us—again because of the clouds—and we were on the way home and looking for a secondary target. We were flying at 26,000 feet, which was considerably higher than our usual 20,000. We were met head-on by German 109s and 190s, and although we took several attacks, the first one did all the damage. This one made a slicing head-on pass, hitting a main spar about fifteen or twenty feet from the right wingtip, knocked out No. 3 and No. 4 engines, knocked out the nose turret just above me, and hit me just above the ankle plus the intercom, all on the first pass. A couple of our guns were frozen and the nose was out, so while we may have made some hits, it was too late. We were going down and like a rock, with drag and no power on one side. I don't know why we weren't spinning, but we weren't.

"The nose turret operator, Dixon, got out of the shattered turret and crawled back to the flight deck. I knew that I had lost a leg, because it was barely hanging on. I took off my oxygen mask to talk to the navigator about giving me a shot of morphine from the nose first aid kit and putting a tourniquet on my leg. I then opened the nose wheel hatch in case we had to get out in a hurry. Popkiss did get the tourniquet partially on, but he was a little nervous by this time and dropped the morphine out the nose wheel hatch. From the nose compartment one can see the feet and legs of the pilot and copilot. About this time I saw the copilot get up and leave, so I guessed we were bailing out and told Popkiss to bail out, and he did. Although I wasn't in any pain, I still thought I ought to have some morphine, so I removed the small first aid kit from the parachute harness. Then I saw through the controls the pilot get out. I put the small first aid kit in a chest pocket of my GI coveralls and got down on the floor of the nose compartment to bail out. I checked the altimeter. It read about 17,000 feet.

"Unfortunately my loose parachute harness caught on a dot fastener as I bailed out, rip cord ready to go, and I found my head, hands, and feet out of the plane, with my rear still attached and no one left in the plane! I managed to squirm around and get my arms back inside and crawled back and unhooked the strap. For some reason I looked at the altimeter again, but I do not remember opening the chute. I assume that I had been without oxygen long enough to pass out and that the opening of the parachute probably jerked me back to consciousness."

"The next thing I knew I was sitting comfortably in that loose harness and the noise of gunfire and planes went quickly away. There were still the solid clouds below, and although it was difficult to be sure, I thought I could see nine chutes falling off in the distance. There was no question, I was the last one out and I was really quite lucky. I thought I should have that morphine and I reached into my pocket, but it was gone. Apparently it fell out when the chute opened. But under the flap in the pocket was a package of Lucky Strike cigarettes and a box of wooden matches. So, although I took three matches to get a light, I smoked a cigarette on the way down."

Lieutenant Manning landed beside a farmhouse and was helped by the Austrian farmers. He spent a year in German hospitals before being repatriated in February 1945.

Later on the German Messerschmitt plant at Regensburg was plastered, and it was finally abandoned and ceased to be a target. Ploesti continued to be a tough target. The 449th hit it eleven times.

In the summer of 1944 a Tunisian sort of USO-type troupe showed up at the base and gave a rouser of a show. The orchestra consisted of four Arabs in robes and a belly dancer named Rouhia dressed in next to nothing at all. Everybody cheered. But Africa exported more than low comedy. The French sent a unit to Italy, and the Senegalese and the Italian civilians fought. A nurse at Taranto told men of the 449th that there were an average of eighteen knifings every night.

Officially and unofficially, Rome became a port of leave. The trouble with "having engine trouble" around Rome was that the runway was too short for B-24s.

Lieutenant Kinsinger was a young man in a hurry. He had come in April and by September was winding up a tour that lasted just one day over four months. Fifty missions! On many of these a Colonel Gent had ridden copilot. On one in heavy flak their deputy leader was shot down, and their turbos were shot out so that they could not hold altitude going into the bomb run. But they bombed and came back.

August 15, 1944 was one of Lieutenant Kinsinger's last missions. The day before, activity began at the intelligence office that pointed to a new mission. Before night fell aircraft engines were turning over and jeeps were rushing about the airfield. The aircrews came to the room for the midnight briefing and looked at the big briefing map that showed the route to the target. Everyone knew it was an important occasion, because General Rush, the wing commander, showed up to make a speech. Next day would be D-day for the invasion of southern France, and the 449th was going to fly cover for the invasion. The troops would land at eight o'clock in the morning. The B-24s' job was to attack German emplacements and barriers to the landing.

Takeoff for the mission began at 2:30 in the morning. The whole base was awakened at about 3 a.m. when one of the B-24s crashed on takeoff. It could not gain altitude as it left the ground, so it struck telephone wires along the Taranto-Grottaglie road. Twelve men were lost, including the pilot, who was flying his last mission.

Once the other planes were airborne, life quieted down and the bases waited. The planes returned at about 11 a.m. to report that a huge number of aircraft from the Mediterranean Air Force were in the air over the target area and the sea offshore was full of the warships bombarding something. As the 449th planes bombed and left the area, they saw paratroops coming down from the C-4 troop transports. Because of this, which involved a mix-up in timing, Lieutenant Kinsinger returned to base without dropping his bombs.

And so Lieutenant Kinsinger got ready to go home. He had taken just one weekend of time off in four months. He had sometimes flown six missions in a row. Once he passed out in the pay line and was grounded for three days. He was an eager beaver, no doubt about it. When he wasn't flying missions, he was test-flying aircraft. But he was also one of the most skillful pilots, chosen by Colonel Gent to lead the pack and coming off the missions with a perfect record. No member of his crew was killed or wounded.

Lieutenant Kinsinger went home, but at Grottaglie the war went on. On August 17 came a new mission against "Big P" (Ploesti), with the welcome news that the Germans were hurting desperately for oil. August 18 brought another Ploesti mission. One airplane was badly hit by flak, but the pilot came home on three engines. All the other planes remained airborne, circling while the damaged ship came in to land. As the pilot banked toward the field, he lost another engine, and the plane smashed, burning, into the ground. Seven men survived, but three of them died in the next few minutes and the other four were badly burned and out of the war.

Here is the story of the mission through the eyes of an aerial photographer, Sergeant James E. Wiess of the 719th Squadron.

Sergeant Wiess was awakened at 2:45 a.m. by the operations clerk, who announced briefing time at 3:45. It was hard to get up, but he did, and after dressing and smoking a cigarette he made his way to the S-2 office. At the briefing he learned they were going back to Ploesti. Just the day before, Sergeant Wiess had been to Ploesti for the fifth time.

He went to the photo lab and learned he was to fly with either plane No. 12 or No. 15 (it turned out to be No. 12). He went back to his tent, picked up his mess kit, and went over for breakfast: fried eggs, cereal, prunes, bread, butter, jam, and coffee. He would have to last on that until late afternoon if all went well. He decided to take a K ration to eat on the way home.

He picked up his flight gear and went to the parachute room, where he picked up a chute harness and Mae West jacket. Then he got onto a truck and rode out to the aircraft. Most of the crew was already there, checking. Someone broke out a pack of cigarettes, and they all lit up. Sergeant Wiess began scribbling notes:

"There is a certain tenseness over the crew. Most of us have been to our target for today several times, and a lot of our buddies went there but didn't return. This is no milk run. We were hit yesterday, and they threw everything but the kitchen sink at us. I thought I saw one of those go by the right waist window, but I couldn't swear to it."

At 5:30 the aircraft began taking off. The dust and mist were so thick he couldn't see the hangar 200 yards way. The sun was just peeking over the hills to the cast.

At 5:50 the last planes of the first section were off. Plane No. 12 was the third in the second section. The pilot taxied into position. With a deafening roar from the four engines, they started down the runway. "Agonizingly slow at first, we pick up speed until at the halfway mark the ship is bouncing along, toying with the earth as if reluctant to leave. It is at this point that I always breathe a prayer, and some seconds later, just as we become airborne, another prayer of thanks."

As they rose the air grew cooler. Sergeant Wiess climbed into flying clothes (khaki pants and a T-shirt) first. Then he put on a pair of heavy electrically heated trousers and a coat to match. He added a pair of heavy socks and electrically heated shoes. Over the electric shoes he put on heavy fleece-lined flying boots. On his hands he wore silk gloves with electrically heated gloves over them. The shoes, pants, coat, and gloves all snapped together, and a cord plugged into a 24c volt outlet heated the unit.

At 7:50 they flew over the Italian coastline at 13,000 feet. It was time to go on oxygen.

At 8:10 the pilot told the gunners to test-fire their guns, and they did so.

After gun check came an oxygen check, because a man could die from lack of oxygen and no one would know it until too late. Now the plane climbed to 15,000 feet. The temperature had fallen to 0° centigrade inside the aircraft. The navigator said they were on course to the target.

"We're coming to the initial point, and I just finished checking the camera. It is really getting cold. The first bursts of flak are visible, and hell will break loose any second now. No enemy fighters visible, and there are P-51s skating around looking for trouble. The flak is right ahead of us at twelve o'clock, and the bombardier says it is right at our altitude.

"My God, we are in it now! The entire ship is being tossed around by the bursts. They really have our range today. They have spotted the target, and I will be glad when we get rid of these bombs.

"Bombs away at 10:04, and I start taking pictures. It takes about thirty seconds for the bombs to hit, and I can see them hitting all through the target. This is awful! Won't they ever run out of scrap iron to throw at us? I can hear the sharpnel tearing through the ship.

"The bombardier just said that he was hit. Thirty seconds later and the bombardier calls that he was hit again. My God, aren't we ever going to get out of this stuff? I JUST SAID A PRAYER, AND I ONLY WISH THAT I KNEW HOW TO PRAY BETTER.

"Oh Lord! A piece just tore through the side of the ship about ten inches from my head. I want to go home. Let's get the hell out of here. I am scared, and I don't give a damn who knows it. When that piece hit, it was just as if someone had fired a .45 right by my ear. It would be a hell of a note to get shot down now, after being so near finished. Funny thing—I just happened to think about how I used to blast away at quail in Arkansas. I guess I know how they felt now.

"No point in just kneeling here waiting for it to stop. I'll take some pictures of the flak.

"We rally to the right. We are out of flak and circling around the town. No fighters in sight except our own, and I hope there are none around. Fighters will be sort of like the straw that broke the camel's back, so to speak. I got some beautiful shots of flak bursting. Should be in sound so you could hear it. Wish that I had a movie camera with me.

"We just found out that engines No.1, No.2, and No.3 have been hit, and maybe No.4. When it rains, it pours. No.3 engine is smoking, and I think the pilot is going to feather it. The enemy has a nice habit of jumping ships with only three engines, so we may have some more action. There goes No. 3. They put four engines on these babies, and I really love to see all of them working.

"Pilot decided that No. 3 will stand running, so he just started it again. I just saw a B-24 crash and explode at seven o'clock. I didn't see a single chute blossom. God, I hope by some miracle they got out.

"I see the Adriatic ahead of us. The rest of the formation is way off to the left. I made a little tour of the ship and saw that we sort of resemble a colander. You know, one of those things that Mother grates vegetables over. We still have all four engines, though. No. 15 is having trouble. He had his ailerons shot away. Lucky thing that I picked No. 12 today.

"We have been off oxygen since leaving Yugoslavia, and it feels great to be alive. Just came out of all this burdensome equipment, and it is nice and cool. Had my first cigarette since 7:30 this morning, and it tastes great. I noticed that I have a little trouble holding the thing. Wonder why!

"Just sighted the field and made our turn. My God, a B-24 just crashed and burst into flames a mile from the field. Wonder if it could be No.15. He had a lot of trouble today. It doesn't look as if anybody came out of that alive. So close to home, too.

"We just let the landing gear down and are on our base leg. We will be on sweet dear mother earth in a few minutes now. That B-24 that crashed is off to our right as we come in for landing and is scattered all over the countryside.

"Here we come! This is another breathless time for a trip, the landing. The wheels hit with only a slight jar, and we are slowing as we near the end of the runway. Another job almost completed. As we turn off the landing strip, the smoke from the crash is billowing a thousand or so feet in the air.

"On the ground at last. It really feels nice and solid. It is difficult to hear for a few minutes. Here come the guys from the lab to pick up the cameras. In a matter of minutes the pictures I took today will be on their way to Air Force.

"There is a truck waiting to take us to the hangar where we will be interrogated. No one knows for sure, but everyone thinks that No. 15 crashed. Here we go to interrogation.

"Well, interrogation is over, and we have iced tea and donuts. It was No. 15 that crashed, and I hear that four got out alive.

"Just got back to the tent, and humble as it is, it's swell to be safely back in it. The crew that was in No. 15 had their tent seventy-five feet away from mine. It is enough to give a man the creeps, never knowing when his number is coming up. On well, tomorrow is another day, but I do hope we don't go back there for a couple of days anyway. Hard on the nervous system, you know.

"On looking back at what I have scribbled all day, it does sound very tough. If you multiply this day by 50 you will get a vague idea of what a combat tour consists of in the Fifteenth Air Force. Just a job that has to be done and will be done. It could be worse, you know. We could be in the infantry."

August 24, 1944, brought big news: Rumania had surrendered to the Russians and was out of the war. That meant no more missions to ever-dangerous Big P. The news was read at the morning briefing, and the crowd broke out in cheers.

The mission of the 449th changed. Now they were supporting the Russians by cutting off German reinforcements.

On August 27 a report came down on the group's losses. There were 640 fliers missing in action. Of these, 98 had made their way back to the Allied lines, and 168 were known to be prisoners. That left 374 men still unaccounted for. (Ultimately some of them were found to be POWs.)

In August the 449th flew nineteen missions, most of them in the Balkans. In September the group attacked the Brenner Pass line and factories in the Munich area and sent several missions in support of the Russians who were fighting in Hungary.

In October 1944, Colonel Gent left for Hollywood to be technical advisor for a movie on the bombing of Ploesti. But the really big news was that at last all squadrons had arranged for showers on the base!

In October the mission changed again, as the war did. On October 12, the entire Fifteenth Air Force sent planes against Bologna, the center of Marshal Kesselring's force in the Po Valley. The roughest mission of the month was against the marshaling yards at Vienna North, which was ringed with flak. Many planes were damaged, and aircraft landed all the way down the Allied line from Ancona to Foggia. Captain John B. Wright of the 717th Squadron was hit by three bursts of flak over Vienna. One burst exploded in the cockpit, killing the copilot and wounding Captain Wright in the arm. Wright flew to Foggia to make a forced landing with only one hand and a flat tire. He was awarded the Distinguished Service Cross.

# FIFTY-ONE

# Fire!

Life at Grottaglie was very rough in the beginning and never got to be luxurious for anyone. But for all the other squadrons of the 449th Group it got better as time went on, while for the 716th it got worse. The reason was the great fire of November 10, 1944, which knocked the 716th out of its comparatively luxurious old German barracks and put the squadron on the same basis as the others.

In the fall of 1944 it began to get cold in the barracks, so Staff Sergeant Donald Tuttle and the men in his barracks decided to build a stove. They built one of parts from the boneyards: an old bomb casing in a sandbox, fired by aviation fuel in a drum outside with tubing coming into the stove, regulated by a shutoff valve. The fuel dripped onto the sand inside the stove and kept the fire burning.

After a few explosions the previous year, the order had come down that all stoves had to be approved, and so the group got the administrative officer in charge of such matters to approve the stove.

"Fine stove," he said. "Well built."

So all was well, and that night the men went to bed in the comfort of the warmth of their new stove, which was located at the foot of Sergeant Tuttle's bed.

On October 10 at 5 a.m., Sergeant Tuttle was awakened by a tremendous explosion which set his bed on fire and leaped to the dry wooden walls of the barracks. He woke up the man next to him, who pulled the blankets up over his head and told Tuttle to put the fire out.

By this time the walls were blazing.

Sergeant Tuttle grabbed a blanket and ran the length of the barracks shouting "Fire!" and out to the back of the barracks where a Lister bag stood full of water. He plunged the blanket into the Lister bag and soaked it, and then went back to beat out the fire. But the fire was really roaring by the time he got back, and men were throwing their belongings out the windows.

He put the blanket around his shoulders and checked beds. Everyone was out. By then it was time for him to get out. As he left the barracks he took one last look. He saw his uniform burning on the wall, and his gunner's wings dropping off.

He grabbed up the barracks mascot, a little dog called Static, and ran out. Static escaped from his arms and ran back into the building and did not come out again.

Sergeant Tuttle had been scheduled along with some of the others in the barracks for the day's mission, but the 716th had to be scratched because the fire spread to the squadron's other three barracks. They were dispossessed, and almost all their gear was lost. The day was spent getting new issue and pitching tents. Thus equality came to the 449th Bomb Group.

# FIFTY-TWO

# *Hollandia*

In April 1944 the First Fighter Control Squadron moved up to New Guinea for the Hollandia operation. This was a major move in MacArthur's plan to sweep across New Guinea and prepare for landings in the Philippines. It had taken the Americans and Australians a year to move the 240 miles from Buna in southeastern New Guinea to command the Vitiaz Strait.

The rate of advance was slowed by the limited range of Allied land-based fighter planes. MacArthur's navy, the Seventh Fleet, had no carriers and practically no capital ships. It borrowed from the Pacific Fleet when an operation was in progress, but all too soon the capital naval vessels had to be sent back again. The Hollandia operation was based on the bypassing of Madang, Wewak, and other bases, moving in one swoop 800 miles up the coast. MacArthur said this would advance his time schedule for conquest of New Guinea by six months.

The operation at Hollandia was called Reckless. The primary objective was to take three airstrips above Lake Sentani using a pincers-like movement. General Horace Fuller's Forty-first Infantry Division would land at Humboldt Bay, near Hollandia, and move inland. General Fred Irving's Twenty-forth Division would land at Tanahmerah Bay, 30 miles along the coast, and take a trail back through the Cyclops Mountains. Fifty-six officers and men of the first Fighter Control Squadron were tapped to provide communications between air and ground forces. (Airman Driest was one of the men loaded aboard an LST for the mission.)

The ships assembled made up the largest force yet mounted

in the South Pacific, 37,500 combat troops. They had transports, LSTs, and other landing craft, and special craft called Buffaloes and Alligators, vehicles that were part boat and part tractor, for movement across swamps and coral reefs. And they had a flotilla of navy escort carriers with fighter bombers.

The force moved through the Vitiaz Strait, then on a wide detour to fool the enemy, and finally to Hollandia. Everyone was aware of the time factor, for the schedule demanded that the next move from Hollandia be staged by May 15.

D-day was April 22. No one knew what the Japanese knew about the invasion. The bombardment began before dawn, bright flashes lighting up the sky.

A navy air controller had been assigned to the LST of the first Fighter Control Squadron, and he made contact from the deck with the navy planes that were sweeping over the landing beaches. There were no Japanese fighters—245 enemy planes had been destroyed, mostly on the ground, the day before.

It soon became apparent that the Allies had totally surprised the enemy. Rocket landing craft hit the shore, with no answer from the Japanese. Then waves of landing craft came in to make the assault.

At Humboldt Bay the Japanese defenders were surprised at their morning meal. They fled into the jungle, leaving half-finished bowls of rice and tea kettles still boiling on the fires. At Tanahmerah Bay the Japanese fled into the jungle to escape the bombardment of the shore.

The troops landed on two beaches at Tanahmerah: Red Beach 2 and Red Beach 1 (Depapre). The latter was a tiny cove where the Japanese had built a jetty. It was very useful to the Japanese, but constricted for the Allied purposes. The cove was shallow, with a coral bottom, and a mountain ran almost straight up behind the beach. When the landing site had been suggested to the navy, they had hooted. But General Irving wanted the Depapre beach, and General Robert Eichelberger, the land commander, backed him in this. Their reason: only by going over the steep mountain trails could the men get inland to seize the air bases which were the reason for the whole operation.

The landings were simultaneous. Three reinforced rifle teams of Lieutenant Colonel Jock Clifford landed there. They earned the sobriquet Clifford's Cowboys because they clambered and crawled up the mountain trail, a 60 degree slope.

The Americans could tell that the Japanese had expected to defend this terrain, because fire lanes had been cut and prepared positions had been located to control the trails. But there were no Japanese. They had disappeared with the bombardment.

By nightfall the troops were six miles inland.

Red Beach 2 was supposed to be easy. But there the Americans were in for a big surprise. Aerial photographs had been the basis for the decision to land here, but the jungle in the photos concealed the fact that the beach was really an island, with no exits to the mainland. Thirty yards behind the welcoming sandy beach was mangrove swamp—the area that had been designated as supply dumps! When the troops reached the swamp, one man walked in and was immediately swallowed by the swamp before anyone could save him. Others stepped in and fell into deep sinkholes from which they were extricated by their comrades.

The landing here moved to high gear because of the sloping beach, and the goods piled up on the beach. The men frantically searched for exists that did not exist. Natives had reported that the Japanese had built a road from Red 2 to Depapre, but troops took twenty-four hours to travel two miles through jungle and swamp. They did not find a road, because none existed.

The landings succeeded, but not quite in the way that the planners had planned.

At Humboldt Bay the Alligators and Buffaloes really came into play, moving out of the sea, five miles overland to Lake Sentani, and down the lake thirteen miles toward the airfields.

Tanks and jeeps had come ashore but could not move through the jungle, so everything had to be hand-carried: food, weapons, ammunition. The handful of narrow trails were overcrowded, and the pressure of the enemy so great that it took forty-eight hours for stretcher parties carrying the wounded to get back to the beach. It was slog, slog, slog through mud, across swollen streams, slipping, being hit by dirt slides.

At Humboldt Bay, on D + 1, came tragedy: a Japanese bomber slipped through the antiaircraft network and bombed an ammunition dump which had been captured by the Americans from the Japanese. The dump went up in a series of booms and set fire to the gasoline dump. Soon the supply dumps were all blazing, and twenty-four American troops were killed. The fire burned for two days, destroying 80 percent of the supplies unloaded.

In the Sentani area, after a few hours many of the troops were out of contact. On the fourth day the leading element had outrun its supply, and had to be resupplied by B-17s from the Lake Sentani airfield.

With Hollandia, General MacArthur's plan to isolate the big Japanese base at Rabaul by surrounding it with Allied airfields was nearly complete. Concurrently he was planning to move northward preparatory to attacking the Philippines. While the navy had been carrying the Pacific war through the Central Pacific in 1943 and 1944, General MacArthur had consistently argued for the reoccupation of the Philippines as the next step after capture of the Mariana Islands. In the summer of 1944, MacArthur had flown to Hawaii to meet with President Franklin D. Roosevelt and Admiral Chester Nimitz, and at this historic meeting MacArthur had convinced Roosevelt that his plan of liberating the Philippines next was both politically and militarily sound.

On May 17, the new invasion was on. Airman Driest's LST beached in the Kobon area. On leaving the boat, the men discovered that while the water was shallow at the beaching place, it deepened thereafter. So the LST pulled off and beached at again. Even so, there was a great deal of water between the ramp and the shore, and a number of vehicles drowned out and had to be towed ashore by bulldozers.

The landing was a mess. Action had to be stopped while bulldozers built a jetty and reinforced it with sandbags. Then the beach party was so eager to get vehicles off onto the beach that they were taken out of the sequence that had been prepared. Trailers were attached to the wrong vehicles going to the wrong places, and some trailers were stranded aboard the LST while their propelling vehicles were driven ashore.

All this caused delay in the establishment of the Goblet Fighter Control Center. The one problem the troops did not face was serious enemy action. They did not need it; they had plenty of internal problems. By noon they did manage to have a squad tent up and were operating the field from another tent. By 5 p.m. operations were transferred to the operations tent. Antiaircraft guns were placed, and the communications network was put together. The squadron was ready for action.

On the night of May 19 the area erupted in furious gunfire, shouting, and noise. A red alert!

What was going on?

The 191st Field Artillery Battalion had released a red target balloon, which the artillery began firing on without telling anyone. A ground observer had then mistakenly reported enemy aircraft overhead.

The confusion was sorted out, but thereafter the control squadron GIs did not have much faith in the ground observers.

Next crisis: A ground observer reported a Japanese barge approaching. Since the battle of the Bismarck Sea, in which Allied air power had decimated a Japanese convoy, the Japanese had supplied that garrison in New Guinea exclusively by barge. Consequently everyone in the Southwest Pacific was alert to barge movement, A barge might contain fifty Japanese soldiers or more, plenty to give a headache.

The observer indicated that a red alert was in order, but investigation showed that the enemy barge was a floating log.

An observer reported "aircraft engines" overhead at night. The aircraft engines turned out to be PT boats along the shore.

To hear the observers, the command would believe the unit was under threat from air and sea. Actually, no aircraft were reported, and no Japanese vessels came along.

By this time the Japanese in the South and Southwest Pacific had been badly hit by disease and Allied action, particularly bombing, and their effectiveness was minimal. The impetus of the war was shifting, to points much nearer the Japanese inner empire.

# FIFTY-THREE

# Morotai

Curtis Krogh enlisted in the U.S. Army Air Corps in the fall of 1942 and began training to become an air crewman early the next year. Soon he was sent to Albion College in Michigan, which was really a stall by the air corps because it was having some trouble assimilating all the cadets in the training programs. So Cadet Krogh studied college subjects and trained in a Piper Cub for several months.

While at Albion, Cadet Keogh was recruited as "an A-2 man, which meant I secretly reported weekly by mail in coded language any unusual or subversive personnel activities of anyone on the base. Every base I was on, I was always approached in a clandestine manner by an officer in the intelligence section of the Air Force to 'do my thing.' "

In February 1944, Cadet Krogh was selected for multiple engine training at Lubbock, Texas. On April 15, class 44D was graduated and he got his wings and the gold bars of a second lieutenant. Then he learned to tow gliders behind the C-47. Suddenly he was switched to flying the C-46 Commando and kept at Syracuse for six months. He went overseas from San Francisco aboard a troop transport, zigzagging all the way to Hollandia, New Guinea, where the unit arrived in November 1944. Not long afterward they went to Biak, which General MacArthur had secured several months before.

The Second Combat Cargo Group spent six months at Biak.

"We flew many long, weary flights to places like Hollandia,

Finschhafen, Peleliu, Morotai, Port Moresby, Samar, and so forth. We flew mostly anywhere from New Guinea to areas of the Philippines. Some were fortunate enough to get "fat cat" flights to Australia, and occasionally these crews brought back milk which generally had started to sour. They also brought back liquor, wines, and so forth, which helped stock our "Seventh Heaven" officers' club bar. Our loads consisted of litter patients and jeeps, weapons carriers, food, gasoline, and other war material. We also carried GIs and Red Cross personnel and sometimes VIPs.

"We were awakened at 3 a.m. and dressed and went to the mess tent for powdered eggs, powdered milk, and coffee. Food wasn't too great. The plane usually was outfitted with 10-in-1 rations, mostly canned bacon, canned eggs, and dry crackers. These became quite palatable because we became adept at heating the rations on our hot plate in the plane.

"We were briefed at 5 a.m. and took off at 6 a.m. We flew in any kind of weather. Weather was our biggest enemy, although the Japs gave us a hard time too. Our planes were capable of flying at about 18,000 feet with a load, so we could never get over the storms. We would look for light areas and go through. Inevitably we got buffeted around and this we dreaded, especially at night. Sometimes we opted to skim the ocean to avoid the turbulence."

For a month they were stationed on Morotai and assigned to fly gasoline in 55-gallon drums to Mindoro in the Philippines.

"We were bombed by the Japs every night, and I had my first foxhole experience there. Very little sleep. Left the island at 12:30 for Mindoro. I could hardly ever find the lead plane [which carried a navigator], so I would take off on my own. I would put the copilot and the radio operator to work trying to guide us across Mindanao and up to Mindoro. This was tough navigating, and we almost got lost several times. When we got near Mindoro there was always a red alert, which meant that Jap fighters were attacking Mindoro Field. They came down from Clark Field in Luzon and harassed us every morning. Finally we were given the all-clear and could fly the last fifty miles and land on this dusty, bombed-out airstrip and unload our volatile cargo and then head back, always landing at Tacloban on Leyte before proceeding back to Morotai."

By the time the group got navigators for every aircraft, they were managing pretty well without them; they had learned to use loran (a long-range navigational system employing radio signals), along with the radio compass. With navigators things were even easier. The C-46 crew in the southwest Pacific consisted then of pilot, copilot, navigator, radio operator, and crew chief. The last was responsible for keeping the plane in good condition. It made the rest of the crew feel secure to have the crew chief fly with them; "It was his neck too."

# FIFTY-FOUR

# The Twentieth

The Twentieth Air Force was activated in Washington on April 4, 1944, for the specific purpose of sending B-29 Superfortresses to bomb Japan. The Twentieth Bomber Command was established to carry out the mission, and the Fifty-eighth Bomb Wing, with four bombardment groups, was soon scheduled for Calcutta, and then Chengdu in western China, in the hope that the Chinese airfields would be adequate for the job. By May 1, four airfields in the Chengdu area were ready for the big bombers. Major Gen. Laverne G. Saunders became commanding general of the Twentieth Bomber Command, and on July 7, 1944, fourteen B-29s bombed Sasebo, Omura, and Tobata in the first raid on Japan since the Doolittle raid in April 1942. On July 29, seventy B-29s from Chengdu bombed the Showa Steel Works at Anshan, Manchukuo; Taku, on the Chinese coast; and Chinwangdao. The first B-29 to fall to the enemy was shot down by five Japanese fighters near Chenghsien.

Almost as soon as the B-29s arrived in the China-Burma-India Theater, General H. H. Arnold realized that this had been a mistake. The distance was too great to Japan. From the western China airfields the big bombers could reach only Manchuria, Kyushu, and Formosa. They could not bomb the real Japanese industrial heartland of Honshu Island's Kanto plain. Even the raids they did make out of Chengdu were hampered by weather, and by limited bomb capacity because of extra gasoline required. From the Calcutta area, the B-29s did bomb targets in Southeast Asia successfully, but in terms of the war effort these were all secondary targets.

The problem was being solved that summer of 1944, with the Central Pacific Drive that took the U.S. Navy to the Mariana Islands. Saipan was attacked in June, and work began as soon as the shooting died down to rebuild the Japanese air bases there, on Tinian, and on Guam, to accommodate the B-29s. On August 24 General O'Donnell's Seventy-third Bomb Wing moved headquarters to the Marianas, and soon the Twenty-first Bomber Command was established in the Marianas under General Hansell. Meanwhile Major General Curtis LeMay was moved from the Eighth Air Force in England to take over the Twentieth Bomber Command in China.

The bombers still worked out of the Chengdu airfields, against Anshan and other Manchukuo targets. Ninety big bombers hit Anshan on September 8, but this raid and one on September 26 were not very satisfactory. High altitude, small bomb capacity, and weather did not help. The Japanese, aroused, conducted a series of bombing raids on the Chengdu airfields which destroyed and damaged a number of B-29s.

The emphasis was definitely shifting from China to the Pacific. On October 12, 1944, *Joltin' Josie*, piloted by General Hansell, became the first B-29 to arrive at Saipan.

Still the bombing from Chengdu continued. In October bombers hit Japan again several times. But on October 28 the Twenty-first Bomber Command flew its first raid to Dublon, bombing Japanese submarine pens. They repeated this raid twice in the next few days. Bombers from the Calcutta area began to hit Southeast Asia targets harder.

In November the B-29s truly became a force to reckon with when they bombed Iwo Jima. This softened the island up for the coming invasion, and also put the big dry dock at Singapore out of commission for three months.

On November 24, General O'Donnell led the first Twenty-first Bomber Command mission against Tokyo, 111 B-29s making the raid. The Japanese were having a great deal of difficulty combatting the B-29s, because they bombed from above 25,000 feet, which was the maximum range of the antiaircraft guns, and also the maximum altitude for Japanese fighters. But by stripping off armament and all extras, the Japanese put some planes higher, and one of them rammed a B-29 that day, shearing off the elevator and right horizontal stabilizer. The B-29 crashed in the sea off Honshu—the first big bomber casualty over Japan.

In this period the Twenty-first Bomber Command was carrying out instructions from Admiral Nimitz to hit airfields and aircraft factories, but without signal success. The factories were well protected, the aircraft on the fields were well dispersed, and the bombing from 25,000 feet and above was not very accurate.

Then, on December 18, 1944, General Curtis LeMay engineered a B-29 raid on the Hankow docks, flying low and using incendiaries. The result was spectacular. The wooden city of Hankow blazed. A new technique was born, although not immediately recognized. It was to be an improvement in destructive capacity on the deadly quality of the Hamburg and Dresden firebomb raids.

The B-29s continued to operate from Calcutta and Chengdu, although it was now recognized that the Chengdu operation was very expensive in terms of aircraft, maintenance, and fuel. On January 17, about eighty B-29s from the Chengdu fields set out to bomb targets in Taiwan. One of these was the B-29 No. 42-24494, called *Mary Ann*, stationed at the A-7 airfield. The pilot was Major Clarence C. McPherson.

The mission began at 4:45 in the morning. The B-29 carried twenty-seven 500-pound bombs. The weather was foul, so the takeoff was on instruments in the darkness, and the aircraft set course and climbed.

At 6500 feet the flight engineer, Lieutenant Stanley Gray, reported that the oil cooler shutter on the No. 3 engine was inoperative. It would not work on either manual or automatic settings.

Major McPherson leveled off and throttled back the No. 3 engine. The engineer then checked the fuse. It was fine, so something else had to be wrong. McPherson swung into a 180-degree turn to return to base. The No. 3 engine was left running at minimum rpms, but the flight engineer was instructed to notify the major if the oil pressure dropped.

The pilot then returned to the field and circled, coming down to 3000 feet (1500 feet above the field). He made an instrument approach through heavy cloud, but he discovered that the alignment with the field was improper, and had to abort the landing. He slammed home the throttles on the three good engines, and they responded for another go-around as the gear went back up. But in a few moments the aircraft began to settle, so Major McPherson applied power to the No. 3 engine. He increased rpm and manifold pressure to takeoff power, and then raised the flaps to 25 degrees. Their line of flight from the field was three hundred and sixty degrees, airspeed 150 mph and altitude 100 feet above the ground. He got the airspeed up to 175 mph and the altitude above ground to 300 feet. Then the flight engineer announced that the nose oil pressure on the No. 3 engine had dropped to zero. McPherson told copilot Lieutenant William Smith to feather the No. 3 engine, but just then the propeller ran away and the engine would not feather. With the windmilling, the altitude dropped to 260 feet and the airspeed to 160 mph.

He increased the manifold pressure again to takeoff power on the three good engines and trimmed the plane, but he knew the engines would not stand that power setting for very long. The plane would not go up.

On Major McPherson's order, the bombardier, Lieutenant Donald Irby, salvoed the bombs. At least part of the bomb load blew up, although the pins were still in the bombs. The plane was so close to the ground that the front bomb bay bulkhead door was blown in and shrapnel splattered all around them. Pilot McPherson could feel the blast of heat from the bombs through his open side window. The shrapnel cut the rudder cables and damaged the aircraft's tail, and the ship lurched to the right. Major McPherson thought the plane was going to crash immediately, so he flipped on the emergency bell and ordered the copilot to bail out. He used the ailerons to roll the plane out of the right bank, and put the nose down to prevent a stall. He was turning into the hills. The blast had one helpful effect: it blew the plane up to 500 feet above the ground.

The aircraft was very sluggish and required full left aileron to maintain level attitude but then it again began to settle. The airspeed was 150 mph.

At this point Staff Sergeant Dennis P. Shannon, the radio operator, bailed out. Then bombardier Irby bailed out. Flight engineer Gray went out next. Copilot Smith bailed out next, and then the navigator, Captain Martin D. Roe, asked the major if he was going to bail out. Major McPherson was fighting the controls, totally on instruments, trying to keep the plane from stalling out. He yelled at the navigator to get out. The navigator disappeared through the nose wheel well.

Major McPherson than started to bail out himself. His earphone cord caught in the parachute harness and stopped him from getting out of the seat. He grabbed the control column, leveled the plane, jerked the cord loose, and jumped out of the seat, just as he thought he saw a hill looming up ahead. He pulled the rip cord ring free of the container as he went into the wheel well, dropped to the bottom rung of the ladder, and fell free. As soon as he felt the slipstream he jerked the rip cord and saw the parachute stream out. It opened with a sharp crack, the risers jerked hard, and it seemed that he stopped in midair for a second or two. The plane hit the ground and exploded. He heard screeching metal and exploding oxygen bottles and ammunition, and saw a sheet of flame.

"I had a sudden sensation of moving backwards rapidly and the ground coming up at me. Just as I started to pull on my risers, I heard a crackling sound of branches and felt myself going through the branches of a tree. When the din died away I found myself swinging gently in my chute, which was hanging in a tree, and my toes could just touch the bank of the ravine I had landed in. I left my chute hanging in the tree, and in the darkness made my way slowly to the burning plane close by. The aircraft had crashed in a lake, and the top gun turret, a wheel, and burning gasoline were catapulted onto land. I reached the scene at the same time as the navigator, who landed okay. It was just then breaking daylight in the east."

Major McPherson and the navigator then found radio operator

Shannon and Staff Sergeant John J. Cole, the senior gunner, who had bailed out safely. They also found the bodies of Lieutenant Irby and Lieutenant Gray. Irby's parachute had not opened and he was killed on impact. Gray had been strangled in his shroud lines. The survivors picked up the bodies and took them back to the A-1 base, north of their own A-7. There they found that the other survivors had already come in and returned to A-7. They were the left gunner, Staff Sergeant Frank A. Langlois, and the radar operator, Staff Sergeant James P. Loftus. The right gunner and the tail gunner were also killed when their chutes did not open.

In the fall of 1944 the North Burma campaign was over and the British took over most operations in the area. American air activity moved north into China for the most part, and the 530th Fighter Squadron was reassigned to the Fourteenth Air Force and stationed at Chengdu in western China, where the B-29s had been operating. After the capture of Saipan, Tinian, and Guam, B-29 activity was centered in the Marianas, for operation against the Japanese homeland.

The primary mission of the P-51 squadrons became the interdiction of Japanese railroad traffic on the eastern China seaboard. The 530th squadron shot up some three hundred locomotives in the spring and summer of 1945. And then, after twenty months and seventy-two missions, the war ended for Lieutenant Cruikshanks.

# FIFTY-FIVE

# *Mindoro*

At the end of 1944, Airman Driest's detachment was in Leyte, waiting for the invasion of Mindoro to establish an air base to cover later landings at Lingayen Gulf on Luzon Island. Their mission would be to go in with the landing forces on Mindoro. The men were loaded in LST 1036 and LST 1025. One group would go in on D-day and set up a control operation within the first few hours. The second group would join up on D+1.

So they loaded—and they sat off Leyte. D-day was postponed for twelve days.

Twelve days aboard an LST can be a very long time, Airman Driest learned:

"Since few men had prepared for more than a few days aboard ship and the facilities of an LST are not designed to accommodate a large number of men comfortably, baths and changes of clothing were few during this period. Beards often remained unshaven, clothes became very dirty and grease-streaked, and a miasma of body odor came up from down below through the open door-ways and vents of the landing craft. Bunks were assigned to the enlisted men on a ratio of eight bunks to thirty-two men; consequently most of the men slept above deck. The sleeping quarters in the hold were for the most part unventilated, and after a few days the air became foul and fetid. Water faucets were turned on for only a few minutes each morning to permit hasty ablutions."

The convoy set sail on December 12. On the voyage to Mindoro it was attacked by Japanese aircraft a number of times. The antiaircraft guns boomed and the Allied fighters overhead moved in to hit the enemy planes. Planes of Marine Air Group 12, Fifth Air Force fighters, and navy aircraft from Rear Admiral Felix Stump's escort carriers protected the invasion force.

But on the second day out of Leyte, a Japanese reconnaissance plane discovered the invasion convoy at about nine in the morning. That afternoon the kamikazes came. They arrived at three o'clock as the convoy was about to turn around the southern cape of Negros Island into the Sulu Sea. An Aichi dive bomber zoomed down to crash into the cruiser *Nashville*, near the cabin of Rear Admiral A. D. Struble. The flag bridge was wrecked and 133 men were killed, including Struble's chief of staff and several high-ranking officers, Colonel John T. Mutha, commander of the 310th Bombardment Wing, among them. Another 190 men were wounded and the *Nashville* was out of the battle.

Two hours later, Airman Driest and his fellows aboard the LSTs watched another kamikaze attack. Three fighters escorted seven kamikazes. The combat air patrol intercepted the Japanese a dozen miles out, but three kamikazes broke through the screen. One was shot down by a destroyer, another was shot down by a cruiser, but the third plowed into the destroyer *Harden*, killing fourteen men, wounding twenty-four, and putting that destroyer out of action.

There were more attacks that day, but all of them were fended off.

On December 14 the Japanese planned to destroy the convoy, and sent 186 planes to find it. But the planes missed the convoy, and their attacks were diluted elsewhere. The convoy steamed on to Mindoro.

The landings on Mindoro began early on the morning of December 15. First the destroyers and landing craft equipped with rockets hit the beaches. The mission was to establish a perimeter around the village of San Jose, and begin airstrip construction at the four Japanese airstrips in the area.

Airman Driest was in LST 1025, under Captain M. Bonfoey, in the forward detachment of the First Fighter Control Squadron.

They landed at Blue Beach near Agustin, virtually on the bank of the Bugsanga River.

The LST pulled right up to the sandy beach, and the men landed with dry feet and began unloading. It was very quiet, there being no enemy opposition.

In the afternoon Captain John Johnson's second echelon was landed at White Beach. Johnson decided to try to link up with the first echelon, so he got in a jeep and began traveling. But he discovered there was no road to Blue Beach, and soon he was driving along a rail track toward San Jose. He passed a line of men who told him they had just gotten out ahead of the advance infantry patrol. Captain Johnson turned about and retreated to the beach to wait.

Airman Driest's detachment was already setting up equipment two miles back from the beach, and fighter control was in operation by five o'clock in the evening of D-day. That night the Japanese came again, in a series of air raids that kept the men tumbling into their foxholes. On December 16, they moved up to San Jose and established a temporary fighter sector in a building with a bowling alley! Driest was billeted in a nearby house.

From that day on the squadron operated, although there were many air raids. Every morning a radio jeep was driven to a hill overlooking San Jose valley and the air cover was vectored out visually to intercept incoming Japanese planes.

A few days later, as the air raids persisted, the commanding officer decided to move the center to the hills, where they could spread out and be safe from attack. They had no tents, so they slept on cots under the trees on the hillside.

The commander of the First Fighter Control Squadron must have been prescient, for even as he moved his forces to the hills, the Japanese navy was preparing a major attack on Mindoro's beachhead. Imperial General Headquarters ordered a naval bombardment and an infantry raid on the island beachhead.

On Christmas Eve, the Japanese force, including a heavy cruiser, a light cruiser, and six destroyers, set out from Camranh Bay in Indochina, under command of Rear Admiral Masanori Kimura.

Airman Driest's squadron learned of the Japanese on the afternoon of December 26, when navy Lieutenant Paul F. Stevens, piloting a B-24 Liberator patrol bomber, spotted the force 180 miles northwest of the beachhead and reported in. Later he landed at San Jose and made sure that Brigadier General William Dunckel, commander of the Twenty-fourth Division at Mindoro, knew about the coming of the Japanese. Stevens then took off and began shadowing the Japanese force, reporting frequently. By this time fighters and B-25 medium bombers had moved in to the airfields, and a force consisting of ninety-two fighters, thirteen B-25s, and a couple of dozen P-61 night fighters was dispatched to attack the Japanese.

At 8:30 on the night of December 26, another Liberator pilot sighted the Japanese force again, this time fifty miles northwest of San Jose.

There were no Allied warships in the area, only nine serviceable PT boats and the aircraft of the airfields: the thirteen B-25s of the Seventeenth Reconnaissance Squadron, forty-four P-38s of the Eighth Fighter Group, twenty-eight P-47s of the Fifty-eighth Fighter Group, and twenty P-40s of the 110th. These aircraft began taking off at about dusk and continued to move into action.

Meanwhile the PT boats set out to attack the Japanese as well, but the wily Japanese, who had been through much trouble with PT boats at the battle of Surigao Strait in October, avoided them. They could not, however, avoid the stingers of the Air Force, which began harrying them as they came up. Admiral Kimura carried out his mission, shelling San Jose, Beach Red, and the airfield for forty minutes. The Japanese also set the Liberty ship *James H. Breasted* afire. But the damage done overall was not too great, largely because of the aircraft. They stung like wasps, hitting the Japanese ships with bombs and strafing, disturbing the aim of the Japanese gunners. But the cost to the airmen was not low: three B-25s were lost, as well as seven P-38s, ten P-47s, and six P-40s.

After forty minutes the Japanese began to withdraw and were so doing when they fell afoul of two American PT boats off Dongon Point. *PT-223* put a torpedo into the Japanese destroyer *Kiyoshima*, which had already been severely damaged by the air attack. The destroyer went dead in the water and soon sank. The Japanese then retired.

For the rest of the month the Japanese harried Mindoro from the air. The First Fighter Control Squadron had its hands full, with a hundred red alerts and a hundred air raids.

At the end of the month a convoy from Dulag carrying airfield construction materials was attacked by kamikazes, and two crashed the Liberty ships *William Sharon* and *John Burke*. The plane that hit the *John Burke* made a ten-strike; the ammunition ship blew up, creating an enormous white cloud which hid an empty sea. The *John Burke* went down immediately with all hands. The *William Sharon* burned but was towed back to Leyte.

The kamikazes also wrecked the tender *Orestes*, and two of them hit the destroyer *Pringle* and the destroyer *Gansevoort*. These attacks were repelled by fighters controlled by the First Squadron, and the night fighters in particular scored heavily against the Japanese. But the Japanese kept coming. On December 30 the Liberty ship *Hobart Baker* was sunk off the Mindoro beachhead. On the last day of 1944 two Liberty ships were hit and run aground on a reef off Mindoro, and more supply ships were hit as well. Another ammunition ship went up with a bang.

But by the end of December, Mindoro was secured, and the only problem was in finding the materials to replace the destroyed supplies to build the airfields. Army Airways Communications Group took over communications, and the First Fighter Control Squadron prepared to move to Luzon.

# FIFTY-SIX

# Tragedy

Once in a while the airmen's weapons backfired on them. One of the most poignant stories of disaster was a self-inflicted tragedy that struck the fortieth Bombardment Group of B-29s at Chakulia, India, on January 14, 1945.

That morning the group was preparing for takeoff for a bombardment mission against Formosa. Following orders from higher headquarters, the operations officer Major Eigenmann instructed the armorers to load the B-29s with 500-pound fragmentation bombs. After this was done, a new order came changing the loading to 500-pound general demolition bombs. No sooner was the change made, when a new order came to change back to fragmentation bombs.

By this time the men were very tired. But again came a change order: Unload the frags and load up again with demolition bombs.

At this point Captain Redler, the armament officer, went to see Major Neil Wemple, squadron commander, to protest. This changing was wearing out the bombs, he said, and it was also wearing out the men. Major Eigenmann and Captain Redler argued, and in the end Redler was ordered to make the change for the third time—otherwise the planes would not be ready in time for the mission.

A discouraged Captain Redler went back to the line to give his boys the bad news. After all this they would probably be too tired to attend the base concert being given that Sunday night by Andre Kostelanetz, the orchestra leader and pianist, and Lily Pons, the operatic soprano.

When Captain Redler reached the line, he told the men they would have to do the work again.

Captain Redler did not like the M-47 cluster antipersonnel bombs they were being asked to reload. Each one consisted of ten fragmentation bombs, fixed in two clusters of five, which were secured by steel bands. The bombs were extremely dangerous to handle because they were fully armed to detonate on impact. In the captain's opinion—and he had said as much to Major Wemple—the bombs had already been handled too much and should not be touched again.

After the change was made for the last time, the men on the line were exhausted.

The planes moved off from the loading area, except for two B-29s No. 582 and No. 269, which were loaded with bombs but not scheduled. Two spare planes were loaded up for every mission in case others aborted. But this day one of the spares aborted: Aircraft No. 582 was scratched when Crew Chief Carmine Merolla discovered a crack in one of the superchargers.

After the mission planes got off, orders came to unload the M-47s from the two superfluous aircraft.

Captain Redler again protested that further handling of the bombs was dangerous. He suggested that the two aircraft take off and unload their bombs on the bombing practice range. He was overruled and ordered to unload the bombs from the two spare aircraft.

He gave the orders.

Two bomb crews of three men each, ragged and weary after a long hard day, came up to unload the planes.

On the hardstand next to No. 582 stood No. 394, fully gassed but carrying no bombs. That aircraft had been placed on jacks for the removal of wheels and some repairs. Crew chief Nathan Kritzer was "shooting the breeze" with crew chief Merolla while the armorers had the bomb bay doors of No. 582 open and were gingerly bringing down the dual cluster bombs. Suddenly one of the bands that held the fragmentation bombs broke in the hands of a loader, and the bomb exploded under the bomb bay.

Kritzer recalled, "Still to this day I do not know exactly what happened. I do know that all hell broke out. Merolla started to run toward his plane, but I grabbed him as there was nothing he could do over there. I also saw that there was nothing I could do with my plane either, as it was on jacks, so I could not start engines and taxi it away. We took off and got out of range of fire and explosion."

Sergeant Ed Connelly, one of the armament men, was killed instantly by the first explosion. More explosions followed as the other clusters in that aircraft went up. Within seconds all the men of the unloading crew were dead or seriously wounded. Bomb fragments penetrated the gas tanks of No. 582, setting them afire, and they exploded in all directions. The flames spread to No. 394, still on its jacks.

A second series of explosions ripped the area. The group chaplain, Father Bartholomew Adler, came up in a jeep. By this time ten men of the crash crew and two men from the Twenty-fifth Squadron who had come running over to help were down. The clothes of some of them were on fire. Father Adler recalled:

"Four or five men were lying on the ground. They were badly burned, with wisps of smoke floating from their clothing. Several men were trying to drag them to safety; other men were trying to rescue those still trapped beneath the bomb bay. I joined in that effort. I distinctly remember helping Corporal Aloysius Schumacher to get away from the plane, assisting him to crawl under a command car that was parked some distance away. Although badly wounded, he kept asking me to help his buddy, Sergeant Edward Donnelly, who was still back at the plane [dead]."

Then came another explosion. Someone jumped into the command car and drove it off, leaving Corporal Schumacher totally exposed.

Fire trucks and ambulances began to come to the scene. Sergeants Charles McCarthy and Stephen D' Addio, both medics, and Private Cleo Askins, a cook at the dispensary, brought an ambulance up to the exploding planes. They parked the ambulance seventy-five yards away and went to the tail of the plane, where five men lay on the ground. Sergeant D'Addio injected them with morphine, in spite of the exploding bombs and ammunition of the aircraft, which were now going off in all directions. Private Askins helped Sergeant D'Addio and then began to get the walking wounded cases into the ambulance. Sergeant McCarthy was bandaging the more seriously hurt.

Corporal Irvin Miller, who was working on his plane when the explosions began, dragged two injured men from the aircraft, although he was injured himself. Private First Class Elias Flessor, who was also working on the aircraft, joined two others running away from the aircraft. When one man fell, Flessor ran to McCarthy's ambulance, found another enlisted man and got a stretcher, and went back for the fallen man. He started for the planes again, but by this time the explosions and fire had become general and he was driven back.

The firefighting unit had arrived. Believing it was a fuel fire, the men of the crew drove their truck up too close, and most of them became casualties of the explosions, too.

Ambulances and trucks began picking up men and taking them to the base hospital. Soon there were several bodies in the morgue and ninety patients filling three hospital wards.

They brought in Corporal Schumacher and Private Edwin Elefant. Schumacher had been hit in the stomach by shrapnel, but he told the medics to take care of Elefant first. Elefant died that night, and Schumacher died the next day.

Squadron Commander Wemple, having transmitted the orders from higher authority, had gone back to his administrative duties at the squadron headquarters that morning when he heard a muffled explosion from the line area. He ran to his jeep, jumped in, and drove to the B-29 parking area, hearing more explosions as he drove. He saw several B-29s on fire, and explosions rocking the whole area. People were running in all directions, and ambulances were taking off for the hospital. He just stood and watched—there was nothing else to do. His heart fell as he considered: he would have to write letters to the next of kin and try to explain.

*     *     *

Captain Redler wished that he were dead, for having obeyed the orders to unload these bombs. All along he had suspected what might happen and he had said so, his views greeted by hints that he was insubordinate.

After the explosions began, his armament men balked at unloading the other B-29 of its fragmentation bombs. Rather than see them face courts-martial, Captain Redler and a sergeant did the job by themselves, securing each cluster with a GI web belt to be sure the band did not snap and repeat the tragedy. The job took most of the rest of the day. Then an exhausted Captain Redler reported to Major Wemple and offered his resignation, which was ignored.

Sergeant Richard Bornholdt of the Forty-fifth Squadron was a patient in the hospital that day. He recollected:

"We had one surgeon in the base hospital. As I remember, he was a refugee from Greece who had escaped to the U.S. and had volunteered for the Army Medical Corps. He did major surgery continuously for some twelve to fifteen hours before a surgical team was flown in. After the relief team took over, he spent several hours walking around the hospital area as if in a trance.

"One of those who didn't make it didn't have a scratch on him. He arrived at the hospital in a state of shock. His turn for medical assistance came after the surgery was completed. He was obviously in pain, and the medical team determined that his kidneys were not functioning. They catheterized and obtained nothing from one kidney and a teaspoon full of bright red blood from the other. He was flown out to a larger hospital, but he only made it a couple days after arrival. Then he died."

That Sunday night, as scheduled, Lily Pons and Andre Kostalanetz performed at the base theater. Then they visited the sick and wounded at the hospital.

A few hours after the tragedy, scarcely after the flames along the flight line had died down and the dead had all been removed, came new orders from Washington. The scientists at Aberdeen Proving Grounds in Maryland had suddenly discovered what the airmen had known all along: the M-47 cluster bomb was jerry-built and extremely unsafe. Headquarters ordered the immediate abandonment of use of these bombs. And even later, higher head-quarters placed a limitation on the number of load changes that could be made for a specific mission.

In retrospect, Major Wemple had this to say:

"All of this . . . brings to light the incompetence and inefficiency of higher headquarters, but. . . ."

# FIFTY-SEVEN

# The Seventh

Not very many Americans have ever heard of the Seventh United States Army Air Force of World War II, although that air force, along with the Fifth and the Thirteenth, played an important role in the Allied drive back across the Pacific to recapture territory taken by the Japanese in the opening days of the war.

The Seventh Air Force was created from the old Hawaiian Air Force on February 5, 1941. Its major mission in the Central Pacific phase of the war was to support the amphibious landings, which it did from Tarawa to Iwo Jima. After the capture of the Marshall Islands early in 1944, the Seventh Air Force had the task of sealing off the important Japanese air bases at Mille, Wotje, Maloelap, and Jaluit. Then they went to work on Truk, the biggest Japanese naval base outside Singapore. The bombing was done by B-25 Mitchell medium bombers and B-24s. For the most part the bombers flew without fighter escort until the last days of the war.

July 1, 1945, was an historic day for the Seventh Air Force. For the first time since Jimmy Doolittle's raid from a carrier task force in April 1942, B-25s of the Forty-seventh and Forty-eighth bomb squadrons flew from Okinawa to raid the Japanese Chiran Airfield on the southern tip of Kyushu.

The squadrons had recently arrived at Okinawa, and when the aircraft were delivered they got orders for the Kyushu flight. Here is an account from the Forty-seventh Squadron records:

"The night before the mission the air was filled with coral dust from the heavy traffic. Out on the line the armorers worked until well after dark. There was a bright sunset. A truckload of musicians came down to the alert line and played some hot jazz. The men looked up from their planes. The music faded away, and they went back to work. The fourteen forward-firing .50s on the new model B-25s were all loaded."

Up at the living area the crews were getting briefed in the wide spot where they showed movies.

Someone turned to Major N. S. Wood, who would lead the mission.

"Hey Curly," he said, "do you realize that the last man to hold your job made lieutenant general?" He was referring to Jimmy Doolittle, who was jumped from lieutenant colonel to brigadier general after the famous Doolitle B-25 raid on Japan.

The fliers concentrated on the briefing. They were told they were heading for rough flak country. They were told to expect 20 percent casualties. After the briefing they sat through Deanna Durbin in *Christmas Holiday*, a film most of them had already seen.

Next morning at 3:30 the whistle traveled up and down between the tent rows. A line started forming in the dark by the mess hall. After breakfast the half-ton trucks filled up with crew members and crew chiefs going down to the flight line. Each man picked up his parachute and walked down to where his plane was parked. Crew members and intelligence officers stood around and talked that early Sunday morning, looking and sounding like a bunch of excited young high school kids taking off for a basketball tournament.

As time passed the tension grew. Finally the word came. The ground men said, "Let's pull 'em through." They wound up the props, and the racket of preflight check followed.

It was getting light as the planes taxied out of their bunkers. By sunup they were all off the new white coral strip that was like so many strips before. They circled the field once—planes from two squadrons loaded with clusters of frag bombs—and then they were off for Japan.

The ground crews sweated it out. It was another hot day, and the men waited in the shadows under the bomber wings. At mid-morning the planes appeared and were counted. No casualties. Nobody had even been wounded!

What a change in the war! They met no opposition in the air over Japan and practically no antiaircraft fire, although they bombed at 7500 feet.

The air war was winding down.

# FIFTY-EIGHT

# The Hero of the 100th

In February 1945, Colonel Jeffrey was promoted out of the command of the 100th and Colonel Frederick Sutterlin took over. The Eighth Air Force missions continued—big missions, involving a thousand planes—as the war moved toward the defeat of Germany. The Russians were very close to Berlin, and the mission on February 3 was to the marshaling yards to prevent the Germans from resupplying the troops there.

Major Rosenthal, at the head of the Third Division, led that mission.

At 9:20 that morning the planes headed out to sea. They reached the Dutch coast north of Amsterdam at 9:55. At 11:15 Major Rosenthal turned into the target area at 25,000 feet. A few moments later the lead plane was hit by flak in the gas tank and bomb bay. Major Rosenthal flew on and bombed, but by the time the bombs were away, dense white smoke was coming out of the cockpit. Rosenthal directed the deputy leader, Major D. K. Lyster:

"Take over, Dave."

Then Rosenthal's plane dropped out of formation. The plane flew level for a few moments while the crew bailed out and then went into a spin at 15,000 feet. The plane continued to go down.

So Major Robert Rosenthal was gone, on his fifty-second mission. No one knew what happened to him. Vernon Sheedy wrote: "Major Rosenthal is a legend here at station 139, and the entire base felt bad about it."

Everyone thought Rosenthal was dead.

*     *     *

Rosenthal had ridden the plane down to 1000 feet, saw that everyone had jumped who could (the bombardier had been decapitated), and then jumped. There was just time for his parachute to open before the plane exploded nearby and bounced him around in the air.

He landed hard, rebreaking the arm which had been broken in his last crash-landing. He got out his .45 caliber revolver and waited to see who would pick him. As he was on the edge of Berlin, it could be Russians or it could be German soldiers; worst of all it, could be German civilians, who quite often these days were killing Allied fliers who parachuted into their areas.

He had landed on the right bank of the Oder River. A vehicle drove up, and he recognized the jeep and the men in it as Russian army. They were suspicious, but contact was at last made. They took him to a Russian headquarters where the general sent him to a hospital. Here his broken arm was set.

Rosenthal's crew had been scattered (most of them had landed inside the German lines and been captured). He could not go west—that way lay the Germans. So after four days in the hospital, the Russians sent Major Rosenthal east. For a week he was billeted at a Russian air base. He collected a Russian soldier's hat. He was wearing flight boots and a green flying jacket. Those were all the clothes he owned.

Next he moved into Poland, where he was billeted with the family of a former Polish army officer who spoke some English. He stayed there about a week, and then was taken to Moscow. Here Major Rosenthal was a welcome oddity for the diplomatic corps. He was entertained by U.S. Ambassador Averill Harriman. He had a box at the opera, and at the ballet he sat very near the Japanese ambassador. After a few more days, Major Rosenthal took a train to Kiev and then to Poltava. Then he went to Tehran, Cairo, Athens, and Naples, and from Italy was flown back to Thorpe Abbotts, to report in from his fifty-second mission.

More missions, more bombs delivered, more B-17s down. On April 20, twenty-nine B-17s of the 100th bombed Oranienburg, completing mission No. 306—the last. Then came VE-day.

# FIFTY-NINE

# Singapore

It was a photographic mission on February 26, 1945, and the original crew of B-29 No. 804 of the Fortieth Bomb Group was not available, so the crew of pilot James Lyons was called to replace it.

Pilot Lyons was deeply involved in a poker game the night of February 25 when he was called to the operations office at Chakulia, India, and told that he would be flying the photo mission to Singapore. He did not have a full crew so a scratch crew was put together.

The mission itself was ordinary enough; good weather, no opposition, and the pictures would be good, according to the aerial photographer. Everybody was relaxed as they started back to base. But suddenly, about an hour after they started back, everything changed. Pilot Lyons had changed seats with copilot Mills Bale and was relaxing, when opposition appeared. The pilot saw only one Japanese fighter, but left gunner Louis L. Sandrick spotted two. One was approaching from one o'clock high. Copilot Bale turned into him, and the forward guns began to fire.

On the first pass the Japanese fighter put a shell into the nose compartment that started a hydraulic fire and knocked out the right inboard engine—and also made a human torch of Bombardier William Kintis.

Bale and flight engineer Frank Thorp feathered the engine, while pilot Lyons and radio operator Joseph Dimock put out the cockpit fire with extinguishers and doused bombardier Kintis, who was unconscious. Pilot Lyons burned his hands in the process, but such was the tension that he did not even know it at the time.

Either the first fighter or another made several more passes and set the bomb bay gas tank on fire. Then the attack was broken off—perhaps because the fighters were low on fuel.

While pilot Lyons took over, copilot Bale and navigator Nathan Teplick and Dimock went to the bomb bay and tried to drop the bomb bay tank, but it would not release. They finally chopped it loose, but as it fell it damaged the bomb bay doors so they would not close. To pilot Lyons this meant they could not ditch the aircraft.

He thought they might make it back to base, particularly after another B-29 came by and gave an accurate position and course. But as they flew along he saw a small spot on the leading edge of the wing next to the No. 2 feathered engine. He realized the wing was on fire inside.

The crew prepared to bail out but kept going, slowly losing altitude. Suddenly when he tried to release the wheel, pilot Lyons saw that he was leaving skin on the wheel, and he turned the wheel over to copilot Bale. He rigged a line to bombardier Kintis's chute and pushed him out. Gunners J. M. Moffit and J. J. Carney jumped, but they wore chest-type chutes and probably were trapped in them when they hit the water. These three men were lost. It was about 2 p.m.

The other nine members of the crew all got out safely. The plane exploded before pilot Lyons hit the water. He dropped free of the chute but too high above the water, and he went deep. When he came up, the gas cylinders of the Mae West did not work. He managed to inflate the vest manually, and then he kicked off his shoes, dumped his wallet (with his poker winnings of 3000 rupees, or about $1000), and worked to survive. Four of the crew had been dropped within shouting distance of one another, and they got together and tied themselves together.

They were afloat for twenty-five hours.

Before they bailed out, radio operator Dimock had sent a distress call, and it was picked up at Strategic Air Force Command. Soon rescue craft, both American and British, were on their way.

Three B-29s from the Fortieth Group and several British Catalina flying boats (PBYs) were sent to search for the survivors. Two of the B-29s took off immediately, but the third was delayed with mechanical problems. The first two Superfortresses exhausted their gas and had to turn homeward, but the third, coming late, spotted a mirror flashing on the water, made a descent, and dropped two rafts with provisions. The B-29 crew saw one of the survivors climb into a raft before the plane had to leave the area.

Teplick, Lester, and Dimock got onto one raft, but radar operator Topolski was all alone. Although for a time he was aware of the presence of others, he eventually drifted away from them. Here is his story:

"A Mae West does not keep you afloat. You have to keep fighting to stay afloat every minute. You can't let your legs drag or you will go under. I got bumped by sharks several times. You bob like a cork on a fishing line. You have to keep the back of your head to the waves, and you have to fight constantly to do this. If the water is said to be calm during the day, the swells are really strong at night. You can feel all the big swells building up as much as an hour before they arrive to hit you.

"One of the PBY search planes flew around the area looking one way and then banking to look the other and trying to see directly below the plane. It seemed like the plane was within fifty feet of me. I waved and tried to signal to them, but they did not see me and eventually flew away.

"The desperateness of being alone in the water can't be described. . . . You search in vain for something—anything—to hold onto, even a pencil or a twig, but there is nothing."

On the second day, five of the men were located by a British flying boat. Pilot Lyons, copilot Bale, right gunner Anthony Peleckis, left gunner Louis Sandrick, and flight engineer Thorp were picked up and taken back to Calcutta and the hospital.

But four others were still out there somewhere.

So was HMS *Seadog*, a British submarine commanded by Lieutenant E. A. Hobson. Here is the *Seadog*'s tale, as taken from British Public Records Office in Kew, England.

At about 3:48 p.m. on February 27 the *Seadog* sighted a B-29 orbiting over the sea and sailed toward it. The submarine tried to attract the attention of the plane by firing flares and grenades, but did not succeed. Reluctantly the captain told the radio operator to break radio silence and signal the plane.

The aircraft commander called for the submarine to fire a red flare, but the signalman found that he had used all his red flares but one, that one malfunctioned.

Captain Hobson was dismayed, but ordered out the big ensign to signal the B-29, finally the flare worked. The airmen were sighted, and so the submarine picked up a raft carrying Dimock, airman Vernon Lester, and navigator Teplick.

Realizing that the raft would be downwind of the crash site, skipper Hobson began a northward patrol. He knew that the rest of the survivors would have only Mae Wests to sustain them. The submarine captain then sighted through the periscope what was thought to be a shark fin and turned toward it, since perhaps it was a shark after a man in the water. It was not a shark, but a man, waving at the submarine.

Here is Topolski's account of the rescue:

"The worst was seeing the B-29 making its last circle. I knew they could not stay any longer, but they never saw me. I said to myself: I'll never last another night. I know that you can never give up or you're lost, but I was ready to give up, when this giant submarine surfaced directly in front of me. The submarine crew threw me a line. I resolved that I was never going to let go of that line. I began swinging around toward the stern of the sub, and there was concern that I would be sucked into the propellers. One of the sub crewmen dove in and pulled me away."

The submarine skipper recalled, "He was utterly exhausted and clearly would not have lasted another night."

The *Seadog* continued to search for survivors for several hours. A B-29 was spotted and then a PBY, and the flying boat was signaled, came down, landed, and picked up the survivors from the submarine. That evening the skipper of the *Seadog* searched until dark, and then gave up the hunt and resumed the submarine's war patrol. Nine of the twelve-man crew of B-29 No. 804 were rescued that day and all taken to a hospital. By the time they were released, the Fortieth Bombardment Group had moved from India to Tinian Island in the Marianas.

# SIXTY

# *Galfo*

On March 2, 1945, the B-17 named *Something for the Boys* was one of 1159 heavy bombers of the Eighth Air Force making a daytime strike against German industry. The target of the 401st Bombardment Group was the synthetic oil plant at Bohlen near Leipzig. Here is the recollection of Corporal Armand J. Galfo, the airplane's radio operator on this mission:

"I was asleep. The pilot's voice was blaring over the intercom: 'We're on the final approach.'

"We can't be. We had been told that our old bucket of bolts which we named *Something for the Boys* was but a fill-in should another plane abort the mission because of mechanical failure. We were to fly just to the English Channel and return.

"Did I fall asleep because I was tired from that 2 A.M. wake-up call? Or would a psychologist find a deeper meaning? All members of the crew including myself found this amusing: the usual 'kid' radio operator, an electronic whiz, oblivious to the real world.

"The 'kid'—me—was barely twenty years old. But the pilot—my God, was he really twenty-one and the copilot twenty-two?

"I wondered why wars are fought by the young. The question was a frequent source of discussion. Sometimes we argued that it must be because of youth's ability of mind and body. Or was it because we had less to lose? Or maybe it was to take advantage of the competitive macho bravado that is part of being young. It seemed significant to us that the only one of our crew who expressed the fear we all felt was 'the old man,' Adam the tail gunner.

Adam was twenty-six years old. He drank my double shot of after-mission whiskey as well as his own."

"The missions were stretching to ten, twelve hours. Why were we bombing so close to the eastern front? Why help the Russians? Why weren't we helping our own armies in their drive to the east? Weren't we going to be fighting the Russians soon? Shouldn't Ike unleash Patton? He'd make the Russians think twice about our determination to have a free Europe.

"But the Russians were on our side, weren't they? Didn't they hold off Hitler and sap the German strength?

"That's the sort of discussion we had in the barracks at night. The ambivalence concerning the role of the Soviet Union in the war continued to be hotly debated. There were even rumors that the end of the war with Germany would not find us going home but moving to the continent to set up bases for the bombing of Russian targets."

"Our planes cruised at an airspeed of 150 knots, but when we tried to bomb Bohlen our flight into the target had to be at an angle to the 200-mile-per-hour jet stream. If we had tried to fly straight in, as first planned, we would have been going backward. As it was, we could only manage an over-the-ground speed of 25 knots, and it seemed as if we would never reach the target. All the while German 88s were filling the sky with ominous black puffs.

"From the doorway between the radio room and the bomb bay I was watching the bombs dropping toward the snow-covered countryside.

"Then came sounds: first like a firecracker, then a rapid series of pings like pebbles hitting a tin roof. The realization that we had been hit by spent pieces of flak shattered my false sense of security.

" 'Don't worry,' the briefing officer had said. 'The jet stream will screw up their aim.' That thought had sustained my courage. "I slammed the door shut, but the absurdity of trying to shut out the war with a quarter-inch plywood door struck me so funny that I could not stop laughing.

"Almost over the target at last. There was some flak, but it looked like one of the more recent milk runs, a quiet round of deadly delivery."

"What a strange war. Two days ago a bit of tennis with some English friends and, in the evening, a few beers in a pub in Kettering. Now we were on our way to 'Work.' The job: to carpet parts of a city with 500-pound bombs.

"How do those gunners down there think of us? Do they hate us? We don't hate them, even though we are supposed to. Maybe if we could see their faces we could hate them."

" 'Fighters at one o'clock.'

"Fighters—what do you mean fighters? We haven't seen any fighters since January, and even then they didn't attack. Maybe I'll get to fire at something just once before the war is over.

"Holy Smoke! ME-262 jets!

"ME-262s. There was no doubt about it! As they turned toward us, they looked exactly like the silhouettes that we had been shown in countless briefings: sleek cockpit, a jet pod hanging below each wing. They're sliding toward the tail. Maybe Adam will get off a few rounds.

"Some of our planes are going down! There, low at three o'clock, a B-17 in a slow, flat spin. It must have been hit.

"Come on guys, get the hell out before she rolls over—before it's too late!

"Thank God some chutes are opening. But we didn't just lose some planes; a friend won't get back, another radio operator.

"The jets did a lot of damage with just one pass. The jet pilot who loosed the rockets that did the damage must have aimed at us! His rockets didn't have time to converge.

"Luck—it has to be part of war! What if he had shot sooner? What if we hadn't pounded their refineries in Bohlen? What if those thousands of jets that Hitler is supposed to have weren't grounded by the lack of fuel?

"What if the man who made up the rosters of newly formed B-17 crews last year in Tampa had put me on my friend's plane and him on mine? What if . . . ? What if . . . ?"

# SIXTY-ONE

# The Home Front

While others were fighting the war, east and west, Corporal Jake Jones was fighting the home front in the Army Air Force training command.

"At Roswell Army Air Field once in a while our airplane would be chosen for a long-distance cross-country flight, since one requirement of the course for the pilots was to fly 1200 miles from base, stop overnight, and return. That was the theory. Practically, this requirement gave the instructors a chance to go home for a night, for 1200 miles from Roswell included some very good sized, satisfying cities, without military bases. These were plums. We always hoped to go someplace where the girls were plentiful and the GIs few.

"Well, I saw some nice towns, but never did find all those loose women out there. As usual I wound up drunk and sometimes without a hotel room, so it was sleep in the lobby of the hotel until time to go out to the airplane again."

Towards the end of 1944, the Air Force priorities shifted as it was apparent the European war was about to end in victory, and the Japanese war was still going strong.

"Our base started bringing in B-29s and getting rid of the B-17s. My last mission in a B-17 was on January 8, 1945. With the B-29s we adopted a whole new training course. We still had flight engineers, but for the B-29s they were all commissioned officers. All of a sudden we enlisted men were out of a job where we were 'somebody,' and just peons again. Not one of us was chosen to go to B-29 flight engineering school. For some reason the Air Force chose to take ground pounders and make them into flight engineers, instead of taking flight engineers and making them into officers. What a heartbreak it was for us!"

Some of the old flight engineers were sent to Amarillo for mechanic's training on the B-29. Among them was Corporal Jones, who ended up as an "R-3350 engine specialist."

"Phooey!" he said, "I wanted to fly."

Crew training at Roswell was different. The pilot, copilot, and flight engineer trained together and became the nucleus of the flight crew that would fly the airplane in combat.

But in fact the system did not work out quite as planned. When Corporal Jones returned to Roswell from Amarillo he found that even with all the rank aboard, a GI was still needed to do the dirty work: pull the chocks, bring the coffee and the water, and watch takeoffs and landings for safety factors.

In the training command, most of the B-29 missions were takeoffs and landings. The aircraft were pressurized, but they never went to high altitude, practiced formation flying, or addressed any long-range navigational problems.

The B-29 still had some bugs, like a tendency for the engines to catch fire, and for electrical systems to fail at critical moments. It was an all-electric airplane: flaps, landing gear, oil cooler, shutters, and cowl flaps all depended on the engine generators. In case of generator failure the landing gear, flaps, and all could become inoperative. To provide an extra safety margin, Boeing installed a small gasoline engine with a generator in the after end of the airplane's waist that was known as the "putt-putt," Corporal Jones's new main task was to operate this "putt-putt" on takeoff and landing.

The flight crew would be ready for takeoff. Corporal Jones would announce "putt-putt on the line, sir," and life could go on. Then Jones would sit in one of the gunner's side blisters in the waist, to observe the landing gear and flaps in operation, and on every takeoff and landing he would report to the pilot on the intercom, confirming that all was going properly.

\*        \*        \*

In 1945 Corporal Jones had a little taste of the real war when "war wearies" were shipped back to the United States, mostly from the China-Burma-India theater. Some of these planes were YB-29s used on bombing missions from the Calcutta and Chengdu areas, but most of them were veterans of "the Hump," used to fly fuel from India to China. These were camouflaged to avoid the Japanese fighters. Instead of having bombing missions painted on the nose, they bore rows of camels to show how many supply missions they had made.

Now at Roswell they were flying two shifts. One ran from 3 A.M. to 2 P.M. and the other from 2 P.M. to 3 A.M. The missions became longer—ten or twelve hours—but it was all the same, bump-bump-bump, low level and turbulence.

Corporal Jones's station was in the waist, at the end of a long pressurized tunnel that ran through the unpressurized bomb bay. He was a long way from the center of gravity of the aircraft, so the bumping was worse than it had been in the B-17. There was nothing left of the romance of flying now. The B-17 had been important and glamorous, but the B-29 was just a bombing machine, and the enlisted men, in particular, were just grease for its wheels. Now, in 1945, it became a question of sweating out the end of the war, piling up hours.

"VE-day came in May, but I was flying that day and so I didn't get to take part in any wild celebrations and kiss all the women, like it showed in the newsreels."

# SIXTY-TWO

# VE-day

Corporal Galfo and the men of the B-17 *Something for the Boys* finished out the European war with the 401st Bomb Group. Galfo recalled VE-day this way:

"We were ordered to conduct a series of low-level flights over the continent to allow the 'ground pounders' to see what the air had wrought. The only members of the aircrew who were required to fly the missions were the pilots, copilots, and radio operators.

"Eager to see as much as possible, I took the little bombardier seat in the nose of *Something for the Boys*. The Plexiglas bubble was an ideal place to see it all.

"We were instructed to maintain an altitude of 300 feet and to stay in formation.

"Three hundred feet and formation? Hell, the war was over —at least for a while, until we would have to go to the South Pacific. Twenty-year-olds find little fun in flying formation at 300 feet, and this was a day to celebrate.

"As soon as we had cleared the Channel, it was everyone for himself. *Something for the Boys* headed first for the Lowlands. As we swept over Brussels at tree-top level, it seemed that everyone in the city was in the streets celebrating, waving all kinds of flags. Where did they get them?

"I could actually look into the startled and joyous faces. We waved at one another.

"Can that middle-aged lady in the black kerchief still see my face? Why the black kerchief? Was her husband killed by the Germans?"

*     *     *

"On to Paris, and the scene was repeated. There—to the left—the top of the Eiffel Tower *above* us. One of our crazy pilots was bringing *Something for the Boys* in a slow banking circle around the tower. Talk about a fool stunt! But man, what a sight to remember!

"Now, on toward Germany, but first a buzzing of a French farm. My God, the pilots have really lost their senses. Our plane is so low that if the wheels were lowered we would touch the ground!

" 'Harry! Bob! There's a herd of cows ahead. Pull up or we'll hit them!'

"Foolhardy, stupid, no discipline. We were read the riot act by the squadron commander over the radio."

"By the time we started to fly over Germany the mood had turned sombre. Cologne—nothing, nothing standing but the cathedral, and it had a hole in the roof.

"But the people—where were the people? Was there no one in Cologne other than that old ragged lady pulling a small wagon? She wasn't even looking up.

"City after city it was the same thing. How would the Germans ever recover? They couldn't, that's for sure!"

"Two weeks later we were back in the States, ready to take on the Japanese. But their August surrender short-circuited that prospect.

"What did we, the combatants, learn about war? Everything, and nothing."

# SIXTY-THREE

# Tokyo Raid

Since the summer of 1943, when the 308th Heavy Bombardment Group and other units of the Fourteenth Air Force had lost so many aircraft in attacking the big Japanese-held port of Hankow, the Yangtze River ports had been a major problem for the Allies. But in the fall of 1944, when Major General Curtis LeMay was transferred from the Eighth Air Force Third Division to command B-29s in China, all that changed. General LeMay had developed some strong ideas on strategic bombardment, ideas that made some of his fellow airmen wince. The way to defeat the enemy, LeMay said, was to hit him as hard as possible without quarter. If civilians got in the way, that was too bad for them.

In the Far East, General LeMay first tested his theory at Hankow. On December 18, 1944, flying out of Chengdu's airfields in western China, eighty-four B-29s plastered the dock area of Hankow with firebombs. The result was an enormous conflagration which destroyed Hankow as a major Japanese river port. Of course, the principal victims of the firebombing were the Chinese civilians who lived in Hankow, but they were the servants of the Japanese, no matter how unwilling, and in this new no-holds-barred aerial warfare they were the unfortunate.

Soon General LeMay was transferred to Saipan to manage the B-29 bombing campaign against Japan. That campaign had not been producing very good results. The B-29s had been concentrating for months on the Japanese aircraft industry, bombing Tokyo, Osaka, and other cities and concentrating on such war industry as the big Mitsubishi complex at Nagoya. But the Japanese were so well entrenched that the high-altitude bombing did relatively little damage. Japanese aircraft production, stepped up in the fall of 1944 after the virtual demise of the Japanese navy, had actually increased during the period of the bombings.

The rationale for the destruction of whole Japanese cities by firebombing—if one was needed after all the atrocities that had occurred by 1945—was that Japanese war production, and particularly the aircraft factories, depended very heavily on Japanese cottage industry. In their home workshops in the cities, Japanese men and women were building parts for military equipment. By the Japanese government's own dicta, this was total war, and there were no "innocent civilians" anymore. School children were working in military factories, even making hand grenades. Enough said, then, about guilt and innocence.

In the early hours of March 10, 1945, the Twentieth Air Force B-29s firebombed Japan. Of the 334 Superfortresses that set out on the raid, some dropped out, and ultimately 279 bombers hit Tokyo, concentrating on an industrial and dock area of ten square miles between the Sumida and Ara rivers.

That night the airmen were blessed and the Japanese cursed with high winds over Tokyo. The winds fanned the fires ignited by the incendiary bombs into a firestorm that leaped from block to block, engulfing whole buildings and tens of thousands of people. The final death toll in that horrible night in Tokyo was put by the U.S. Air Force at 83,000 people, by the Japanese government at well over 100,000 people; it may actually have been closer to 200,000 people. The true figures will never be known, because when the B-29s had begun bombing Japan regularly from the Marianas, more than half the people of Tokyo had fled the city. The number of houses destroyed was known to be 270,000, or a quarter of the buildings in Tokyo, most of them residential buildings. As to people, in big Meiji Theater near the Sumida River, for example, thousands of people died when they mistakenly believed the concrete walls would be a shelter; instead the theater became an oven. Thousands upon thousands more were killed in the rivers as they sought safety from the fire in the water and drowned, or suffocated by smoke that hung down on the surface, or were scalded to death. Those bodies that were not washed out to sea lay stacked like driftwood on the banks of the rivers and canals.

So great was the destructive success of the firebombing of Tokyo that the whole B-29 program was adapted to that end. The notion of "military targets" was largely forgotten; all Japan, and particularly its major cities, was a military target now. And the burning of Japan continued. Osaka, Nagoya, and Kobe were primary targets along with Tokyo.

On May 23, 1945, at 11 a.m., Captain Eino Jenstrom and his crew of the B-29 *Eddie Allen* assembled in the briefing room of the Fifty-eighth Bombardment Wing on Tinian in the Mariana Islands. They were about to go back to Tokyo with firebombs in the biggest B-29 raid of the war. A total of 562 Superfortresses were assigned to make the raid. Pathfinder aircraft, the elite crews of the Twenty-first Bomber Command, would lead, going in at low level to mark the targets in the urban-industrial area south of the Imperial Palace, on the west side of Tokyo harbor. The palace, which was of course, off-limits for bombing, was easily recognizable, with its stone-walled moat, more than three hundred acres of open land inside one of the largest cities, and certainly the most crowded, in the world. Most of the houses were built of wood and paper, guaranteed to go up in bursts of flame when ignited by the firebombs.

At the briefing Captain Jenstrom learned that he was to bomb from 9000 feet. This was a distinct change from the first firebomb raid on Tokyo, when the B-29s went in at low level; but since that March day the Japanese air defenses had become more sophisticated.

In mid-afternoon the eleven-man combat crew of the *Eddie Allen* was delivered by truck to the flight line. This was to be the penultimate mission for the *Eddie Allen*, a Superfortress financed for the U.S. Air Force by the men and women who worked at Boeing Aircraft Company's Wichita plant. It was named in honor of a Boeing director of aerodynamics and flight research who had been killed testing a B-29 in the early days. This mission and one more would make twenty-five in all, after which, like an aircrewman after his string, the *Eddie Allen* would be returned to the United States to become a memorial.

On the flight line, crew chief John Mahli informed pilot and aircrew that the airplane was ready, three engines in their second hundred hours, one "high time" engine to be watched. They had forty clusters of incendiary bombs aboard and a full supply of ammunition of the .50 caliber machine guns.

The aircrew then went to work checking out their aircraft. The bombardier checked the incendiary clusters. The flight engineer checked fuel and oil for the engines. The radar operator checked his instrument and the radioman checked his radio. The gunners checked their guns and the ammunition supplies at each station.

Pilot Jenstrom and his copilot, Lieutenant Louis Bicknese, got in their seats and started the preflight check. More than 100 aircraft would take off from the two parallel runways on Tinian. For this long flight there was not much margin for error: a thirty-minute extra supply of gasoline for a fifteen-and-a-half-hour flight. If they missed their assigned position by not being ready, they would go to the end of the takeoff line, which would cut seriously into the fuel margin.

Slowly, the *Eddie Allen* moved to the runway and then to the takeoff line. Captain Jenstrom put on the brakes, and then applied full power to the engines. The plane shook and strained like a dog trying to shake its leash. Copilot Bicknese counted down the last ten seconds and then the brakes were released and the plane surged forward, flaps down. The plane scurried along the runway, gaining momentum until the nose came up. They moved off the end of the runway in a swirl of coral dust, and up over the marine encampment on the ridge above the runway, and then they dipped down. The flaps came up, the airspeed indicator went up, and the B-29 began to climb.

Dusk came and then darkness, as the Superfortress slid over the top of the clouds. They reached Iwo Jima, the first checkpoint and emergency landing field for the Superfortresses, and traveled through a front east of Japan, coming out of it well before they reached Tokyo.

The city was alight from fires set by other aircraft. The next checkpoint was a town about thirty miles southwest of the capital. They could see aircraft over the southern end of Tokyo Bay. Searchlight fingers probed until they found a plane, passed, came back and tried to hold it in the glare. The antiaircraft guns below boomed away. The B-29s were trying to hold steady courses for the target, a difficult task in the searchlight glare and the buffeting of flak. Suddenly left waistgunner Corporal Vic Braeunig shouted a warning. A dark shape, another Superfortress, passed few feet below the *Eddie Allen*, so swiftly they could not have done anything about it if they had had to. There was no need—the plane was already gone.

As they neared the town that was their initial point, the aircraft ahead of them was pinned by a searchlight. Flak began to blossom around it as the pilot weaved to try to get out of the searchlight glare. Off to the right another Superfortress was pinned to the cloud ceiling by searchlights. The *Eddie Allen* was five hundred yards behind that plane. One searchlight found the plane in front of them and one the plane just behind them, but they remained in the murk.

Ahead and to the left pilot Jenstrom saw a B-29 blow up, hit perhaps by flak, perhaps by a kamikaze. The pieces arced away and downward, slowly, gracefully. There were no parachutes. Jenstrom saw another B-29, trailing a plume of white smoke from one wing, turning away from the target and out toward the sea.

Ahead the target was south central Tokyo, largely residential but with some industry. The first forty bombers had carried clusters of M-47 antipersonnel bombs and firebombs, but the rest of the bombers carried the six-pound M-69 bombs which were so effective in clinging to tile roofs, burning through, and demolishing the flimsy wooden Japanese houses.

By the time the *Eddie Allen* reached it, the target area was obscured by an enormous pall of smoke. The aiming point was the edge of the fire. The bombardier, Lieutenant Fred Billingsley, took over. For the next three minutes the *Eddie Allen* was committed to straight, steady flight, no matter the flak or fighters.

Now came the flak. A shell passed in front of bombardier Billingsley's nose compartment, soared up, and exploded a hundred feet above and behind the aircraft.

Billingsley shouted, "Wow!" and then "Bombs away! Bomb bay doors closed!"

Just then the *Eddie Allen* lurched and the left wing jumped. The tail gunner, Corporal Jim Taliaferro, shouted, "We're hit," and then there was silence from him . . . ominous silence.

The top gunner, Sergeant Dan Thorne, broke in over the intercom, "Tail Gunner! Tail Gunner, this is Central Fire Control. Come in! Come in!"

"I'm okay. We're hit. Can't see much."

Another flak burst lifted the *Eddie Allen*, and the aircraft slid to the right, diving. Pilot Jenstrom turned out toward the sea, accelerating until the needle of the airspeed indicator approached the red line. The aircraft was still pinned by the searchlights and still surrounded by flak bursts, but soon they began to fall behind. Pilot Jenstrom pulled up, cut the speed and headed east as he leveled off. The plane slid into the darkness of the weather front.

Captain Jenstrom turned over the controls to the copilot and went aft to the front bomb bay to inspect the damage. He saw fluid dripping from a broken hydraulic line. It was the same at the rear bomb bay. They had been pasted nicely, but the all important radar gear that lay between the bomb bays was unhurt.

In the aft gunner's compartment the gunners had taken a real beating, but no one was hurt. The plane was full of flak holes, which they had stuffed with cushions. The right gunner, Corporal Bob Mautner, had had a narrow escape: A piece of flak had buried itself in his seat.

It became apparent to Jenstrom why tail gunner Taliaferro had shouted. A hole a yard in diameter had been blown in the elevator, six feet from the tail gunner's position. Structurally the elevator seemed all right; the critical point would come on landing.

Pilot Jenstrom started forward again. He was met by the navigator, flight officer Frank Moch, at the front end of the crew tunnel.

"Captain, the leading edge of the left wing outboard of No. 2 is red hot."

Captain Jenstrom stuck his head up into the astrodome and looked at the left wing. A foot behind the leading edge was a long red line which feathered back toward the back of the wing, and a wisp of smoke peeled back from the No. 1 engine.

The left gunner, Braeunig, called, "Smoke from No. 1 increasing. More sparks."

Jenstrom decided, "Feather No. 1."

The engine feathered without fail. The propeller turned edges into the wind and stopped. All secure. "How's the smoke?" Copilot Bicknese asked Braeunig.

"Seems to be thinning. Fewer sparks."

The flight engineer, Corporal Olan Garrett, asked permission to transfer the fuel from the No. 1 fuel cells to avoid fire.

"Roger. Start pumping," said the pilot.

Braeunig broke in, "Smoke real thin now. Hardly any sparks."

They flew on. When the transfer of fuel was completed, flight engineer Garrett reported again. There should have been 1100 gallons of fuel in that set of fuel cells, but he had pumped only 800 gallons; the 300 that had been lost to leakage had been their reserve. This meant they would have to let down at Iwo Jima on the way home.

They flew on steadily on three engines until they were fifty miles out of Iwo Jima. Then the radio operator, Sergeant Ralph Desch, called Iwo radio reporting battle damage and asked for weather soundings and clearance to land.

Iwo answered:

"Iwo weather zero zero. Expected to remain for the next six hours. Crashed aircraft on the runway. Iwo closed to all aircraft. Enter Orbit Area Charlie. Stand By."

Six hours! They could not last that long. It might be possible to reach Tinian on three engines, although the fuel reserve for four-engine flight was lost. Nobody knew. They might have to ditch in the sea. Certainly they did not want to ditch around Iwo in the fog. Better to try for sunny Tinian. They radioed for an escort. Navigator Moch fired a flare from a Very pistol to mark their position, and a few moments later an answer came from a B-29. They had an escort, so at least they would not go down unmarked in the desolate sea.

Pilot Jenstrom headed for Tinian, throttling back to the minimum. For once he sought the tall cumulus clouds, with their turbulence that lifted them—50 feet, 100 feet, even 300 feet—and kept the pressure off fuel consumption.

They watched the fuel gauges drop, drop, drop, but dropping more slowly than the performance charts had indicated. Navigator Moch had predicted that they would ditch at a Point X, but they passed Point X and were still in the air.

And suddenly, there ahead in the sunshine was Tinian. They could see the steady stream of aircraft with four engines that had passed them by on the journey home. The landing pattern was full.

Radioman Desch got on the horn: "West Tower. Victor One Nine. Emergency landing. Battle damage. Minimum fuel. Flare marks position."

The flare went up. Radio Tinian ordered the approaches cleared, and the runway was *Eddie Allen*'s. The wheels went down without trouble. The elevator seemed to be holding. The flaps went halfway down, but without much effect.

They were going in. The gear hit with the usual sliding creak, and the weight went onto all wheels. The right wing dropped as it should, but the left wing hung "like the wing of a mallard duck," pilot Jenstrom said.

He taxied the plane slowly and carefully to Hardstand 11, and they were home free. Mission Number 24 for the *Eddie Allen* was completed.

When the aircrew got down, they and crew chief John Mahli looked over the aircraft. A hole in the lower surface of the left wing near the root of engine No. 1 was big enough for the crew chief to stick head and shoulders into. He could see the whole wing structure. The dividing wall between the fuel cells was burned away; it seemed miraculous that the fuel had not flamed. The shell had been a dud but had still done its damage. They checked the fuel remaining—less than fifty gallons.

The crew agreed on one thing: The *Eddie Allen* would never fly mission No. 25 and would never go home to be a memorial. Instead the aircraft was stripped and moved to the group training area. There it became a classroom for teaching emergency procedures.

In a way Eddie Allen had his memorial anyhow. That left wing, weakened to the point that it tested out as only at one-half its specified hardness, had supported the plane all the way home and had proved out Eddie Allen's maxim. As he had once told his Boeing staff, "Remember, it is not enough that these planes fight the enemy. They must endure; they must bring their crews home."

As Major General Tom Jeffrey was to say of the B-17 after flying it all through the European operations of World War II, the B-29 was "a very forgiving airplane." In the end, that was Eddie Allen's memorial. He had made it so.

Based on "The Last Mission of the *Eddie Allen*" by Col. Eino E. Jenstrom, USAF (Ret.). Reprinted by permission from *Air Force* Magazine. Copyright 1980 the Air Force Association.

# SIXTY-FOUR

# *Torpedoing*

Sergeant John Mahan was the tail gunner on a B-25J with the Forty-seventh Squadron of the Forty-first Bomb Group in the Seventh Air Force. In July 1945, after working their way across the Pacific, the Forty-seventh Squadron was operating out of Okinawa, sometimes flying conventional bombardment missions against the southern Japanese island of Kyushu.

But these B-25s had also been modified to carry "glide torpedoes." These were standard torpedoes, but equipped with a wing and tail assembly. When dropped at a given airspeed, the torpedo would glide one mile for every 1000 feet of altitude. The gyros were preset to perform maneuvers. Some zigzagged when they hit the water, some performed helix circles, some did figure eights. The idea was to bomb in a harbor or bay that held a concentration of ships, and the torpedoes would run until they hit something or ran out of fuel and sank to the bottom.

"This is a good theory," said Sergeant Mahan, "and we did hit a couple of ships: an aircraft carrier and some smaller ships."

The technique was for the pilot, not the bombardier, to control the torpedo drop. In fact, in the B-25J that the Forty-seventh flew, all the positions and the nomenclatures were screwed up. The pilot also controlled the twelve forward firing .50 caliber machine guns, which had been modified from a bomber with a bombardier's compartment in the Plexiglas nose, to become a strafing machine. The pilot also controlled the bomb bay doors, and dropped the bombs if bombs were carried.

"The tit buttons are located on the yoke. . . . I guess they did that to keep the pilot busy when he was doing nothing but flying the plane and taking evasive action. The bombardier was dual-rated, as was every crew member of our B-25s, so his classification was bombardier/navigator, and he was not doing any bombing any more.

"In our flight only one plane carried a bombsight—this was a normal B-25, with a normal bombardier located in the nose cone. All the other B-25s were strafing models with the machine guns in the bombardier's compartment. So the wing planes dropped off the lead plane."

By this point in the war the use of B-25s was so changed from the original concept that many of the bombardier/navigators had never dropped a bomb. Besides, the Forty-seventh was now a torpedo squadron!

On July 31, the B-25s of the Forty-seventh Squadron flew a mission against Sasebo Bay in Kyushu, seeking out shipping at Sasebo Naval Base. Here is Sergeant Mahan's story:

"Watch for fighters. Here comes the flak. Not bad. Seen it a lot worse. The bay is sheltered by mountains.

"Our assigned target is in a cove in Sasebo Bay. Our flight of B-25s is approaching the target. We have strong head winds—that will affect the drop. Releasing the torpedo into a strong head-wind will increase the airspeed of the torpedo and cause it to glide a further distance.

"Throttle back. Slow down our airspeed. Watch the lead plane: When he drops, we drop.

"There it goes. The pilot hits the tit button, and our flying fish drops away.

"We watch our fish as it glides away. Some of the other torpedoes are entering the water. We see their wings fly off. They are armed. (There is a device that trails behind and below the torpedo. When this strikes the water, it releases the wing assembly and arming wire.) These other torpedoes are now on their search missions in the water, looking for something to hit. Our fish is still in the air. What has happened? It should be in the water with the rest of them, but it's still flying, still streaking across the cove.

"All the other fish are searching, searching, but our bird still flies and is now racing over the land!

"We lose sight of it for a few seconds in the background of the land area. Suddenly we see a tremendous explosion. Our fish with its 2000-pound warhead has made history. The torpedo exploded with all its fury about halfway up the mountain side.

"For Christ's sake, we torpedoed a mountain!!!

"We torpedoed a stinking mountain!!

"That torpedo must have gotten caught in a gust of that head wind or maybe an updraft. We go home hoping at least it hit somebody's fish pond, perhaps with a rowboat in it."

The fish dropped by the other B-25s did better that day, sinking some small ships in the bay. Next day the squadron was back, in Nagasaki this time, torpedoing the dock area.

# SIXTY-FIVE

# Cargo Group

In 1945, they were flying 80 to 130 hours per month. They got into Clark Field in January, after the Lingayen Gulf invasion, and they were still dodging bomb craters. One day Lieutenant Krogh flew from Clark Field over Manila and realized that below him the Americans and Japanese were fighting for possession of Manila. They landed at Neilsen Field and walked into Manila to see a wrecked city, for an element of the Japanese defense had decided to fight to the last ditch, although General Yamashita had ordered the city evacuated.

When Okinawa was invaded, the Second Combat Cargo Group of the Fifth Air Force was soon flying Lingayen-Okinawa. This was difficult because they had to stay within a corridor to avoid Japanese kamikazes, fighters, and antiaircraft fire. They would fly to Yontan airstrip, unload, and fly back to the Philippines. From the air, Lieutenant Krogh watched the progress of the conquest of Okinawa by the marines and the army, fighting around Naha and the southern third of the island. Finally they got to stay overnight after bringing in a load of cargo. They slept first in bunkers; later, when the danger of bombing or shelling was not so great, they set up cots under the wings of their plane. But in May the Seabees would work all night with the lights on, until an air raid alert sounded. Then all lights went out. There was a sign on the field that said, "Every night at Yontan is the Fourth of July."

Late in the spring of 1945 Lieutenant Krogh's Second Combat

Cargo Group got word that they were going to move from Dulag to Okinawa.

"This was a tough move, because life at Dulag was quite tranquil and pleasant when we weren't flying. We tore down all our nice wooden floored tents and then went up to Okinawa where we plunked down some tents on a hillside. Our floors were coral, and there were no luxuries. It was back to canteens, mess gear, and C rations. It didn't matter too much, because we were flying day and night."

Finally, on September 2, the men of Lieutenant Krogh's group learned that the war was over. The next day Krogh flew sixty-two fully equipped soldiers of the Thirty-second Division for occupation duty. For several days they flew in troops, three hours each way from Ie Shima to Kanoya, Kyushu. That was the end of Lieutenant Krogh's war. Soon he was a member of the occupation force, and in November he had enough points to be shipped home.

# SIXTY-SIX

# The Last Patrol

Just before the Pacific war ended, Lieutenant (J.G.) Layer was finishing up the final stages of training at Corpus Christi and getting ready for final checkout as first pilot of a new PBM. One day he took a plane off the ramp into the water, ready for takeoff, but the starboard engine kept cutting out and he could not develop enough power for lift-off. He called operations and was told to start all over and try again. So he revved up the engines and got five feet off the water, when the starboard engine cut out again and the PBM came down into the water like a ruptured duck. Operations told him to bring the aircraft in and he taxied toward the ramp, but as he was making his turn into the ramp the bad engine cut out once more, throwing the hull pontoon up against the edge of the ramp and ripping it. He gunned the good engine and got the aircraft onto the ramp—barely. Then as the horrified handlers looked on, before they could put a line on the PBM, it slid slowly and majestically back into the water.

The water came into the ruptured hull—glug-glug-glug—and the PBM sank in twelve feet of water. Skipper Layer and his bedraggled crew struggled ashore. Not long afterward Layer was grounded for the careless destruction of government property. He remained grounded as his squadron mates took off for Alameda, and then for Pearl Harbor and the war zone once again.

Lieutenant Layer was feeling unwanted and unloved and very much out of it, even though he had learned that he had been the object of the operations officer's pique: that particular aircraft's starboard engine had been acting up all week, and no one had mentioned it to him.

His squadron mates, in three sections of five planes each, were heading for Pearl Harbor. It was August 14, Pacific Daylight Time, and some of them were tuned into radio station KRON in San Francisco, listening to Glenn Miller records and wondering if the world would ever be the same again without him.

An announcer cut in: "We interrupt this program with a news bulletin. The Japanese have surrendered. The war is over! I repeat: The Japanese Emperor has announced the surrender of Japan!"

And then the PBM squadron suddenly separated into two segments, the eager beavers and the hostilities-only people. The eager beavers flew straight and fast to their Pearl Harbor destination, looking forward to Pacific duty for a couple of years at least. But the volunteer soldiers immediately had other ideas, and suddenly some of the aircraft began to develop problems. Engines acted up, the fuel consumption rate suddenly became adverse, and planes began turning back toward Alameda.

Yes, the war was over. They were going home to a brave new world.

# SIXTY-SEVEN

# Sic Transit Gloria Mundi

On VJ-day, Corporal Jake Jones was flying another of those twelve-hour training missions out of Roswell, New Mexico, preparing B-29 skeleton crews for a war they would no longer have to fight.

"Again, no wild celebrations for us. Rather, a feeling of numbness, because flying at our bases stopped just about overnight."

Not long after VJ-day, most of the B-29s from the 509th Bombardment Squadron came back to Roswell—including the *Enola Gay*, which had dropped the atomic bomb on Hiroshima, and *Bock's Car*, which had dropped the atomic bomb on Nagasaki. They were moved into the squadron parking area and stayed there, but to the men of the Roswell base they were just another bunch of B-29s.

Now that the war was over, Corporal Jake Jones was out of a job again, but because Roswell Air Base was designated as a separation center, he found a new one, doing paperwork. He was put into a unit set up to encourage officers to stay in the reserve after discharge from active duty. With the new job Corporal Jones got a promotion—sort of. He was advanced to sergeant, but whereas he had been a corporal on flight pay, making $99 a month, as a sergeant with no more flight pay, he made $78 a month, and it was hard to see the promotion as very significant.

Fortunately, for the first time since he had been in the service Sergeant Jones had a commanding officer he liked. "The officer in charge of our section, Second Lieutenant Steve Wiesnieski, was the only officer I encountered during the entire war that ever treated me like I was a person and not a "thing.'"

Sergeant Jones had no love for his job, and from this point on he started counting days "like guys in prison." He still did not know for sure when he would get out, because his not having been overseas had not only made it a very dull war for him, but had put him in a very low position on the point system for discharge.

By the end of 1945, Roswell Air Base had finished its task as a separation center, and late in January 1946 most of the enlisted men were flown to California. On February 3, 1946, Sergeant Jones was discharged at Fort MacArthur, California, with $200 in mustering out pay, his last month's $79, train fare back to Washington, and an Honorable Discharge from the Army of the United States.

So ended the story of the airmen of World War II.

# Chapter Notes

## Chapter 1

This chapter depended on the World War II autobiography of Corporal Jake Jones, 13144734, who although disappointed in his ambition to become a pilot, at least managed to become an aircrew member. When the war ended, Jake Jones went to college and afterwards secured a commission in the United States Air Force, where he served until his retirement.

## Chapter 2

I first became aware of the Spanish Civil War long ago through tales told by Jay Allen of the *Chicago Tribune*, who had witnessed the bombing of Barcelona and several other cities as a correspondent. I used Seagrave's *Soldiers of Fortune* for this chapter.

## Chapter 3

The Flying Tigers and General Claire Chennault were legendary when I was in China in 1944 and 1945. I used Seagrave's book and Gregory Boyington's *Baa, Baa, Black Sheep* for this chapter, plus materials I gathered in China and conversations with Graham Peck, who spent much of the war in Kunming and Guilin as a writer and with the U.S. Office of War Information. He knew the Tigers very well.

## Chapter 4

Vern Haugland's book *The Eagle Squadrons* was a source for this chapter about the Battle of Britain and the Americans who volunteered to fight for

Britain in the air. Two other sources were C. G. Grey's *The Luftwaffe* and Williamson Murray's *Luftwaffe*.

Pilot Dunn's personal account is from *The Eagle Squadrons*, as are pilot Daniel's and pilot Fessler's (reprinted from *The Eagle Squadron* by Vern Haugland. Copyright © 1979, Ziff Davis Publishing Company).

### Chapter 5

Jake Jones's personal account was vital to this chapter.

### Chapter 6

The discussion of President Roosevelt and the preparations for the Pacific war is from materials I gathered for *Japan's Triumph*, the account of the first six months of the war. I also used Gordon Prange's *At Dawn We Slept*, and Admiral Edwin T. Layton's *And I Was There*. The story of the early morning of December 7, 1941 is from the admiral's book, as is the story of Private McDonald and Lieutenant Tyler. The story of Commander Ramsey's activity is from my *How They Won the War in the Pacific*. The story of Colonel Farthing is from Jablonski's *Flying Fortress*. The story of pilots Taylor and Welch is from *And I Was There*. The story of the Naval airmen at San Diego is from Frederick Mears's book *Carrier Combat*.

### Chapter 7

The research for this chapter was done at the MacArthur Memorial Museum in Norfolk, Virginia. The materials about the squadrons come from Major General Richard Sutherland's collection of reports and papers there. The material about the Japanese plans for the attack on the Philippines is from the Japanese Defense Agency's 101-volume history of the Pacific war. The material about the Pearl Harbor attack notice is from the Sutherland papers and the CincPac files. The tales of the airmen at this time are from the squadron reports in the Sutherland papers. The story of Captain Colin Kelly comes from three sources: Jablonski's *Flying Fortress*, my book *How They Won the War in the Pacific*, and Saburo Sakai's *Samurai!* The story of the movement of the Far Eastern Air Force is from materials gathered for *Japan's Triumph* and from the Sutherland papers. The material about General George Brett is from *Flying Fortress*.

### Chapter 8

The material about the fighter squadrons in the Philippines is from the Sutherland papers. The material about Lieutenant Grashio is from his own book. The material about Bataan is from *Death March* and from Samuel Grashio's *Return to Freedom*. The stories of the Japanese are from the Japanese official war history.

### Chapter 9

The story of Lieutenant Kane and the *U-701* is from the records of the Eastern Sea Frontier in the Naval History Center, Washington, D. C.

### Chapter 10

The story of the battle for Java is from the Sutherland papers and reports. The stories about the B-17s are from *Flying Fortress*. The material about the Fifth Air Force is from William Leary's *We Shall Return!*

### Chapter 11

Edison Vail's experiences were told to me by Vail in an interview.

### Chapter 12

The material about early flights over the Hump is from William Tunner's *Over the Hump*. Other tales of airmen flying the Hump are from the memorial book. The verse by Bill Wise is from The Hump Pilots Association's memorial book (see bibliograpy).

### Chapter 13

The story of Gordon Cruickshanks was told to me by Gordo in an interview.

### Chapter 14

The stories about Frederick Mears and his friends are from his book.

### Chapter 15

The tales of the carrier *Hornet* are from the Mears book.

### Chapter 16

The story of Jimmy Doolittle's raid comes from a long interview I had with the general in 1972 when I was working with Lowell Thomas on a book about the general, which was never published. Other sources were materials in the naval history files that I used for *How They Won the War in the Pacific*.

## Chapter 17

Much of the material here is from the Mears book and from the Naval History Center's records regarding Midway.

## Chapter 18

The material about the battle is from the CincPac records, the Mears book, and the Japanese official war history.

## Chapter 19

The story of the adventures of the *Enterprise* is from the Naval History Center records and from the Mears book. The story of the action off Guadalcanal is from the Morison history and from Mears.

## Chapter 20

The material about Frank Jack Fletcher is from Admiral Dyer's book *The Amphibians Came to Conquer* and the CincPac records. The opinion that Fletcher caused the attenuated battle for Guadalcanal and totally relinquished the surprise and strength factor of the invasion is my own. The material about the Japanese is from the Japanese naval and army records in the official war history.

## Chapter 21

The general material about the Guadalcanal situation is from the Dyer book and from materials gathered for *South Pacific*, part of my series on the Pacific war. Mears's adventures come from his book.

## Chapter 22

This chapter depended on an extended interview with General Jeffrey.

## Chapter 23

For this chapter I used the Air Force chronology of World War II, *Flying Fortress*, and R. J. Overy's *The Air War, 1939–1945*.

## Chapter 24

For this chapter I used Morison, the Japanese official war history, and *We Shall Return!* plus materials collected for my *Jungles of New Guinea* that included volumes of the U.S. Army History and the U.S Air Force History dealing with the Southwest Pacific campaign. The records of General Sutherland also have several accounts by pilots of this battle.

## Chapter 25

This chapter depended on materials I gathered in Tokyo on the death of Admiral Yamamoto (which I used more fully in *Yamamoto*). Burke Davis's *Get Yamamoto* has a complete account of the event. My own opinion is that it was a very risky effort, endangering the security of the breach of the Japanese naval codes for a grandstand play, an opinion shared by Admiral Halsey, at least after the fact. But as with the Doolittle Raid, there were considerations other than the events at hand, and the death of Yamamoto certainly did create negativism and upset in Japan, particularly in the navy, where Yamamoto's predictions of disaster for Japan were well known.

## Chapter 26

Jimmy Doolittle told me the story of his flight to North Africa prior to the invasion. The story of Joseph Yuhasz and his adventures in the Sicily campaign comes from a manuscript written by Yuhasz which he kindly let me use. Other material in this chapter about the Eighty-second Airborne Division came from research at Fort Bragg, North Carolina, in connection with my book *Airborne*, published some years ago.

## Chapter 27

The Jeffrey interview was central to this chapter. So was the story of the 390th Bombardment Group and the 390th's anthology. I drew several battle experience stories from the anthology, including Wilbert Richarz's account. The Air Force chronology and Overy were also useful here.

## Chapter 28

This chapter depended on my interview with General Jeffrey.

## Chapter 29

Ray Stone's account of the fighter strike on Kukiang came from a letter he wrote in response to my request for information.

## Chapter 30

Henry Brady's account of the Hankow mission comes from information he sent me in response to a request.

## Chapter 31

Chester W. Driest's account of his sinking in the southwest Pacific is from his unpublished manuscript dealing with his experiences in World War II.

## Chapter 32

I used the 390th book and General Jeffrey's interview here, plus Williamson Murray's *Luftwaffe*. I also used LeStrange and Varian's books dealing with the Bloody Hundredth. Lieutenant Crosby was one of the most effective diarists and writers about the activities of the group. Lieutenant Robert Rosenthal soon became one of the most distinguished of the bomber pilots in Britain. The German account of the bombing of Münster comes from Ian Hawkins's book *Münster: The Way It Was*. Permission for use of the Bloody Hundreth was kindly granted by Harry Crosby.

## Chapter 33

I used the Air Force chronology for this chapter, as well as the personal account Sergeant Anderson sent to me.

## Chapter 34

Captain Robert Sellers sent me this account of his volunteer mission of January 29, 1944.

## Chapter 35

I interviewed Kenneth Kinsinger at his home in Williamsburg, Virginia, and he lent me the volume of reminiscences published by the 449th Bomb Group Association after the war. Part of this chapter comes from an account in the book.

## Chapter 36

Sergeant Lewis's story comes from the 449th record.

## Chapter 37

Sergeant Szablinski's story also comes from the 449th book. His remarkable odyssey was possible because he spoke German.

## Chapter 38

Sergeant Watkins wrote me his story of the raids as a photographer, and he also put me in touch with Kenneth Kinsinger.

## Chapter 39

To the men of the 449th Bombardment Group the mission of April 4, 1944, against Bucharest will always stand out, for it was on this mission that the group cracked open the Rumanian air force, which after this day was never again the same dangerous enemy. The mission was costly to the Americans, too, as can be ascertained in the reading of this account from the 449th book.

## Chapter 40

The Grudaugh story also comes from the collection of tales in the 449th book.

## Chapter 41

Jakes Jones longed to be in combat, and instead he was relegated to a training command. From Jake's point of view, as he told me, the only asset was that at least he got to fly.

## Chapter 42

Much of this material comes from a paper written by Colonel William Parkhill in response to claims by the airborne troops that the troop carrier aircraft pilots were inept and did not take them where they were supposed to go. From my study for *Airborne* I know the charge to be true. Many men of the Eighty-second Airborne died because they were dropped into land the Germans had flooded and they were so tightly packed in their rigging that they could not escape their own equipment. Actually, the very confusion of the airdrops militated for their success, because the Germans were more confused than the airborne troops. Yet Colonel Parkhill has a point insofar as his own squadron was concerned, and as far as I know this is the first time it has been made public.

## Chapter 43

The material for this chapter comes from several of the books about the Bloody 100th and from Murray's *Luftwaffe* and Grey's *The Luftwaffe*. The sad story of Ralph Cotter was too often repeated during the war. The morale of the Bloody 100th hit some new lows in April. What was needed was some new blood in command to revive morale.

## Chapter 44

The story of the plane called *Patches* is from the 390th book and from Sergeant Jahnke's privately printed book.

## Chapter 45

The story of life in Stalag 17B is from the Jahnke book.

## Chapter 46

The tales in this chapter are from my conversation with General Jeffrey and the various books on the 100th Bombardment Group.

## Chapter 47

The source for the stories about Chick's Crew is the book of that title written by Benjamin Smith, Jr., after the war.

## Chapter 48

The further adventures of the 449th Bombardment Group come from the second volume of their book of memorabilia and from Kenneth Kinsinger.

## Chapter 49

Joe Layer's story of the war in the Pacific as seen by a patrol plane pilot comes from a long conversation. The material about the fleet and Marc Mitscher is from conversations with Admiral Arleigh Burke.

## Chapter 50

The story of the joint Eighth and Fifteenth Air Force raid on Ploesti comes from the 449th book and from General Jeffrey. The tales of the Regensburg raid are from the 449th book and from Kenneth Kinsinger.

**Chapter 51**

The story of the great Grottaglie fire is from the group's book.

**Chapter 52**

The story of the Hollandia operations continues the odyssey of Airman Driest and is from his unpublished manuscript.

**Chapter 53**

Curtis Krogh's story is also from an unpublished manuscript.

**Chapter 54**

The material about the Twentieth Air Force comes from Air Force records which I studied when doing research for my book about the firebombing of Japan several years ago, from several books about flying the Hump, and from a newsletter published by the 40th Bombardment Group Association.

**Chapter 55**

Airman Driest's story continues in this chapter, from his unpublished recollections of the war.

**Chapter 56**

The story of the Chakulia tragedy is from the 40th Bomb Group Association's newsletter.

**Chapter 57**

The material about the Seventh Air Force is from a newsletter of that organization.

**Chapter 58**

The story about Major Rosenthal is from the 100th's book of memorabilia.

**Chapter 59**

The story of the Singapore mission is from the Fortieth Bomb Group newsletter.

### Chapter 60

The Galfo story was supplied by Professor Armand J. Galfo.

### Chapter 61

This continuation of Jake Jones's story was supplied by him.

### Chapter 62

Corporal Galfo supplied me with this story of VE-day.

### Chapter 63

The material about General LeMay is from the records of the Twentieth Air Force. The material about the firebomb raid on Tokyo of March 10, 1945, is from Japanese official records. The story of Captain Eino Jenstrom and the *Eddie Allen* is from material supplied by Jenstrom. He wrote an article about that raid which was published in *Air Force Magazine*, whose editors granted me permission to use it.

### Chapter 64

Sergeant John Mahan's story about the torpedoing of a Japanese mountain comes from a letter he wrote me.

### Chapter 65

This chapter concludes Lieutenant Krogh's story.

### Chapter 66

The source here is the interview with Joe Layer.

### Chapter 67

The conclusion of Jake Jones's story is from his manuscript.

# Bibliography

## UNPUBLISHED MANUSCRIPTS

Driest, Chester W. *World War II History of the 1st Fighter Control Squadron, 5th Air Force, 85th Fighter Wing.*
Jones, Jake. *Jake Jones, 13144734 USAAF, 1942–46.*
Krogh, Curtis. *World War II: My Personal Story.*
Mahan, John. *The Day We Torpedoed a Mountain.*
Parkhill, William. *Account of the Airborne Landings at Normandy.*
Yuhasz, Joseph J. *My Part in the Invasion of Sicily.*

## PERIODICALS

Eino E. Jenstrom. "The Last Mission of the Eddie Allen." *Air Force Magazine*, August 1980.
*40th Bomb Group Association Newsletters.*
*7th Air Force Newsletter.*

## BOOKS

Boyington, Gregory. *Baa, Baa, Black Sheep.* New York: G.P. Putnam's Sons, 1958.
Brewer, James F., et al., eds. *The Hump*, vol. 1. Poplar Bluff, Mo.: China-Burma-India Hump Pilots Assn., 1980.
Carter, Kit, and Robert Mueller, compilers. *The Army Air Corps in World War II: Combat Chronology.* Washington, D.C.: Office of Air Force History, 1973.
Davis, Burke. *Get Yamamoto.*
Duke, Neville, and Edward Lanchbery. *The Saga of Flight.* New York: John Day, 1961.
Dyer, George Carroll. *The Amphibians Came to Conquer: The Story of Admiral Richmond Kelly Turner.* Washington, D.C.: Office of Naval History, undated.
449th Bomb Group Association. *Grottaglie and Home.* Privately printed, 1989.
Grashio, Samuel C. *Return to Freedom.* Tulsa, Ok.: MCN Press, undated.
Grey, C. G. *The Luftwaffe.* London: Faber and Faber, 1944.
Haugland, Vern. *The Eagle Squadrons.* New York: Ziff Davis Flying Books, 1979.
Hawkins, Ian. *Münster: The Way It Was.* Anaheim, Calif.: Privately printed, 1984.

Hess, William N. *Pacific Sweep.* New York: Zebra Books, 1974.

Howton, Harry G., et al., eds. *China Airlift—The Hump,* Vols. I and II. Poplar Bluff, Mo.: China-Burma-India Hump Pilots Association, Vol. I, 1980. Vol II, 1983. (Copyrighted by The China-Burma-India Hump Pilots Association, Inc.)

Hoyt, Edwin P. *Airborne.* New York: Stein and Day, 1977.

——*How They Won the War in the Pacific.* New York: Weybright and Talley, 1968.

——*Japan's Triumph.* New York: Avon Books, 1989.

Jablonski, Edward. *Flying Fortress.* Garden City, N.Y.: Doubleday and Co., 1965.

Jahnke, George. *And There I Was.* Augusta, Mont.: Privately printed, 1989.

Knox, Donald. *Death March.* New York: Harcourt Brace Jovanovich,1981.

Layton, Edwin T. *And I Was There.* New York: William Morrow, 1985.

Leary, William M., ed. *We Shall Return!* Lexington, Ky.: University of Kentucky Press, 1988.

Le Strange, Richard. *Century Bombers: The Story of the Bloody Hundredth.* Norfolk, England: 100th Bomb Group Memorial Museum, 1989.

Mears, Frederick. *Carrier Combat.* New York: Doubleday and Co., 1944.

Morison, Samuel Eliot. *History of United States Naval Operations in World War II.* Boston: Atlantic-Little Brown, 13 vols.

Murray, Williamson. *Luftwaffe.* London: Allen and Unwin, 1945.

O'Brien, Howard V. *The Story of the 390th Bombardment Group.* New York: Privately Printed, 1947.

Overy R. J. *The Air War 1939–45.* New York: Stein and Day, 1981.

Prange, Gordon. *At Dawn We Slept.* New York: McGraw-Hill, 1981.

Richarz, W. H., et al., compilers. *The 390th Bomb Group Anthology.* Tucson: 390th Memorial Museum Foundation, Inc., 1983.

Sakai, Saburo. *Samurai!* New York: Bantam Books, 1978.

Scott, Robert Lee, Jr. *Flying Tiger: Chennault of China.* Garden City, N.Y.: Doubleday and Co., 1959.

Seagrave, Sterling. *Soldiers of Fortune.* Alexandria, Va.: Time-Life Books, 1981.

Smith, Benjamin, Jr. *Chick's Crew.* Tallahassee Fla.: Privately printed, 1978.

Sommerville, Donald. *World War II, Day by Day.* Greenwich, Conn.: Brompton Book Corporation, 1989.

Stafford, Edward P. *The Big E.* New York: Random House, 1962.

Thomas, Gordon, and Max Morgan. *Enola Gay.* New York: Stein and Day, 1977.

Thorne, Bliss K. *The Hump.* Philadelphia: J. B. Lippincott, 1965.

Tunner, William H. *Over the Hump.* New York: Duell Sloan and Pearce, 1964.

Turner, Damon. *Tucson to Grottaglie—The 449th Bomb Group History: And This Is Our Story.* Privately printed, 1984.

Varian, Horace L., ed. *The Bloody Hundredth.* 100th Bomb Group Committee, 1979.

# Name Index

# Subject Index

| DATE | | | |
|---|---|---|---|
|  |  |  |  |
|  |  |  |  |
|  |  |  |  |
|  |  |  |  |
|  |  |  |  |
|  |  |  |  |
|  |  |  |  |
|  |  |  |  |
|  |  |  |  |
|  |  |  |  |
|  |  |  |  |
|  |  |  |  |